Choc. Eclair Cake

(1) 1 lb. Box Graham Crackers
(2) pkgs. Instant French Van. Pudding
3½ c milk   (1) 8 oz cont. Cool Whip

(2) pks. Nestles Pre-melted Choc.
(2) tblsp. corn syrup
(2) tsp vanilla
(2) tblsp. milk
1½ c powdered sugar
2 tblsp. Soft butter

Blend ~~to~~ "tog"

Mix pudding c milk - let sit. Add cool whip. Layer 9x13 pan c graham crackers. Place ½ of pudding mixture on top, then crackers, then remaining pudding, ending c crackers.

Spread choc. mixture on top.
Refrigerate for (3) days! Don't cover

from Dolores / HIP

WOMAN'S DAY
DESSERTS

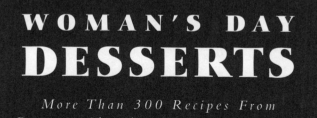

WOMAN'S DAY
DESSERTS

*More Than 300 Recipes From
Brownie Shortbread to Apple Sorbet
to Lemon Meringue Pie*

*Kathy Farrell-Kingsley
and the Editors of Woman's Day*

A ROUND STONE PRESS BOOK

VIKING

VIKING
Published by the Penguin Group
Penguin Putnam Inc., 375 Hudson St., New York, New York 10014, U.S.A.
Penguin Books Ltd, 27 Wrights Lane, London W8 5TZ, England
Penguin Books Australia Ltd, Ringwood, Victoria, Australia
Penguin Books Canada Ltd, 10 Alcorn Avenue, Toronto, Ontario, Canada M4V 3B2
Penguin Books (N.Z.) Ltd, 182–190 Wairau Road, Auckland 10, New Zealand

Penguin Books Ltd, Registered Offices: Harmondsworth, Middlesex, England

First published in 1997 by Viking Penguin, a member of Penguin Putnam Inc.

10 9 8 7 6 5 4 3 2 1

Woman's Day ® is a registered trademark of Hachette Filipacchi Magazines, Inc.

WOMAN'S DAY STAFF:
Editor-in-Chief: Jane Chesnutt
Creative Director: Brad Pallas
Managing Editor: Sue Kakstys
Senior Editor, Service: Christopher Canatsey
Executive Food Editor: Elizabeth Alston
Food Editor: Holly Sheppard
Associate Food Editor: Ellen R. Greene
Test Kitchen Director: Nancy L. Dell'Aria
Associate Editors: Terry Grieco-Kenny, Christine Makuch
Test Kitchen Assistant: Dionisia Colon
Assistant to the Food Editor: Marisol Vera

ROUND STONE PRESS STAFF:
Directors: Marsha Melnick, Susan E. Meyer, Paul Fargis
Development Editor: Nick Viorst
Project Manager: Amy Mintzer
Design: Wendy Palitz
Production Design: Smythtype
Copyeditor: Dolores Simon
Illustrations: Wendy Wilson
Index: Andrea Chesman
Nutritional Analysis: Hill Nutrition Associates, Inc.

Special thanks to Mary Goodbody, Antoinette Higgins, Wendy Kalen, Shirley Sarvis,
and Karen Berman.

Photograph credits will be found on page 350 and constitute an extension
of this copyright page.

ISBN 0-670-87444-2
CIP data available.

This book is printed on acid-free paper. ∞

Printed in the United States of America
Set in Bembo

CONTENTS

A Word from WOMAN'S DAY
  by Jane Chesnutt, Editor-in-Chief **7**

In the WOMAN'S DAY Kitchens
  by Elizabeth Alston, Executive Food Editor **8**

COOKIES & BARS **11**

**ICE CREAMS &
FROZEN DESSERTS** **51**

PIES & TARTS **89**

**PUDDINGS,
CUSTARDS & MOUSSES** **137**

CAKES **161**

FRUIT DESSERTS **215**

SILLY CAKES **247**
  Fanciful cakes for kids' parties, holidays, and other lighthearted special occasions

HOLIDAY DESSERTS **275**
  *Fresh ideas for sweet finishes at Valentine's Day, Easter, Passover,
  Fourth of July, Halloween, Thanksgiving, Hanukkah, and Christmas,
  plus Gifts from the Kitchen*

APPENDIX
  Equipment, Ingredients & Techniques **318**
  Guide to Chocolate **328**
  Glossary **331**
  Equivalents & Conversions **336**

Index **337**

Credits **350**

A WORD FROM WOMAN'S DAY

MOST OF US LIKE TO END A MEAL WITH SOMETHING sweet. Who could imagine a dinner party without dessert? A birthday party or baby shower without a cake? Thanksgiving without pie? Or the Fourth of July without ice cream? Not me. I love dessert, whether it's a fresh peach, a bowl of frozen yogurt, or, especially, a spectacular chocolate mousse. (A confessed chocolate-lover, I've been known to head to the test kitchen for a handful of chocolate chips when a sweets craving hits mid-afternoon.) So when readers ask why we often show desserts on the cover of WOMAN'S DAY magazine, the answer is easy: Because we love them as much as you do.

Like many of you, I don't have time to make dessert during the week. But weekends frequently find me in the kitchen trying a new recipe, often one I've seen in the magazine's test kitchens. I'm proud of the boundless creativity of WOMAN'S DAY's food editors and of the extraordinary care our test kitchens give to each recipe. As a cook, I enjoy experimenting with main dishes, but one thing I've learned from experience is that many desserts do not lend themselves to improvisation. Especially with baked goods such as cookies and cakes, it is essential to follow the recipe precisely. Happily, our kitchens have done such a thorough job that you can relax.

Why in this age of healthy eating is WOMAN'S DAY doing a dessert book? First, you will find lots of great-tasting low-fat desserts in this book. But second, I believe that dessert is good for the soul. While many people prepare food and eat just because it's necessary for survival, dessert is for fun. When you prepare a homemade dessert, it's for the pleasure of making it, the pleasure of seeing it received with joy, and, of course, the pleasure of eating it. That's the philosophy behind *Woman's Day Desserts*. Enjoy!

Jane Chesnutt, Editor-in-Chief

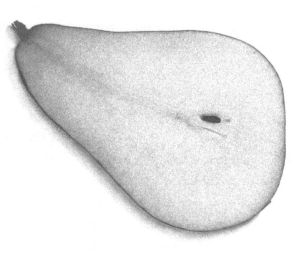

IN THE WOMAN'S DAY KITCHENS

DESSERT IS ONE OF LIFE'S PLEASURES. IN THIS book, you'll find ideas and recipes that allow you to enjoy sweet pleasures often, from quick weeknight fixes and low-fat treats, to festive cakes for holidays and spectacular party desserts. *Woman's Day Desserts* includes more than 300 recipes. Many require no baking; others are low-fat versions of old favorites. There are cakes that can be baked in the microwave and recipes that are ideal to make with your children or are easy enough for the kids to make on their own. We also include the very best renditions of classic and holiday desserts, along with some new twists on those vintage favorites.

The book is organized to help you easily locate a recipe that meets your needs. There are individual chapters on cookies, cakes, and pies. The chapter on ice creams includes WOMAN'S DAY's fabulous ice cream cakes and other frozen desserts perfect for summer. Fruit Desserts celebrates the glories of fresh seasonal produce, while the recipes in Puddings, Custards & Mousses satisfy our taste for those smooth, comforting confections. The chapter called Silly Cakes is packed with fun-to-make novelty cakes designed to delight our children—and the child in all of us—or to commemorate a special occasion. Finally, we've included dozens of recipes for holiday desserts that, over the years, have inspired our readers to create new traditions while affirming those that already exist.

Of course, you can always browse through the book or scan the recipe lists at the opening of each chapter. But if you have some specific requirements in mind, our categories and chapter indexes can help you find the dessert that best meets your needs. Let's

say you have friends coming for a barbecue on a summer Saturday. Something with fruit sounds appealing (after all, it's high season) but you don't want to spend all day in the kitchen while you have company. Turn to the opening page of the Fruit Desserts chapter and check the categories Easy, Quick, and 1 Hour. Then again, maybe a cake seems more in the barbecue spirit. If you want to treat your friends to something special while keeping a promise to yourself to avoid high-fat treats, you can look at the opening of the Cakes chapter to see which recipes appear in both the categories Decadent and Low Fat. (Yes, such desserts exist!) If you're browsing through the book, you'll see that the same category information appears in a blue banner above each recipe. Here are the details on what our categories mean:

EASY: Recipes that call for a limited number of ingredients and very little effort. These are perfect for super-busy nights, as well as for the beginning cook.

QUICK: From peeling to cooking, 30 minutes is all it takes to complete these desserts. (Our countdown begins when all the ingredients are ready to be chopped, diced, sifted, measured, or otherwise prepared.)

1 HOUR: Nearly as simple as the Quick recipes, 1 Hour recipes require a little more preparation time or a little more cooking time, or both.

LOW FAT: To qualify, a recipe has to have no more than 9 grams of fat per serving. A cookie can have a maximum of 3 grams of fat and a bar cookie a maximum of 5 grams. When enjoying any dessert labeled "low fat," do be aware of its ingredients and, especially, of portion size. A sorbet made entirely of fruit, sugar, and water will be fat-free no matter how much of it you eat, but if you eat six cookies made with butter and eggs (or if you make those cookies three times as large as we recommend), the fat grams will add up quickly.

CLASSIC: These are traditional recipes that have stood the test of time. Some are quick to prepare, others require more time and planning; some are homey, some are elegant.

OLD FASHIONED: These are comforting, traditional desserts, just as appealing today as they were long ago.

DECADENT: Some recipes have earned this designation by being sinfully high in fat and calories; others just taste that way. All are wickedly delicious.

Of course, few recipes fall into just one category—an easy recipe may also be low-fat, for example. Every recipe is listed in all applicable categories.

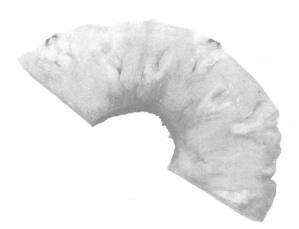

NUTRITIONAL INFORMATION

Each one of the recipes (and every Variation) in this book carries information on its calorie, protein, carbohydrate, fat, sodium, and cholesterol content. Please keep in mind that all nutritional data are approximate and based on averages. Also, many of the recipes include optional (raisins instead of chocolate chips, for example) or alternative ingredients (e.g., regular or nonfat sour cream). While it is not possible to include nutritional information for every possible combination within a recipe, we have provided nutritional information where a variation significantly affects the calorie, fat, sodium, or cholesterol count. The nutritional information can help you appreciate the relative values of each recipe so that you can decide whether it's appropriate for you and your family. Rich desserts tend to carry high fat tags, but that's not necessarily a reason to forget them. If you're watching fat intake, remember that it's the percentage of fat in your diet over the course of a day or a week that counts, not the number of grams of fat in any one dish. This is particularly important to remember when selecting a dessert! (I love an occasional rich dessert, but I have two rules: If it isn't worth the calories, I skip it, and if it is, I don't have to eat the whole thing.)

BEFORE TRYING A NEW RECIPE

• Read the recipe all the way through (this is especially important when baking), checking to see that you have all the necessary ingredients, tools, and equipment. Make sure you understand the instructions, especially if there's a new-to-you technique involved.

• Allow yourself plenty of time: Preparation and cooking times, as well as baking and chilling/cooling/freezing times, are included with every recipe. (Preparation begins after the ingredients are assembled. Cooking is any time on top of the stove. For those few recipes prepared primarily in the microwave, microwave cooking time is listed.) Remember that not everyone slices, chops, measures, or stirs at the same pace. And a recipe always takes longer the first time you make it.

• Take advantage of the make-ahead and storage information set off by a blue "bullet" in the body of each recipe. You may be able to make all or part of a recipe well in advance of when you plan to serve it—a great convenience.

• Experienced bakers know that advance organization is the best way to avoid making mistakes. Measure all ingredients and line them up in the order you'll use them before you begin to cook. That way, if you are interrupted, you will know whether or not you have added a particular ingredient.

AND LAST...

Most of us love to cook, but hate to clean up. The best advice I can give (and I freely admit, I don't always practice it) is: Clean up as you go. In fact, before you begin, clear the counter as much as possible and make sure the sink is empty. Put away ingredients as you finish with them. Soak bowls and tools in a sinkful of soapy water. When you have a minute or two, rinse the utensils and put them in the dishwasher or wash them and put them away. When you've finished cooking, the kitchen will be in relatively good shape and clean-up won't seem like a burden.

We hope you enjoy this cookbook as much as we at WOMAN'S DAY have enjoyed testing and (best of all) tasting the recipes you will find in it.

Elizabeth Alston, Executive Food Editor

COOKIES
& BARS

"How do they taste?
They taste like more."
H. L. MENCKEN

Children may love them, but cookies and bars are not just kid stuff. They're infinitely varied, and most are equally appropriate for packing in a lunch bag or serving with coffee.

Cinnamon–Peanut Butter Cookies, Molasses Crinkle Cookies, or Lemon-Ginger Crisps will add a little spice to the cookie jar. Chocolate lovers can make four delicious kinds of chocolate cookies from one dough. There are also crisp, buttery shortbreads, sophisticated biscotti, pecan-studded blondies and several kinds of brownies.

The methods for making them are varied, too: easy drop-style cookies, no-fuss bar cookies perfect for parties, bake-when-you-want icebox cookies, and cookies and bars that don't require any baking at all. Whatever the method, the recipes and tips in this chapter will enable even a novice to bake cookies like a pro.

EASY

Almond Shortbread, 43
Blondies, 26
Brownie Nut Slices, 48
Caramel Clusters, 50
Chocolate Leaves, 41
Chocolate Nut Brownies, 23
Chocolate Pretzels, 41
Chocolate Sandwiches, 41
Chocolate Shortbread, 43
Chocolate Walnut Chunk Cookies, 14
Chocolate-Peanut Rounds, 46
Cinnamon-Peanut Butter Cookies, 15
Congo Bars, 31
Crispy Apricot Bars, 49
Double Chocolate Jumbles, 14
Fudgy Low-Fat Brownies, 24
Lemon Softies, 22
Lemon-Ginger Crisps, 47
Mexican Wedding Cakes, 38
Molasses Crinkle Cookies, 42
Nutty Granola Cookies, 20
Oatmeal-Chocolate Chip Cookies, 18
Orange-Hazelnut Shortbread, 44
Peanut Butter and Jelly Cookies, 49
Pecan Thumbprint Cookies, 43
Praline Chip Cookies, 18
Raspberry-Hazelnut Bars, 30
Soft Sugar Cookies, 21
Walnut Thumbprint Cookies, 42
White Chocolate Walnut Chunk
   Cookies, 14
Whole-Wheat Raisin Cookies, 19
Zebras, 25

QUICK

Caramel Clusters, 50
Peanut Butter and Jelly Cookies, 49

1 HOUR

Almond Shortbread, 43
Apple Kuchen Bars, 28
Blondies, 26
Cherry Cobbler Bars, 28

Chocolate Walnut Chunk
    Cookies, 14
Chocolate Shortbread, 43
Cinnamon–Peanut Butter Cookies, 15
Congo Bars, 31
Double Chocolate Jumbles, 14
Fudgy Low-Fat Brownies, 24
Lacy Oatmeal Cookies, 16
Lemon Softies, 22
Molasses Crinkle Cookies, 42
Nutty Granola Cookies, 20
Oatmeal–Chocolate Chip Cookies, 18
Orange-Hazelnut Shortbread, 44
Pecan Thumbprint Cookies, 43
Praline Chip Cookies, 18
Raspberry-Hazelnut Bars, 30
Soft Sugar Cookies, 21
Walnut Thumbprint Cookies, 42
White Chocolate Walnut Chunk
    Cookies, 14
Whole-Wheat Raisin Cookies, 19
Zebras, 25

LOW FAT

Caramel Clusters, 50
Chocolate Crackle Tops, 39
Chocolate Leaves, 41
Cinnamon-Peanut Butter Cookies, 15
Cornmeal Shortbread Cookies, 40
Fig Bar Cookies, 37
Flaky Cinnamon Twists, 45
Fudgy Low-Fat Brownies, 24
Lemon Softies, 22
Lemon-Ginger Crisps, 47
Molasses Crinkle Cookies, 42
Raspberry-Hazelnut Bars, 30

CLASSIC

Almond Shortbread, 43
Blondies, 26
Chocolate Crackle Tops, 39
Chocolate Nut Brownies, 23

Cinnamon-Almond Biscotti, 44
Congo Bars, 31
Lemon Bars, 28
Mexican Wedding Cakes, 38
Oatmeal Spice Cookies, 17
Soft Sugar Cookies, 21

OLD FASHIONED

Apple Kuchen Bars, 28
Cherry Cobbler Bars, 28
Chocolate Crackle Tops, 39
Cinnamon-Peanut Butter Cookies, 15
Cornmeal Shortbread Cookies, 40
Fig Bar Cookies, 37
Flaky Cinnamon Twists, 45
Lacy Oatmeal Cookies, 16
Lemon Bars, 28
Lemon Softies, 22
Lemon Softies with Lemon Icing, 22
Oatmeal Spice Cookies, 17
Oatmeal-Chocolate Chip Cookies, 18
Pecan Thumbprint Cookies, 43
Soft Sugar Cookies, 21
Walnut Thumbprint Cookies, 42
Whole-Wheat Applesauce Bars, 32

DECADENT

Black and White Brownies, 27
Brownie Nut Slices, 48
Brownie Shortbread, 29
Chocolate Cherry "Ravioli," 41
Chocolate Lemon Bars, 29
Chocolate Nut Brownies, 23

Chocolate Sandwiches, 41
Chocolate Walnut Chunk Cookies, 14
Double Chocolate Jumbles, 14
White Chocolate Walnut Chunk
    Cookies, 14
Zebras, 25

NO-BAKE COOKIES

Caramel Clusters, 50
Crispy Apricot Bars, 49
Peanut Butter and Jelly
    Cookies, 49

ICEBOX COOKIES

Brownie Nut Slices, 48
Chocolate-Peanut Rounds, 46
Cornmeal Shortbread Cookies, 40
Lemon-Ginger Crisps, 47
Oatmeal Spice Cookies, 17

FOR THE COOKIE JAR

Brownie Nut Slices, 48
Chocolate Pretzels, 41
Chocolate-Peanut Rounds, 46
Cinnamon-Peanut Butter Cookies, 15
Cornmeal Shortbread Cookies, 40
Double Chocolate Jumbles, 14
Lemon-Ginger Crisps, 47
Nutty Granola Cookies, 20
Oatmeal Spice Cookies, 17
Oatmeal-Chocolate Chip Cookies, 18
Praline Chip Cookies, 18
Whole-Wheat Raisin Cookies, 19

CHOCOLATE WALNUT CHUNK COOKIES

Makes 36 cookies

Preparation time: 20 minutes

Baking time: 15 minutes per batch

You can find bags of chocolate chunks alongside the chocolate chips in your market, or you can coarsely chop a bar of your favorite semisweet chocolate. In this recipe, golden raisins add chewiness and flavor as well.

> *10 tablespoons plus 2 teaspoons (2/3 cup) butter or*
> *margarine (see page 321), softened*
> *2/3 cup granulated sugar*
> *1/3 cup packed dark brown sugar*
> *1 large egg, at room temperature*
> *1 teaspoon vanilla extract*
> *1½ cups all-purpose flour*
> *1 cup (6 ounces) semisweet chocolate chunks or*
> *mini kisses*
> *1 cup (4 ounces) walnuts, chopped*
> *½ cup golden raisins*

1. Heat the oven to 325°F. Lightly grease 1 or more cookie sheets.

2. In a large (mixer) bowl, beat the butter, both sugars, the egg, and vanilla with an electric mixer until pale and fluffy. With the mixer on low speed, gradually add the flour, beating just until blended. Stir in the chocolate, walnuts, and raisins.

3. Drop heaping tablespoonfuls of the dough 2 inches apart onto the prepared cookie sheet(s).

4. Bake until the tops look dry, about 15 minutes. Cool the cookies on the sheet on a wire rack for 5 minutes, then remove to the rack to cool completely. • The cookies can be kept in an airtight container or plastic bag at cool room temperature up to 3 days or frozen up to 1 month.

Per cookie with butter: 120 cal, 1 g pro, 7 g fat, 15 g car, 40 mg sod, 15 mg chol.
With margarine: 50 mg sod, 6 mg chol

VARIATION

WHITE CHOCOLATE WALNUT CHUNK COOKIES

Coarsely chop 6 ounces white chocolate and use instead of the semisweet.

Per cookie with butter: 120 cal, 1 g pro, 7 g fat, 15 g car, 40 mg sod, 15 mg chol. With margarine: 50 mg sod, 6 mg chol.

• EASY • 1 HOUR
• DECADENT

COOK'S TIP

If using only 1 cookie sheet, allow it to cool between batches so the cookies will not spread too much.

DOUBLE CHOCOLATE JUMBLES

Makes 18 cookies

Preparation time: 20 minutes

Baking time: 13 minutes per batch

These easy-to-make, rich dark cookies deliver a wallop of chocolate. They're especially good made with mint chocolate chips.

1 stick (½ cup) butter or margarine (see page 321), softened
¾ cup granulated sugar
1 large egg, at room temperature
1 teaspoon vanilla extract
⅓ cup unsweetened cocoa powder
1 cup all-purpose flour
¾ cup (4½ ounces) chips: mint chocolate, semisweet,
    vanilla-milk, or a combination

1. Heat the oven to 350°F. Have ready 1 or more ungreased cookie sheets.

2. In a large (mixer) bowl, beat the butter, sugar, egg, and vanilla with an electric mixer until well blended. With the mixer on low speed, beat in the cocoa, then the flour, just until blended. Stir in the chips.

3. Drop heaping tablespoonfuls of the dough onto the cookie sheet(s), spacing them about 2 inches apart.

4. Bake until the tops look dry, 11 to 13 minutes. (The cookies will feel soft.) Cool the cookies on the sheet on a wire rack for 5 minutes, then remove to the rack to cool completely. ● The cookies can be kept in an airtight container or plastic bag at cool room temperature up to 3 days or frozen up to 1 month.

Per cookie with butter: 140 cal, 2 g pro, 8 g fat, 19 g car, 60 mg sod, 26 mg chol. With margarine: 60 mg sod, 12 mg chol

PEANUT BUTTER
In 1890, a doctor in St. Louis invented peanut butter as a protein substitute for patients with poor teeth. A local food manufacturer mechanized the process and in 1903 a patent was issued for the first peanut butter machine. One year later, peanut butter was being promoted as a health food at the St. Louis World's Fair.

EASY • 1 HOUR • LOW FAT • OLD FASHIONED

CINNAMON–PEANUT BUTTER COOKIES

Makes 48 cookies
Preparation time: 15 minutes
Baking time: 12 minutes per batch

Cinnamon gives these classic cookies a new flavor. If you like the old-fashioned crisscross look, flatten the cookie dough with the tines of a fork to make a cross-hatch pattern before baking.

1 stick (½ cup) butter or margarine (see page 321), softened
½ cup packed dark brown sugar
½ cup granulated sugar
½ cup creamy peanut butter
1 large egg, at room temperature
1 teaspoon vanilla extract
1 teaspoon ground cinnamon
½ teaspoon salt
1 cup all-purpose flour

1. Heat the oven to 350°F. Have ready 1 or more ungreased cookie sheets.

2. In a large (mixer) bowl, beat the butter, both sugars, the peanut butter, ▶

egg, vanilla, cinnamon, and salt with an electric mixer until well blended. With the mixer on low speed, gradually add the flour, beating just until blended.

3. Drop heaping teaspoonfuls of the dough about 1½ inches apart onto the cookie sheet(s).

4. Bake just until lightly golden, 10 to 12 minutes. (Be careful not to overbake.) Cool the cookies on the sheet on a wire rack for 5 minutes, then remove to the rack to cool completely. • The cookies can be kept in an airtight container or plastic bag at cool room temperature up to 3 days or frozen up to 1 month.

Per cookie with butter: 60 cal, 1 g pro, 3 g fat, 7 g car, 60 mg sod, 10 mg chol.

With margarine: 4 mg sod

1 HOUR • OLD FASHIONED

LACY OATMEAL COOKIES

Makes 40 cookies

Preparation time: 20 minutes

Baking time: 9 minutes per batch

These wonderful old-fashioned cookies can be tricky even for an experienced baker and are best eaten on the day they are made. Be sure to use light-brown sugar and real butter, and don't bake them on a rainy or humid day. If, however, some of these delicate cookies do crumble, just sprinkle the crumbs over ice cream.

1 stick (½ cup) butter (not margarine), cut into pieces

½ cup packed light brown sugar

2 tablespoons milk

1 cup (4 ounces) pecans, finely chopped

½ cup uncooked old-fashioned or quick-cooking oats

¼ cup all-purpose flour

½ teaspoon vanilla extract

1. Heat the oven to 350°F. Line 1 or more cookie sheets with foil.

2. Put the butter, sugar, and milk into a 1- to 1½-quart saucepan. Stir over low heat just until the butter melts. Remove from the heat. Stir in the pecans, oats, flour, and vanilla until blended. Let cool for 10 minutes.

3. Drop slightly rounded teaspoonfuls of the dough on the prepared cookie sheet(s), spacing 3 inches apart. Flatten the cookies with the back of a spoon.

4. Bake until the cookies spread, look lacy, and are lightly browned, 8 to 9 minutes.

5. Cool the cookies on the sheet on a wire rack for 1 to 1½ minutes, until they harden slightly. Using a broad metal spatula, remove the cookies to the rack to cool completely. If the cookies become too hard to remove from the foil, return to the oven for 15 to 30 seconds to soften, then try again. • Freeze the cookies in an airtight freezer container between layers of waxed paper up to 1 month. Thaw at room temperature.

Per cookie: 60 cal, 0 g pro, 4 g fat, 4 g car, 20 mg sod, 6 mg chol

---

DOUBLE DUTY

You can successfully bake two sheets of cookies at the same time if you follow these simple guidelines:

◆ Space the oven racks well apart (one in the upper position and one in the lowest).

◆ Do not put the cookie sheets directly over each other, if possible.

◆ Allow enough room for air to circulate between the edges of the cookie sheets and the oven walls.

◆ For even baking, switch the position of the sheets up and down and back to front halfway through baking.

OATMEAL SPICE COOKIES

Makes 60 cookies
Preparation time: 25 minutes plus at least 4 hours to chill
Baking time: 12 minutes per batch

Icebox- or refrigerator-style cookies, where you mix the dough and chill it, then slice and bake from the log of chilled dough at any time, are a favorite of busy moms. While these spicy, chewy cookies bake, your kitchen will be filled with the aromas of cinnamon, nutmeg, and cloves. Keep the wrapped dough in the coldest part of your refrigerator.

> 2 sticks (1 cup) butter or margarine (see page 321),
>   softened
> 1 cup granulated sugar
> 1 cup packed light or dark brown sugar
> 2 large eggs, at room temperature
> 1 teaspoon vanilla extract
> 1 teaspoon baking soda
> 1 teaspoon salt
> 1 teaspoon ground cinnamon
> 1/4 teaspoon grated nutmeg
> 1/8 teaspoon ground cloves
> 1 1/2 cups all-purpose flour
> 3 cups uncooked old-fashioned or
>   quick-cooking oats
> 1 cup (4 ounces) walnuts, chopped

1. In a large (mixer) bowl, beat the butter and both sugars with an electric mixer until light and fluffy. Beat in the eggs, vanilla, baking soda, salt, cinnamon, nutmeg, and cloves until well blended. Stir in the flour, then the oats and nuts.

2. Shape the dough into two 8-inch-long rolls. Cover tightly with plastic wrap and chill until firm, about 4 hours; or place in the freezer for 2 hours and let stand for 20 minutes at room temperature before slicing. • The dough can be made up to this point and refrigerated up to 3 days or wrapped in foil and frozen up to 3 months. If frozen, remove to the refrigerator for 2 hours before baking.

3. Heat the oven to 350°F. Lightly grease 1 or more cookie sheets.

4. With a sharp, thin knife, using a sawing motion, slice the dough into 1/4-inch-thick rounds. Place the slices 1 inch apart onto the prepared cookie sheet(s).

5. Bake until lightly browned, 10 to 12 minutes. Cool the cookies on the sheet on a wire rack for 5 minutes, then remove to the rack to cool completely. • The cookies can be kept in an airtight container or plastic bag at cool room temperature up to 3 days or frozen up to 1 month.

Per cookie with butter: 95 cal, 1 g pro, 5 g fat, 12 g car, 90 mg sod, 15 mg chol.
With margarine: 7 mg chol

COOK'S TIP

To shape the dough into long rolls, divide it roughly in half. Put each half onto a square of plastic wrap or waxed paper. Using the wrap as a guide, shape the dough into a long, fat, sausagelike shape. Enclose the dough in the wrapping, then mold it into an even shape.

OATMEAL–CHOCOLATE CHIP COOKIES

Makes 40 cookies

Preparation time: 15 minutes

Baking time: 13 minutes per batch

Oatmeal and chocolate chip cookies might well be America's finest contribution to the dessert world. Here, the two are combined for a marvelously rich and chewy treat that is sure to become a family favorite.

1 stick (½ cup) unsalted butter or margarine (see page 321), softened
1 cup packed light or dark brown sugar
1 large egg, at room temperature
2 teaspoons vanilla extract
½ teaspoon baking soda
½ teaspoon baking powder
¼ teaspoon salt
1 cup all-purpose flour
1½ cups uncooked old-fashioned oats
1 cup (6 ounces) mini semisweet chocolate chips

1. Heat the oven to 350°F. Lightly grease 1 or more cookie sheets.

2. In a large (mixer) bowl, beat the butter and sugar with an electric mixer until light and fluffy. Beat in the egg, vanilla, baking soda, baking powder, and salt until well blended. With the mixer on low speed, gradually add the flour, beating just until blended. Stir in the oats and chocolate chips.

3. Roll tablespoonfuls of the dough into balls and place 2 inches apart on the prepared cookie sheet(s). Slightly flatten the cookies with the palm of your hand.

4. Bake until the edges are lightly browned, 12 to 13 minutes. Cool the cookies on the sheet on a wire rack for 2 to 3 minutes, then remove to the rack to cool completely. • The cookies can be kept in an airtight container at cool room temperature up to 3 days or frozen up to 1 month.

Per cookie with butter: 90 cal, 1 g pro, 4 g fat, 13 g car, 40 mg sod, 12 mg chol.

With margarine: 65 mg sod, 5 mg chol

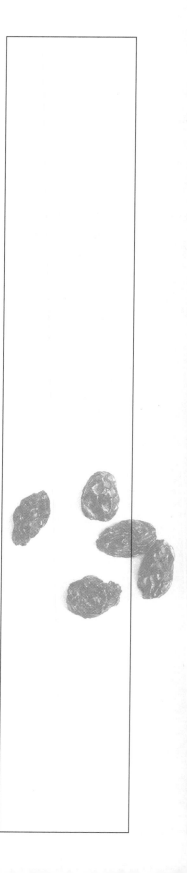

PRALINE CHIP COOKIES

Makes 20 cookies

Preparation time: 20 minutes

Baking time: 13 minutes per batch

The brown sugar and pecans in these cookies make them taste like praline candies. They are the ultimate snack with a cold glass of milk.

½ cup (1 stick) butter or margarine (see page 321), softened
¾ cup packed light or dark brown sugar
1 large egg, at room temperature
1 teaspoon vanilla extract
½ teaspoon baking soda
1¼ cups all-purpose flour
⅔ cup (3⅓ ounces) pecans, coarsely chopped
⅔ cup (4 ounces) chips: semisweet chocolate, butterscotch, peanut butter,
*   vanilla-milk, or a combination*

1. Heat the oven to 350°F. Have ready 1 or more ungreased cookie sheets.
2. In a large (mixer) bowl, beat the butter, sugar, egg, vanilla, and baking soda with an electric mixer until well blended. With the mixer on low speed, gradually add the flour, beating just until blended. Stir in the pecans and chips.
3. Drop heaping tablespoonfuls of the dough 2 inches apart on the cookie sheet(s).
4. Bake until the edges are lightly browned, 11 to 13 minutes. The tops will feel soft. Cool the cookies on the sheet on a wire rack for 2 to 3 minutes, then remove to the rack to cool completely. ● The cookies can be kept in an airtight container or plastic bag at cool room temperature up to 3 days or frozen up to 1 month.
Per cookie with butter and chocolate chips: 160 cal, 2 g pro, 10 g fat, 19 g car, 80 mg sod, 23 mg chol. With margarine: 90 mg sod, 11 mg chol

EASY • 1 HOUR

WHOLE-WHEAT RAISIN COOKIES
Makes 22 cookies
Preparation time: 20 minutes
Baking time: 15 minutes per batch

Whole-wheat flour contains several nutrients that all-purpose flour doesn't, and this recipe offers whole-grain nutrition in a very delicious package. Just don't be tempted to eliminate the all-purpose flour in favor of the whole-wheat; the result will be heavy rather than hearty.

10 tablespoons plus 2 teaspoons (⅔ cup) butter or
*   margarine (see page 321), softened*
1 cup granulated sugar
1 large egg, at room temperature
1 teaspoon vanilla extract
½ teaspoon baking powder
1½ cups whole-wheat flour
1 cup all-purpose flour
⅔ cup raisins
⅔ cup (4 ounces) chips: semisweet chocolate, butterscotch,
*   peanut butter, vanilla-milk, or a combination*

▶

1. Heat the oven to 350°F. Have ready 1 or more ungreased cookie sheets.

2. In a large (mixer) bowl, beat the butter, sugar, egg, vanilla, and baking powder with an electric mixer until well blended. With the mixer on low speed, gradually add the whole-wheat and all-purpose flours, beating just until blended. Stir in the raisins and chips.

3. Drop heaping tablespoonfuls of the dough 2 inches apart on the cookie sheet(s).

4. Bake until the edges are lightly browned, 13 to 15 minutes. The tops will feel soft. Cool the cookies on the sheet on a wire rack for 2 to 3 minutes, then remove the cookies to the rack to cool completely. ● The cookies can be kept in an airtight container or plastic bag at cool room temperature up to 3 days or frozen up to 1 month.

Per cookie with butter and chocolate chips: 170 cal, 2 g pro, 7 g fat, 26 g car, 70 mg sod, 25 mg chol. With margarine: 80 mg sod, 10 mg chol

EASY • 1 HOUR

NUTTY GRANOLA COOKIES

Makes 36 cookies

Preparation time: 15 minutes

Baking time: 12 minutes per batch

Better than any granola bars you can buy, these wholesome cookies are crisp on the outside and chewy within.

*1 stick (½ cup) unsalted butter or
   margarine (see page 321), softened*
½ cup packed light or dark brown sugar
½ cup granulated sugar
1 large egg, at room temperature
½ teaspoon vanilla extract
½ teaspoon baking soda
¼ teaspoon baking powder
¼ teaspoon salt
1 cup all-purpose flour
2½ cups granola cereal with nuts

1. Heat the oven to 350°F. Lightly grease 1 or more cookie sheets.

2. In a large (mixer) bowl, beat the butter and both sugars with an electric mixer until light and fluffy. Beat in the egg, vanilla, baking soda, baking powder, and salt. Stir in the flour, then the granola until blended.

3. Roll the dough into 1-inch balls, using about 1 tablespoon for each. Place 2 inches apart on the prepared cookie sheet(s).

4. Bake until lightly browned, about 12 minutes. Cool the cookies on the sheet on a wire rack for 5 minutes, then remove cookies to the rack to cool completely.

COOK'S TIP

Be sure not to overmix any cookie dough once you have added the flour. If you overwork the flour, you will end up with tough cookies.

• The cookies can be kept in an airtight container or in plastic bags at cool room temperature up to 3 days or frozen up to 1 month.

Per cookie with butter: 100 cal, 2 g pro, 4 g fat, 13 g car, 40 mg sod, 13 mg chol. With margarine: 70 mg sod, 6 mg chol

EASY • 1 HOUR • CLASSIC • OLD FASHIONED

SOFT SUGAR COOKIES

Makes 18 cookies
Preparation time: 20 minutes
Baking time: 12 minutes per batch

Charmingly old-fashioned and simple, these sugar-coated cookies will evoke fantasies of porch swings and lemonade.

½ stick (¼ cup) unsalted butter or margarine (see page 321),
*   softened*
¾ cup plus ⅓ cup granulated sugar
½ teaspoon baking soda
½ teaspoon freshly grated lemon peel
½ teaspoon grated nutmeg
½ teaspoon vanilla extract
Pinch salt
1 large egg, at room temperature
1¼ cups all-purpose flour
½ cup regular, reduced-fat, or nonfat sour cream

1. Heat the oven to 350°F. Lightly grease 1 or more cookie sheets.

2. In a large mixer bowl, beat the butter, ¾ cup of the sugar, the baking soda, lemon peel, nutmeg, vanilla, and salt until well blended. Beat in the egg. Scrape down the sides of the bowl.

3. With the mixer on low speed, beat in half the flour, then the sour cream, then the remaining flour. Beat just until blended.

4. Spread the remaining ⅓ cup of sugar on a sheet of waxed paper. Using a small rubber spatula and a measuring tablespoon, scrape 1 tablespoon of the dough onto the sugar. Repeat 2 more times. Sprinkle some of the sugar over the tops. Gently roll the dough balls in the sugar to coat. Place the balls 2 inches apart on the prepared cookie sheet(s). Repeat with the remaining dough and sugar. (You will have sugar left over.)

5. Bake the cookies until golden brown, 10 to 12 minutes. Cool the cookies on the sheet on a wire rack for 2 to 3 minutes, then remove the cookies to the rack to cool completely. • The cookies can be kept in an airtight container or plastic bag at cool room temperature up to 3 days or frozen up to 1 month.

Per cookie with butter and sour cream: 120 cal, 1 g pro, 4 g fat, 19 g car, 50 mg sod, 22 mg chol. With margarine and nonfat sour cream: 110 cal, 2 g pro, 3 g fat, 80 mg sod, 12 mg chol

COOK'S TIP

When you're baking several batches of cookies you can speed up the process by dropping the cookie dough onto sheets of foil or parchment paper on your countertop while one batch is baking. You can slide the foil or parchment right onto the cooled baking sheet.

EASY • 1 HOUR • LOW FAT • OLD FASHIONED

LEMON SOFTIES

Makes 48 cookies
Preparation time: 15 minutes
Baking time: 11 minutes per batch

Sour cream in the dough makes the cookies tender and light, and chopped almonds and golden raisins give them a nice chewy texture.

1 stick (½ cup) unsalted butter or margarine
  (see page 321), softened
1 cup granulated sugar
1 large egg, at room temperature
½ cup regular sour cream
2 teaspoons baking powder
½ teaspoon baking soda
½ teaspoon grated nutmeg
½ teaspoon salt
¼ teaspoon vanilla extract
2 cups all-purpose flour
½ cup (2 ounces) blanched almonds, finely chopped
⅓ cup golden raisins
1½ tablespoons freshly grated lemon peel

1. Heat the oven to 375°F. Have ready 1 or more ungreased cookie sheets.
2. In a large (mixer) bowl, beat the butter and sugar with an electric mixer until light and fluffy. Beat in the egg, sour cream, baking powder, baking soda, nutmeg, salt, and vanilla until blended. Stir in the flour, then the nuts, raisins, and lemon peel.
3. Drop heaping teaspoonfuls of the dough about 2 inches apart on the cookie sheet(s). (The cookies will spread.)

VARIATION

LEMON SOFTIES WITH LEMON ICING

• Make the cookies as directed.
• In a medium-size (mixer) bowl, beat 3 tablespoons softened unsalted butter with a pinch of salt until creamy. Beat in 2 tablespoons fresh lemon juice, ½ teaspoon vanilla extract, and 1½ cups confectioners' sugar until blended. (Additional confectioners' sugar may be added, if necessary, to achieve a spreading consistency.)
• Spread the tops of the cooled baked cookies with the icing and let the icing harden before storing the cookies.

Per cookie with butter: 90 cal, 1 g pro, 4 g fat, 13 g car, 60 mg sod, 13 mg chol. With margarine in the cookie and butter in the icing: 84 mg sod, 7 mg chol

• OLD FASHIONED

SECRETS FOR SUPERIOR COOKIES

◆ Many recipes call for room-temperature ingredients because they're easier to beat. Leave butter out of the refrigerator or soften it carefully in a microwave. (Just don't melt it.)
◆ Measure ingredients carefully. Press and pack down brown sugar into a cup measure. Spoon flour lightly into an exact cup measure. Fill to overflowing (don't tap or press down) and sweep across with a straightedge to level.

◆ There is no need to sift flour and other dry ingredients unless a recipe tells you to do so.
◆ For rolled dough, cut cookies as close together as possible. Collect the trimmings and press—don't knead—them together, then reroll. Cookies from re-rolled dough will be a little less tender.
◆ If you bake cookies immediately after mixing dough that is supposed to be chilled, the cookies will spread out more.

◆ Unrimmed cookie sheets are best for even browning. Make sure the cookie sheets are at least 2 inches smaller than your oven dimensions on all sides, so heat can circulate better and the cookies will bake evenly. Don't use sheets with high sides; they'll simply deflect the heat and make the cookies hard to remove.
◆ If you run out of cookie sheets, use the underside of inverted baking pans.

4. Bake until just lightly golden, about 11 minutes. (Be careful not to overbake.) Cool the cookies on the sheet on a wire rack for 5 minutes, then remove to the rack to cool completely. ● The cookies can be kept in an airtight container or plastic bag at cool room temperature for 1 day or frozen up to 1 month.

Per cookie with butter: 70 cal, 1 g pro, 3 g fat, 9 g car, 60 mg sod, 11 mg chol.

With margarine: 90 mg sod, 5 mg chol

CHOCOLATE NUT BROWNIES

Makes 24 squares

Preparation time: 18 minutes

Baking time: 45 minutes

These decadent, super-chocolatey brownies are topped by a crisp crust.

4 cups (two 12-ounce bags) semisweet chocolate chips
¼ cup water
1 stick (½ cup) plus 3 tablespoons butter or margarine (see page 321), softened
1½ cups granulated sugar
4 large eggs, at room temperature
1½ cups all-purpose flour
½ teaspoon baking powder
½ teaspoon salt
¼ teaspoon baking soda
1 cup (4 ounces) walnut pieces

1. Heat the oven to 350°F. Grease a 13 x 9-inch baking pan.

2. Put 3 cups of the chocolate chips and the water into a medium-size saucepan. Place over low heat and stir occasionally until melted (the mixture will be slightly grainy). (Or microwave the chocolate and water in a microwave-safe bowl, uncovered, on High for 1 minute. Stir the mixture, microwave for 30 seconds more, and stir again. Repeat as necessary until the chocolate is melted and the mixture is smooth.)

3. Scrape the mixture into a large (mixer) bowl. Add the butter and beat with an electric mixer until smooth and glossy. Beat in the sugar, then the eggs until blended.

4. In a small bowl, whisk together the flour, baking powder, salt, and baking soda. With the mixer on low, gradually add the flour mixture to the chocolate mixture, beating just until blended. Stir in the remaining chocolate chips and the nuts.

5. Scrape the batter into the prepared pan and smooth the top.

6. Bake until a toothpick inserted in the center comes out moist, not wet, 40 to 45 minutes. Cool the brownies completely in the pan on a wire rack before cutting into bars. ● The brownies can be kept in an airtight container at cool room temperature up to 3 days or frozen up to 2 months.

Per brownie with butter: 300 cal, 4 g pro, 17 g fat, 38 g car, 130 mg sod, 50 mg chol.

With margarine: 36 mg chol

BROWNIE BASICS
There may be some argument over what makes a perfect brownie: should it be fudgy and chewy or cakelike? One thing everyone does agree on is that brownies should be slightly underbaked in the center. Test brownies for doneness by touching the surface lightly with your fingertip. If it feels set, then test it with a toothpick, inserting it in the center. If it emerges with a few moist crumbs clinging to it, it's time to remove the pan from the oven.

EASY • 1 HOUR • LOW FAT

FUDGY LOW–FAT BROWNIES

Makes 16 squares
Preparation time: 10 minutes
Baking time: 22 minutes

These delightful brownies are fudgy and low in fat. The use of unsweetened cocoa powder, vegetable oil, and egg whites reduces the fat content but not the flavor.

½ cup packed light brown sugar
½ cup granulated sugar
¼ cup vegetable oil
1 large egg, at room temperature
Whites of 3 large eggs
1 teaspoon espresso powder
2 teaspoons vanilla extract
½ teaspoon baking powder
⅔ cup unsweetened cocoa powder
⅓ cup all-purpose flour
2 tablespoons sliced unblanched (natural) almonds

1. Heat the oven to 350°F. Coat an 8-inch square pan with cooking spray.

2. In a medium-size bowl, mix the sugars, oil, egg, egg whites, espresso powder, vanilla, and baking powder until blended. Stir in the cocoa and flour until blended.

3. Scrape the batter into the prepared pan. Sprinkle the surface with the almonds.

4. Bake until a toothpick inserted in the center comes out clean, 20 to 22 minutes. Cool the brownies completely in the pan on a wire rack before cutting into squares. • The brownies can be kept in an airtight container layered between sheets of waxed paper at cool room temperature up to 3 days or frozen up to 2 months.

Per brownie: 110 cal, 2 g pro, 5 g fat, 17 g car, 30 mg sod, 13 mg chol

C OOK'S TIP

For an extra-special low-fat dessert, serve these brownies topped with a scoop of low-fat or fat-free vanilla or coffee frozen yogurt.

STORING BROWNIES

Cool brownies in the pan completely before cutting them, no matter how tempting a tiny taste may be. Brownies that include nuts need to be cooled even longer because the nuts retain heat. Cutting nutty brownies before they cool completely will only cause the nuts to fall out and the brownies to crumble. Letting brownies rest for a minimum of 6 hours at room temperature, and preferably overnight, is ideal, as it allows flavors to blend and the butter or margarine, chocolate, and sugar to set. (Most blondies, however, taste better warm.) It's amazing how significantly brownies improve in taste and texture when stored overnight. Most brownies, particularly fudgy and chewy types, actually improve after 24 hours— if they last that long! Most fudgy brownies will last, uncut, in the pan, covered tightly and refrigerated, for up to three days. Unfrosted brownies may also be cut into squares, wrapped in plastic wrap, and stored in an airtight container at room temperature for up to three days. Before wrapping brownies, trim off any dried edges with a serrated knife. Blondies are best eaten within 24 hours of baking.

EASY • 1 HOUR • DECADENT

ZEBRAS

Makes 24 bars
Preparation time: 20 minutes
Baking time: 30 minutes

Dark and light layers give these delicious treats their whimsical name. The kids will be charmed by the name, and they'll love the taste too.

1½ cups (9 ounces) semisweet chocolate chips
2 sticks (1 cup) butter or margarine (see page 321), softened
1 cup packed light brown sugar
2 large eggs, at room temperature
1 teaspoon vanilla extract
1 teaspoon baking powder
2 cups all-purpose flour
¾ cup walnuts, coarsely chopped

1. Heat the oven to 350°F. Line a 13 x 9-inch baking pan with foil, letting the ends extend above both ends of the pan. Lightly grease the foil.

2. In a small saucepan, melt 1 cup of chocolate chips over low heat, stirring until melted. Remove from the heat and let cool slightly. (Or microwave the chocolate in a small microwave-safe bowl, uncovered, on High for 30 seconds. Stir until melted and smooth. Repeat as necessary, microwaving for 20 seconds at a time, then stirring until melted. Let cool slightly.)

3. In a large (mixer) bowl, beat the butter and brown sugar with an electric mixer until fluffy. Beat in the eggs one at a time, beating well after each addition. Beat in the vanilla and baking powder. Stir in the flour just until blended. Scoop half the dough into a second bowl.

4. Stir the melted chocolate into the remaining batter until blended. Spread the chocolate batter in the prepared pan. Drop tablespoonfuls of the plain batter over the chocolate layer. Spread carefully in an even layer. Sprinkle with the remaining ½ cup of chocolate chips and the walnuts.

5. Bake until the edges begin to pull away from the sides of the pan, about 30 minutes.

6. Cool completely in the pan on a wire rack. Lift the foil by the ends onto a cutting board. Remove the foil. Cut into bars. ● The zebras can be kept layered between sheets of waxed paper in an airtight container at cool room temperature up to 3 days or frozen up to 2 months.

Per bar with butter: 220 cal, 3 g pro, 13 g fat, 25 g car, 110 mg sod, 38 mg chol.
With margarine: 120 mg sod, 18 mg chol

BLONDIES

Makes 9 squares
Preparation time: 12 minutes
Baking time: 35 minutes

A blondie is a chewy brown-sugar bar cookie—like a brownie without the choco-late. This one is packed with pecans and chocolate chips, though any kind of nuts will do. Raisins would also be a delicious addition.

1 stick (½ cup) butter or margarine (see page 321), softened
1 cup packed light brown sugar
1 large egg, at room temperature
1 teaspoon vanilla extract
1 cup all-purpose flour
½ teaspoon baking powder
¾ cup (4½ ounces) semisweet chocolate chips
¾ cup (3 ounces) pecans, toasted and coarsely chopped
* (see page 325)*

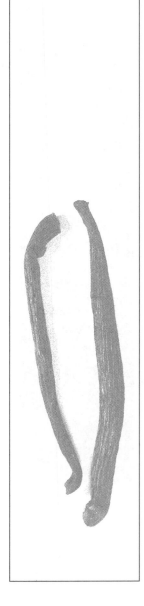

1. Heat the oven to 325°F. Line an 8-inch square baking pan with foil, letting the ends extend above the pan on 2 sides. Grease the foil.

2. In a medium-size (mixer) bowl, beat the butter, brown sugar, egg, and vanilla with an electric mixer until pale and fluffy. Stir in the flour, baking powder, choco-late chips, and nuts. Spread the mixture evenly in the prepared pan.

3. Bake until a toothpick inserted into the center comes out clean, 30 to 35 min-utes. Cool the blondies completely in the pan on a wire rack.

4. Lift the foil by the ends onto a cutting board. Remove the foil. Cut the blondie into squares. • The blondies can be kept layered between sheets of waxed paper in an airtight container at cool room temperature up to 3 days or frozen up to 2 months.

Per blondie with butter: 370 cal, 4 g pro, 21 g fat, 46 g car, 150 mg sod, 51 mg chol. With margarine: 160 mg sod, 24 mg chol

COOKIE MAILING TIPS

◆ Wrap highly decorated cookies indi-vidually in plastic wrap, then together in bubble wrap.

◆ Use shoe boxes for cookies if you run out of tins. Cookies must be well cush-ioned inside their container.

◆ Mail your cookie container inside a sturdy mailing carton big enough to leave space all around for cushioning.

◆ Cushion the box with crumpled news-paper, foam pellets, sheets of bubble plastic, or shredded paper.

◆ Don't use popcorn, cereal, or other edibles for the filler. They attract insects and may pick up noxious fumes.

◆ Close the carton and shake carefully before sealing. If you hear a rattle, add more cushioning.

◆ Mark the carton "Open Immediately—Edible," or "Fragile," or both, and mail it for the quickest delivery possible.

DECADENT

BLACK AND WHITE BROWNIES

Makes 16 squares

Preparation time: 25 minutes

Baking time: 45 minutes

These rich, fudgy, moist brownies are swirled with a luscious cream cheese mixture that makes these bar cookies to die for.

6 ounces semisweet chocolate, chopped

1 stick (½ cup) butter

3 large eggs, at room temperature

1 cup granulated sugar

1 teaspoon vanilla extract

⅔ cup all-purpose flour

⅛ teaspoon salt

CREAM CHEESE MIXTURE

1 package (8 ounces) cream cheese, softened

⅓ cup granulated sugar

1 large egg, at room temperature

1 teaspoon vanilla extract

1. Heat the oven to 350°F. Line an 8-inch square baking pan with foil, letting the ends extend above the pan on 2 sides.

2. In a small saucepan, melt the chocolate and butter over low heat, stirring until melted and smooth. Let cool. (Or microwave the butter and chocolate in a medium-size microwave-safe bowl, uncovered, on High for 1 minute. Stir the mixture. Repeat as necessary, microwaving for 20 seconds at a time, then stirring until the mixture is smooth and melted. Let cool.)

3. Meanwhile, make the cream cheese mixture: In a medium-size (mixer) bowl, beat the cream cheese and sugar with an electric mixer until smooth. Beat in the egg and vanilla until blended. Scrape down the bowl. Set aside.

4. In a medium-size (mixer) bowl, beat the eggs with an electric mixer until frothy. Beat in the sugar and vanilla. Beat in the cooled chocolate mixture until blended. Stir in the flour and salt.

5. Spread two-thirds of the chocolate mixture into the prepared pan. Spoon the cream cheese mixture over it, then spread to the edges of the pan. Cover with the remaining chocolate mixture. Swirl gently with a thin knife to marbleize the batter.

6. Bake until the top is dry but a toothpick inserted into the center comes out with traces of moist crumbs, about 45 minutes. Cool completely in the pan on a wire rack. Lift the foil by the ends onto a cutting board. Remove the foil. Cut into squares. ● The brownies can be kept layered between sheets of waxed paper in an airtight container at cool room temperature up to 3 days or frozen up to 2 months.

Per brownie: 250 cal, 4 g pro, 15 g fat, 28 g car, 130 mg sod, 84 mg chol

1 HOUR • OLD FASHIONED

CHERRY COBBLER BARS

Makes 18 bars

Preparation time: 30 minutes

Baking time: 30 minutes

All the flavor of cherry pie without the fuss of making a pie crust. Flouring your fingers makes it easier to position the sticky dough.

1 stick (½ cup) butter or margarine (see page 321), softened
1 cup confectioners' sugar
1 large egg, at room temperature
1 teaspoon freshly grated lemon peel
½ teaspoon baking powder
1½ cups all-purpose flour
1 can (21 ounces) cherry-pie filling
For garnish: confectioners' sugar

1. Heat the oven to 350°F. Grease an 11 x 7-inch baking pan.
2. In a large (mixer) bowl, beat the butter and confectioners' sugar with an electric mixer until pale and fluffy. Beat in the egg, lemon peel, and baking powder. With the mixer on low speed, gradually beat in the flour just until blended. Reserve ⅔ cup of the dough. With floured fingers, pat the remaining dough over the bottom of the prepared pan.
3. Spread the cherry-pie filling over the dough to the edges of the pan.
4. Roll the reserved dough into 1-inch balls. Flatten the balls slightly and place, evenly spaced, over the pie filling.
5. Bake until the top is golden brown, about 30 minutes.
6. Cool completely in the pan on a wire rack. Dust with confectioners' sugar before cutting into bars. • The bars can be kept layered between sheets of waxed paper in an airtight container at cool room temperature up to 3 days or frozen up to 2 months.

Per bar with butter: 150 cal, 2 g pro, 6 g fat, 24 g car, 70 mg sod, 26 mg chol.
With margarine: 80 mg sod, 12 mg chol

CLASSIC • OLD FASHIONED

LEMON BARS

Makes 24 bars

Preparation time: 25 minutes

Baking time: 45 minutes

A classic among cookies, these tangy bars are an irresistible treat. For a new dimension, try the chocolate variation.

VARIATION

APPLE KUCHEN BARS

• Proceed as directed through step 2. Omit the cherry-pie filling. Instead, drain 1 can (20 ounces) apple slices. Mix the apples with ½ cup golden raisins and 1 teaspoon ground cinnamon. Spread the mixture over the dough, using a rubber spatula to break up apples if needed to cover the surface of the dough.
• Roll the remaining dough into long ropes and lay them diagonally across the filling to create a lattice effect. Proceed as directed in step 5 and step 6.

Per bar with butter: 150 cal, 2 g pro, 6 g fat, 23 g car, 70 mg sod, 26 mg chol. With margarine: 80 mg sod, 12 mg chol

• 1 HOUR
• OLD FASHIONED

VARIATION

CHOCOLATE LEMON BARS

• Prepare the pan as directed.

• In a food processor, process 1½ cups all-purpose flour, ½ cup confectioners' sugar, ¼ cup unsweetened cocoa powder, and ½ teaspoon salt until blended. With the machine running, gradually add 2 sticks (1 cup) cold butter or margarine, cut into small pieces. Process until the mixture clumps and leaves the side of the bowl. Press the dough evenly over the bottom of the prepared pan.

• Bake the crust at 350°F. until it looks dry on the top, about 20 minutes.

• Proceed as directed from step 4.

Per bar with butter: 280 cal, 3 g pro, 15 g fat, 35 g car, 210 mg sod, 72 mg chol. With margarine: 230 mg sod, 35 mg chol

• DECADENT

CRUST

1½ sticks (¾ cup) butter or margarine (see page 321), softened
1½ cups all-purpose flour
½ cup confectioners' sugar

LEMON TOPPING

4 large eggs, at room temperature
2 cups granulated sugar
¼ cup all-purpose flour
1 teaspoon baking powder
2 teaspoons freshly grated lemon peel
⅓ cup fresh lemon juice
For garnish: confectioners' sugar

1. Heat the oven to 350°F. Line a 13 x 9-inch baking pan with foil, letting the ends extend above both ends of the pan. Grease the foil.

2. Make the crust: In a food processor or with an electric mixer, process or beat the butter, flour, and confectioners' sugar until the mixture holds together and forms a dough. Press the dough over the bottom of the prepared pan.

3. Bake until lightly golden and firm when gently pressed, about 15 minutes. Do not turn the oven off.

4. Meanwhile, make the topping: In a food processor or with an electric mixer, process or beat the eggs, sugar, flour, baking powder, lemon peel, and lemon juice until blended. Pour the mixture over the hot crust.

5. Bake until the top is golden brown and the filling is set, 25 to 30 minutes. Cool completely in the pan on a wire rack. Dust with confectioners' sugar before cutting into bars. • The lemon bars can be kept between layers of waxed paper in an airtight container at cool room temperature up to 3 days or frozen up to 2 months.
Per bar with butter: 170 cal, 2 g pro, 7 g fat, 27 g car, 90 mg sod, 51 mg chol.
With margarine: 100 mg sod, 35 mg chol

DECADENT

BROWNIE SHORTBREAD

Makes 24 bars
Preparation time: 45 minutes
Baking time: 40 minutes

These delectable bars combine shortbread pastry with a brownie topping.

SHORTBREAD CRUST

1 stick (½ cup) unsalted butter or margarine (see page 321), softened
1 cup all-purpose flour
¼ cup granulated sugar
¼ teaspoon salt

▶

BROWNIE LAYER

1 stick (½ cup) unsalted butter or
  margarine (see page 321)
3 ounces unsweetened chocolate
2 large eggs, at room temperature
¾ cup granulated sugar
3 tablespoons all-purpose flour
½ teaspoon baking powder

1. Heat the oven to 350°F. Grease an 11 x 7-inch baking pan.

2. Make the crust: In a food processor or with an electric mixer, process or beat the butter, flour, sugar, and salt until the mixture holds together and forms a dough. Press the dough over the bottom of the pan.

3. Bake until light golden and firm when touched, about 20 minutes.

4. Meanwhile, make the brownie layer: In a small saucepan, heat the butter and chocolate over low heat, stirring often, until melted. Remove from the heat and let cool for 5 minutes. (Or microwave the butter and chocolate in a small microwave-safe bowl, uncovered, on High for 1 minute. Stir the mixture. Repeat as necessary, microwaving for 20 seconds at a time, then stirring until the mixture is smooth and melted. Let cool for 5 minutes.) In a medium-size bowl, whisk the eggs, sugar, flour, and baking powder until blended. Whisk in the cooled chocolate mixture.

5. Remove the shortbread from the oven (leave the oven on) and pour the brownie mixture over the shortbread base. Return to the oven and bake until top feels firm, about 20 minutes. Cool completely in the pan on a wire rack. Cut into bars. ● The brownie bars can be kept in an airtight container between layers of waxed paper at cool room temperature up to 3 days or frozen up to 2 months.
Per bar with butter: 150 cal, 2 g pro, 10 g fat, 14 g car, 40 mg sod, 38 mg chol.
With margarine: 130 mg sod, 18 mg chol

COOK'S TIP

Bar cookies can also be stored right in the same pan they are baked in. Cover tightly with plastic wrap.

EASY • 1 HOUR • LOW FAT

RASPBERRY–HAZELNUT BARS

Makes 48 bars
Preparation time: 20 minutes
Baking time: 25 minutes

These nut-sprinkled bar cookies are pretty enough to grace a holiday table or sturdy enough to pack in a lunch box or for a picnic.

1 stick (½ cup) butter or margarine (see page 321), softened
⅓ cup granulated sugar
1 large egg, at room temperature
2 cups all-purpose flour
¾ cup seedless raspberry jam
½ cup skinned toasted hazelnuts, coarsely chopped (see page 325)

1. Heat the oven to 350°F. Line a 13 x 9-inch baking pan with foil, letting the ends extend above both ends of the pan. Lightly grease the foil.

2. In a large (mixer) bowl, beat the butter and sugar with an electric mixer until light and fluffy. Beat in the egg. With the mixer on low speed, gradually add the flour, beating just until blended.

3. Pat the dough evenly into the prepared pan. Spread the jam over the dough almost to the edges. Sprinkle with the nuts.

4. Bake until the edges are just golden, 20 to 25 minutes. Cool completely in the pan on a wire rack. Lift the foil by the ends onto a cutting board. Remove the foil. Cut into bars. • The bars can be kept in an airtight container between layers of waxed paper at cool room temperature up to 1 week or frozen up to 2 months.
Per bar with butter: 60 cal, 1 g pro, 3 g fat, 9 g car, 20 mg sod, 10 mg chol.
With margarine: 4 mg chol

EASY • 1 HOUR • CLASSIC

CONGO BARS

Makes 24 bars
Preparation time: 15 minutes
Baking time: 25 minutes

These moist bar cookies are made with sweetened condensed milk and generously studded with chocolate chips, coconut, and almonds.

½ stick (¼ cup) butter or margarine
1½ cups graham-cracker crumbs
1 can (14 ounces) regular or nonfat sweetened condensed milk
 (not evaporated milk)
1 cup (6 ounces) semisweet chocolate chips
1 cup sweetened flaked coconut
½ cup sliced almonds

1. Heat the oven to 350°F. Line a 13 x 9-inch baking pan with foil, letting the ends extend above both ends of the.

2. Put the butter in the prepared pan and place it in the oven to melt.

3. Remove the pan from the oven and stir in the graham-cracker crumbs. Press the crumbs into an even layer with a rubber spatula.

4. Pour the sweetened condensed milk evenly over the crumb layer. Sprinkle with the chips, then the coconut, then the almonds. Press down gently with your fingertips.

5. Bake until the top is golden, about 25 minutes. Cool completely in the pan on a wire rack. Lift the foil by the ends onto a cutting board. Remove the foil. Cut into bars. • The bar cookies can be kept in an airtight container between layers of waxed paper at cool room temperature up to 4 days or frozen up to 2 months.
Per bar: 160 cal, 3 g pro, 8 g fat, 21 g car, 90 mg sod, 11 mg chol.
With margarine and nonfat sweetened condensed milk: 150 cal, 6 g fat, 1 mg chol

SWEETENED CONDENSED MILK
Sweetened condensed milk is an all-natural blend of fresh milk and cane sugar cooked until most of the water is evaporated. It was invented in 1853 by Gail Borden and was the first product sold by Borden Inc.

OLD FASHIONED

WHOLE–WHEAT APPLESAUCE BARS

Makes 24 bars
Preparation time: 15 minutes
Baking time: 30 minutes

Soft, sweet, and packed with walnuts and raisins, these bars are the perfect snack to pack in a lunch box or enjoy with a cup of hot tea or coffee. The cream cheese icing adds a delectable finish, but the cookies can also be served with a dusting of confectioners' sugar.

⅔ cup packed dark brown sugar
5 tablespoons plus 1 teaspoon (⅓ cup) butter or
  margarine (see page 321), softened
2 large eggs, at room temperature
⅔ cup unsweetened plain applesauce
¾ teaspoon ground allspice
½ teaspoon ground cinnamon
¼ teaspoon baking soda
½ cup all-purpose flour
½ cup whole-wheat flour
⅓ cup golden raisins
⅓ cup (3⅓ ounces) walnuts, chopped

CREAM CHEESE ICING
1 package (3 ounces) cream cheese, softened
1 cup confectioners' sugar
1 teaspoon vanilla extract

1. Heat the oven to 350°F. Line an 8- or 9-inch square pan with foil, letting the ends extend above the pan on 2 sides. Lightly grease the foil.

2. In a large (mixer) bowl, beat the brown sugar, butter, eggs, applesauce, allspice, cinnamon, and baking soda with an electric mixer until well blended.

3. With the mixer on low speed, add both flours, the raisins, and nuts, and beat just until blended.

4. Spread the mixture in the prepared pan. Bake until a toothpick inserted near the center comes out clean, 25 to 30 minutes. Cool completely in the pan on a wire rack.

5. Meanwhile, make the icing: In a medium-size (mixer) bowl, beat the cream cheese, confectioners' sugar, and vanilla with an electric mixer until smooth and creamy.

6. Lift the foil by the ends onto a cutting board. Remove the foil. Spread the icing over the top. Cut into bars. ● The bars can be kept in an airtight container in the refrigerator up to 1 week.

Per bar with butter: 140 cal, 2 g pro, 7 g fat, 18 g car, 60 mg sod, 28 mg chol.
With margarine: 22 mg chol

COOK'S TIP

Whole-wheat flour has a shorter shelf life than all-purpose flour because it contains part of the wheat's oil-rich germ and bran. Buy small quantities and store it airtight in the refrigerator up to 6 months, or in the freezer up to 1 year.

These fabulous Fig Bar Cookies (p.37), here decorated with fruit-shaped cereal, are both delicious and healthful.

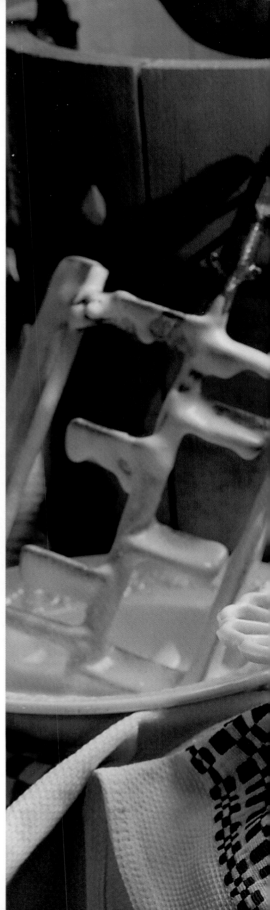

Chocolate, coconut, and almonds make Congo Bars (p.31), below, a treat that disappears quickly. Bake two batches and freeze one for later; they keep wonderfully.

Good things like simple, old-fashioned bar cookies never go out of style. These Blondies (p.26), right, prove the point deliciously.

Cookies are easy to make, and the fun of mixing, rolling, and shaping the dough brings out the kid in everyone.

These Molasses Crinkle Cookies (p.42) not only taste terrific, they're also great for dunking.

FIG BAR COOKIES
Makes 64 bars
Preparation time: 15 minutes plus 1 hour to chill
Cooking time: 25 minutes
Baking time: 35 minutes

COOK'S TIP

Figs (both fresh and dried) are a good source of iron and calcium. Store dried figs (and all dried fruit) in a plastic bag in the refrigerator, and they will keep from 6 months to 1 year.

There is no first bite as luxurious as that of a fig bar cookie. Moist and chewy, these will remind you of the fig cookies of your childhood—only better.

DOUGH
10 tablespoons plus 2 teaspoons (⅔ cup) butter or margarine (see page 321), softened
1 cup packed light or dark brown sugar
1 large egg, at room temperature
Yolk of 1 large egg
2 teaspoons vanilla extract
1 teaspoon baking powder
¼ teaspoon salt
2½ cups all-purpose flour

FIG FILLING
2 packages (8 ounces each) dried Mission figs, stems removed
  and figs finely chopped (2½ cups)
1⅔ cups orange juice
¼ cup honey
¼ teaspoon ground cinnamon

For garnish: confectioners' sugar

1. Make the dough: In a large (mixer) bowl, beat the butter and sugar with an electric mixer until smooth. Beat in the egg, egg yolk, vanilla, baking powder, and salt until well blended. With the mixer on low speed, beat in the flour just until blended.

2. Divide the dough in half. Wrap with plastic and refrigerate until firm enough to roll out, about 1 hour.

3. Meanwhile, make the filling: In a large nonstick skillet or saucepan, mix the figs, orange juice, honey, and cinnamon. Bring to a boil over medium-high heat. Reduce the heat to medium-low and simmer, uncovered, for 20 minutes, until the mixture is reduced to a thick paste. Spread over an ungreased cookie sheet to cool.

4. Heat the oven to 375°F. Line a 13 x 9-inch baking pan with foil, letting the ends extend above both ends of the pan. Grease the foil.

5. On a lightly floured surface with a lightly floured rolling pin, roll out half the dough to a 13 x 9-inch rectangle. Roll the dough loosely around the rolling pin, then unroll into the prepared pan (if the dough tears, simply patch it together). Spread the filling over the dough. Roll out the remaining dough as directed and lay over the filling.

▶

6. Bake until the top is golden brown, 30 to 35 minutes. Cool completely in the pan on a wire rack.

7. Lift the foil by the ends onto a cutting board. Remove the foil. Cut crosswise into 8 equal strips. Cut each strip into 8 rectangles. Dust with confectioners' sugar.
• The bars can be kept between layers of waxed paper in an airtight container at cool room temperature up to 1 week or frozen up to 3 months.
Per bar with butter: 80 cal, 1 g pro, 3 g fat, 14 g car, 40 mg sod, 12 mg chol.
With margarine: 7 mg chol

EASY • CLASSIC

MEXICAN WEDDING CAKES

Makes 66 cookies
Preparation time: 10 minutes
Baking time: 18 minutes per batch

In Oaxaca, Mexico, these rich and tender cookies are festively wrapped and given as favors to guests at weddings. They are liberally coated with confectioners' sugar, so you may want to have a clothes brush handy when you eat them. Or warn anyone within reach of these cookies to pop them into their mouths whole. (You'll get no arguments.)

½ cup (2 ounces) whole unblanched (natural) almonds
½ cup (2 ounces) pecans
2 sticks (1 cup) cold unsalted butter or
   margarine (see page 321), cut into small pieces
1¾ cups confectioners' sugar
1 teaspoon vanilla extract
2 cups all-purpose flour
1 teaspoon anise seeds

1. Heat the oven to 325°F. Have ready 1 or more ungreased cookie sheets. Process the nuts in a food processor for 1 minute, or until very finely ground. (Don't overprocess or you'll have a paste.) Add the butter and process until smooth and creamy, scraping down the bowl as necessary. Add ¼ cup of the confectioners' sugar and the vanilla. Process until blended. Add the flour and anise seeds; process until well blended.

2. Roll the dough into 1-inch balls and place 1 inch apart on the cookie sheet(s).

3. Bake until the bottoms of the cookies are light brown, about 18 minutes. Cool on the cookie sheets on a wire rack for 15 minutes. Put the remaining confectioners' sugar on a plate and gently (the cookies are fragile) roll the warm cookies in the sugar. Cool on a wire rack, then roll in the sugar again.
Per cookie with butter: 60 cal, 1 g pro, 4 g fat, 6 g car, 0 mg sod, 8 mg chol.
With margarine: 30 mg sod, 0 mg chol

COOK'S TIP

Anise seeds (also spelled aniseed) have a licorice-like flavor. They are popular in Scandinavian and German baked goods such as cookies, cakes, and breads and in the classic Italian biscotti. Store anise seeds airtight in a dark, cool place up to 1 year.

LOW FAT • CLASSIC • OLD FASHIONED

CHOCOLATE CRACKLE TOPS

Makes 56 cookies
Preparation time: 30 minutes plus 1 hour to chill
Baking time: 14 minutes per batch

A gem of a cookie—they're soft when hot but firm and chewy when cool.

> 1 stick (½ cup) butter or margarine (see page 321), softened
> 1½ cups granulated sugar
> 3 large eggs, at room temperature
> 4 ounces unsweetened chocolate, melted and cooled
> 1 teaspoon vanilla extract
> 2 teaspoons baking powder
> 1 teaspoon ground cinnamon
> 2 cups plus 2 tablespoons all-purpose flour
> ½ cup confectioners' sugar

1. In a large (mixer) bowl, beat the butter and granulated sugar with an electric mixer until the mixture looks like wet sand. Beat in the eggs until blended, then beat in the chocolate, vanilla, baking powder, and cinnamon. With the mixer on low speed, gradually add the flour, beating until well blended.

2. Wrap the dough in waxed paper or plastic wrap and chill for 1 hour or until firm enough to handle, about 1 hour.

3. Heat the oven to 350°F. Lightly grease 1 or more cookie sheets.

4. Shape heaping teaspoonfuls of the dough into balls (it's a bit messy). Roll the balls in confectioners' sugar. Place 1½ inches apart on the prepared cookie sheet(s). ▶

COOKIE STORAGE

Homemade cookies are so irresistible, they may not be around for long. If you do store them, however, keep these hints in mind:
◆ Store all cookies after they have completely cooled.
◆ Store most cookies airtight in tightly closed plastic bags, foil wrap, plastic storage containers, tins, or cookie jars with tight-fitting lids.
◆ Don't store crisp and soft cookies together. While soft cookies need an airtight container to stay moist, crisp cookies do best in a loosely covered container kept in a dry place to maintain crispness. (If you live in a humid climate, do keep crisp cookies tightly covered. If they soften anyway, recrisp them in a 300°F oven for about 5 minutes.) If the cookies are moist or sticky, store them with waxed paper between the layers. If soft cookies dry out, add an apple wedge on a piece of waxed paper to the container and replace it every few days.
◆ Don't store cookies with incompatible flavors together, and don't store strongly flavored cookies with mild ones. Sugar cookies kept in a tin with gingerbread cookies will end up tasting of the spices.
◆ It is better to freeze cookies in freezer storage containers or wrapped in heavy-duty foil than to keep them for longer than suggested at room temperature.
◆ Always label containers headed for the freezer with the date.
◆ Unwrap frosted or glazed frozen cookies before you thaw them. Otherwise, the icing may stick to the wrapping.

5. Bake until the cookie tops are puffed, slightly cracked, and soft to the touch and do not spring back when gently pressed, 12 to 14 minutes. Cool the cookies on the sheet on a wire rack for 2 to 3 minutes. Using a spatula, remove the cookies to the rack to cool completely. • The cookies can be kept in an airtight container or plastic bag at cool room temperature up to 3 days or frozen up to 1 month.

Per cookie with butter: 760 cal, 1 g pro, 3 g fat, 11 g car, 40 mg sod,16 mg chol.

With margarine: 11 mg chol

LOW FAT • OLD FASHIONED

CORNMEAL SHORTBREAD COOKIES

Makes 64 cookies

Preparation time: 15 minutes plus 2 hours to chill

Baking time: 18 minutes per batch

The crunch of cornmeal adds an unexpected bite to these rich cookies. While any kind of cornmeal will work in this recipe, you'll appreciate the flavor most if you use stone-ground, which contains bits of the outer bran layer.

> *2 sticks (1 cup) unsalted butter, softened*
> *1 cup confectioners' sugar*
> *1½ teaspoons vanilla extract*
> *¼ teaspoon salt*
> *1 large egg, at room temperature*
> *Yolk of 1 large egg*
> *1⅓ cups yellow cornmeal*
> *1¾ cups all-purpose flour*

1. In a large (mixer) bowl, beat the butter and sugar with an electric mixer until fluffy. Beat in the vanilla and salt. Beat in the egg and egg yolk until well blended. With the mixer on low speed, add the cornmeal, then the flour, beating just until blended.

2. On a lightly floured surface, form the dough into a ball, then divide in half. Roll each half into a 12-inch log. Wrap each in plastic wrap. Refrigerate until firm, at least 2 hours, or freeze for 30 minutes. • The dough can be made up to this point and refrigerated up to 3 days or wrapped in foil and frozen up to 3 months. If frozen, remove to the refrigerator for 2 hours before baking.

3. Heat the oven to 350°F. Have ready 1 or more ungreased cookie sheets.

4. Cut each log into 32 slices. Place the slices 1½ inches apart on the cookie sheet(s). Bake until pale gold on the top and pale brown on the bottom, 15 to 18 minutes. Cool the cookies on the sheet on a wire rack for 2 to 3 minutes, then remove to the rack with a spatula to cool completely. • The cookies can be kept in an airtight container or plastic bag at cool room temperature up to 1 week or frozen up to 1 month.

Per cookie : 60 cal, 1 g pro, 3 g fat, 7 g car, 10 mg sod, 14 mg chol

Ⓒ OOK'S TIP

Store cornmeal in an airtight container in a cool, dry place for up to 6 months or in the refrigerator or freezer up to 1 year.

FOUR CHOCOLATE COOKIES FROM ONE DOUGH

With a single versatile chocolate dough, you can make Chocolate Leaves, Chocolate Pretzels, Chocolate Sandwiches, and Chocolate Cherry "Ravioli." Make just one variety per batch of dough, or divide the dough and make a few of each.

Preparation time: 15 minutes plus 1 hour to chill
Baking time: 10 to 15 minutes per batch (depending on cookie)

1 stick (½ cup) butter or margarine (see page 321), softened
½ cup packed light brown sugar
½ teaspoon vanilla extract
1 large egg, at room temperature
2 ounces unsweetened chocolate, melted and cooled
½ teaspoon baking powder
2 cups all-purpose flour

1. In a large mixer bowl, beat the butter, sugar, and vanilla with an electric mixer until pale and fluffy. Beat in the egg, then the chocolate and baking powder. With the mixer on low speed, gradually add the flour, beating just until blended.
2. Pat the dough into a disk, wrap in plastic, and chill until firm enough to shape or roll out, about 1 hour.
3. Follow the instructions for one of the variations below.

EASY• LOW FAT

CHOCOLATE LEAVES
1. Heat the oven to 350°F. Have ready 1 or more ungreased cookie sheets.
2. Roll out the dough on a lightly floured surface with a floured rolling pin to ¼-inch thickness. Cut the dough with a 3-inch leaf-shaped cookie cutter, or cut out leaves with the tip of a knife. Mark veins with the back of a knife.
3. Place 2 inches apart on the cookie sheet(s). Bake 10 to 12 minutes, until the cookies feel firm. Cool the cookies on the sheet on a wire rack for 2 minutes, then remove to the rack to cool completely.

Makes 40. Per cookie with butter: 60 cal, 1 g pro, 3 g fat, 8 g car, 30 mg sod, 12 mg chol. With margarine: 40 mg sod, 5 mg chol

EASY

CHOCOLATE PRETZELS
1. Heat the oven to 350°F.
2. Roll the dough into a log and cut into 28 equal pieces. Roll each piece into an 8-inch-long rope. Twist into pretzel shapes. Place 1 inch apart on ungreased cookie sheet(s).
3. Brush with beaten egg white, then sprinkle with nonpareils or coarse sugar. Bake until the cookies feel firm, about 12 minutes. Cool the cookies on the sheet on a wire rack for 2 minutes, then remove to the rack with a spatula to cool completely.

Makes 28. Per cookie with butter: 90 cal, 1 g pro, 5 g fat, 11 g car, 50 mg sod, 16 mg chol. With margarine: 8 mg chol

EASY • DECADENT

CHOCOLATE SANDWICHES
1. Heat the oven to 350°F. Have ready 1 or more ungreased cookie sheets.
2. Roll out the dough on a lightly floured surface with a floured rolling pin to ⅛-inch thickness. Cut the dough with a plain or scalloped 2½-inch round cookie cutter. Reroll the scraps. Place 2 inches apart on the cookie sheet(s).
3. Bake until cookies feel firm, about 10 minutes. Cool the cookies on the sheet on a wire rack for 2 minutes, then remove to the rack with a spatula to cool completely.
4. Sandwich 2 cookies together with ready-to-spread milk chocolate frosting (you'll need about ⅔ cup). To decorate, melt ½ cup semisweet chocolate chips and drizzle cookies with the melted chocolate.

Makes 18. Per cookie with butter: 210 cal, 3 g pro, 10 g fat, 28 g car, 90 mg sod, 26 mg chol. With margarine: 12 mg chol

DECADENT

CHOCOLATE CHERRY "RAVIOLI"
1. Heat the oven to 350°F. Have ready 1 or more ungreased cookie sheets.
2. Roll out the dough on a lightly floured surface with a floured rolling pin to ⅛-inch thickness. Cut the dough into 2½-inch squares. Spoon 1 heaping teaspoon canned cherry-pie filling (you'll need about ⅔ cup) in the center of half the squares. Brush the edges with beaten egg white. Top with the remaining squares (the dough may crack slightly). Press the edges with a fork to seal. With a sharp knife, cut an X in the center of the tops.
3. Place 2 inches apart on the cookie sheet(s). Bake until the cookies feel firm, about 15 minutes. Cool the cookies on the sheet on a wire rack for 2 minutes, then remove to the rack with a spatula to cool completely.

Makes 18. Per cookie with butter: 150 cal, 2 g pro, 7 g fat, 21 g car, 70 mg sod, 26 mg chol. With margarine: 12 mg chol

EASY • 1 HOUR • LOW FAT

MOLASSES CRINKLE COOKIES

Makes 36 cookies

Preparation time: 18 minutes

Baking time: 12 minutes per batch

These spicy cookies are true to their name. Bake them until they "crinkle" on top and "crackle" in your mouth.

¾ cup plus 3 tablespoons granulated sugar
½ cup light molasses
2 tablespoons vegetable oil
Whites of 2 large eggs
1½ teaspoons ground ginger
1 teaspoon ground cinnamon
¾ teaspoon baking soda
½ teaspoon salt
¼ teaspoon ground cloves
2 cups all-purpose flour

1. Heat the oven to 350°F. Coat 1 or more cookie sheets with vegetable oil cooking spray.

2. In a medium-size bowl, whisk together ¾ cup of the sugar, the molasses, oil, egg whites, ginger, cinnamon, baking soda, salt, and cloves just until blended. Stir in the flour.

3. Put the remaining 3 tablespoons of sugar into a small bowl. Roll tablespoonfuls of dough into 1-inch balls. Roll the balls in the bowl of sugar. Place 2 inches apart on the prepared cookie sheet(s).

4. Bake until crackled on top and firm to the touch, 12 minutes. Cool the cookies on the sheet on a wire rack for 2 to 3 minutes, then remove to the rack to cool completely. • The cookies can be kept in an airtight container or plastic bag at cool room temperature up to 3 days or frozen up to 1 month.

Per cookie: 70 cal, 1 g pro, 1 g fat, 14 g car, 60 mg sod, 0 mg chol

MOLASSES

This thick brown syrup is made by boiling the juices pressed during sugar cane and sugar beet processing. There are three types of molasses: Light molasses is produced by the first boiling and has a mild flavor. The second boiling produces dark molasses, which has a more assertive flavor and darker color. The final product is called blackstrap molasses. High in iron, it is very thick and dark with almost no sweetness and is rarely used in cooking.

EASY • 1 HOUR • OLD FASHIONED

WALNUT THUMBPRINT COOKIES

Makes 28 cookies

Preparation time: 25 minutes

Baking time: 20 minutes per batch

These butter-rich cookies are shaped with your thumb (or you can use a thimble). Fill the hollows with your favorite jam or an assortment of colors and flavors. Unsweetened all-fruit spread would work just as well.

1 stick (½ cup) butter or margarine (see page 321), softened
⅓ cup granulated sugar
Yolk of 1 large egg
¾ teaspoon vanilla extract
1 cup all-purpose flour
⅛ teaspoon salt
½ cup (2 ounces) walnuts, finely chopped
5 tablespoons fruit jam (strawberry, peach, or raspberry)

1. Heat the oven to 350°F. Have ready 1 or more ungreased cookie sheets.

2. In a medium-size (mixer) bowl, beat the butter and sugar with an electric mixer until fluffy. Beat in the egg yolk and vanilla until blended.

3. With the mixer on low speed, add the flour, salt, and nuts, beating just until blended.

4. Shape the dough into 1-inch balls and place 2 inches apart on the cookie sheet(s). With a lightly floured thumb or thimble, make a depression in the center of each cookie.

5. Bake for 10 minutes. Remove the sheet from the oven and fill each depression with about ½ teaspoon of jam. Return to the oven and bake until the cookies just begin to turn golden, about 10 minutes more.

6. Cool the cookies on the sheet on a wire rack for 3 minutes, then remove to the rack to cool completely. ● The cookies can be kept loosely covered at cool room temperature up to 2 days or frozen in an airtight freezer container up to 2 weeks.

Per cookie with butter: 80 cal, 1 g pro, 5 g fat, 9 g car, 50 mg sod, 16 mg chol.
With margarine: 50 mg sod, 8 mg chol

EASY • 1 HOUR • CLASSIC

ALMOND SHORTBREAD

Makes 12 cookies
Preparation time: 20 minutes
Baking time: 30 minutes

Shortbread is not a bread at all, but a thick, rich, crisp cookie of Scottish origins. It contains a high proportion of butter or "shortening," which is how it got its name. This tender version and the flavored variations share a richness that is hard to resist.

1 cup all-purpose flour
¼ cup confectioners' sugar
1 tablespoon cornstarch
1 stick (½ cup) cold unsalted butter or margarine (see page 321),
*   cut into small pieces*
1 teaspoon almond extract
½ teaspoon vanilla extract
For decoration: almond slices (optional)

▶

VARIATION

PECAN THUMBPRINT COOKIES

Substitute ½ cup finely chopped pecans for the walnuts and proceed as directed.

Per cookie with butter: 80 cal, 1 g pro, 5 g fat, 9 g car, 50 mg sod, 16 mg chol. With margarine: 60 mg sod, 8 mg chol

- EASY • 1 HOUR
- OLD FASHIONED

VARIATION

CHOCOLATE SHORTBREAD

Add ⅓ cup unsweetened cocoa powder to the flour mixture and increase the confectioners' sugar to ½ cup; omit the almond extract. Proceed as directed.

Per cookie with butter: 130 cal, 2 g pro, 8 g fat, 15 g car, 0 mg sod, 21 mg chol. With margarine: 90 mg sod, 0 mg chol

- EASY • 1 HOUR

1. Heat the oven to 325°F. Have ready 1 ungreased cookie sheet.

2. To make the dough in a food processor: Process the flour, sugar, and cornstarch a few seconds to blend. Scatter the butter over the surface and process with on/off turns 4 or 5 times until the mixture resembles coarse crumbs. Sprinkle with the almond and vanilla extracts and process with on/off turns 2 or 3 times until the mixture clumps together.

To make the dough by hand: In a medium bowl, mix the flour, sugar, and cornstarch. Cut in the butter with a pastry blender until the mixture resembles coarse crumbs. Stir in the almond and vanilla extracts.

3. Put the dough in the center of the cookie sheet. Using your hands, pat the dough into an even circle, 8 inches in diameter. With a blunt knife (or the back of a knife), score the dough into 12 wedges, cutting about halfway through. Prick the dough all over with a fork. Press 3 almond slices at the end of each wedge.

4. Bake until the shortbread looks dry but not browned, 25 to 30 minutes. Put the shortbread on the sheet on a wire rack. Cut the wedges all the way through with a sharp knife, taking care not to scratch the surface of the cookie sheet. Cool the shortbread completely. • The cookies can be kept in an airtight container at cool room temperature up to 3 days or frozen up to 2 months.

Per cookie with butter: 120 cal, 1 g pro, 8 g fat, 11 g car, 0 mg sod, 21 mg chol.
With margarine: 90 mg sod, 0 mg chol

VARIATION

ORANGE-HAZELNUT SHORTBREAD

Add 1 teaspoon freshly grated orange peel to the flour mixture; eliminate the almond extract. Proceed as directed. Decorate each wedge with 2 hazelnuts before baking.

Per cookie with butter: 160 cal, 2 g pro, 12 g fat, 12 g car, 0 mg sod, 21 mg chol. With margarine: 90 mg sod, 0 mg chol

• EASY • 1 HOUR

CLASSIC

CINNAMON–ALMOND BISCOTTI

Makes 80 cookies

Preparation time: 10 minutes plus 1 hour to chill

Baking time: 1 hour

Biscotti are a traditional Italian treat; they are crisp and hard but soften without crumbling when dunked into a cup of hot coffee, hot tea, or hot cocoa. Their name, related to the word "biscuit," means "twice-cooked"—which is how they are made.

1¾ cups granulated sugar
1¼ sticks (½ cup plus 2 tablespoons) butter or margarine (see page 321), softened
1¼ teaspoons ground cinnamon
1 teaspoon baking powder
1 teaspoon baking soda
5 large eggs, at room temperature
1 tablespoon vanilla extract
2 ounces unsweetened chocolate, grated or finely ground in food processor or blender
4 cups all-purpose flour
1½ cups whole unblanched (natural) almonds, toasted and coarsely chopped

EGG GLAZE
1 egg beaten with 1 teaspoon water

COOK'S TIP

Skinned, toasted hazelnuts (1½ cups) could be used instead of the almonds.

1. In a large (mixer) bowl, beat the sugar, butter, cinnamon, baking powder, and baking soda with an electric mixer until blended.

2. Add the eggs and extract and beat until smooth. Stir in the grated chocolate. With the mixer on low speed, beat in the flour, half at a time, until blended. Stir in the almonds. Cover the dough and refrigerate until firm enough to shape, about 1 hour.

3. Adjust the oven racks to divide oven into thirds. Heat the oven to 350°F. Lightly grease 2 cookie sheets.

4. Divide the dough in fourths. On a lightly floured surface, roll out each portion of dough into a 12-inch log. Place 2 logs 4 inches apart on each cookie sheet. In a small bowl, mix the egg and water. Brush the dough with the egg glaze.

5. Bake until the logs feel firm, 25 to 30 minutes, switching the cookie sheets halfway through baking. Loosen the logs and cool on the sheets for 10 minutes. Reduce the oven temperature to 275°F.

6. Slide the logs onto a cutting board. With a long serrated knife, carefully cut each log diagonally into 20 slices. Arrange the slices upright on the cookie sheets.

7. Bake until dry, 25 to 30 minutes. Cool the cookies on the sheet on a wire rack for 2 minutes, then remove to the rack to cool completely. ● The cookies can be kept in an airtight container at cool room temperature up to 1 week or frozen up to 1 month.

Per cookie with butter: 80 cal, 2 g pro, 4 g fat, 10 g car, 40 mg sod, 20 mg chol.
With margarine: 16 mg chol

LOW FAT ● OLD FASHIONED

FLAKY CINNAMON TWISTS

Makes 40 cookies
Preparation time: 20 minutes plus at least 1 hour to chill
Baking time: 16 minutes per batch

The dough for these cookies, made from butter and cream cheese, produces a tender, flaky, irresistible treat. They are pretty to serve and can be presented arranged on a plate or standing on end in a glass or any upright container.

> *1 stick (½ cup) cold unsalted butter or margarine (see page 321),*
>   *cut into small pieces*
> *1 package (3 ounces) regular or fat-free cream cheese,*
>   *cut into small pieces*
> *⅛ teaspoon salt*
> *1 cup all-purpose flour*
> *¼ cup granulated sugar*
> *¼ teaspoon ground cinnamon*
> *2 tablespoons heavy (whipping) cream or milk*

1. To make the dough in a food processor: Process the butter, cream cheese, salt, and flour with on/off turns until the mixture comes together in a ball. ▶

To make the dough by hand: Soften the butter and cream cheese to room temperature. In a large (mixer) bowl, beat the butter, cream cheese, and salt until blended. Stir in the flour to make a smooth, soft dough.

2. Gather the dough into a ball and shape into a 6 x 4-inch rectangle. Wrap in plastic and refrigerate until firm, about 1 hour. • The dough can be made up to this point and refrigerated up to 1 day.

3. Heat the oven to 375°F. Line 1 or more cookie sheets with foil.

4. In a small bowl, mix the sugar and cinnamon. On a lightly floured surface with a lightly floured rolling pin, roll the dough out to a 15 x 10-inch rectangle. Brush the dough with the cream, then sprinkle with the cinnamon sugar.

5. Trim the edges of the dough. With a pastry wheel or sharp knife, cut the dough crosswise into 20 equal strips. Then cut the dough in half lengthwise. Twist each piece of dough and place on the prepared cookie sheet(s).

6. Bake until golden, 14 to 16 minutes. Cool the cookies on the sheet on a wire rack for 2 minutes, then remove to the rack to cool completely. • The cookies are best eaten on the day they are made but can be frozen in an airtight freezer container or freezer bags up to 1 month.

Per cookie with butter: 50 cal, 1 g pro, 3 g fat, 4 g car, 40 mg sod, 10 mg chol.
With margarine: 3 mg chol

EASY

CHOCOLATE–PEANUT ROUNDS
Makes 32 cookies
Preparation time: 15 minutes plus at least 4 hours to chill
Baking time: 15 minutes per batch

The classic combination of chocolate and peanuts makes for great-tasting cookies. Be sure to use unsalted peanuts. If you prefer plain peanut cookies, just omit the cocoa and add an additional 2 tablespoons of flour in its place.

1 stick (½ cup) butter or margarine (see page 321), softened
⅔ cup granulated sugar
¼ cup creamy peanut butter
1 large egg, at room temperature
2 tablespoons unsweetened cocoa powder
½ teaspoon baking powder
¼ teaspoon salt
2 cups all-purpose flour
½ cup (2 ounces) unsalted peanuts,
  coarsely chopped

1. In a large (mixer) bowl, beat the butter, sugar, and peanut butter with an electric mixer on medium until fluffy. Beat in the egg, then the cocoa, baking powder, and salt. With the mixer on low speed, gradually add the flour, beating just until blended.

2. Shape the dough into a log 12 inches long and 1½ inches thick. Spread the nuts on a sheet of waxed paper. Roll the log in the nuts until coated fairly evenly. Wrap the log in the waxed paper, transfer to a cookie sheet, and refrigerate until firm, at least 4 hours, or freeze for 45 minutes. ● The dough can be made up to this point and refrigerated up to 3 days or wrapped in foil and frozen up to 3 months. If frozen, remove to the refrigerator for 2 hours before baking.

3. Heat the oven to 350°F. Lightly grease 1 or more cookie sheet(s).

4. Cut the log into 32 slices. Place the slices 1 inch apart on the prepared cookie sheet(s). Bake until cookies feel firm, 12 to 15 minutes. Cool the cookies on the sheet on a wire rack for 2 to 3 minutes, then remove to the rack with a spatula to cool completely. ● The cookies can be kept in an airtight container at cool room temperature up to 4 days or frozen up to 1 month.

Per cookie with butter: 100 cal, 2 g pro, 5 g fat, 11 g car, 70 mg sod, 14 mg chol.
With margarine: 7 mg chol

EASY ● LOW FAT

LEMON–GINGER CRISPS

Makes 96 cookies
Preparation time: 20 minutes plus at least 4 hours to chill
Baking time: 12 minutes per batch

These refrigerator cookies, crisp, tender, and decidedly lemon-flavored, are accented by finely chopped pistachio nuts. Some cookies may be made for milk, but these are perfect with tea.

2 sticks (1 cup) butter or margarine (see page 321), softened
1¼ cups granulated sugar
1 tablespoon freshly grated lemon peel
1½ teaspoons ground ginger
½ teaspoon baking soda
1 large egg, at room temperature
2½ cups all-purpose flour
½ cup (2 ounces) pistachio nuts, finely chopped

1. In a large (mixer) bowl, beat the butter, sugar, lemon peel, ginger, and baking soda with an electric mixer until fluffy. Beat in the egg. With the mixer on low speed, beat in half the flour. Add the remaining flour, beating until blended.

2. Divide the dough in half. Roll each half into a 9-inch log. Spread the nuts on a sheet of waxed paper. Roll in the nuts until the logs are 12 inches long. Wrap each log in waxed paper or plastic wrap. Refrigerate until firm, at least 4 hours, or freeze for 45 minutes. ● The dough can be made up to this point and refrigerated up to 3 days or wrapped in foil and frozen up to 3 months. If frozen, remove to the refrigerator for 2 hours before baking.

3. Heat the oven to 350°F. Lightly grease 1 or more cookie sheet(s). ▶

4. Cut each log into 48 slices. Place the slices 1 inch apart on the prepared cookie sheet(s). Bake until the cookies are firm and the edges are barely golden, 10 to 12 minutes. Cool the cookies on the sheet on wire a rack for 2 to 3 minutes, then transfer the cookies to the rack to cool completely. • The cookies can be kept in an airtight container or plastic bag at cool room temperature up to 1 week or frozen up to 1 month.

Per cookie with butter: 40 cal, 1 g pro, 2 g fat, 5 g car, 30 mg sod, 7 mg chol.
With margarine: 2 mg chol

EASY • DECADENT

BROWNIE NUT SLICES

Makes 40 cookies

Preparation time: 20 minutes plus at least 4 hours to chill

Baking time: 10 minutes per batch

Look out—these are addictive. As with all icebox cookies, the dough keeps in the refrigerator for several days, so they can be baked and enjoyed at a moment's notice.

> 2 sticks (1 cup) butter or margarine (see page 321), softened
> 1¼ cups granulated sugar
> ½ teaspoon baking soda
> 1 large egg, at room temperature
> 2 cups all-purpose flour
> ½ cup unsweetened cocoa powder
> ½ cup (3 ounces) mini semisweet chocolate chips
> ½ cup (2 ounces) walnuts, finely chopped

1. In a large (mixer) bowl, beat the butter, sugar, and baking soda with an electric mixer until fluffy. Beat in the egg. With the mixer on low speed, add the flour and cocoa, half at a time, beating until blended. Stir in the chocolate chips.

2. Divide the dough in half. Roll each half on a lightly floured surface into a 7-inch log. Spread the nuts on 2 sheets of waxed paper and roll the logs in the nuts until the logs are 10 inches long. Wrap each log in the waxed paper or plastic wrap. Refrigerate until firm, at least 4 hours, or freeze for about 45 minutes. • The dough can be made up to this point and refrigerated up to 3 days or wrapped in foil and frozen up to 3 months. If frozen, remove to the refrigerator for 2 hours before baking.

3. Heat the oven to 350°F. Lightly grease 1 or more cookie sheets.

4. Cut each log into 20 slices. Place the slices 1 inch apart on the prepared cookie sheet(s). Bake just until the cookies are set and the tops look dry, 8 to 10 minutes. Cool the cookies on the sheet on a wire rack for 2 to 3 minutes, then remove to the rack to cool completely. • The cookies can be kept in an airtight container at cool room temperature up to 1 week or frozen up to 1 month.

Per cookie with butter: 110 cal, 1 g pro, 6 g fat, 13 g car, 60 mg sod, 18 mg chol.
With margarine: 70 mg sod, 5 mg chol

COOKIE SPREAD
There are two good ways to keep cookies from spreading. One is to be sure to use a cool cookie sheet and the other is to chill the dough before forming the cookies. A chilled dough limits spreading as the cookie bakes.

PEANUT BUTTER AND JELLY COOKIES

Makes 24 cookies

Preparation time: 15 minutes plus 15 minutes to set

These chewy, gooey no-bake cookies are as easy as…peanut butter and jelly! Make them in a saucepan in just minutes.

1 bag (10 ounces) peanut butter chips
2 tablespoons butter or margarine (see page 321)
2 tablespoons smooth peanut butter
3½ cups sweetened oat and wheat bran cereal,
    such as Kellogg's Cracklin' Oat Bran, finely crushed
¼ cup jelly (such as grape or strawberry)
¼ cup unsalted roasted peanuts, finely chopped

1. In a heavy saucepan, stir the peanut butter chips, butter, and peanut butter over very low heat until melted and smooth. Add the cereal and stir until blended. Remove from the heat.

2. Drop level tablespoonfuls of the mixture 2 inches apart on waxed paper. Press into flat 2-inch round cookies. Let stand at room temperature until firm, about 15 minutes.

3. Spoon the jelly into a cup and stir until runny. Generously drizzle the jelly over the cookies, then sprinkle with the nuts. • The cookies can be kept in an airtight container at cool room temperature up to 1 week.

Per cookie with butter: 140 cal, 4 g pro, 7 g fat, 15 g car, 80 mg sod, 3 mg chol.

With margarine: 0 mg chol

CRISPY APRICOT BARS

Makes 16 bars

Preparation time: 5 minutes plus 1½ hours to chill and set

Cooking time: 7 minutes

This no-bake cookie recipe mingles the tartness of dried apricots with the creamy sweetness of white chocolate.

1½ cups (9 ounces) dried apricots
⅔ cup packed light brown sugar
1 stick (½ cup) cold butter or margarine (see page 321), cut into small pieces
4 ounces white chocolate, coarsely chopped
3 cups crisp rice cereal

1. Line an 8-inch square baking pan with foil, letting the ends extend above the pan on 2 sides.

2. In a food processor, process the apricots and brown sugar with on/off turns until finely chopped. Scrape into a heavy medium-size saucepan. Add the butter and half the white chocolate.

3. Stir over medium-low heat until the butter and chocolate are melted, the sugar is dissolved, and the apricots are coated. Remove from the heat. Stir in the cereal until blended.

4. Scrape the mixture into the prepared pan and cover with waxed paper. Place another 8-inch square baking pan or a heavy book on top. Press to compact the mixture into an even, firm layer. Refrigerate until cool, about 30 minutes.

5. Melt the remaining white chocolate in a small saucepan over very low heat, stirring frequently. (Or microwave in a small microwave-safe bowl on Medium for 1 minute. Remove from the microwave and stir until melted and smooth.)

6. Drizzle the melted white chocolate over the cereal mixture, cover loosely, and let stand at room temperature until the cereal mixture is firm, about 1 hour. Lift the foil by the ends onto a cutting board. Remove the foil. Cut into bars. • The cookies can be kept in an airtight container at cool room temperature up to 2 days.
Per bar with butter: 180 cal, 1 g pro, 8 g fat, 27 g car, 120 mg sod, 16 mg chol.
With margarine: 0 mg chol

FREEZING DROP COOKIE DOUGH

Drop the dough onto cookie sheets and freeze uncovered until firm. Remove the frozen unbaked cookies, pack into freezer bags, and freeze up to 1 month. Arrange the frozen dough on cookie sheets and let thaw for about 45 minutes before baking.

EASY • QUICK • LOW FAT

CARAMEL CLUSTERS

Makes 50 cookies
Preparation time: 15 minutes plus 15 minutes to set

If you don't want to dirty a lot of bowls or heat up the kitchen by turning on the oven, but you crave a sweet homemade treat, these rich clusters provide the answer.

1 bag (14 ounces) caramels, unwrapped
¼ cup milk
5 cups granola cereal

1. In a medium-size saucepan, stir the caramels and milk over low heat until the caramels melt and the mixture is smooth. Remove from the heat. Add the cereal and stir until coated.

2. Drop level tablespoonfuls of the mixture onto waxed paper. Let cool and set before serving, about 15 minutes. • The clusters can be kept in an airtight container at cool room temperature up to 2 weeks.
Per cookie: 90 cal, 2 g pro, 3 g fat, 13 g car, 20 mg sod, 1 mg chol

ICE CREAMS
& FROZEN DESSERTS

"Too much of a good thing can be wonderful."

MAE WEST

If you've never tasted homemade ice cream (or better yet, if you have), you're in for a treat. The ice creams on these pages—from Fabulous Vanilla to Cappuccino-Chocolate Chunk—are rich, smooth, and flavorful. The same is true for low-fat flavors such as Blueberry-Lemon and Chocolate. For a more intense, usually fruit, flavor, without the fat of cream or other dairy products, there are icy sorbets and granitas.

Ice creams and frozen desserts are great all year round, but they're a special favorite during the warm summer months. And with a variety of shapes—cakes, pies, tortes, bombes, and loaves—ice cream, store-bought or homemade, becomes the centerpiece of a whole repertoire of easy, no-bake desserts. Or choose from the selection of soda fountain specialties and make your own sensational sundaes, shakes, and sodas.

EASY

Apple Sorbet, 63
Banana Shake, 87
Blueberry-Lemon Ice Cream, 58
Cappuccino-Chocolate Chunk
    Ice Cream, 56
Coffee Granita, 64
Coffee-Almond Ice Cream, 54
Fabulous Vanilla Ice Cream, 54
Frozen Strawberry Daiquiri Pie, 66
Ice Cream Bombe, 82
Kiwi-Lime Sorbet, 60
Ladyfinger Ice Cream Loaf, 79
Low-Fat Banana Shake, 87
Low-Fat Chocolate Ice Cream, 58
Low-Fat Orange-and-Cream Soda, 87
Mint Julep Sorbet, 62
Mocha Ice Cream Soda, 88
No-Bake Brownie Ice Cream Loaf, 77
Orange-and-Cream Soda, 87
Orange Sherbet Loaf with Chocolate
    Sauce, 80
Orange-Strawberry Swirl Pie, 66
Peach Ice Cream, 55
Peach Melba Sundaes, 83
Peach-Raspberry Ice Cream Pie, 65
Piña Colada Sorbet, 59
Pineapple-Coconut Ice Cream, 54
Raspberry-Lemon Granita, 63
Strawberry Ice Cream, 54
Strawberry-Banana Ice Cream, 57
Strawberry-Grapefruit Sorbet, 61
Super-Rich Chocolate Ice Cream, 55

QUICK

Banana Shake, 87
Kiwi-Lime Sorbet, 60
Low-Fat Banana Shake, 87
Low-Fat Chocolate Ice Cream, 58
Low-Fat Orange-and-Cream Soda, 87
Mocha Ice Cream Soda, 88
Orange-and-Cream Soda, 87
Peach Melba Sundaes, 83
Piña Colada Sorbet, 59
Strawberry-Grapefruit Sorbet, 61

1 HOUR

Blueberry-Lemon Ice Cream, 58
Cappuccino-Chocolate Chunk Ice
    Cream, 58
Peach Ice Cream, 55
Pineapple-Banana Sorbet, 60
Super-Rich Chocolate Ice Cream, 55

LOW FAT

Apple Sorbet, 63
Banana Split with Fudge Sauce, 86
Blueberry-Lemon Ice Cream, 58
Frozen Chocolate Meringue Torte, 67
Frozen Strawberry Daiquiri Pie, 66
Kiwi-Lime Sorbet, 60
Layered Melon Sherbet Cake, 81
Low-Fat Banana Shake, 87
Low-Fat Chocolate Ice Cream, 58
Low-Fat Orange-and-Cream Soda, 87
Mint Julep Sorbet, 62
Orange Sherbet Loaf with Chocolate
   Sauce, 80
Orange-Strawberry Swirl Pie, 66
Peach Ice Cream, 55
Peach Melba Sundaes, 83
Pineapple-Banana Sorbet, 60
Raspberry-Lemon Granita, 63
Strawberry-Banana Ice Cream, 57
Strawberry-Grapefruit Sorbet, 61

CLASSIC

Banana Shake, 87
Fabulous Vanilla Ice Cream, 54
Ice Cream Bombe, 82
Peach Melba Sundaes, 83
Super-Rich Chocolate Ice Cream, 55

OLD FASHIONED

Banana Shake, 87
Banana Split with Fudge Sauce, 86
Fabulous Vanilla Ice Cream, 54
Mocha Ice Cream Soda, 88
Orange-and-Cream Soda, 87
Peach Ice Cream, 55
Strawberry Ice Cream, 54
Super-Rich Chocolate Ice Cream, 55

DECADENT

Banana-Toffee Ice Cream
   Cake, 78
Cappuccino-Chocolate
   Chunk Ice Cream, 56
No-Bake Brownie Ice
   Cream Loaf, 77
Seven-Layer Brownie Ice
   Cream Cake, 77
Super-Rich Chocolate Ice
   Cream, 55

THE SODA FOUNTAIN

Banana Shake, 87
Banana Split with Fudge Sauce, 86
Butterscotch Ice Cream Sauce, 85
Chocolate-Peanut Butter Ice
   Cream Sauce, 84
Hot Fudge Sauce, 84
Lemon-Blueberry Ice Cream
   Sauce, 85
Low-Fat Banana Shake, 87
Low-Fat Orange-and-Cream Soda, 87
Mocha Ice Cream Soda, 88
Orange-and-Cream Soda, 87
Peach Melba Sundaes, 83
Ruby-Red Ice Cream Sauce, 83

ICY TREATS

Apple Sorbet, 63
Coffee Granita, 64
Kiwi-Lime Sorbet, 60
Mint Julep Sorbet, 62
Piña Colada Sorbet, 59
Pineapple-Banana Sorbet, 60
Raspberry-Lemon Granita, 63
Strawberry-Grapefruit
   Sorbet, 61

ICE CREAM CAKES AND PIES

Banana-Toffee Ice Cream Cake, 78
Frozen Chocolate Meringue Torte, 67
Frozen Strawberry Daiquiri Pie, 66
Ladyfinger Ice Cream Loaf, 79
Layered Melon Sherbet Cake, 81
No-Bake Brownie Ice Cream Loaf, 77
Orange Sherbet Loaf with Chocolate
   Sauce, 80
Orange-Strawberry Swirl Pie, 66
Peach-Raspberry Ice Cream Pie, 65
Seven-Layer Brownie Ice Cream
   Cake, 77

ICE CREAM SAUCES

Butterscotch Ice Cream Sauce, 85
Chocolate-Peanut Butter
   Ice Cream Sauce, 84
Hot Fudge Sauce, 84
Lemon-Blueberry Ice Cream
   Sauce, 85
Ruby-Red Ice Cream Sauce, 85
Toasted Almond-Apple Ice Cream
   Topping, 84

FABULOUS VANILLA ICE CREAM

Makes 6 cups (12 servings)
Preparation time: 5 minutes plus at least 4 hours to chill and freeze

It's incredibly delicious, unbelievably easy to make, and you don't even need an ice cream maker. The variations that follow are also sensational.

½ cup cold milk
1 tablespoon vanilla extract
1 can (14 ounces) nonfat sweetened
  condensed milk (not evaporated milk)
⅛ teaspoon salt
2 cups heavy (whipping) cream

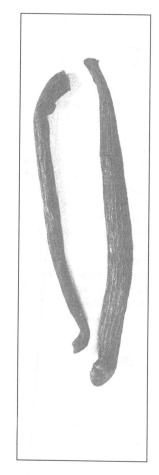

1. In a medium-size bowl, mix the milk, vanilla, condensed milk, and salt.

2. In a large (mixer) bowl, beat the cream with an electric mixer until stiff peaks form when the beaters are lifted. Gently stir (fold) in the milk mixture with a rubber spatula. Pour into a shallow 1½-quart metal bowl or pan.

3. Cover and freeze at least 4 hours, stirring once after 2 hours or when the edges start to harden.

4. Serve right away or pack into an airtight freezer container and keep frozen up to 1 month.

Per ½ cup serving: 240 cal, 4 g pro, 15 g fat, 22 g car, 80 mg sod, 58 mg chol

FABULOUS ICE CREAM VARIATIONS

STRAWBERRY ICE CREAM
Omit the ½ cup milk and the vanilla. Mash 4 cups hulled and halved ripe strawberries with 2 tablespoons light corn syrup; stir into the sweetened condensed milk. Proceed as directed. Makes 8 cups.

Per ½ cup serving: 190 cal, 3 g pro, 11 g fat, 21 g car, 60 mg sod, 43 mg chol

PINEAPPLE-COCONUT ICE CREAM
Toast 1½ cups sweetened flaked coconut at 350°F for 8 to 10 minutes, until golden. Omit the ½ cup milk and the vanilla. Stir one 8-ounce can juice-packed crushed pineapple into the sweetened condensed milk. Proceed as directed. After folding the milk mixture into the whipped cream, fold in the coconut. Freeze as directed. Makes 6 cups.

Per ½ cup serving: 290 cal, 4 g pro, 19 g fat, 28 g car, 80 mg sod, 57 mg chol

COFFEE-ALMOND ICE CREAM
Stir 2 tablespoons instant coffee powder or granules into the ½ cup milk-vanilla mixture until dissolved. Proceed as directed. After folding the milk mixture into the whipped cream, fold in 1 cup toasted sliced almonds (see page 325). (The almonds may sink to the bottom, but will be redistributed when stirred after 2 hours.) Makes 6½ cups.

Per ½ cup serving: 270 cal, 5 g pro, 18 g fat, 22 g car, 70 mg sod, 54 mg chol

EASY • 1 HOUR • CLASSIC • OLD FASHIONED • DECADENT

SUPER–RICH CHOCOLATE ICE CREAM

Makes 4 cups (8 servings)
Preparation time: 5 minutes plus 40 minutes to chill and freeze
Cooking time: 7 minutes

You can vary the flavor of this very creamy ice cream by using mint-flavored or raspberry-flavored semisweet chocolate chips.

Yolks of 3 large eggs
1¾ cups milk
½ cup granulated sugar
⅔ cup (4 ounces) semisweet chocolate chips
1 ounce unsweetened chocolate, chopped
1 cup heavy (whipping) cream
1 teaspoon vanilla extract

1. In a small bowl, whisk the egg yolks until blended.
2. In a medium-size saucepan, stir the milk and sugar over medium heat until the mixture comes to a gentle boil. Whisk about ½ cup into the yolks, then whisk the yolk mixture back into the saucepan. Whisk constantly over medium-low heat until the mixture looks as if it's just about to boil, 1 to 2 minutes. (The eggs will be pasteurized at a temperature of 160°F and will slightly thicken the milk.)
3. Remove from the heat and immediately add the semisweet and unsweetened chocolates, stirring until melted.
4. Stir in the cream and vanilla. Refrigerate for 20 minutes.
5. Pour into an ice cream maker and freeze according to the manufacturer's instructions, or use the still-freeze method (see page 62).
6. Serve right away or pack into an airtight freezer container and keep frozen up to 1 month.

Per ½ cup serving: 680 cal, 4 g pro, 21 g fat, 126 g car, 40 mg sod, 128 mg chol

EASY • 1 HOUR • LOW FAT • OLD FASHIONED

PEACH ICE CREAM

Makes 4 cups (8 servings)
Preparation time: 10 minutes plus 40 minutes to chill and freeze
Cooking time: 7 minutes

A century ago, our great-grandmothers cracked peach pits and simmered them to extract their almondlike flavor. Here, a little almond extract—a perfect flavor complement to peach—will do the same for you. This recipe is a great way to use up soft or overripe peaches.

▶

3 large ripe peaches (about 1½ pounds), peeled, pitted,
   and cut into chunks (1½ cups)
¼ cup granulated sugar
1 tablespoon fresh lemon juice
1 teaspoon vanilla extract
⅛ teaspoon almond extract

CUSTARD
Yolks of 3 large eggs
1 pint (2 cups) half-and-half
¼ cup granulated sugar

1. In a medium-size bowl, mash the peaches with a potato masher until only small chunks of peach remain. Stir in the sugar, lemon juice, and vanilla and almond extracts. Let stand at room temperature while making the custard.

2. Make the custard: In a small bowl, whisk the egg yolks with a fork until blended. In a small saucepan, stir 1 cup of the half-and-half and the sugar over medium heat until the mixture comes to a gentle boil. Whisk about ½ cup of the hot half-and-half into the yolks, then whisk the yolk mixture back into the saucepan. Whisk constantly over medium-low heat until the mixture looks as if it's just about to boil, 1 to 2 minutes. (The eggs will be pasteurized at 160°F and will slightly thicken the half-and-half.)

3. Remove the saucepan from the heat and immediately stir in the remaining 1 cup of half-and-half.

4. Stir the custard into the peach mixture until well blended. Refrigerate for about 20 minutes.

5. Pour into an ice cream maker and freeze according to the manufacturer's instructions, or use the still-freeze method (see page 62).

6. Serve right away or pack into an airtight freezer container and keep frozen up to 1 month.

Per ½ cup serving: 180 cal, 3 g pro, 9 g fat, 23 g car, 30 mg sod, 102 mg chol

> **RIPENING ICE CREAMS**
> Many desserts should be made as close to serving time as possible, but ice creams with custard bases benefit from having time to "ripen." The base can be refrigerated for up to 2 days before freezing. (Just keep it tightly covered.) After the ice cream is frozen, it can ripen up to 4 hours in the freezer. Both of these standing times will improve the texture and develop the flavors of homemade ice cream.

EASY • 1 HOUR • DECADENT

CAPPUCCINO–CHOCOLATE CHUNK ICE CREAM

Makes 4 cups (8 servings)
Preparation time: 5 minutes plus 40 minutes to chill and freeze
Cooking time: 7 minutes

Enjoy a scoop of this sophisticated custard-based ice cream on a hot summer day and you can dream you're sitting in a piazza in Venice or Florence. Add chunks of chocolate or nuts to ice cream after it's almost frozen, and they will distribute evenly and not all sink to the bottom. The recipe calls for bittersweet chocolate, but you could use a good-quality semisweet chocolate here also.

Yolks of 3 large eggs
1½ cups milk
⅔ cup granulated sugar
3 tablespoons instant coffee granules
½ teaspoon ground cinnamon
1 cup heavy (whipping) cream
1 teaspoon vanilla extract
3 ounces bittersweet chocolate, chopped into small pieces

1. In a small bowl, whisk the egg yolks until blended.

2. In a medium-size saucepan, whisk the milk, sugar, coffee granules, and cinnamon over medium heat until the mixture comes to a gentle boil. Whisk about ½ cup into the yolks, then whisk the yolk mixture back into the saucepan. Whisk constantly over medium-low heat until the mixture looks as if it's just about to boil, 1 to 2 minutes. (The eggs will be pasteurized at 160°F and will slightly thicken the milk.)

3. Remove from the heat and immediately stir in the cream and vanilla. Refrigerate for about 20 minutes.

4. Pour into an ice cream maker and freeze according to the manufacturer's instructions, adding the chocolate chunks during last few minutes of freezing time, or use the still-freeze method (see page 62).

5. Serve right away or pack into an airtight freezer container and keep frozen up to 1 month.

Per ½ cup serving: 270 cal, 4 g pro, 18 g fat, 26 g car, 40 mg sod, 127 mg chol

EASY • LOW FAT

STRAWBERRY–BANANA ICE CREAM
Makes 6½ cups (13 servings)
Preparation time: 10 minutes plus 4 hours to freeze

This recipe starts with store-bought ice cream, but then becomes "homemade" with the addition of coarsely mashed strawberries and banana. For the best flavor, use the ripest strawberries you can find.

1 pint (12 ounces) ripe strawberries, rinsed and hulled
1 large banana (about 7 ounces), cut into chunks (about 1 cup)
2 teaspoons fresh lemon juice
½ teaspoon grated nutmeg
1 quart vanilla ice cream, slightly softened

1. In a large bowl, mash the berries, banana, lemon juice, and nutmeg with a potato masher to a slightly chunky purée.

2. Stir in the ice cream until well blended. Transfer to a freezer container. Cover and freeze for at least 4 hours, or until firm. (The ice cream can be frozen up to 2 weeks.)

Per ½ cup serving: 100 cal, 2 g pro, 5 g fat, 14 g car, 30 mg sod, 18 mg chol

LOW–FAT CHOCOLATE ICE CREAM

Makes 4 cups (8 servings)

Preparation time: 5 minutes plus 20 minutes to freeze

This ice cream is sinfully rich in taste and texture, but very low in fat. For an extra-luscious (but still low-fat) dessert, serve the ice cream topped with the Fudge Sauce used for our Banana Split (page 86) and a spoonful of light nondairy whipped topping.

> 1 (4-serving) package instant chocolate-pudding mix
> ¼ cup granulated sugar
> 1 can (12 ounces) evaporated skim milk (not sweetened condensed)
> 1 cup skim milk

1. In a medium-size bowl, combine the pudding mix and sugar. Whisk in the evaporated milk and skim milk until blended.

2. Pour into an ice cream maker and freeze according to the manufacturer's instructions, or use the still-freeze method (see page 62).

3. Serve right away or pack into an airtight freezer container and keep frozen up to 1 month.

Per ½ cup serving: 120 cal, 5 g pro, 0 g fat, 25 g car, 260 mg sod, 2 mg chol

BLUEBERRY–LEMON ICE CREAM

Makes 3½ cups (7 servings)

Preparation time: 5 minutes plus 40 minutes to chill and freeze

Cooking time: 12 minutes

By using evaporated skim milk and egg substitute, this luscious ice cream delivers the flavor of berries and cream with almost no fat calories.

> 1 pint (12 ounces) fresh blueberries, picked over and rinsed
> ½ cup granulated sugar
> 1 tablespoon cornstarch
> 1 can (12 ounces) evaporated skim milk (not sweetened condensed)
> ½ cup egg substitute (equivalent to 2 large eggs), thawed if frozen
> 1 teaspoon freshly grated lemon peel
> 2 tablespoons fresh lemon juice
> ½ teaspoon vanilla extract

1. In a medium-size saucepan, stir the blueberries and ¼ cup of the sugar over medium heat for 6 minutes, or until the sugar dissolves and the blueberries release their juices.

ICE CREAM OVERRUN

When filling an ice cream machine, leave at least 2 inches at the top of the canister for the ice cream to expand. As the machine churns, it incorporates air (called overrun) that improves the texture of the ice cream.

COOK'S TIP

Do not rinse the blueberries (or any berries) until just before using to prevent them from becoming water-logged and bruised.

2. Set a strainer over a bowl. Pour in the blueberry mixture and press the berries through the strainer with the back of a spoon. Scrape the puréed berries from the outside of the strainer into the bowl. Discard the blueberry skins. Refrigerate the berry purée.

3. Rinse and dry the saucepan. Put in the remaining ¼ cup of sugar and the cornstarch. Whisk in about ⅔ cup of the evaporated milk. Whisking constantly, bring to a gentle boil over medium heat and boil for about 1 minute, until the mixture is almost as thick as pudding.

4. Remove from the heat and whisk in the egg substitute, then the remaining evaporated milk.

5. Stir the milk mixture into the blueberry purée. Stir in the lemon peel, lemon juice, and vanilla until blended. Refrigerate for about 20 minutes.

6. Pour into an ice cream maker and freeze according to the manufacturer's instructions, or use the still-freeze method (see page 62).

7. Serve right away or pack into an airtight freezer container and keep frozen up to 1 month.

Per ½ cup serving: 140 cal, 6 g pro, 0 g fat, 28 g car, 90 mg sod, 2 mg chol

EASY • QUICK

PIÑA COLADA SORBET

Makes 4 cups (8 servings)

Preparation time: 3 minutes plus 20 minutes to freeze

This icy sorbet, made with canned pineapple chunks and coconut milk, is great after a spicy meal. Look for coconut milk in large supermarkets or Asian markets and do not confuse it with sweetened "cream" of coconut. The rum is optional; it will give the sorbet a softer consistency as well as a grown-up "kick."

1 can (20 ounces) pineapple chunks in heavy syrup,
  not drained
¼ cup granulated sugar
1 can (about 15 ounces) unsweetened coconut milk
  (not cream of coconut)
2 tablespoons dark or light rum (optional)

1. Process the pineapple with syrup and the granulated sugar in a food processor or blender until smooth.

2. Pour into a medium-size bowl. Whisk in the coconut milk and rum.

3. Pour into an ice cream maker and freeze according to the manufacturer's instructions, or use the still-freeze method (see page 62).

4. Serve right away, or pack into an airtight freezer container and keep frozen up to 1 month. Before serving, let stand at room temperature 10 to 15 minutes to soften slightly.

Per ½ cup serving: 180 cal, 1 g pro, 11 g fat, 22 g car, 10 mg sod, 0 mg chol

1 HOUR • LOW FAT

PINEAPPLE–BANANA SORBET

Makes 8 cups (16 servings)
Preparation time: 15 minutes plus 20 minutes to freeze

The flavors of these two tropical fruits are delicious together, and the fresh pineapple gives the sorbet a wonderful slushy texture. To save time, make the sugar syrup ahead; it will keep indefinitely in the refrigerator.

  2 cups granulated sugar
  2 cups water
  1 large ripe pineapple (3½ pounds),
      peeled, cored, and cut into small chunks (5 cups)
  2 large ripe bananas, peeled and
      cut into small chunks (2 cups)
  ¼ cup fresh lemon juice
  ¼ cup fresh orange juice
  For garnish: fresh pineapple wedges and mint leaves

1. In a medium-size saucepan, stir the sugar and water over medium-high heat until the sugar is completely dissolved and the mixture is clear. Cool the syrup to room temperature or refrigerate.

2. Process the pineapple and bananas in batches in a food processor or blender until almost smooth. Add the lemon juice and orange juice and process until smooth.

3. Pour the mixture into a large bowl. Stir in the sugar syrup. Pour into an ice cream maker and freeze according to the manufacturer's instructions, or use the still-freeze method (see page 62).

4. Serve immediately, or pack into an airtight freezer container and keep frozen up to 2 weeks. Before serving, let stand at room temperature 10 to 15 minutes to soften slightly. Garnish with pineapple and mint.

Per ½ cup serving: 140 cal, 0 g pro, 0 g fat, 36 g car, 0 mg sod, 0 mg chol

EASY • QUICK • LOW FAT

KIWI–LIME SORBET

Makes 4 cups (8 servings)
Preparation time: 5 minutes plus 20 minutes to freeze

This green-hued sorbet, flecked with tiny black edible kiwi seeds, packs not only a tart and refreshing flavor but a good measure of vitamin C as well. If all you can find is very firm kiwifruit, keep it at cool room temperature for a few days to ripen. Once ripened, kiwi can be kept in the refrigerator for several days.

COOK'S TIP

To cut a fresh pineapple into chunks, slice off the crown and the bottom, then cut the fruit lengthwise into quarters. Trim away and discard the central core from each piece. Cut the flesh into chunks all the way to the skin, then slip the knife just above the skin to cut them free.

4 ripe kiwifruit (about 1 pound),
  peeled and quartered
½ cup granulated sugar
2 cups water
1 can (6 ounces) frozen limeade concentrate,
  not thawed

1. Process the kiwifruit, sugar, and ¼ cup of the water in a food processor or blender just until smooth.

2. Put ½ cup of the remaining water and the limeade concentrate in a medium-size bowl and stir until slushy. Stir in the remaining 1¼ cups of water and the kiwifruit purée.

3. Pour into an ice cream maker and freeze according to the manufacturer's instructions, or use the still-freeze method (see page 62).

4. Serve right away, or pack into an airtight freezer container and keep frozen up to 1 month. Before serving, let stand at room temperature 10 to 15 minutes to soften slightly.

Per ½ cup serving: 130 cal, 1 g pro, 0 g fat, 33 g car, 0 mg sod, 0 mg chol

EASY • QUICK • LOW FAT

STRAWBERRY–GRAPEFRUIT SORBET

Makes 5 cups (10 servings)
Preparation time: 5 minutes plus at least 20 minutes to freeze

The flavor and color of this sorbet depend upon the ripeness of the berries, so enjoy it when the strawberry season is at its peak—from April through July. Use pink grapefruit juice to intensify the color.

2 pints (1½ pounds) ripe strawberries,
  rinsed and hulled
1 cup granulated sugar
1 cup grapefruit juice

1. Process the strawberries, sugar, and ¼ cup of the grapefruit juice in a food processor or blender until smooth.

2. Pour the mixture into a medium-size bowl. Stir in the remaining grapefruit juice until blended.

3. Pour into an ice cream maker and freeze according to the manufacturer's instructions, or use the still-freeze method (see page 62).

4. Serve right away, or pack into an airtight freezer container and keep frozen up to 2 weeks. Before serving, let stand at room temperature 10 to 15 minutes to soften slightly.

Per ½ cup serving: 110 cal, 0 g pro, 0 g fat, 27 g car, 0 mg sod, 0 mg chol

MINT JULEP SORBET
Makes 5 cups (10 servings)
Preparation time: 15 minutes plus at least 3½ hours to stand and freeze

You don't have to wait for the Kentucky Derby to enjoy this icy springtime treat, a take-off on the old Southern cocktail.

2 cups bite-size ripe honeydew melon chunks
2 cups loosely packed fresh mint leaves
1½ cups plus 1 tablespoon granulated sugar
1 cup boiling water
½ cup fresh lemon juice
¼ cup bourbon (optional)
2 pints (1½ pounds) fresh strawberries, rinsed,
*   hulled, and sliced (5 cups)*
For garnish: sprigs of fresh mint and confectioners' sugar

1. Freeze the melon chunks in a single layer on a cookie sheet for about 1 hour, or until hard. Also put an 8- or 9-inch square metal pan in the freezer.

2. Meanwhile, put the mint leaves and the 1½ cups of sugar into a medium-size bowl. Add the boiling water and let steep for 30 minutes. Pour the mixture through a fine strainer set over a small bowl. Discard the mint leaves. Stir in the lemon juice and bourbon.

3. In a medium-size bowl, mix the strawberries with the remaining tablespoon of sugar. Cover and refrigerate for at least 1 hour.

4. Process the frozen melon chunks and mint syrup in a food processor or blender until smooth (the mixture will be slushy). Scrape into the chilled pan. Freeze for 1 hour, or until firm enough to scoop.

5. To serve, moisten the rims of goblets or glass serving bowls. Dip the rims into confectioners' sugar to coat. Spoon the strawberries into the goblets. Top with scoops of the sorbet. Garnish with mint sprigs. Serve right away.

Per serving: 200 cal, 0 g pro, 0 g fat, 51 g car, 10 mg sod, 0 mg chol

THE STILL-FREEZE METHOD

You don't need an expensive machine to make wonderful homemade ice creams and sorbets. Just clear some space in your freezer and follow the directions.

◆ Pour the prepared ingredients into a metal loaf pan or an 8-inch square baking pan.

◆ Cover with plastic wrap or foil and place in the freezer.

◆ Freeze for 1 to 2 hours or until solid.

◆ Break the frozen mixture into pieces with a fork. Spoon into a food processor or a large bowl.

◆ Process, or beat with electric mixer on medium-high speed, until soft but not melted. Repeat the freezing and processing or beating 1 or 2 times, if desired for smoothness.

◆ Stir in any chopped chocolate or other small pieces, such as nuts. Return to the freezer to firm up.

EASY • LOW FAT

APPLE SORBET

Makes 4 cups (8 servings)

Preparation time: 10 minutes plus 55 minutes to chill and freeze

This sorbet takes a little work, but it's worth it. The color and intensity of flavor will vary with the variety of apple used. Fuji, Cortland, Granny Smith, Gala, McIntosh, and Red Delicious are all wonderful choices. If you use a very sweet apple, you might want to decrease the sugar to ⅔ cup.

> 1 cup granulated sugar
> 1 cup water
> 2 tablespoons light corn syrup
> 3 large apples (1½ pounds)
> ⅓ cup fresh lemon juice

1. In a small saucepan, stir the sugar and water over medium heat until the sugar dissolves.

2. Increase the heat to medium-high and bring the mixture to a boil. Remove from the heat and stir in the corn syrup.

3. Refrigerate in the saucepan for 30 minutes or until the mixture cools.

4. When the syrup is cool, quarter and core the apples (don't peel). Cut the quarters in half and put into a food processor with the lemon juice. Process until it becomes a fine purée, about 2 minutes. With the motor running, gradually add the cooled sugar syrup. Process until blended.

5. Pour the mixture through a fine sieve set over a medium-size bowl. Press the mixture to extract as much liquid as possible. Discard the pulp.

6. Pour the apple liquid into an ice cream maker and freeze according to the manufacturer's instructions, or use the still-freeze method (see page 62).

7. Serve right away, or pack into an airtight freezer container and freeze up to 2 weeks. Before serving, let stand at room temperature 10 to 15 minutes to soften slightly.

Per ½ cup serving: 160 cal, 0 g pro, 0 g fat, 41 g car, 10 mg sod, 0 mg chol

EASY • LOW FAT

RASPBERRY–LEMON GRANITA

Makes 4¾ cups (9 servings)

Preparation time: 15 minutes plus at least 8½ hours to chill and freeze

A granita, unlike most frozen desserts, isn't smooth, but has the coarse texture of ice crystals. The name comes from the Italian word *grana,* meaning grainy. To get the right texture, stir the granita every 20 minutes. A fork is the best utensil to use for stirring because the tines can be used to break up the large ice chunks.

▶

3 cups water
1½ cups granulated sugar
Peel of 2 lemons, removed with a vegetable peeler
3 tablespoons red-raspberry preserves
½ cup fresh lemon juice
½ pint (6 ounces) fresh red raspberries,
  rinsed and picked over (1¼ cups)
For garnish: fresh raspberries

1. In a medium-size saucepan, bring the water, sugar, lemon peel, and preserves to a boil. Reduce the heat and simmer for 5 minutes. Refrigerate until cool, about 30 minutes. Stir in the lemon juice. Pour through a strainer into an 8- or 9-inch square metal pan. Discard the peel.

2. Holding the strainer over the pan, press the raspberries through with the back of a spoon. Scrape the purée from outside the strainer into the pan. Stir the purée into the lemon–raspberry preserve mixture until blended.

3. Place in the freezer. When mixture starts to freeze, scrape the frozen sides into the center of the pan every 20 minutes with a fork. Cover the pan with foil and freeze for at least 8 hours or until firm.

4. At serving time, move the pan from the freezer to the refrigerator for 20 minutes to thaw slightly. To serve, scrape the surface with a spoon and mound the granita into serving dishes or use an ice cream spade or scoop. Garnish with raspberries.
Per serving: 240 cal, 0 g pro, 0 g fat, 62 g car, 0 mg sod, 0 mg chol

EASY

COFFEE GRANITA

Makes 3 cups (6 servings)
Preparation time: 10 minutes plus at least 3 hours to freeze

Here's an icy treat that's packed with flavor but low in fat. Serve this granita as a refreshing "dessert and coffee" in one.

FRUIT BLIZZARD

When it's so hot that you want to stick your head in the freezer, go ahead. You might even find one of these refreshing frozen snacks and desserts in there.

◆ NIPPY NIBBLES: Spread fresh blueberries, seedless grapes, or ½-inch-thick banana slices on a jelly roll pan. Freeze for 8 hours or until hard, then pop into zipper-lock freezer-storage bags. When you get the urge to snack, grab a handful.

◆ SUGARED SPLIT BANANAS: Make a lengthwise slit in an unpeeled ripe banana. Spread the skin apart and sprinkle in 2 tablespoons brown sugar. Close and wrap in foil. Freeze for at least 8 hours. To enjoy, let the banana almost thaw (about 1 hour out of the freezer), then scoop banana up with a spoon.

◆ CHOCOLATE-COVERED FROZEN BANANA: Insert a popsicle stick into one end of a peeled banana. Dip banana into melted semisweet chocolate or coat with chocolate "hard-shell" topping. Place on waxed paper and freeze until firm. Let soften slightly before serving.

COOK'S TIP

Use brewed coffee or mix 4 teaspoons instant coffee granules with 1½ cups hot water.

1½ cups strong black coffee
¼ cup granulated sugar
1 cup heavy (whipping) cream
For garnish: sprigs of fresh mint

1. In a small bowl, mix the coffee and sugar until the sugar dissolves.

2. Pour into an 8- or 9-inch metal pan and freeze for at least 3 hours or until solid.

3. When frozen, move the pan from the freezer to the refrigerator for 10 minutes to thaw slightly. With a fork, break up the coffee ice into 1- to 2-inch chunks.

4. Put the chunks into a food processor or blender (you may need to do this in 2 batches) and process with on/off turns until finely chopped. Serve immediately or pack into an airtight freezer container and freeze up to 2 weeks.

5. At serving time, move the granita to the refrigerator for 10 to 15 minutes to thaw slightly. Meanwhile, in a medium-size (mixer) bowl, beat the cream with an electric mixer until stiff peaks form when the beaters are lifted. To serve, scrape the surface of the granita with a spoon and mound into stemmed glasses. Top with whipped cream and mint sprigs.

Per ½ cup serving: 170 cal, 0 g pro, 15 g fat, 10 g car, 20 mg sod, 54 mg chol

EASY

PEACH–RASPBERRY ICE CREAM PIE

Serves 8

Preparation time: 10 minutes plus at least 3 hours to freeze

A nice dessert for a special family dinner on a hot summer night. When you put the ice cream, sorbet, and fresh peaches together in a ready-to-fill graham-cracker crust, you have an elegant dessert with little effort.

1 pint raspberry sorbet, slightly softened
1 pint vanilla ice cream or low-fat frozen yogurt, slightly softened
1 (9-ounce) ready-to-fill graham-cracker pie crust
1 cup thinly sliced peaches, fresh, drained canned, or frozen and thawed
½ pint (6 ounces) fresh raspberries, picked over and rinsed (1¼ cups)
⅓ cup raspberry pourable fruit
2 cups slightly sweetened whipped cream
   or frozen nondairy whipped topping, thawed

1. Spoon the sorbet and ice cream alternately into the crust. Smooth the surface with a spatula, mounding it slightly in the center. Freeze for at least 3 hours or overnight.

2. At serving time, in a small bowl mix the peaches, raspberries, and pourable fruit. Top the pie with whipped topping, then spoon the fruit mixture over the top.

Per serving with ice cream and whipped cream: 380 cal, 3 g pro, 20 g fat, 49 g car, 190 mg sod, 55 mg chol. With low-fat frozen yogurt and whipped topping: 300 cal, 9 g fat, 2 mg chol

A WORD ABOUT ICE CREAM MACHINES

The least expensive ice cream machine is the hand-crank model, which uses either salt and ice or a prefrozen canister of artificial coolant to freeze the ice cream mixture. The electric-crank machines are chilled by the same methods mentioned above and spare your arm constant churning. The ultimate ice cream machine and the most expensive is the automatic-crank machine with a built-in freezing unit. This machine yields excellent results in a relatively short period of time and with little or no advance chilling.

EASY • LOW FAT

ORANGE–STRAWBERRY SWIRL PIE

Serves 12

Preparation time: 15 minutes plus at least 5 hours to freeze

Here's a pretty dessert that features just three ingredients: poundcake, orange sherbet, and strawberry jelly. Because it has to be made ahead, it's the perfect dessert to serve at a party, so you can spend time with your guests rather than in the kitchen.

Half a purchased 10¾-ounce loaf poundcake,
  cut crosswise into six ½-inch-thick slices
¼ cup strawberry jelly
1 quart orange sherbet, slightly softened
For garnish: strawberry halves and canned mandarin orange sections

1. Cut each slice of poundcake diagonally in one direction, then diagonally in the other direction to form 4 triangles.
2. Cover the bottom of a 10-inch straight-sided porcelain quiche dish with 12 triangles. Stand the remaining 12 triangles, points up, around the sides of the dish.
3. Stir the jelly with a fork until syrupy and no lumps remain.
4. Put the sherbet into a medium-size bowl. Stir with a spatula or wooden spoon until the sherbet is smooth and spreadable. Spoon into the cake-lined dish, then gently spread into an even layer.
5. Drop teaspoonfuls of jelly 1 inch apart over the sherbet. Draw the tip of a pointed knife through the jelly to make decorative swirls in the sherbet.
6. Freeze for at least 5 hours or overnight.
7. Just before serving, arrange the strawberry halves and orange sections around the edge.

Per serving: 150 cal, 1 g pro, 4 g fat, 30 g car, 80 mg sod, 31 mg chol

COOK'S TIP

You can use a 10-inch deep-dish pie plate instead of a quiche dish.

EASY • LOW FAT

FROZEN STRAWBERRY DAIQUIRI PIE

Serves 12

Preparation time: 15 minutes plus at least 2 hours to freeze

A strawberry daiquiri that you can eat with a spoon—and it won't make you a bit tipsy! If you can't find mango sorbet, use a citrus-flavored sorbet such as lemon or orange. The granola crust is quick and easy to make, or you can use a ready-made graham-cracker crust instead.

CRUST
3 cups (10½ ounces) low-fat granola cereal without raisins
3 tablespoons light corn syrup

1 pint mango sorbet
2 pints vanilla frozen yogurt
1 can (10 ounces) frozen nonalcoholic strawberry-daiquiri mixer
1 pint (12 ounces) ripe strawberries, rinsed and hulled
For garnish: sprigs of fresh mint

COOK'S TIP

Choose fresh strawberries
that are bright red, shiny,
and plump with fresh
green leaves. Small
berries will have more
flavor than bigger ones.
Refrigerate the berries in
well-ventilated baskets.
Wash them just before
using, then remove the
stems and hulls.

1. Lightly spray a 9-inch pie plate with vegetable oil cooking spray.

2. In a small bowl, mix the granola cereal with the corn syrup to coat. Moisten your fingertips with water and press the cereal mixture evenly over the bottom and up the sides of the prepared pie plate. Freeze until firm, about 1 hour.

3. Let the sorbet and frozen yogurt soften at room temperature for 15 to 20 minutes. Spread the mango sorbet over the bottom of the crust.

4. Put the vanilla frozen yogurt into a medium-size bowl. Spoon in all but ½ cup of the frozen-daiquiri mixer. With a rubber spatula, swirl it through the frozen yogurt to create a marble effect. Spread the mixture over the mango sorbet. Cover and freeze until ready to serve, at least 1 hour or up to 4 days.

5. Put the remaining ½ cup of daiquiri mixer in a medium-size bowl. Mash ½ cup of the strawberries into the daiquiri mixer. Slice the remaining berries in half and add to the mixture, stirring to blend. Cover and refrigerate up to 8 hours.

6. Just before serving, top the pie with some of the chilled strawberry mixture. Garnish with mint sprigs. Serve the remaining berry mixture to spoon over the wedges.

Per serving: 270 cal, 5 g pro, 3 g fat, 60 g car, 110 mg sod, 3 mg chol

LOW FAT

FROZEN CHOCOLATE MERINGUE TORTE

Serves 12

Preparation time: 20 minutes
plus at least 4 hours to freeze
Baking time: 2 hours 15 minutes

Surprise: The easy meringue layers are made from angel-food cake mix. Though this recipe is not complicated, it takes a long time: the meringue layers bake for 2 hours—and you'll have to bake two batches unless you have a double oven. The assembled torte then needs to freeze for at least 4 hours. The meringue layers can be made well ahead, however, and the torte quickly assembled on the day you plan to serve it.

MERINGUE LAYERS

1 package (about 16 ounces) angel-food cake mix
1 cup cold water
¾ cup granulated sugar

½ gallon nonfat chocolate frozen yogurt

▶

For garnish: unsweetened cocoa powder, chocolate syrup,
  chocolate curls (see page 329), raspberries, mint leaves

1. Place 1 rack in the middle of the oven and another rack in the lowest position. Heat the oven to 200°F. If you have 2 ovens, use both. Line 4 cookie sheets with foil. (Do not grease cookie sheets or foil and do not put 2 meringue layers on 1 cookie sheet.) On 3 of the cookie sheets outline a 9-inch circle by pressing a 9-inch cake pan, pie plate, or salad plate into the foil.

2. In a large bowl with an electric mixer on high speed, beat the contents of the cake mix package with the 1 cup water. Add the granulated sugar and beat on high speed for 2 minutes longer. (Makes about 10 cups meringue.)

3. Spoon about 2½ cups of the meringue in each outlined circle. Spread evenly to the edges. Drop the remaining meringue by spoonfuls on the unmarked foil (or pipe rosettes using a ½-inch star tip).

4. Place 1 cookie sheet on each oven rack. (The other 2 can wait their turn.) Bake until the meringue is crisp and dry, about 2 hours 15 minutes for the layers, 1 hour 50 minutes for the small meringues. Cool the meringues on the foil on the cookie sheets.

5. Lift off the small meringues. Carefully peel the foil off the layers. (Any cracks won't show when the torte is assembled.) • The meringues can be baked up to 3 days ahead and stored loosely covered at room temperature, or wrapped airtight and frozen up to 2 months.

6. To assemble, soften the frozen yogurt slightly. Place one meringue layer on a serving platter. Spread with half the yogurt. Repeat with another meringue layer, the remaining yogurt, and the third layer. Immediately cover the torte and freeze for at least 4 hours.

7. Up to 15 minutes before serving, arrange the small meringues on the torte. Dust the torte with cocoa, drizzle with chocolate sauce, then finish with chocolate curls, raspberries, and mint leaves. Refrigerate until ready to serve.

8. To serve, remove the small meringues to plates. Cut the cake with a sharp knife.
Per serving: 320 cal, 6 g pro, 0 g fat, 73 g car, 390 mg sod, 0 mg chol

TORTES

A dessert torte is a round construction of alternating layers of cake and filling. Typically, the cake layers are made with ground nuts or bread crumbs and very little flour. Savory tortes feature layers of cheese, meat, and vegetables, usually in a pastry crust.

Your guests don't need to know that this festive Ice Cream Bombe (p. 82) is assembled from purchased ingredients in just 20 minutes.

Peach Ice Cream (p. 55), Kiwi-Lime Sorbet (p. 60), and Strawberry-Grapefruit Sorbet (p. 61), left, are cool ways to capture the essence of fruit.

This Raspberry-Lemon Granita (p. 63), above, is elegant, refreshing, and entirely fat-free.

Now you can enjoy the classic American ice cream treat Banana Split with Fudge Sauce (p. 86), above, without feeling guilty. Our version is low in fat, but every bit as delicious. Friends and family will appreciate the rich, creamy flavor of homemade Fabulous Vanilla Ice Cream (p.54), right, or one of the easy variations, such as Coffee-Almond or Strawberry.

Ice cream cakes are always popular, and Banana-Toffee Ice Cream Cake (p.78), right, will be no exception. Made with chocolate pound cake, butter-pecan ice cream, bananas, toffee bars, and caramel topping, it's sure to win raves.

Don't wait for the Kentucky Derby to enjoy this refreshing Mint Julep Sorbet (p.62), left. Any lazy, warm afternoon will do.

Orange-Strawberry Swirl Pie (p.66), above, is a fitting finale for a casual summer meal. And you can make it ahead.

Nothing beats the simple pleasure of icy sorbets and granitas—and you don't need an ice cream machine to make them.

Looks can be deceiving. This pretty Ladyfinger Ice Cream Loaf (p.79) takes only 15 minutes to prepare.

• Line a 9 x 5 x 3-inch loaf pan with plastic wrap, letting enough wrap extend above the sides of the pan to cover the top when filled. Trim 4 whole chocolate-flavored (not chocolate-coated) graham crackers to fit side by side (long sides touching) in the bottom of the lined pan. (Do not place in the pan.) Put the pan in the freezer for 10 minutes.

• At the same time, take out 3 pints coffee ice cream or low-fat frozen yogurt to soften slightly.

• Trim 8 more graham crackers to fit in the pan. Remove the pan from the freezer. Cover the bottom of the pan with 4 trimmed crackers. Spoon 1 cup of ice cream on top. Spread evenly with the back of a spoon.

• Gently press 4 more crackers onto the ice cream. Freeze for 5 minutes. Repeat the layers using the remaining ice cream and crackers.

• Fold the plastic wrap tightly over the loaf. Freeze for at least 5 hours or overnight.

• Serve and garnish the loaf as directed.

Per serving with ice cream: 190 cal, 3 g pro, 9 g fat, 28 g car, 150 mg sod, 30 mg chol. With low-fat frozen yogurt: 150 cal, 3 g fat, 5 mg chol

• EASY
• DECADENT

DECADENT

SEVEN–LAYER BROWNIE ICE CREAM CAKE

Serves 12

Preparation time: 45 minutes plus at least 5 hours to freeze

Baking time: 32 minutes

Disks of brownie cookies separate layers of ice cream in this special-occasion cake. If time is short, try the no–bake variation. To reduce fat, use frozen yogurt. The cake will be just as spectacular.

BROWNIE LAYERS
1/4 cup unsweetened cocoa powder
3 tablespoons water
1 large egg
1 teaspoon vanilla extract
1 stick (1/2 cup) butter or margarine (see page 321), softened
1 cup granulated sugar
1 1/3 cups all-purpose flour

3 pints coffee ice cream or low-fat coffee frozen yogurt, slightly softened

For garnish: whipped cream, raspberries, crushed chocolate-covered toffee candy bars

1. Trace an 8-inch circle on a piece of waxed paper, using a cake pan or plate as a guide. Place on a stack of 6 more pieces of waxed paper. Using the traced circle as a guide, cut through all the pieces of paper, giving you seven waxed paper rounds. (Or use seven 8-inch nonstick baking pan liners.)

2. Heat the oven to 375°F. Have ready 2 cookie sheets and an 8-inch springform pan.

3. Make the brownie layers: In a small bowl, whisk the cocoa, water, egg, and vanilla until blended and smooth. In a large (mixer) bowl, beat the butter and sugar with an electric mixer until pale and fluffy, about 3 minutes. Beat in the cocoa mixture (the batter may look curdled). With the mixer on low speed, gradually add the flour and beat until well blended (the batter will be very stiff).

4. Spread the 7 rounds of waxed paper out on a countertop. Drop a level 1/3 cup of batter in the center of each round. Divide the remaining 1/3 cup of batter between the rounds (about 2 teaspoons each).

5. Slightly dampen a cookie sheet with water. Place 2 waxed paper rounds on the cookie sheet (the water will stop them from slipping). Spread the batter almost to the edges of the rounds.

6. Bake until the surface looks dry and set but is slightly springy to the touch, about 8 minutes. (While the first batch bakes, spread out the batter for next 2 layers.)

7. Set the baked layers on the cookie sheet on a wire rack to cool for 3 minutes. Remove the layers, on the waxed paper, to the rack. Let cool completely. ▶

8. Bake and cool the remaining layers.

9. To assemble: Line the springform pan with plastic wrap, letting enough wrap extend above the sides of the pan to cover the top when filled. Peel the waxed paper off the cooled brownie layers. Place one brownie layer in the bottom of the pan. Spread evenly with 1 cup of ice cream. Top with another brownie layer, then another cup of ice cream. Repeat with 5 more brownie layers and the ice cream, ending with a brownie layer on the top. Fold the plastic wrap over the top and freeze for at least 5 hours, or wrap airtight and freeze up to 1 month.

10. To serve, remove the sides of the pan and peel the plastic wrap down from the sides. Lift the cake off the plastic wrap onto a serving plate. Garnish with whipped cream, raspberries, and crushed toffee. Refrigerate for about 20 minutes before cutting and serving.

Per serving with butter and ice cream: 330 cal, 5 g pro, 16 g fat, 44 g car, 140 mg sod, 67 mg chol. With margarine and low-fat frozen yogurt: 280 cal, 10 g fat, 23 mg chol

DECADENT

BANANA–TOFFEE ICE CREAM CAKE

Serves 12

Preparation time: 30 minutes plus at least 9 hours to freeze

No one will ever guess how easy it is to assemble this scrumptious ice cream cake. It is made in a springform pan, so the pan sides can be removed to show off the multi-layers.

> *1 chocolate poundcake (15 to 16 ounces)*
> *3 medium-size ripe bananas, cut into ¼-inch-thick slices*
> *¼ cup bottled caramel topping (from a squeeze bottle)*
> *1½ quarts (3 pints) butter-pecan ice cream*
> *3 chocolate-covered toffee bars (about 1.4 ounces each), coarsely chopped (¾ cup)*
> *For garnish: whipped cream, chopped toffee bars, caramel topping*

1. Have an 8-inch springform pan ready.

2. Trim the ends off the poundcake. Cut the cake into twelve ½-inch-thick slices. Cut a pie-shaped wedge, 2 inches across the top, from each slice. Wrap the wedges in plastic wrap and reserve.

3. Cover the bottom of the springform pan with the remaining cake pieces, pressing them together to make an even layer with no gaps. (You may not need all the cake.)

4. Scatter the bananas over the cake in the pan, then drizzle with the caramel sauce. Cover and freeze until the bananas are firm, about 1½ hours.

5. Soften 1½ pints (3 cups) of the ice cream and spread evenly over the bananas. Sprinkle with the chopped toffee bars, cover, and freeze until the ice cream is firm, at least 1½ hours.

6. Soften the remaining ice cream and spread over the toffee layer. Freeze until firm, about 1 hour.

7. Arrange the reserved cake wedges, points toward the center, over the ice cream layer. Cover and freeze for at least 5 hours or up to 5 days.

8. To serve, remove the sides of the pan and set the cake on a serving plate. Decorate the cake with the garnishes.

Per serving: 380 cal, 5 g pro, 21 g fat, 47 g car, 200 mg sod, 114 mg chol

EASY

LADYFINGER ICE CREAM LOAF

Serves 12

Preparation time: 15 minutes plus at least 5 hours to freeze

This triple-decker indulgence tastes as good as it looks. If you use a glass loaf dish, chill it well in the freezer so the first sherbet layer won't melt while you're assembling the other layers. Look for ladyfingers in the cookie or baked good section of your supermarket, and be sure to buy the ones that are not filled.

1 package (3 ounces) unfilled ladyfingers (12 ladyfingers)
1 pint raspberry, strawberry, or orange sherbet, slightly softened
1 pint vanilla ice cream or low-fat vanilla frozen yogurt, slightly softened
1 pint chocolate ice cream or low-fat chocolate frozen yogurt, slightly softened
1 cup heavy (whipping) cream, whipped stiff with 1 tablespoon granulated sugar,
*   or 2 cups nondairy whipped topping*
For garnish: cooled melted semisweet chocolate or chocolate ice cream sauce

1. Tear off two 20-inch lengths of regular-thickness aluminum foil. Place on top of each other and fold over the sides to make a 9-inch-wide strip. Fit into a 9 x 5 x 3-inch loaf pan, letting the ends of the foil extend above the sides of pan to cover the top when filled.

2. Split the ladyfingers apart and separate the tops from the bottoms.

3. Spoon the raspberry sherbet into the foil-lined loaf pan. Press into an even layer with the back of a spoon.

4. Arrange 12 ladyfinger halves over the sherbet. Top with an even layer of vanilla ice cream.

5. Repeat the layers with the remaining ladyfingers and the chocolate ice cream.

6. Fold the foil tightly over the top of loaf. Freeze for at least 5 hours or overnight.

7. To serve, fold back the foil. Loosen the ends of loaf from the pan with a thin knife. Holding the foil, carefully lift the loaf from the pan. Invert onto a serving dish and peel off the foil.

8. Just before serving, spread the whipped cream over the top of the loaf and drizzle with the chocolate.

Per serving with ice cream and whipped cream: 230 cal, 3 g pro, 13 g fat, 27 g car, 70 mg sod, 72 mg chol. With low-fat frozen yogurt and whipped topping: 180 cal, 4 g pro, 6 g fat, 30 mg chol

ORANGE SHERBET LOAF WITH CHOCOLATE SAUCE

Serves 16

Preparation time: 25 minutes plus at least 5 hours to freeze

If you like the combination of chocolate and orange, you'll love this tasty low-fat treat. It's the perfect ending to a rich meal. The low-fat chocolate sauce is also wonderful served over low-fat frozen yogurt.

1 fat-and-cholesterol-free chocolate loaf cake
  (15 ounces)
½-gallon block orange sherbet

CHOCOLATE SAUCE
¼ cup unsweetened cocoa powder
¼ cup granulated sugar
3 tablespoons water
1 teaspoon vanilla extract
1 teaspoon vegetable oil

1. Tear off two 20-inch lengths of regular-thickness aluminum foil. Place on top of each other and fold over the sides to make a 9-inch-wide strip. Fit into a 9 x 5 x 3-inch loaf pan, letting the ends of the foil extend above the sides of pan to cover the top when filled.

2. With a long serrated knife, cut the cake horizontally into 4 layers. Cut the rounded top layer crosswise into thirds.

3. Open up the sherbet carton. Cut through the side seams so the box lies flat under the sherbet block. With a serrated knife, cut the sherbet crosswise into twelve ½-inch-thick slabs.

4. Place 3 slabs into the foil-lined pan. Press into an even layer with a spatula.

5. Top with 1 cake layer and one of the 3 small pieces of cake. Add another 3 slabs of sherbet and pack firmly with a spatula.

6. Repeat with the remaining cake and sherbet.

7. Fold the foil tightly over the top. Freeze at least 5 hours. (For longer storage, wrap in additional foil and keep frozen up to 1 month.)

8. Make the sauce: In a small bowl, whisk the cocoa powder, sugar, water, vanilla, and oil until thoroughly blended and the sugar dissolves. Cover and refrigerate for at least 2 hours (the sauce will thicken slightly) or until ready to serve.

9. To unmold, fold back the foil. Loosen the ends of the loaf from the pan with a thin knife. Holding the foil, carefully lift the loaf from the pan. Invert onto a serving dish and peel off the foil.

10. Just before serving, stir the sauce. Dip the tines of a fork in the sauce and drizzle some over the top of the loaf. Serve the remaining sauce at the table.

Per serving: 220 cal, 3 g pro, 2 g fat, 48 g car, 170 mg sod, 5 mg chol

LAYERED MELON SHERBET CAKE

Serves 12

Preparation time: 20 minutes plus at least 3 hours to freeze

Cooking time: 13 minutes

This super-refreshing "cake" made with layers of homemade cantaloupe, honeydew, and watermelon sherbet is perfect for the long, hot summer. If you'd rather not make your own sherbet—which is easier than it sounds—you can use 1 quart each of store-bought raspberry, orange, and lemon or lime sherbet or sorbet—or any other flavors that appeal.

1½ cups granulated sugar
1½ cups water
2 pounds ripe cantaloupe, rind cut off, seeded,
*   and cut into 1-inch pieces (about 4 cups)*
3 tablespoons fresh lemon or lime juice
¾ cup light cream or half-and-half
2 pounds ripe honeydew melon, rind cut off, seeded,
*   and cut into 1-inch pieces (about 4 cups)*
2 pounds watermelon, rind cut off, seeded, and
*   cut into 1-inch pieces (about 4 cups)*
For garnish: thin watermelon wedges,
*   sliced carambola (star fruit) and nectarines,*
*   fresh strawberries and raspberries*

1. Have ready an 8- or 9-inch springform pan about 3 inches high.

2. In a medium-size saucepan, mix the sugar and water. Stir over medium-high heat until the sugar dissolves. Bring to a boil, reduce the heat, and simmer, without stirring, for 5 to 8 minutes, until syrupy. Remove from the heat and cool completely. (You'll have 2 cups of syrup.)

3. In a food processor or blender, process the cantaloupe chunks until almost smooth. Add ⅔ cup of the syrup, 1 tablespoon of lemon juice, and ¼ cup of cream. Process until completely smooth.

4. Freeze in an ice cream maker following manufacturer's directions. Or pour into 9-inch square pan, cover with plastic wrap, and freeze until nearly solid. Break into chunks and process in a blender or food processor until smooth.

5. Spoon the mixture into the springform pan, packing it down into an even layer, and freeze until firm, about 1 hour.

6. Repeat steps 3 and 4 using the honeydew melon. Pack it down evenly over the cantaloupe layer and freeze until firm, about 1 hour.

7. Repeat steps 3 and 4 with the watermelon. Pack it down evenly over the honeydew layer. Cover with plastic wrap and freeze at least 1 hour before serving or wrap and freeze up to 1 week.

▶

8. To serve, turn the springform pan upside down on a serving plate. Remove the pan sides and top. If the "cake" has been frozen more than a few hours, refrigerate it for 30 minutes or until soft enough to slice. Just before serving, arrange the garnishes on top.

Per serving: 160 cal, 1 g pro, 3 g fat, 35 g car, 10 mg sod, 10 mg chol

---

EASY • CLASSIC

ICE CREAM BOMBE

Serves 12

Preparation time: 20 minutes plus at least 10½ hours to freeze

A visual as well as a taste treat, this frozen dessert contains layers of cherry-vanilla ice cream, chocolate cake, and creamy orange sherbet all covered with a hard chocolate coating. It's easy to assemble and looks so spectacular it's sure to become the focal point of a special celebration.

> *2 pints cherry-vanilla ice cream or 1 pint each low-fat cherry*
> *and low-fat vanilla frozen yogurt, slightly softened*
> *1 package (8 ounces) frosted devil's food cakes (12 pieces)*
> *1 pint vanilla ice cream-orange sherbet combination,*
> *or 1 cup each low-fat vanilla frozen yogurt and*
> *orange sherbet, slightly softened*
> *1 container (7 ounces) chocolate "hard-shell" ice cream topping*
> *For garnish: maraschino cherries*

1. Line a deep, narrow 1½-quart bowl or mold with plastic wrap, letting enough wrap extend above the rim to cover the top when filled.

2. Spoon the cherry-vanilla ice cream into the lined bowl. Press with the back of a spoon until the bowl is lined with a ¾-inch-thick layer.

3. Gently press the devil's food cakes in a layer into the ice cream, overlapping if necessary. Freeze until firm, at least 1 hour.

4. Pack the ice cream-sherbet mixture into the center of the mold.

5. Fold the plastic wrap over the top. Freeze for at least 8 hours or overnight.

6. Several hours before serving, fold back the plastic wrap. Holding the wrap, carefully lift the bombe from the bowl. Invert it onto a plate and peel off the plastic wrap. Return to the freezer for 1 hour.

7. Pour the chocolate topping over the bombe, tilting the plate so the bombe is completely covered with the chocolate. (The topping will set as it hits the ice cream.) Return to the freezer until the chocolate shell is very hard, about 30 minutes.

8. To serve, cut around the base of the bombe to release the hardened coating from the plate. With a spatula, carefully lift the bombe to a serving dish. Surround with the cherries.

Per serving with ice cream: 300 cal, 3 g pro, 41 g car, 14 g fat, 26 mg chol, 121 mg sod. Per serving with yogurt and sherbet: 280 cal, 4 g pro, 45 g car, 9 g fat, 5 mg chol, 100 mg sod

COOK'S TIP

To quickly soften frozen ice cream, put it in the microwave on Medium-Low for 30 seconds. Insert a thin knife into the ice cream to test for softness.

EASY • QUICK • LOW FAT • CLASSIC

PEACH MELBA SUNDAES

Serves 6

Preparation time: 15 minutes

Fresh peaches become more delectable with the flavorful addition of raspberries and vanilla. The colors of this sundae are beautiful, too. If you like, add a spoonful of chilled whipped topping.

½ cup red raspberry preserves
1 tablespoon orange juice
2 teaspoons water
3 medium-size ripe peaches (about 1¼ pounds),
  halved, pitted, and cut into bite-size chunks
1¼ cups fresh raspberries or partially thawed frozen
  no-sugar-added raspberries
1 pint nonfat vanilla frozen yogurt
⅓ cup pistachio nuts, coarsely chopped

1. In a small bowl, mix the preserves, orange juice, and water.
2. In a medium-size bowl, mix the peaches and raspberries.
3. To serve, scoop the frozen yogurt into 6 dessert glasses. Top each with the fruit, preserve mixture, and pistachios. Serve right away.

Per serving: 220 cal, 4 g pro, 4 g fat, 45 g car, 40 mg sod, 0 mg chol

SUPER SUNDAES

There are no hard and fast rules about making sundaes; they are only limited by your imagination and the size of the dish. Just consider using contrasting colors for visual appeal and flavors that complement one another. Here are some ideas using the recipes in this chapter:

◆ **LOW-FAT CHOCOLATE SUNDAE:** Low-Fat Chocolate Ice Cream (page 58), Chocolate Sauce (page 80), and fat-free nondairy whipped topping

◆ **TROPICAL SUNDAE:** Pineapple-Coconut Ice Cream (page 54), Butter-scotch Ice Cream Sauce (page 85), and toasted chopped macadamia nuts or sweetened flaked coconut
◆ **GEORGIA PEACH SUNDAE:** Peach Ice Cream (page 55), Butterscotch Ice Cream Sauce (page 85), and pecans
◆ **RED, WHITE, AND BLUE SUNDAE:** Blueberry-Lemon Ice Cream (page 58), Ruby-Red Ice Cream Sauce (page 85), and whipped cream. Or Strawberry Ice

Cream (page 54), Lemon-Blueberry Ice Cream Sauce (page 85), and whipped cream or topping
◆ **MOCHA CHOCOLATE SUNDAE:** Coffee-Almond Ice Cream (page 54), Hot Fudge Sauce (page 84), whipped cream, and chocolate shavings
◆ **DOUBLE CHOCOLATE-PEANUT BUTTER CUP SUNDAE:** Super-Rich Chocolate Ice Cream (page 55), Chocolate-Peanut Butter Ice Cream Sauce (page 84), and whipped cream

ICE CREAM SAUCES

Ice cream sauces are always popular and are an easy way to make a scoop of ice cream extra–special. In addition to these delectable sauces, don't forget about other toppings such as crushed fruit, crushed cookies, toasted nuts, and mini marshmallows.

HOT FUDGE SAUCE
Makes 1½ cups
Preparation time: 5 minutes
Cooking time: 15 minutes

This decadent fudge sauce is the old-fashioned type that hardens and turns chewy as it comes in contact with cold ice cream.

2 ounces unsweetened chocolate, coarsely chopped
2 tablespoons unsalted butter
½ cup boiling water
1 cup granulated sugar
1 tablespoon unsweetened cocoa powder
2 tablespoons light corn syrup
2 teaspoons vanilla extract

1. Put the chocolate and butter in a heavy medium-size saucepan. Stir frequently over medium-low heat until melted and smooth.
2. Slowly stir in the boiling water, then the sugar, cocoa, and corn syrup. Bring the mixture to a boil over medium heat, stirring often. Gently boil over medium-low heat, without stirring, for 8 to 9 minutes.
3. Remove from the heat and let cool for 5 minutes. Stir in the vanilla.
4. Serve warm, or pour into an airtight container and refrigerate up to 2 weeks. Reheat in a saucepan over low heat or microwave in a microwave-safe bowl, loosely covered, on Medium-Low power for 1 to 2 minutes, stirring once or twice.

Per ¼ cup serving: 240 cal, 1 g pro, 9 g fat, 42 g car, 10 mg sod, 10 mg chol

CHOCOLATE–PEANUT BUTTER ICE CREAM SAUCE
Makes 2 cups
Preparation time: 15 minutes
Cooking time: 5 minutes

For a quick dessert that children will love, use this sauce to make an ice cream sundae or a banana split.

¾ cup packed dark brown sugar
½ cup unsweetened cocoa powder
1 tablespoon cornstarch
1⅓ cups skim milk
¼ cup reduced-fat creamy peanut butter spread
1 teaspoon vanilla extract

1. In a medium-size saucepan, whisk together the brown sugar, cocoa, and cornstarch (the mixture will be lumpy).
2. Gradually whisk in the milk until blended. Bring to a boil over medium heat, stirring occasionally. Boil, stirring constantly, until thick, about 1 minute.
3. Remove from the heat and whisk in the peanut butter spread and vanilla until blended.
4. Serve right away, or cool and pour into an airtight container and refrigerate up to 2 weeks. Reheat in a saucepan over low heat, stirring often, or microwave in a microwave-safe bowl, loosely covered, on Medium-Low power for 1 to 2 minutes, stirring once.

Per ¼ cup serving: 160 cal, 4 g pro, 4 g fat, 30 g car, 70 mg sod, 1 mg chol

TOASTED ALMOND-APPLE ICE CREAM TOPPING
Makes 1⅓ cups
Preparation time: 10 minutes
Cooking time: 6 minutes

This warm and spicy fruit topping is not only wonderful with vanilla ice cream but also delicious over pancakes, waffles, or slices of poundcake.

¼ cup (1 ounce) sliced almonds
1 tablespoon butter or margarine
2 large McIntosh apples (about ¾ pound), peeled, cored, and cut into ¼-inch-thick slices
2 tablespoons packed light brown sugar
¼ teaspoon ground cinnamon
Pinch grated nutmeg
Pinch ground cloves
¼ cup apple juice

1. In a nonstick medium-size skillet, toast the almonds over medium heat, stirring occasionally, until golden. Remove to a small bowl.
2. In the same skillet, melt the butter over medium heat. Add the apples, brown sugar, cinnamon, nutmeg, and cloves. Cook, stirring often, until the apples are tender, 3 to 4 minutes. Stir in the apple juice and bring to a boil over medium-high heat.
3. Remove from the heat and let cool slightly. Just before serving, stir in the toasted almonds. Serve right away.

Per ⅓ cup serving with butter: 140 cal, 2 g pro, 7 g fat, 21 g car, 30 mg sod, 8 mg chol. With margarine: 40 mg sod, 0 mg chol

RUBY-RED ICE CREAM SAUCE

Makes 5 cups
Preparation time: 5 minutes
Cooking time: 10 minutes

This dessert sauce is also delightful over poached pears or sliced oranges.

1 can (16 ounces) tart cherries in juice
2 bags (12 ounces each) fresh or frozen cranberries
1 bag (12 ounces) frozen raspberries
1 cup granulated sugar
1 cup light corn syrup
½ cup orange juice
2 tablespoons orange-flavored liqueur (optional)

1. Drain the juice from the cherries into a large saucepan. Add the cranberries, raspberries, sugar, corn syrup, and orange juice.
2. Bring to a boil over medium-high heat and boil until thickened slightly, 6 to 8 minutes. Remove from the heat and let cool for about 10 minutes.
3. Purée the mixture in batches in a food processor or blender. Press through a fine strainer set over a medium-size bowl; discard the solids. Stir in the cherries and liqueur.
4. Serve right away, or pour into an airtight container and refrigerate up to 2 weeks.

Per ¼ cup serving: 120 cal, 0 g pro, 0 g fat, 32 g car, 20 mg sod, 0 mg chol

BUTTERSCOTCH ICE CREAM SAUCE

Makes 2½ cups
Preparation time: 5 minutes
Cooking time: 10 minutes

Pour this buttery sauce over a scoop of your favorite ice cream for an irresistible treat on a hot day. For extra flavor, sprinkle with some toasted chopped pecans.

1 cup packed dark brown sugar
½ stick (¼ cup) unsalted butter, cut into small pieces
Pinch salt
1 cup light corn syrup
½ cup heavy (whipping) cream
½ teaspoon vanilla extract

1. Put the brown sugar, butter, salt, corn syrup, and cream into a medium-size heavy saucepan. Cook over medium heat, stirring occasionally, until the mixture is a light caramel color, 7 to 10 minutes.
2. Remove from the heat and stir in the vanilla. Let cool.
3. Serve warm, or cool and pour into an airtight container and refrigerate up to 2 weeks. Reheat in a saucepan over low heat or microwave in a microwave-safe bowl, loosely covered, on Medium-Low power for 1 to 2 minutes, stirring once.

Per ¼ cup serving: 260 cal, 0 g pro, 9 g fat, 47 g car, 70 mg sod, 29 mg chol

LEMON-BLUEBERRY ICE CREAM SAUCE

Makes 2 cups
Preparation time: 10 minutes plus cooling
Cooking time: 11 minutes

Turn plain and simple vanilla ice cream into a festive dessert with this topping that can be made in just 15 minutes. Either fresh or frozen blueberries can be used.

⅓ cup water
¼ cup granulated sugar
2 tablespoons butter or margarine
1 teaspoon freshly grated lemon peel
1 tablespoon fresh lemon juice
1 pint (12 ounces) fresh blueberries, picked over and rinsed (2 cups)

1. Put the water, sugar, butter, lemon peel, and lemon juice into a medium-size saucepan. Bring to a boil over medium-high heat, stirring until the sugar is dissolved.
2. Stir in the blueberries, mashing some of them against the side of the pan. Cook over medium heat, stirring often, until thickened, 5 to 6 minutes for fresh berries, and 13 to 15 minutes for frozen berries.
3. Remove the pan from the heat and let cool completely before serving over ice cream. Pour the sauce into an airtight container and refrigerate up to 1 week.

Per ¼ cup serving: 70 cal, 0 g pro, 3 g fat, 12 g car, 30 mg sod, 8 mg chol. With margarine: 40 mg sod, 0 mg chol

LOW FAT • OLD FASHIONED

BANANA SPLIT WITH FUDGE SAUCE

Serves 4

Preparation time: 10 minutes plus 2 hours to chill

Cooking time: 5 minutes

Yes, it's possible to make a low-fat banana split. Make this fudge sauce with cocoa powder, cornstarch, and 1%-fat milk and use purchased chocolate sorbet. You'll love the flavor and won't miss the calories. Of course, you can make this no-guilt banana split with any flavors of sorbet or fat-free frozen yogurt.

FUDGE SAUCE

1/3 cup Dutch-process unsweetened cocoa powder

1/4 cup granulated sugar

1 tablespoon cornstarch

1/3 cup 1%-fat milk

3 tablespoons light corn syrup

1 tablespoon semisweet chocolate chips (optional)

1/2 teaspoon vanilla extract

4 medium-size ripe bananas

1 pint chocolate sorbet

1/4 cup (1 ounce) dry-roasted salted peanuts, chopped

For garnish: maraschino cherries with stems, reduced-fat whipped topping

1. In a small saucepan, mix the cocoa, sugar, and cornstarch. Whisk in the milk and corn syrup until blended. Bring to a gentle boil over medium heat, whisking often. Remove from the heat, add the chocolate chips, and whisk until melted. Stir in the vanilla extract. Refrigerate until the sauce has thickened and chilled, 2 hours.

2. To serve, cut the peeled bananas in half lengthwise. Put 2 halves on each dessert plate. Top with scoops of chocolate sorbet, fudge sauce, and peanuts. Garnish with cherries and whipped topping.

Per serving: 400 cal, 7 g pro, 6 g fat, 89 g car, 220 mg sod, 1 mg chol

---

STORING ICE CREAM

Ice creams and sorbets should be frozen in airtight containers at 0° to 10°F. If they are left uncovered or not sealed airtight, they will develop ice crystals and pick up freezer odors. Although you can freeze homemade ice cream up to 1 month and sorbet up to 2 weeks, for the best texture both should be eaten within 3 days.

SODA FOUNTAIN HALL OF FAME

An ice cream soda is composed of three ingredients: the flavoring, the soda, such as seltzer or club soda, and ice cream. These favorite soda combinations have been the pride of many a soda jerk:

◆ **Black and White:** Made with chocolate syrup and vanilla ice cream

◆ **Broadway:** Made with vanilla syrup and vanilla ice cream

◆ **Brown Cow:** Made with root beer and vanilla ice cream

◆ **Black Cow:** Made with cola and vanilla ice cream

◆ **Purple Cow:** Made with grape soda and vanilla ice cream

◆ **Strawberry Blondie:** Made with ginger ale and strawberry ice cream

BANANA SHAKE

Serves 1

Preparation time: 10 minutes

Depending on where you live, you may refer to this treat as a milkshake, a frappe, a frosted, or a thick shake. But whatever you call it, the ingredients are always the same: cold milk, ice cream, and a flavoring, blended to a thick and satisfying consistency.

1 cup cold milk
2 small ripe bananas
1 large scoop vanilla ice cream (⅓ cup)
¼ teaspoon vanilla extract
For garnish: whipped cream

1. Put the milk, bananas, ice cream, and vanilla into a blender and blend until smooth.
2. Pour the mixture into a chilled tall glass. Top with whipped cream. Serve right away.

Per shake: 410 cal, 11 g pro, 14 g fat, 65 g car, 160 mg sod, 53 mg chol

ORANGE–AND–CREAM SODA

Serves 1

Preparation time: 10 minutes

Ice cream sodas are made from three basic parts: a flavoring such as a syrup, ice cream, and soda water or a soft drink. Often a spoonful of whipped cream is added as a finishing touch. Here, the flavor combination of orange and vanilla will remind you of Creamsicle ice cream bars.

1 tablespoon frozen orange juice concentrate
1 tablespoon light cream or milk
2 scoops vanilla ice cream (¾ cup)
1 can (12 ounces) orange soda
For garnish: whipped cream

1. Put the orange juice concentrate into a chilled tall glass. Add the cream and stir well.
2. Add the ice cream and add enough of the orange soda to fill the glass. Stir gently and top with whipped cream. Serve right away.

Per soda with cream: 400 cal, 4 g pro, 14 g fat, 69 g car, 130 mg sod, 53 mg chol.
With milk: 11 g fat, 46 mg chol

VARIATION

LOW-FAT BANANA SHAKE

Use skim milk for the milk and nonfat vanilla frozen yogurt instead of ice cream. Proceed as directed.

Per shake: 320 cal, 12 g pro, 1 g fat, 69 g car, 160 mg sod, 5 mg chol

• EASY • QUICK
• LOW FAT

VARIATION

LOW-FAT ORANGE-AND-CREAM SODA

Use skim milk for the cream and nonfat vanilla frozen yogurt instead of ice cream. Proceed as directed.

Per soda: 330 cal, 4 g pro, 0 g fat, 79 g car, 120 mg sod, 0 mg chol

• EASY • QUICK
• LOW FAT

EASY • QUICK • OLD FASHIONED

MOCHA ICE CREAM SODA

Serves 1

Preparation time: 10 minutes

Though "mocha" is simply the name of a variety of Arabian coffee bean, it has come to describe the pairing of coffee and chocolate—one of the world's great flavor combinations. Ice cream sodas are great for dessert on hot summer nights or as a midday pick-me-up.

2 tablespoons chocolate syrup
2 tablespoons light cream or milk
2 scoops coffee ice cream or low-fat frozen yogurt (¾ cup)
About 1 cup seltzer or soda water
For garnish: whipped cream and chocolate shavings (see page 329)

1. Put the chocolate syrup into a chilled tall glass. Add the cream and stir well.
2. Add the ice cream and add enough seltzer to fill the glass. Top with whipped cream and chocolate shavings.

Per soda: 340 cal, 5 g pro, 17 g fat, 50 g car, 130 mg sod, 63 mg chol. With milk and low-fat frozen yogurt: 245 cal, 10 g pro, 3 g fat, 160 mg sod, 13 mg chol

THE SODA JERK

The soda jerk—whose title comes from the jerking motion the hand makes operating the soda spigots—is the person who prepares the confections behind the counter at the soda fountain. A soda jerk's skills were measured by the quality of his or her (usually his) ice cream sodas. A sign of a great ice cream soda was to have the ice cream just touching the soda and hanging on the edge of the glass.

ICE CREAM TREATS

◆ **CHERRY BOMBE:** Press a long-stemmed maraschino cherry into a small scoop of ice cream. Freeze until firm. Squeeze on chocolate "hard-shell" ice cream topping to coat.

◆ **FOURTH OF JULY SUNDAE:** Spoon whipped cream or topping into waffle-cone bowls. Top with a scoop of raspberry or strawberry sorbet. Garnish with blueberries and mint.

◆ **SPACESHIP:** Pour fruit-flavored gelatin into a glass bowl. Chill until set. Scoop out the center. Fill with fruit sherbert or sorbet.

◆ **CARNIVAL CONES:** Dip tops of cones in melted chocolate, then in chopped nuts or sprinkles.

◆ **CITRUS SORBET CUPS:** Cut tops off oranges, lemons, or limes. Scoop out pulp with a serrated grapefruit spoon. Fill with matching sorbets. Wrap and freeze until firm.

◆ **YO-YOS:** Sandwich pretty cookies with softened ice cream. Wrap and freeze until firm.

◆ **SUMMER RAINBOWS:** Dip goblet rims in lime juice, then sugar. Fill with rainbow sherbet.

◆ **WAFFLE SUNDAE:** Toast frozen waffles and cut in half diagonally. Top with butter-pecan ice cream, caramel sauce, toasted pecans, and a berry.

◆ **PARTY CLOWN:** Ruffle a doily on a saucer. Top with a scoop of ice cream and freeze. Decorate with a candy face and refreeze. Stick candies on a cone using tube icing. Dip the tip in whipped topping, then in sprinkles. Top the ice cream with the cone and serve.

◆ **ICE CREAM ZOO:** Sandwich animal crackers with ice cream scooped with a melon baller.

PIES & TARTS

> *"But I, when I undress me*
> *Each night upon my knees,*
> *Will ask the Lord to bless me*
> *With Apple-pie and cheese."*
>
> EUGENE FIELD

On these pages is a collection of irresistible pies and tarts featuring a variety of fillings—fruit, nuts, custard, cream, and more. From a traditional Lemon Meringue Pie to an exotic Mango Custard Tart or a rich and sinful Bittersweet Chocolate Truffle Tart, you'll find just the right dessert for the kids or for dinner guests. In fact, many of the recipes don't require any baking at all. Simply assemble and chill.

Cooks are sometimes daunted by the task of making a crust. They needn't be. It only takes a short time and a few ingredients to produce a perfect crust (see page 93 for tips). And many of the recipes feature easy crusts made from phyllo and puff pastry dough, ground nuts, and cookie crumbs. All these save time—and remember there's nothing wrong with a store-bought pie crust either.

EASY

Apricot Linzer Tart, 135
Banana Custard Tart, 132
Bittersweet Chocolate Truffle
   Tart, 136
Blueberry Pie with Cornmeal
   Crumb Topping, 98
Cherry-Cheese Tart, 128
Chocolate Pastry for a
   Single-Crust Pie, 93
Chocolate Truffle Caramel Pie, 120
Chocolate-Peanut Mousse Pie, 118
Chocolate-Raspberry Chiffon
   Pie, 108
Chocolate-Vanilla Mousse Pie, 119
Flaky Pastry for Tarts, 92
Free-Form Apple Tart, 129
Key Lime Pie, 117
Mango Custard Tart, 123
Maple-Pecan Pie, 107
Nectarine-Raspberry Tart, 126
Pastry for a Double-Crust Pie, 92
Pastry for a Single-Crust Pie, 92
Phyllo Apple Pie, 100
Phyllo Pear Pie, 100
Raspberry Chiffon Pie, 108
Raspberry Linzer Tart, 135
Sour Cream Lemon Pie, 102
Strawberry Mousse Pie, 121
Sweet Pastry for Tarts, 94
Two-Berry Tart, 127
Walnut Pear Upside-Down Tarts, 130
Zucchini "Apple" Pie, 101

QUICK

Chocolate Pastry for a
   Single-Crust Pie, 93
Flaky Pastry for Tarts, 92
Pastry for a Double-Crust Pie, 92
Pastry for a Single-Crust Pie, 92
Sweet Pastry for Tarts, 94

1 HOUR

Phyllo Apple Pie, 100
Phyllo Pear Pie, 100
Walnut Pear Upside-Down
 Tarts, 130

LOW FAT

Phyllo Apple Pie, 100
Phyllo Pear Pie, 100
Rhubarb-Cherry Pie, 96

CLASSIC

Almond Tart, 134
Double Chocolate Cream
 Pie, 105
Free-Form Apple Tart, 129
Key Lime Pie, 117
Lattice Peach Pie, 97
Lemon Meringue Pie, 103
Lime Mousse Schaumtorte, 133
Mississippi Mud Pie, 104
Raspberry Chiffon Pie, 108
Raspberry Linzer Tart, 135
Strawberry Custard Tart, 124

OLD FASHIONED

Apple Cider Pie, 99
Apple Crunch Pie, 99
Banana Custard Tart, 132
Blueberry Pie with Cornmeal
 Crumb Topping, 98
Double Chocolate Cream Pie, 105
Lattice Peach Pie, 97
Lemon Meringue Pie, 103
Mascarpone Lemon Cream
 Tartlets, 131
Rhubarb-Cherry Pie, 96
Sour Cream Lemon Pie, 102

DECADENT

Bittersweet Chocolate Truffle
 Tart, 136
Chocolate Truffle Caramel Pie, 120
Chocolate-Peanut Mousse Pie, 118
Chocolate-Strawberry Tart, 125
Chocolate-Vanilla Mousse Pie, 119
Double Chocolate Cream Pie, 105
Maple-Pecan Pie, 107
Mississippi Mud Pie, 104
Providence Nut Pie, 107

NO-BAKE PIES

Chocolate Truffle Caramel Pie, 120
Chocolate-Peanut Mousse Pie, 118
Chocolate-Raspberry Chiffon
 Pie, 108
Chocolate-Vanilla Mousse Pie, 119
Raspberry Chiffon Pie, 108
Strawberry Mousse Pie, 121

ELEGANT ENTERTAINING

Almond Tart, 134
Apricot Linzer Tart, 135
Bittersweet Chocolate Truffle
 Tart, 136
Chocolate-Strawberry Tart, 125
Lime Mousse Schaumtorte, 133
Mascarpone Lemon Cream
 Tartlets, 131
Raspberry Linzer Tart, 135
Strawberry Custard Tart, 124
Two-Berry Tart, 127

CROWD PLEASERS

Bittersweet Chocolate Truffle
 Tart, 136
Chocolate Truffle Caramel
 Pie, 120
Mascarpone Lemon Cream
 Tartlets, 131
Strawberry Mousse Pie, 121

PASTRY FOR A SINGLE-CRUST PIE

Makes one 9-inch pie crust

Preparation time: 15 minutes

Here's a great all-purpose pie dough. Make several batches to keep in the freezer.

1 cup all-purpose flour
2 tablespoons granulated sugar
⅛ teaspoon salt
¼ cup solid vegetable shortening
1½ tablespoons cold butter or margarine (see page 321), cut into small pieces
3 tablespoons ice water

1. To make the dough in a food processor: Process the flour, sugar, salt, shortening, and butter with on/off turns until coarse crumbs form. With the motor running, add the water through the feed tube and process just until the dough leaves the sides of the bowl. Remove the blade, then the dough.

   To make by hand: In a medium-size bowl, mix the flour, sugar, and salt. Cut in the shortening and butter with a pastry blender until the mixture resembles small peas. Sprinkle with the water, 1 tablespoon at a time, stirring with a fork after each addition, until the mixture clumps together to form a dough.

2. Press the dough into a ball, then flatten into a 1-inch-thick round. • If not using immediately, wrap with plastic and refrigerate up to 3 days or freeze up to 3 months. Thaw in the refrigerator for a day or at room temperature for 30 minutes to 1 hour before using.

PASTRY FOR A DOUBLE-CRUST PIE

• Double all the ingredients for the single-crust pie except for the sugar. Increase the sugar to 3 tablespoons. Prepare the dough as directed.

• Divide the dough in half. Press each half into a ball, then flatten into a 1-inch-thick round. If using immediately, wrap half in plastic wrap or waxed paper to prevent drying while working with the other half. (If not using immediately, wrap each half individually and refrigerate up to 3 days or freeze up to 3 months. Thaw in the refrigerator for a day or at room temperature for 30 minutes to 1 hour before using.)

• EASY • QUICK

FLAKY PASTRY FOR TARTS

Makes one 9- or 10-inch tart shell

Preparation time: 15 minutes

This tender and flaky pastry works equally well for large tarts or individual tartlets.

1¼ cups all-purpose flour
1 stick (½ cup) cold butter or margarine (see page 321), cut into small pieces
3 tablespoons ice water
½ teaspoon finely grated lemon peel
1 tablespoon fresh lemon juice

1. To make the pastry by hand: Put the flour into a medium-size bowl. Cut in the butter with a pastry blender until the mixture resembles small peas. Add the water, lemon peel, and lemon juice. Stir until the dough holds together.

To make in a food processor: Process the flour and butter until coarse crumbs form. With the motor running, add the water, lemon peel, and juice through the feed tube and process just until the dough leaves the sides of the bowl. Remove the blade, then the dough.

2. Gather the dough into a ball, flatten, wrap in waxed paper, and refrigerate for 30 minutes, or just until firm enough to roll out. • If not using immediately, wrap in plastic and refrigerate up to 3 days or freeze up to 3 months. Thaw in the refrigerator for a day or at room temperature for 30 minutes to 1 hour before using.

CHOCOLATE PASTRY FOR A SINGLE–CRUST PIE

Makes one 9-inch pie crust
Preparation time: 15 minutes

Try this pastry with any custard or cream pie, as well as the ones in this chapter.

1 cup all-purpose flour
2 tablespoons unsweetened cocoa powder
2 tablespoons granulated sugar
¼ teaspoon salt
½ stick (¼ cup) cold unsalted butter or margarine (see page 321),
  cut into small pieces
2 tablespoons solid vegetable shortening
Yolk of 1 large egg
2 to 3 tablespoons ice water

1. To make the crust in a food processor: Process the flour, cocoa, sugar, and salt until blended. Add the butter and shortening. Process until coarse crumbs form, about 5 seconds. Add the egg yolk and water and process with on/off turns just until the dough leaves the sides of the bowl. Remove the blade, then the dough. ▶

PIE PANS

For a bottom crust that's as nicely browned as the top, use a glass or dull metal pie plate. The shinier the pie plate, the longer the crust takes to bake. A shiny plate is fine for crumb-crust pies, but will make bottom pastry crusts soggy.

PERFECT PASTRY EVERY TIME

◆ Measure carefully. Too much flour toughens a crust; too much liquid makes it soggy; too much fat makes it greasy and crumbly.
◆ Sprinkle ice-cold liquid over the dry ingredients 1 tablespoon at a time. Toss gently—don't stir—with a fork just until the dough clumps together.
◆ Use a chopping motion to cut the fat

into the flour with a pastry blender.
◆ When rolling out pastry between two sheets of waxed paper, sprinkle the countertop with a few drops of water first to keep the paper from sliding. Flip the pastry occasionally and lift off the top sheet to smooth out any wrinkles.
◆ Chilling pastry makes it easier to handle, but then let it stand at room

temperature just until it's barely soft enough to roll.
◆ Don't stretch pastry to fill a pie or tart pan. Roll it out gently about 2 inches wider than the top of the pan.
◆ If a prebaked shell cracks on the bottom, seal it with a paste made of flour and water. Return the shell to the oven for a few minutes to dry the "glue."

To make by hand: In a medium-size bowl, mix the flour, cocoa, sugar, and salt. Cut in the butter and shortening with a pastry blender until the mixture resembles small peas. Add the egg yolk and water and stir with a fork until the mixture begins to clump together.

2. Press the dough into a ball, then flatten into a 1-inch-thick round. ● If not using immediately, wrap with plastic and refrigerate up to 3 days or freeze up to 3 months. Thaw in the refrigerator for 1 day or at room temperature for 30 minutes to 1 hour.

SWEET PASTRY FOR TARTS

Makes one 9- or 10-inch tart shell
Preparation time: 15 minutes

This buttery, sweet pastry crust will nicely complement a filling of fresh fruit.

1¼ cups plus 1 tablespoon all-purpose flour
2 tablespoons granulated sugar
1 stick (½ cup) cold unsalted butter or margarine (see page 321), cut into small pieces
2 tablespoons cold water
¼ teaspoon vanilla extract

1. To make the pastry in a food processor: Process the flour and sugar to blend. With the machine running, drop the butter through the feed tube and process with on/off turns until coarse crumbs form. Add the water and vanilla and process until the dough leaves the sides of the bowl clean. Remove the blade, then the dough.

To make by hand: In a medium-size bowl, mix the flour and sugar. Cut in the butter with a pastry blender until the mixture resembles small peas. Combine the water and vanilla and sprinkle over the flour mixture, 1 tablespoonful at a time, stirring with a fork after each addition, until the dough holds together.

2. Press the dough into a ball, then flatten into a 1-inch-thick round. ● If not using immediately, wrap in plastic and refrigerate up to 3 days or freeze up to 3 months. Thaw in the refrigerator for 1 day or at room temperature for 30 minutes to 1 hour.

COOK'S TIP

For a crisp bottom crust, bake any single- or double-crust pie in the lower third of your oven. That will help keep the rim or top crust from overbrowning, too. If the top crust starts to get too dark during baking, cover it loosely with foil.

PIE SHELL POINTERS

Lining a Pie Plate: To easily transfer rolled pastry to a pie plate, fold the circle of pastry in half, then into quarters. Put the point in the center of the pie plate and carefully unfold the dough. Ease the dough into the pie plate without stretching, which makes the pastry shrink when it bakes.

Once the pastry is folded under to form a rim, pinch the dough between the thumb and forefinger against the pie plate around the edge to crimp decoratively.
Freezing Pie Shells: Line the pie plate with the dough and flute or crimp the edges. Wrap the pie plate and shell in

plastic, then in a double layer of foil. Freeze up to 1 month. When ready to use, remove from the freezer, unwrap, and let stand at room temperature until thawed, about 30 minutes. You'll probably want to use the foil pie tins available at the supermarket.

Decorative Pie Rims

Besides making a pie more attractive, crimping the edges of the crust seals the pastry, preventing leaks. With little effort, you can make any of these attractive rims for any single- or double-crust pie.

LEAF EDGE: With a sharp knife, cut leaf shapes from pastry trimmings. With the back of knife, mark leaves with veins. Brush rim of pastry with a little cold water. Apply leaves to edge of pastry.

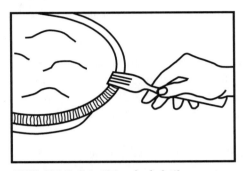

FORK: Lightly flour tines of a fork, then press tines around entire edge of pastry shell.

FLUTED: With thumb and forefinger of one hand, pinch pastry edge into a V shape around the forefinger of the other hand. Repeat around entire edge of pastry shell.

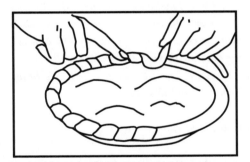

SPIRAL: Cut a long strip of pastry ¾ inch wide. Brush rim of pastry shell with a little cold water. Press one end of strip to rim. Twist strip, pressing into rim after each twist.

SCALLOPED: Pinch pastry edge between thumb and bent forefinger. Repeat around entire edge of pastry shell.

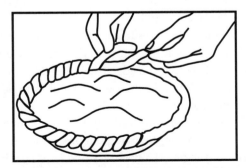

BRAIDED: Cut long strips of pastry ½ inch wide. Brush rim of pastry shell with a little cold water. Braid strips together and apply to edge of shell.

RHUBARB–CHERRY PIE

Serves 10

Preparation time: 30 minutes plus 30 minutes to cool

Cooking time: 5 minutes

Baking time: 55 minutes

It used to be that rhubarb was available only in the spring, and a rhubarb pie was a seasonal treat. Now, with frozen rhubarb on the market, we can enjoy this tart, tangy fruit all year long. (In fact, you can easily freeze fresh rhubarb when it's in season. Spread chunks on a cookie sheet, freeze, then transfer the fruit to a plastic freezer bag.) In this rustic-style pie, the edges of the dough are folded over the fruit.

Pastry for a Single-Crust Pie (page 92)

FILLING

1 cup granulated sugar

2 tablespoons cornstarch

10 ounces fresh rhubarb (without leaves),
stalks cut in half lengthwise, then cut crosswise in
1/2-inch pieces (2 1/4 cups), or 1 bag (16 ounces)
frozen rhubarb, thawed and drained well

1 can (21 ounces) reduced-calorie cherry-pie filling

1/2 teaspoon ground allspice

For garnish: confectioners' sugar

1. Have ready a 10-inch deep-dish pie plate.

2. Make the filling: In a medium-size saucepan, mix the sugar and cornstarch. Stir in the rhubarb, cherry pie filling, and allspice.

3. Bring to a boil over medium–high heat, stirring constantly. Let boil until thickened, about 1 minute. Remove from the heat and cool until warm.

4. Heat the oven to 450°F.

5. On a lightly floured surface with a lightly floured rolling pin, roll the dough out to a 13-inch circle. (Don't worry if edges are a bit uneven.) Line the pie plate with the dough, letting the edge hang over the rim.

6. Spread the filling in the pie shell. Fold the dough around the edge over the filling, letting it form folds naturally.

7. Bake for 10 minutes. Reduce the oven temperature to 350°F and bake until the crust is golden and the filling bubbles, 35 to 45 minutes more.

8. Remove the pie to a wire rack and let it cool completely. Before serving, dust the crust with confectioners' sugar. • The pie can be kept at room temperature on the day it is baked, then covered with plastic and refrigerated up to 3 days.

Per serving with butter in the crust: 250 cal, 2 g pro, 7 g fat, 46 g car, 60 mg sod, 5 mg chol.
With margarine: 0 mg chol

COOK'S TIP

For a bit of a different flavor, try 1/4 teaspoon ground cardamom instead of the allspice.

MAKE YOUR OWN FRUIT PIE

Create your own fruit pie with these few basic rules:

◆ One 9-inch pie will require about 6 cups of raw fruit.

◆ Add approximately 2/3 cup of sugar, depending on the sweetness of the fruit and your own preference.

◆ To thicken the juices, add 2 tablespoons of instant tapioca and 1 tablespoon of cornstarch to the fruit.

LATTICE PEACH PIE

Serves 8

Preparation time: 45 minutes

Baking time: 55 minutes

Juicy fresh peaches are transformed into a seasonal delight: the summer pie. A lattice-top crust shows off the fruit nicely. This pie is best served the day it's made.

Pastry for a Double-Crust Pie (page 92)

FILLING
1 cup granulated sugar
3 tablespoons all-purpose flour
3 pounds ripe peaches (about 9 medium-size),
*   peeled (see Cook's Tip),*
*   halved, pitted, and cut into*
*   1/2-inch-thick wedges (about 7 cups)*
1 tablespoon lemon juice
2 tablespoons butter or margarine
White of 1 large egg mixed with
*   2 teaspoons water*
2 tablespoons granulated sugar

1. Heat the oven to 375°F. Have ready a 9-inch pie plate.

2. Make the filling: In a large bowl, mix the sugar and flour. Add the peaches, sprinkle with the lemon juice, and toss with the sugar mixture until evenly coated.

3. On a lightly floured surface with a lightly floured rolling pin, roll out half the dough to a 12-inch circle. Trim the ragged edges. Line the pie plate with the dough.

4. Spoon the filling into the crust and dot with the butter.

5. Roll the remaining dough out into a 10-inch circle. Cut with a pastry wheel or sharp knife into twelve 3/4-inch-wide strips. Arrange 6 strips across the filling, using the longest in the center. Lay the remaining strips over the top in the opposite direction, weaving them under the bottom strips, if desired. Trim the ends to the inner edge of the pie plate. Press the ends to the edge of the bottom crust. Roll the overhang of the bottom crust up over the edges of the strips to form an even rim. Flute or crimp the edge. Brush the lattice with the egg white mixture, then sprinkle with the sugar.

6. Bake the pie until the pastry is golden brown and the peaches are tender when pierced with a fork, 50 to 55 minutes. Cool the pie on a wire rack for at least 1 hour before serving. • The pie can be kept at room temperature on the day it is baked, then covered with plastic and refrigerated up to 3 days.

Per serving with butter in the crust and filling: 470 cal, 5 g pro, 18 g fat, 75 g car, 130 mg sod, 14 mg chol. With margarine: 0 mg chol

BLUEBERRY PIE
WITH CORNMEAL CRUMB TOPPING

Serves 8 to 10

Preparation time: 15 minutes

Cooking time: 8 minutes

Baking time: 1 hour

Nothing says summer more than a fresh blueberry pie. The cornmeal gives the crumb topping a slight crunch and whole-grain flavor. The topping may seem soggy when the pie is warm, but as it cools it becomes firm.

Pastry for a Single-Crust Pie (page 92)

FILLING

4 cups fresh or frozen and thawed blueberries
¾ cup granulated sugar
3 tablespoons cornstarch
3 tablespoons water
2 teaspoons freshly grated lemon peel
¼ teaspoon ground cinnamon

CORNMEAL CRUMB TOPPING

½ cup yellow cornmeal
½ cup all-purpose flour
½ cup packed light or dark brown sugar
¾ teaspoon ground cinnamon
1 stick (½ cup) cold butter or margarine (see page 321), cut into small pieces

1. Heat the oven to 450°F. Have ready a 9-inch pie plate.

2. On a lightly floured surface with a lightly floured rolling pin, roll the dough out to a 12-inch circle. Trim the ragged edges. Line the pie plate with the dough. Prick the bottom and sides of the pie shell with a fork. Line the pastry with a double thickness of foil. Bake until lightly colored, about 10 minutes. Remove the foil and bake until the crust is golden brown, about 10 minutes more. Cool the pie crust on a wire rack.

3. Reduce the oven temperature to 375°F.

4. Make the filling: In a medium-size saucepan, mix 1 cup of the blueberries and the granulated sugar. Cook, stirring frequently, over medium heat until the sugar is dissolved, 4 to 5 minutes.

5. In a small cup, dissolve the cornstarch in the water. Add to the blueberry mixture and bring to a boil over medium-high heat, stirring constantly, and cook until thickened, about 1 minute. Remove the pan from the heat. Stir in the remaining 3 cups of blueberries, the lemon peel, and the cinnamon.

6. Pour the filling into the prebaked pie shell and set aside.

7. To make the topping in a food processor: Process the cornmeal, flour, brown sugar, and cinnamon for 1 minute, until well blended. Add the butter and process with on/off turns until the mixture is crumbly. Remove the blade, then the topping.

To make by hand: In a medium-size bowl, mix the cornmeal, flour, brown sugar, and cinnamon. Cut in the butter with a pastry blender until the mixture resembles small peas.

8. Sprinkle the topping evenly over the pie. Bake until the filling is bubbly and the topping is golden brown, about 40 minutes. Cool the pie on a wire rack. Serve at room temperature. • The pie can be kept at room temperature on the day it is baked, then wrapped with plastic and refrigerated up to 3 days.

Per serving with butter in the crust and topping: 430 cal, 2 g pro, 18 g fat, 66 g car, 160 mg sod, 33 mg chol. With margarine: 180 mg sod, 0 mg chol

OLD FASHIONED

APPLE CIDER PIE

Serves 8

Preparation time: 45 minutes

Cooking time: 20 minutes

Baking time: 1 hour 15 minutes

Two kinds of apples give this pie a more complex flavor and texture, while apple cider cooked down to a thick syrup gives the filling its concentrated apple essence.

Pastry for a Double-Crust Pie (page 92)

FILLING

3 cups apple cider

¾ cup plus 1 tablespoon granulated sugar

¼ cup all-purpose flour

½ teaspoon ground cinnamon

⅛ teaspoon ground mace or grated nutmeg

*5 large Granny Smith or Braeburn apples
   (about 2½ pounds)*

*3 large Golden Delicious or Cortland apples
   (about 1½ pounds)*

1. Have ready a 9-inch pie plate. Make the filling: In a medium-size heavy saucepan, boil the cider uncovered until it is reduced to ½ cup, about 20 minutes. Remove from the heat and let cool for about 20 minutes.

2. Meanwhile, in a large bowl, mix ¾ cup of the sugar, the flour, cinnamon, and mace. Halve, core, and peel the apples. Cut each half into ½-inch-thick wedges, then cut the wedges in half crosswise. Add the apples to the sugar mixture along with the reduced cider. Toss until evenly coated.

3. Adjust the oven rack to the lowest position. Heat the oven to 425°F. ▶

4. Divide the dough in half. On a lightly floured surface with a lightly floured rolling pin, roll one half of the dough into a 12-inch circle. Line the pie plate with the dough.

5. Spoon the filling into the lined pie plate, mounding it in the center.

6. Roll the remaining dough into a 12-inch circle. Place it over the filling. Press the edges together and roll up to form an even rim. Flute or crimp decoratively. Brush the top of the pie with water and sprinkle with the remaining 1 tablespoon of sugar. Cut a slit in the top for steam to escape.

7. Place the pie on a cookie sheet to catch drips. Bake for 25 minutes. Reduce the oven temperature to 350°F. Bake until the crust is golden brown, the apples are tender when pierced through a slit, and the juices bubble, about 40 to 50 minutes more. Cool the pie on a wire rack. Serve slightly warm or at room temperature.
• The pie can be kept at room temperature on the day it is baked, then covered with plastic and refrigerated up to 3 days.
Per serving with butter in the crust: 520 cal, 4 g pro, 16 g fat, 92 g car, 90 mg sod, 6 mg chol. With margarine: 0 mg chol

EASY • 1 HOUR • LOW FAT

PHYLLO APPLE PIE

Serves 8
Preparation time: 15 minutes
Cooking time: 20 minutes
Baking time: 12 minutes

Middle Eastern-style phyllo pastry makes a flaky crust for this upside-down apple pie. The paper-thin sheets are available frozen. Apple pie couldn't be easier!

FILLING
6 medium-size Granny Smith apples (about 2½ pounds)
¼ cup apple juice
¼ cup packed light brown sugar
⅓ cup granulated sugar
2 tablespoons all-purpose flour
2 tablespoons fresh lemon juice
½ teaspoon ground cinnamon
½ teaspoon grated nutmeg
¼ teaspoon ground ginger

5 sheets phyllo (filo) pastry, thawed if frozen
1 tablespoon butter or margarine, melted
1 tablespoon granulated sugar
Vegetable oil cooking spray

1. Have ready a 9-inch pie plate. Make the filling: Quarter, peel, and core the apples. Cut the quarters crosswise into ½-inch-thick slices. In a large heavy

APPLE PIES
Choose from the following apple varieties for making pies. They have the right tart flavor and a good texture that won't fall apart or turn mushy during baking. Try mixing two or three kinds.
◆ Empire
◆ Gravenstein
◆ Idared
◆ Newtown Pippin
◆ Northern Spy
◆ Rhode Island
◆ Greenings

VARIATION

PHYLLO PEAR PIE

Substitute 5 large ripe pears (about 2½ pounds) for the apples and proceed as directed.

Per serving with butter: 190 cal, 1 g pro, 3 g fat, 44 g car, 80 mg sod, 4 mg chol. With margarine: 0 mg chol

• EASY • 1 HOUR
• LOW FAT

COOK'S TIP

Packaged phyllo can be frozen up to 1 year. Thaw phyllo overnight in the refrigerator. Thawed phyllo dough will keep for 1 month tightly covered in the refrigerator. Once opened, use within a few days. It's important to cover sheets of phyllo with a damp cloth while you're working to keep it from drying out.

saucepan, mix the apples, apple juice, both sugars, the flour, lemon juice, cinnamon, nutmeg, and ginger. Cover and cook about 20 minutes until the apples are tender, stirring occasionally. Spoon the filling into the pie plate. Let cool slightly.

2. Heat the oven to 400°F.

3. Lay 1 sheet of phyllo over the filling. Dab with some of the melted butter and sprinkle with a little sugar. Lay a second sheet of phyllo crosswise over the first. Dab with butter and sprinkle with sugar. Continue with the remaining 3 phyllo sheets.

4. Gather the edges of the phyllo to make a ruffled edge. Spray the edges with vegetable oil cooking spray. Cut slits through the phyllo for steam to escape.

5. Bake until golden brown, about 12 minutes. Cool the pie on a wire rack. Serve slightly warm or at room temperature. ● The pie can be kept at room temperature on the day it is baked, then covered with plastic and refrigerated up to 3 days.

Per serving with butter: 200 cal, 1 g pro, 3 g fat, 45 g car, 80 mg sod, 4 mg chol. With margarine: 0 mg chol

EASY

ZUCCHINI "APPLE" PIE

Serves 8

Preparation time: 20 minutes plus at least 3 hours to chill

Microwave cooking time: 12 minutes

Baking time: 20 minutes

This tasty pie looks and tastes like apple crumb pie, but there's not a bit of apple in it. Zucchini—yes, zucchini—is the main ingredient in the filling.

Pastry for a Single-Crust Pie (page 92)

FILLING

1½ pounds medium-size zucchini, peeled, halved lengthwise, and cut crosswise into thin slices (4 cups)

1 cup granulated sugar

½ cup packed light brown sugar

¼ cup all-purpose flour

3 tablespoons butter or margarine (see page 321), cut into small pieces

2 tablespoons cider vinegar

2 tablespoons water

1 teaspoon fresh lemon juice

½ teaspoon ground cinnamon

½ teaspoon grated nutmeg

CRUMB TOPPING

1 stick (½ cup) cold butter or margarine (see page 321)

½ cup packed light brown sugar

1 cup all-purpose flour

▶

1. Heat the oven to 450°F. Have ready a 9-inch pie plate

2. On a lightly floured surface with a lightly floured rolling pin, roll the dough out to a 12-inch circle. Line the pie plate with the dough. Trim and crimp the edges. Prick the bottom and sides of the pie shell with a fork. Line the pastry with a double thickness of foil. Bake until lightly colored, about 10 minutes. Remove the foil and bake until the crust is golden brown, about 10 minutes more. Cool the pie crust on a wire rack.

3. Meanwhile, make the filling: In a 2-quart microwave-safe bowl, mix the zucchini, both sugars, the flour, butter, vinegar, water, lemon juice, cinnamon, and nutmeg. Microwave uncovered on High for 8 to 10 minutes, stirring 3 times, until thickened. Pour the mixture into the prebaked pie shell.

4. Make the topping: Melt the butter in a 1-quart microwave-safe bowl. Stir in the brown sugar and flour until blended. Cover with vented plastic wrap and microwave on High for 2 to 2½ minutes, stirring twice, until slightly browned and bubbly.

5. Spread the topping out onto a piece of foil. When cool enough to handle, sprinkle evenly over the pie filling.

6. Chill the pie for at least 3 hours before serving. • The pie can be refrigerated, loosely wrapped, up to 3 days.

Per serving with butter in the crust and topping: 570 cal, 5 g pro, 25 g fat, 85 g car, 230 mg sod, 49 mg chol. With margarine: 260 mg sod, 0 mg chol

EASY • OLD FASHIONED

SOUR CREAM LEMON PIE

Serves 8

Preparation time: 20 minutes plus at least 7 hours to chill

Cooking time: 8 minutes

Baking time: 20 minutes

Sour cream provides an extra richness in this tart, refreshing lemon pie. For easy entertaining, prepare the pie up to two days ahead and refrigerate until serving time.

Pastry for a Single-Crust Pie (page 92)

FILLING
⅔ cup granulated sugar
3 tablespoons cornstarch
1 cup milk
Yolks of 3 large eggs
1 teaspoon freshly grated lemon peel
¼ cup fresh lemon juice
½ stick (¼ cup) butter or margarine (see page 321), cut into small pieces
1 cup regular or nonfat sour cream

For garnish: sweetened whipped cream, lemon slices, and fresh mint sprigs

COOK'S TIP

When grating the peel of a lemon, grate only the yellow part of the skin (also called the zest), not the bitter white pith. If you want to increase the lemon flavor of a dessert, add more lemon peel, not lemon juice.

1. Heat the oven to 450°F. Have ready a 9-inch pie plate

2. On a lightly floured surface with a lightly floured rolling pin, roll out the dough to a 12-inch circle. Trim the ragged edges. Line the pie plate with the dough. Trim the overhang of the pastry to ¾ inch. Fold the pastry edge under to form a rim; crimp or flute the rim. Prick the bottom and sides of the pie shell at 1-inch intervals with a fork. Line the pastry with a double thickness of foil. Bake until lightly colored, about 10 minutes. Remove the foil and bake until the crust is golden brown, about 10 minutes more. Cool the pie crust on a wire rack.

3. Meanwhile, make the filling: In a medium-size saucepan, mix the sugar and cornstarch. Whisk in the milk until smooth, then add the yolks and whisk until blended. Stir in the lemon peel and juice. Place the pan over medium heat.

4. Add the butter and whisk constantly just until boiling (5 to 7 minutes). Remove the pan from the heat and stir for 1 minute. Place plastic wrap directly on the surface to keep a skin from forming. Cool to room temperature.

5. Stir in the sour cream until well blended. Pour the mixture into the pie shell. Cover loosely and refrigerate for at least 7 hours or until set. • The pie can be made up 2 days ahead, then loosely covered and refrigerated.

6. Just before serving, garnish with whipped cream, lemon slices, and mint sprigs.

Per serving: 380 cal, 5 g pro, 23 g fat, 39 g car, 150 mg sod, 120 mg chol. With margarine and fat-free sour cream: 340 cal, 6 g pro, 17 g fat, 165 mg sod, 84 mg chol

CLASSIC • OLD FASHIONED

LEMON MERINGUE PIE
Serves 8
Preparation time: 40 minutes plus at least 2 hours to chill
Baking time: 47 minutes

This two-layer pie, a perennial favorite, is best served on the day it is made.

Pastry for a Single-Crust Pie (page 92)

FILLING
1¼ cups granulated sugar
⅓ cup cornstarch
Yolks of 4 large eggs
½ cup fresh lemon juice
2 cups water
3 tablespoons butter or margarine (see page 321), cut into small pieces
1½ teaspoons freshly grated lemon peel

MERINGUE
Whites of 3 large eggs
¼ teaspoon cream of tartar
⅓ cup granulated sugar

COOK'S TIP

To eliminate the cholesterol in this Lemon Meringue Pie, use egg substitute to equal 2 eggs per manufacturer's instructions instead of the 4 large eggs in the filling. You'll also reduce the amount of fat slightly, from 16 to 13 grams per serving.

1. Heat the oven to 425°F. Have ready a 9-inch pie plate.

2. On a lightly floured surface with a lightly floured rolling pin, roll the dough out to a 12-inch circle. Line the pie plate with the dough. Trim the overhang of the pastry to ¾ inch. Fold the pastry edge under to form a rim. Crimp or flute the rim. Prick the bottom and sides at 1-inch intervals with a fork. Line the pastry with a double thickness of foil. Bake until crust is golden brown, 22 to 27 minutes. Set the pie crust on a wire rack to cool.

3. Reduce the oven temperature to 350°F.

4. Make the filling: In a medium-size saucepan, whisk together the 1¼ cups of sugar and the cornstarch. Whisk in the egg yolks and lemon juice until smooth. Stir in the water with a wooden spoon. Place over medium heat and continue stirring until the mixture comes to a full boil. Boil for about 1 minute, stirring constantly, until the filling is translucent and thick. Remove the pan from the heat. Add the butter and lemon peel and stir until the butter melts. Pour the hot filling into the baked pie shell.

5. Make the meringue: In a medium-size bowl, beat the egg whites and cream of tartar with an electric mixer on medium-high speed until soft peaks form when the beaters are lifted. Gradually beat in the sugar, 1 tablespoon at a time, beating well after each addition until the sugar dissolves. Beat for 2 minutes longer or until stiff peaks form when the beaters are lifted.

6. Spoon the meringue around the edge of the filling. Spread to the edge of the crust. Spoon the remaining meringue in the center, spread and swirl with the back of a teaspoon to evenly cover the filling.

7. Bake the pie until the meringue is browned and an instant-read thermometer inserted into the center of the meringue registers 160°F, about 20 minutes.

8. Remove the pie to a wire rack to cool completely, then refrigerate for at least 2 hours or up to 8 hours. To serve, cut with a long-bladed knife dipped in cold water.

Per serving with butter in the crust and filling: 410 cal, 5 g pro, 16 g fat, 63 g car, 130 mg sod, 124 mg chol. With margarine: 106 mg chol

---

CLASSIC • DECADENT

MISSISSIPPI MUD PIE

Serves 8
Preparation time: 20 minutes
Baking time: 45 minutes

A rich, dense chocolate pie that will send you back for more. It derives its name from thick mud along the banks of the Mississippi River. During the dry hot summers, the mud's surface is cracked and dry-looking, similar to what the top of this pie should look like.

Pastry for a Single-Crust Pie (page 92), or
  Chocolate Pastry for a Single-Crust Pie (page 93)

COOK'S TIP

• Because of the small but real chance of salmonella contamination, it's important to cook egg whites completely.

• To keep meringue from shrinking or weeping, drop teaspoonfuls around the edge of the pie, spread it to touch the crust all around, then spread the remaining meringue in the center.

FILLING

2 ounces unsweetened chocolate, coarsely chopped
1 ounce semisweet chocolate, coarsely chopped
1 stick (½ cup) unsalted butter or margarine
  (see page 321)
1 tablespoon instant coffee granules
3 large eggs
1 cup plus 2 tablespoons granulated sugar
¼ cup light corn syrup
1 teaspoon vanilla extract

1. Heat the oven to 350°F. Have ready a 9-inch pie plate.

2. On a lightly floured surface with a lightly floured rolling pin, roll the dough out to a 12-inch circle. Line the pie plate with the dough. Trim the overhang of the pastry to ¾ inch. Fold the overhang under to form a rim. Crimp or flute the rim.

3. Make the filling: In a medium-size saucepan, melt both chocolates with the butter and coffee over low heat, stirring until smooth. Remove the pan from the heat and cool slightly. (Or put both chocolates, the butter, and coffee into a medium-size microwave-safe bowl and microwave, uncovered, on High for 1½ minutes. Stir until smooth and melted. Repeat as necessary, microwaving for 20 seconds at a time, then stirring until smooth and melted.)

4. In a medium-size bowl, whisk together the eggs, sugar, corn syrup, and vanilla. Whisk in the chocolate mixture until blended. Pour the filling into the prepared pie crust.

5. Bake until the filling puffs and the top is cracked and slightly crisp, 40 to 45 minutes. Cool the pie on a wire rack. (The pie will sink as it cools.) Serve at room temperature. • The pie can be kept at room temperature on the day it is baked, then loosely wrapped with plastic and refrigerated up to 3 days.

Per serving with butter in the crust and filling: 470 cal, 5 g pro, 27 g fat, 57 g car, 100 mg sod, 117 mg chol. With margarine: 230 mg sod, 80 mg chol. With chocolate pastry with butter: 153 mg chol. With chocolate pastry with margarine: 106 mg chol

CLASSIC • OLD FASHIONED • DECADENT

DOUBLE CHOCOLATE CREAM PIE

Serves 10

Preparation time: 30 minutes plus at least 3½ hours to chill

Cooking time: 12 minutes

Baking time: 20 minutes

Who can resist the old-fashioned appeal of a cream pie? Here, a smooth chocolate custard is supported by a dark chocolate crust and topped with snowy mounds of whipped cream. This pie is best eaten on the day it is made. For a quicker version, you could use a 9-ounce ready-to-fill graham-cracker or 6-ounce chocolate-crumb crust and nondairy whipped topping.

▶

Chocolate Pastry for a Single-Crust Pie (page 93)

CHOCOLATE CUSTARD
2 cups milk
1 cup heavy (whipping) cream
½ cup granulated sugar
2 large eggs
3 tablespoons cornstarch
6 ounces semisweet chocolate, chopped
½ stick (¼ cup) unsalted butter or margarine (see page 321)
1 teaspoon vanilla extract

TOPPING
¾ cup heavy (whipping) cream
2 teaspoons granulated sugar
½ teaspoon vanilla extract

For garnish: chocolate shavings (see page 329)

1. Make the custard: In a medium-size heavy saucepan, heat 1½ cups of the milk and the cream until tiny bubbles form around the edge. Remove from the heat.

2. In a medium-size bowl, whisk the remaining ½ cup of milk with the sugar, eggs, and cornstarch until smooth. Whisk about ½ cup of the hot milk mixture into the bowl. Repeat with another ½ cup of the milk mixture.

3. Return this mixture to the pan and bring to a boil, whisking constantly. Boil, whisking constantly, for 2 minutes.

4. Remove the pan from the heat and stir in the chocolate, butter, and vanilla until melted and smooth. Place a sheet of waxed paper or plastic wrap directly on the surface of the custard to prevent a skin from forming. Refrigerate until thoroughly cooled, about 30 minutes.

5. Adjust the oven rack to the lowest position. Heat the oven to 425°F. Have ready a 9-inch pie plate.

6. Lightly dust a work surface with cocoa or flour and roll the dough out to a 13-inch circle. Line the pie plate with the dough. Trim the overhang of the pastry to ¾ inch and fold the overhang under to form a rim. Line the dough with a double thickness of aluminum foil.

7. Bake the pie crust for 10 minutes. Reduce the oven temperature to 350°F, remove the foil, and bake until the edges are lightly browned, about 10 minutes more. Remove the pie crust to a wire rack and let cool completely.

8. Pour the custard into the cooled pie shell. Loosely cover and chill for at least 3 hours or up to 12 hours.

9. Just before serving, make the topping: In a medium-size bowl, beat the cream, sugar, and vanilla with an electric mixer until stiff peaks form when the beaters are lifted. Spread the whipped cream over the pie and decorate with chocolate shavings.

Per serving with butter in the crust and filling: 490 cal, 6 g pro, 36 g fat, 40 g car, 110 mg sod, 152 mg chol. With margarine: 220 mg sod, 128 mg chol

COOK'S TIP

Heavy cream whips best when the cream, bowl, and beaters are all cold. Check the stiffness by lifting the beaters often once the cream starts to thicken. (Overbeating turns the cream to butter.)

MAPLE–PECAN PIE

Serves 10

Preparation time: 20 minutes

Baking time: 55 minutes

Maple syrup adds a twist to this hard-to-resist Southern favorite. Top with a scoop of vanilla ice cream or a dollop of whipped cream.

Pastry for a Single-Crust Pie (page 92)
4 large eggs
⅔ cup granulated sugar
½ cup pure maple syrup or maple-flavored syrup
½ cup light corn syrup
6 tablespoons unsalted butter, melted
1 cup pecans, coarsely chopped (4 ounces)

1. Heat the oven to 450°F. Have ready a 9-inch pie plate.
2. On a lightly floured surface with a lightly floured rolling pin, roll the dough out to a 12-inch circle. Trim the ragged edges. Line the pie plate with the dough. Trim the overhang of the pastry to ¾ inch, and fold the overhang under to form a rim. Crimp the rim. Prick the bottom and sides of the pie shell at 1-inch intervals with a fork. Line the pastry with a double thickness of foil. Bake until lightly colored, about 10 minutes. Remove the foil and bake until the crust is golden brown, about 10 minutes more. Cool the pie crust on a wire rack.
3. Reduce the oven temperature to 350°F. In a medium-size bowl, whisk together the eggs and sugar until blended. Stir in the maple and corn syrups, butter and pecans.
4. Pour the filling into the prebaked pie shell. Bake until the filling is still slightly jiggly and the surface is slightly cracked, 30 to 35 minutes. (If the crust becomes too brown after 30 minutes, cover the edge with foil.)
5. Cool the pie on a wire rack. Serve warm or at room temperature. • The pie can be kept at room temperature on the day it is baked, then loosely wrapped in plastic and refrigerated up to 3 days.

Per serving: 420 cal, 5 g pro, 24 g fat, 51 g car, 90 mg sod, 110 mg chol

PROVIDENCE NUT PIE

Serves 8

Preparation time: 30 minutes

Baking time: 45 minutes

A combination of hazelnuts and walnuts gives this pie its crunchy texture. Toasting the nuts first enhances their flavor.

▶

COOK'S TIP

Maple-flavored (pancake) syrup has a slightly thicker consistency and sweeter flavor than pure maple syrup. Both will work in this pie.

Pastry for a Double-Crust Pie (page 92)
3 large eggs
1⅓ cups granulated sugar
1 tablespoon hazelnut liqueur (optional)
1 teaspoon vanilla extract
¾ cup finely chopped toasted hazelnuts (see page 325)
¾ cup finely chopped toasted walnuts (see page 325)
1 tablespoon butter or stick margarine, melted

1. Adjust the oven rack to the lowest position. Heat the oven to 375°F. Have ready a 9-inch pie plate.

2. On a lightly floured surface with a lightly floured rolling pin, roll out half the dough to a 12-inch circle. Line the pie plate with the dough. Trim the overhang of the pastry to ¾ inch. Reserve the trimmings. Fold the overhang under to form a rim. Crimp or flute the rim. Prick the bottom and sides of the pastry shell at 1-inch intervals with a fork. Set aside.

3. In a medium-size bowl, whisk the eggs, sugar, liqueur, and vanilla until well blended. Stir in the hazelnuts and walnuts. Pour the mixture into the lined pie plate.

4. Roll out the remaining dough to a 12-inch circle. Place it over the filling. Press the edges together and turn under to make an even rim. Flute or crimp decoratively.

5. Roll out the reserved trimmings. Cut out little leaves with a cookie cutter or a small sharp knife. Brush the pie with the melted butter. Gently press the leaves in place. Brush with butter. Cut slits in the dough for steam to escape.

6. Bake until the crust is golden brown, 40 to 45 minutes. Cool the pie on a wire rack. Serve warm or at room temperature. • The pie can be kept at room temperature on the day it is baked, then wrapped in plastic and refrigerated up to 3 days.

Per serving with butter in the crust and filling: 580 cal, 9 g pro, 32 g fat, 67 g car, 130 mg sod, 89 mg chol. With margarine: 80 mg chol

EASY • CLASSIC

RASPBERRY CHIFFON PIE
Serves 8
Preparation time: 30 minutes plus at least 4 hours to chill

This no-bake light and creamy raspberry pie makes a refreshing summer dessert. Make our crust or use a purchased 9-ounce graham-cracker crust. Nondairy whipped topping can also be used instead of real whipped cream.

GRAHAM–CRACKER CRUST
1⅓ cups graham-cracker crumbs
(18 graham-cracker squares)
2 tablespoons granulated sugar
½ stick (¼ cup) butter or margarine
(see page 321), melted

▶ *p. 117*

When you're asked to make dessert, surprise everyone with this pretty Nectarine-Raspberry Tart (p.126).

The flavor of fresh apples or pears baked in pastry is hard to improve on, especially in autumn when these fruits are at their peak. For apple lovers, try the Free-Form Apple Tart (p.129), left, or the Apple Cider Pie (p.99), below, with a scoop of vanilla ice cream And for something a little different, the Phyllo Pear Pie (p.100), right, makes a delicious and low-fat dessert.

Keep cool with these luscious no-bake pies. Choose either the Chocolate-Peanut Mousse Pie (p.118) or the Chocolate-Vanilla Mousse Pie (p.119), left, two truly decadent treats.

A layer of tangy smooth lemon curd topped with fluffy white meringue makes classic Lemon Meringue Pie (p.103), above, a perennial favorite of adults and children alike.

Old-fashioned pies and elegant tarts are always tempting and are not difficult to make—the perfect dessert for entertaining.

Sharing a homemade pie or tart with family and friends will turn an ordinary day into a memorable one.

Celebrate the season of fresh strawberries with this striking, elegant, and easy-to-assemble Strawberry Custard Tart (p.124), left.

Everyone will want a piece of old-fashioned Lattice Peach Pie (p.97), below, especially if it's served warm with vanilla ice cream.

This easy-to-make Two-Berry Tart (p.127) showcases both fresh raspberries and blueberries.

FILLING

1 (4-serving) package red-raspberry gelatin
¾ cup boiling water
½ pint (6 ounces) fresh raspberries, picked over and rinsed (1¼ cups)
1 cup heavy (whipping) cream

For garnish: red, black, and/or golden raspberries

1. Lightly grease a 9-inch pie plate.

2. Make the crust: In a medium-size bowl, mix the graham-cracker crumbs and sugar. Add the melted butter and toss with a fork to moisten. Press the mixture evenly over the bottom and up the sides of the pie plate. Refrigerate for about 20 minutes, until firm.

3. Meanwhile, make the filling: Put the gelatin into a medium-size metal bowl. Add the boiling water and stir until completely dissolved. Refrigerate while preparing the raspberries and cream.

4. With the back of a small spoon, press the raspberries through a strainer set over a small bowl. Scrape the purée from outside the strainer into the bowl. Discard the raspberry seeds.

5. In a medium-size (mixer) bowl, beat the cream with an electric mixer until very soft peaks form when the beaters are lifted.

6. When the gelatin has cooled to the consistency of unbeaten egg whites, gently stir in the raspberry purée and whipped cream until completely blended. Spread the mixture into the chilled pie crust. Refrigerate until the filling sets, at least 4 hours.

• The pie can be made up to this point 2 days ahead, covered, and refrigerated.

7. Just before serving, garnish with fresh raspberries.

Per serving with butter: 300 cal, 3 g pro, 18 g fat, 31 g car, 220 mg sod, 56 mg chol. With margarine: 41 mg chol

EASY • CLASSIC

KEY LIME PIE

Serves 10

Preparation time: 20 minutes plus at least 4 hours to chill

Baking time: 45 minutes

This simple pie—tart, creamy, and not too sweet—is perfect for a springtime dessert. Use freshly squeezed lime juice; it makes a noticeable difference in how the filling thickens. Tiny Key limes (as in the Florida Keys) have a wonderful flavor, but they are hard to find and you will have to squeeze a zillion of the little devils to yield enough juice. Stick with regular limes and avoid risking carpal tunnel syndrome.

GRAHAM-CRACKER CRUST

1½ cups fine graham-cracker crumbs (20 graham-cracker squares)
6 tablespoons butter or margarine (see page 321), melted

▶

FILLING

Yolks of 6 large eggs

*1¾ cups (1½ cans) nonfat sweetened condensed skim milk
(not evaporated milk), at room temperature*

1½ teaspoons freshly grated lime peel

¾ cup plus 2 tablespoons fresh lime juice (from 5 to 6 limes)

TOPPING

1 cup heavy (whipping) cream

2 tablespoons sugar

For garnish: thin strips of lime peel

1. Heat the oven to 350°F.

2. Make the crust: Put the graham-cracker crumbs into a medium-size bowl. Add the butter and toss with a fork to moisten evenly. Press the mixture over the bottom and up the sides of the pie plate. Bake the crust for 10 minutes, until set. Remove the crust to a wire rack and let cool. Don't turn off the oven.

3. Meanwhile, make the filling: In a large bowl, beat the egg yolks with an electric mixer until thick and creamy, about 3 minutes. With the mixer on low speed, beat in the condensed milk, lime peel, and lime juice until blended. Pour the filling into the cooled crust.

4. Bake the pie until the filling is set, 30 to 35 minutes. Cool the pie on a wire rack for 30 minutes, then refrigerate for at least 4 hours. • The pie can be made up to this point 4 days ahead, covered, and refrigerated.

5. Up to 2 hours before serving, beat the cream and sugar in a medium-size bowl with an electric mixer until stiff peaks form when the beaters are lifted. Drop spoonfuls of the whipped cream onto the pie, spaced so that each wedge will get some. Refrigerate until serving time. Just before serving, garnish with the lime peel.

Per serving with butter: 420 cal, 8 g pro, 20 g fat, 52 g car, 250 mg sod, 183 mg chol. With margarine: 164 mg chol

---

EASY • DECADENT

CHOCOLATE–PEANUT MOUSSE PIE

Serves 10

Preparation time: 10 minutes plus 1½ hours to chill

An easy, scrumptious confection, this pie appeals to kids of all ages. Adding a topping of crumbled peanut brittle is the crowning finish.

CHOCOLATE LAYER

1¼ cups (7½ ounces) semisweet chocolate chips

1 cup heavy (whipping) cream

1 (6-ounce) ready-to-fill chocolate-flavored crumb crust

COOK'S TIP

• Grate the lime peel before squeezing the juice and moisten the grated peel with a few drops of juice.

• Make the filling in a heavy saucepan that isn't uncoated aluminum. Whisking an acid mixture in an aluminum pan can result in a metallic flavor.

PEANUT LAYER

1 package (8 ounces) light (Neufchâtel) or
   fat-free cream cheese, softened
1/4 cup packed light brown sugar
1/4 cup creamy peanut butter
1/2 cup heavy (whipping) cream
2/3 cup crushed peanut brittle

For garnish: whipped cream, coarsely broken peanut brittle

1. Make the chocolate layer: In a small saucepan, melt the chocolate chips with 1/4 cup of the cream over low heat, stirring until smooth. (Or microwave the chocolate and cream in a small microwave-safe bowl, uncovered, on Medium for 1 to 2 minutes. Stir until melted and smooth. Repeat as necessary, microwaving for 20 seconds at a time, then stirring until melted.) Cool slightly. Scrape the chocolate into a medium-size bowl.

2. In a medium-size (mixer) bowl, beat the remaining 3/4 cup of cream with an electric mixer until soft peaks form when the beaters are lifted. Gently stir (fold) the cream into the chocolate until blended. Spread the mixture into the crust. Refrigerate until set, about 30 minutes.

3. Make the peanut layer: In the same bowl (no need to wash bowl or beaters), beat the cream cheese until smooth. Beat in the brown sugar and peanut butter until smooth, scraping down the sides of the bowl when necessary. Gradually beat in the cream. Stir in the crushed peanut brittle. Spread the mixture over the set chocolate mixture and chill until set, at least 1 hour. • The pie can be made to this point 2 days ahead, covered, and refrigerated.

4. Just before serving, garnish with whipped cream and scatter with brittle.
Per serving: 460 cal, 7 g pro, 31 g fat, 41 g car, 270 mg sod, 61 mg chol. With fat-free cream cheese: 28 g fat, 53 mg chol

EASY • DECADENT

CHOCOLATE–VANILLA MOUSSE PIE
Serves 10
Preparation time: 15 minutes plus 1 hour to chill

This creamy mousse pie makes an elegant dessert. The best part is that there's no baking involved; just assemble the pie and chill until ready to serve.

1 1/4 cups (7 1/2 ounces) semisweet chocolate chips
1 1/4 cups (7 1/2 ounces) vanilla-milk or white chocolate chips
2 cups heavy (whipping) cream
1 (6-ounce) ready-to-fill chocolate-flavored crumb crust

For garnish: whipped cream and fresh strawberries

1. In a small saucepan, melt the chocolate chips with ¼ cup of the heavy cream over low heat, stirring until smooth. Scrape into a medium-size bowl. Wash and dry the saucepan. Repeat with the vanilla chips and another ¼ cup of cream. Scrape into another medium-size bowl. (Or, put the vanilla chips and chocolate chips in separate medium-size microwave-safe bowls. Add ¼ cup of heavy cream to each. Microwave them separately, the chocolate chips first, on High for 45 seconds to 1 minute, or until the cream is steaming hot. Let stand for 1 minute, then stir until smooth.)

2. In a large bowl, beat the remaining 1½ cups of cream with an electric mixer until soft peaks form when the beaters are lifted.

3. Gently stir (fold) half the whipped cream into the vanilla-chip mixture. Then gently stir (fold) the remaining whipped cream into the chocolate-chip mixture.

4. Alternately drop heaping soupspoonfuls (about ⅓ cup) of each mousse into the crust. When it's all in the pie shell, swirl a thin knife through the 2 mousses to create a marbled effect.

5. Refrigerate for at least 1 hour, or until set. ● The pie can be made up to this point 2 days ahead, covered loosely, and refrigerated.

6. Just before serving, garnish the pie with lightly sweetened whipped cream and fresh strawberries.

Per serving: 480 cal, 4 g pro, 34 g fat, 42 g car, 120 mg sod, 65 mg chol

---

EASY • DECADENT

CHOCOLATE TRUFFLE CARAMEL PIE

Serves 12

Preparation time: 30 minutes plus 2 hours 15 minutes to chill

This super-rich, super-sweet pie is as decadent as it gets. Evaporated milk must be ice-cold to beat properly. For best results, pour it into a small metal bowl and place in the freezer for about 15 minutes or until ice crystals are well formed around the edges. Garnish the pie shortly before serving.

½ cup (2 ounces) pecan pieces, toasted (see page 325)
1 (6-ounce) ready-to-fill chocolate-flavored crumb crust

CARAMEL LAYER
1 can (14 ounces) regular or nonfat sweetened condensed milk
  (not evaporated milk)
¾ stick (6 tablespoons) butter or margarine (see page 321)
¼ cup granulated sugar

TRUFFLE LAYER
1½ cups (9 ounces) semisweet chocolate chips
⅔ cup heavy (whipping) cream
3 tablespoons butter or margarine (see page 321)

MOUSSE

1½ cups (9 ounces) semisweet chocolate chips
¾ cup heavy (whipping) cream
⅓ cup ice-cold canned evaporated (but not skim) milk

For garnish: whipped cream and fresh cherries

1. Sprinkle the pecans over the crumb crust.
2. Make the caramel layer: In a medium-size heavy-bottomed saucepan, cook the condensed milk, butter, and sugar over medium-low heat until the butter melts. Increase the heat and bring to a gentle boil. Stirring constantly, boil until thick as pudding, 3 to 6 minutes. (If you are using fat-free sweetened condensed milk, the mixture may have small brown flecks in it, which is OK.) Pour the mixture over the pecans. Refrigerate for about 1 hour, until firm.
3. Make the truffle layer: Put the chocolate chips, cream, and butter into a medium-size microwave-safe bowl. Melt the chocolate chips, cream, and butter in a medium-size heavy saucepan over very low heat, stirring occasionally, until smooth. (Or microwave on High for 1 minute. Let stand for 1 minute, then stir until smooth.) Cool slightly. Pour the mixture over the caramel layer and refrigerate for about 1 hour, until set.
4. Meanwhile, make the mousse: Put the chocolate chips into a medium-size microwave-safe bowl. Melt the chocolate chips in a small heavy saucepan over very low heat, stirring occasionally, until smooth. (Or microwave on High for 1 minute. Let stand for 1 minute, then stir until smooth.) Cool slightly.
5. In a large bowl, beat the heavy cream with an electric mixer until stiff peaks form when the beaters are lifted. Beat the cooled chocolate into the whipped cream until blended.
6. In a small bowl, beat the cold evaporated milk (no need to wash the beaters first) until thick enough for the beaters to leave a trail. Beat into the chocolate mixture.
7. Spread the mousse over the truffle layer and refrigerate for at least 15 minutes, until set. ● The pie can be made up to this point up to 3 days ahead, covered, and refrigerated.
8. Just before serving, garnish the pie with whipped cream and cherries.
Per serving: 620 cal, 6 g pro, 41 g fat, 63 g car, 220 mg sod, 75 mg chol. With nonfat sweetened condensed milk and margarine: 44 mg chol

COOK'S TIP

The chocolate mousse can also be served on its own, spooned into stemmed glasses and garnished with whipped cream and chocolate shavings.

EASY

STRAWBERRY MOUSSE PIE

Serves 12

Preparation time: 30 minutes plus at least 4 hours to chill

Strawberry ice cream, strawberry gelatin, strawberry yogurt, and real strawberries combine for a quadruple berry treat in this no-bake pie. Use the recipe given here to make a graham-cracker crust, or you can purchase a ready-made 9-ounce crust.

GRAHAM–CRACKER CRUST

2¼ cups fine graham-cracker crumbs
   (30 graham-cracker squares)
1 stick (½ cup) butter or margarine (see page 321), melted

STRAWBERRY MOUSSE

1½ cups boiling water
1 (8-serving) package strawberry gelatin
1 pint strawberry ice cream or low-fat strawberry frozen yogurt,
   slightly softened
1 container (6 ounces) custard-style low-fat strawberry yogurt,
   or 1 container (8 ounces) regular low-fat strawberry yogurt
1 cup thawed frozen nondairy whipped topping,
   or ½ cup heavy (whipping) cream, whipped stiff
1 pint (12 ounces) ripe strawberries, hulled, rinsed,
   and cut into small pieces

TOPPING

2 cups thawed frozen whipped topping, or 1 cup heavy
   (whipping) cream whipped stiff with 1 tablespoon granulated sugar
1 cup sweetened flaked coconut, toasted (see page 326)

1. Have ready a 9½- or 10-inch deep-dish pie plate.

2. Make the crust: Put the graham-cracker crumbs into a medium-size bowl. Add the butter and toss with a fork to moisten evenly. Press the mixture over the bottom and up the sides of the pie plate. Refrigerate until firm, at least 30 minutes.

3. Meanwhile, make the mousse: Pour the boiling water into a large bowl. Add the gelatin and whisk until completely dissolved. Stir in the ice cream until melted, then the yogurt until blended. Refrigerate, stirring once or twice, until the mixture starts to set (it should be thick enough to hold its shape when dropped from a spoon), 10 to 15 minutes. Gently stir (fold) in the 1 cup whipped topping and the strawberries until blended.

4. Spread the filling in the prepared crust, mounding it slightly in the center. Refrigerate until firm, at least 4 hours. ● The pie can be made up to this point 2 days ahead, covered, and refrigerated.

5. Up to 1½ hours before serving, spread the 2 cups whipped topping over the mousse and sprinkle with the coconut.

Per serving with butter, ice cream, and whipped cream: 390 cal, 5 g pro, 22 g fat, 41 g car, 280 mg sod, 69 mg chol. With margarine, low-fat frozen yogurt and whipped topping: 330 cal, 5 g pro, 15 g fat, 45 g car, 290 mg sod, 3 mg chol

COOK'S TIP

To line a pie plate with a crumb crust, start by pressing the crumb mixture from the middle of the pie plate over the bottom and then up the sides. Or spread the crumbs in the plate, then press them down with another pie plate.

EASY

MANGO CUSTARD TART

Serves 10

Preparation time: 30 minutes

Baking time: 45 minutes

Puréed ripe mango and sweet, buttery macadamia nuts give this custard tart an exotic tropical flavor. If you can find only salted macadamia nuts, rinse them, pat them dry, and toast as indicated.

MACADAMIA–NUT CRUST

1½ cups (6 ounces) unsalted macadamia nuts, toasted (see page 325)
2 tablespoons granulated sugar
2 to 4 tablespoons all-purpose flour
White of 1 large egg

MANGO FILLING

1 firm ripe mango (1¼ pounds)
3 large eggs
1 cup granulated sugar
1 teaspoon freshly grated lemon peel
¼ cup heavy cream

For garnish: lightly sweetened whipped cream

1. Heat the oven to 375°F. Grease a 9-inch tart pan with a removable bottom.
2. Make the crust: Put the nuts and sugar into a food processor and process until the nuts are finely chopped. Add the flour and egg white and process until the mixture holds together. Remove the blade, then the dough.
3. With wet fingertips, press the nut mixture over the bottom and up the sides of the prepared pan.
4. Bake until the crust pulls away from the sides of the pan, about 15 minutes.
5. Meanwhile, make the filling: Hold the mango on a cutting board and cut a slice along each side of the long flat seed so you have 2 halves. Holding the peel side of 1 half, score the flesh of the mango lengthwise, then crosswise, without cutting through the peel. Bend the scored portion backward, then cut along the peel to loosen the fruit. Cut the peel off the fruit remaining on the seed. Carefully cut off the flesh. Purée the pulp in a food processor.
6. In a medium-size bowl, whisk together the eggs, sugar, and lemon peel. Stir in the mango purée and cream. Pour the filling into the prebaked crust and bake until the filling is puffed and golden and a knife inserted near the center comes out clean, 25 to 30 minutes.
7. Cool the tart in the pan on a wire rack. Serve the tart with whipped cream.
• The tart can be covered and refrigerated up to 2 days.

Per serving: 290 cal, 4 g pro, 16 g fat, 34 g car, 30 mg sod, 72 mg chol

STRAWBERRY CUSTARD TART

Serves 8

Preparation time: 30 minutes plus at least 1 hour to chill
Cooking time: 10 minutes
Baking time: 27 minutes

For this elegant tart, you can substitute raspberries or blueberries for the strawberries if you like—or combine all three.

Flaky or Sweet Pastry for Tarts (pages 92, 94)

CUSTARD

¾ cup granulated sugar
½ cup all-purpose flour
⅛ teaspoon salt
2 cups milk
Yolks of 2 large eggs
5 tablespoons butter or margarine (see page 321),
    or 2 ounces fat-free cream cheese, cut into small pieces
1 teaspoon vanilla extract
¼ cup almond-flavor liqueur, or
    ¾ teaspoon almond extract plus 3 tablespoons milk

TOPPING

2 pints (1½ pounds) ripe strawberries, hulled, rinsed, and patted dry
¼ cup apricot preserves, melted and strained

1. Have ready a 9- or 10-inch tart pan with a removable bottom.
2. Press the tart dough evenly into the bottom and up the sides of the pan.
Cover and chill for 1 hour until very firm. Heat the oven to 425°F. Prick the bottom of the tart shell at 1-inch intervals with a fork. Bake 12 to 15 minutes or
until the crust is set and just beginning to brown. Remove the foil and bake until
the crust is golden brown, 10 to 12 minutes more. Cool the tart shell in the pan
on a wire rack. • The tart shell can be made up to 3 days ahead, covered tightly,
and refrigerated.
3. Meanwhile, make the custard: In a medium-size saucepan, mix the sugar, flour,
and salt. Whisk in the milk until smooth. (Make sure the whisk reaches the corners
of the pan.)
4. Bring to a gentle boil over medium heat, and whisking constantly, boil until
the mixture thickens, 4 to 5 minutes. Remove the pan from the heat. In a small
bowl, whisk the egg yolks. Gradually whisk in about 1 cup of the hot-milk mixture. Pour the egg yolk mixture into the saucepan and, whisking constantly, simmer
until slightly thicker, 2 to 3 minutes. Remove from the heat. Add the butter, vanilla,
and liqueur and stir until the butter is melted. Pour the custard through a fine

FRUIT TART TIPS
A fruit tart with a
soggy bottom crust is
always a disappoint-
ment. Here are some
ways to avoid this:
◆ Brush the prebaked
tart crust with a thin
layer of melted currant
jelly before filling it.
◆ Pat the fruit dry
with paper towels
before placing in the
tart shell.
◆ Always assemble
a fruit tart just before
serving.

strainer set over a medium-size bowl. Place plastic wrap directly on the surface of the custard to keep a skin from forming. Refrigerate until cool, about 1 hour.

5. To assemble: Stir the custard and spread into the prepared crust. Top with the berries, hulled sides down. Brush the berries with the preserves. Serve the tart right away or refrigerate up to 24 hours.

Per serving with butter in the crust and filling: 460 cal, 6 g pro, 23 g fat, 57 g car, 260 mg sod, 112 mg chol. With margarine in the crust and fat-free cream cheese in the filling: 400 cal, 7 g pro, 15 g fat, 240 mg sod, 62 mg chol

CHOCOLATE–STRAWBERRY TART

Serves 8
Preparation time: 30 minutes plus at least 2 hours to chill
Baking time: 16 minutes

Hazelnuts give this pastry its special flavor. Filled with a rich chocolate layer and topped with fresh strawberries, this lovely tart is a real showstopper.

HAZELNUT PASTRY
1¼ cups all-purpose flour
1 stick (½ cup) cold butter or margarine (see page 321), cut into small pieces
⅓ cup finely chopped toasted hazelnuts (see page 325)
1 to 1½ tablespoons cold water

FILLING
1 cup (6 ounces) semisweet chocolate chips
2 tablespoons butter or margarine
¼ cup water
¼ cup confectioners' sugar
2 pints (1½ pounds) ripe strawberries, hulled, rinsed, and patted dry

1. Have ready a 9-inch tart pan with a removable bottom.
2. To make the pastry in a food processor: Process the flour, butter, and hazelnuts with on/off turns until coarse crumbs form. With the motor running, add 1 tablespoon of water and process just until the dough leaves the sides of the bowl. Remove the blade, then the dough. Form the dough into a ball.

To make by hand: In a medium-size bowl, mix the flour and nuts. Cut in the butter with a pastry blender or until the mixture resembles coarse crumbs. Sprinkle with 1 to 1½ tablespoons of water and stir with a fork until blended. Gather and press into a ball.

3. Flatten the ball slightly. Press evenly over the bottom and up the sides of the pan until the pastry extends ⅛ inch above the rim. Prick the bottom and sides all over with a fork. Cover and chill for 1 hour. ▶

COOK'S TIP

Hazelnuts, also called filberts, have a wonderful fragrance and sweet, buttery flavor. When buying hazelnuts, look for ones that are shelled and skinned to save on preparation time.

4. Adjust the oven rack to the lowest position. Heat the oven to 425°F.

5. Bake the crust until light golden, 13 to 16 minutes. Cool the crust in the pan on a wire rack.

6. Meanwhile, make the filling: In a small saucepan, melt the chocolate chips with the butter and water over low heat, stirring until smooth. (Or put the chocolate chips, butter, and water into a medium-size microwave-safe bowl and microwave, uncovered, on High for 1 minute. Stir until smooth and melted. Repeat as necessary, microwaving for 20 seconds at a time, then stirring until smooth and melted.) Whisk in the confectioners' sugar until blended and smooth. Let cool for about 30 minutes (the mixture will be cool but still pourable). Pour the mixture into the crust.

7. Gently press the strawberries, hulled sides down, into the filling. Refrigerate until the filling is set, at least 1 hour. ● The tart can be made up to 1 day ahead, covered, and refrigerated.

8. To serve, remove the sides of the tart pan and place the tart (still on the base) on a serving plate. Let stand at room temperature for 10 minutes before serving.

Per serving with butter in the crust and filling: 370 cal, 4 g pro, 24 g fat, 39 g car, 150 mg sod, 39 mg chol. With margarine: 170 mg sod, 0 mg chol

---

EASY

NECTARINE–RASPBERRY TART

Serves 8

Preparation time: 20 minutes plus at least 1½ hours to chill

Baking time: 30 minutes

To save time, you can use a ready-made refrigerated pie crust. Press into the tart pan as directed below, then bake according to package directions.

Flaky or Sweet Pastry for Tarts
   (pages 92, 94)
½ cup regular or reduced-fat sour cream
1½ tablespoons confectioners' sugar
¼ teaspoon vanilla extract
2 medium-size ripe nectarines (12 ounces)
2 cups fresh raspberries, picked over and rinsed
   (about 1 pint)
3 tablespoons apple jelly, melted

1. Have ready a 9-inch tart pan with a removable bottom.

2. Press the tart pastry over the bottom and up the sides of the tart pan until the pastry extends ⅛ inch above the sides. Prick the bottom and sides at 1-inch intervals with a fork. Cover and chill for at least 1 hour. Meanwhile, adjust the oven rack to the lowest position. Heat the oven to 375°F.

3. Bake the tart shell until lightly browned, 25 to 30 minutes. Cool the tart shell

in the pan on a wire rack. • The tart shell can be made up to 3 days ahead, covered tightly, and refrigerated.

4. To assemble, remove the sides of the pan and place the tart on a serving plate. In a small bowl, mix the sour cream, confectioners' sugar, and vanilla. Spread the mixture in the cooled tart shell. Cut the nectarines into thin wedges. Arrange in a heart shape in the center. Arrange the raspberries around the nectarines. Brush the fruit with melted apple jelly. Refrigerate for 30 minutes to set the glaze.

Per serving: 260 cal, 3 g pro, 15 g fat, 30 g car, 130 mg sod, 37 mg chol. With margarine in the crust and reduced-fat sour cream in the filling: 14 g fat, 140 mg sod, 5 mg chol

EASY

TWO–BERRY TART

Serves 8

Preparation time: 20 minutes

Baking time: 1 hour

Fresh blueberries and raspberries top a cooked blueberry filling in this luscious tart. Serve it with vanilla ice cream and you've got a perfect red, white, and blue dessert for the Fourth of July.

Flaky or Sweet Pastry for Tarts
  (pages 92, 94)
2 tablespoons all-purpose flour
½ cup granulated sugar
⅛ teaspoon ground cinnamon
4 cups (about 1⅓ pints) fresh blueberries,
  picked over and rinsed
½ pint (6 ounces) fresh raspberries,
  picked over and rinsed (1¼ cups)

1. Adjust the oven rack to the lowest position. Heat the oven to 400°F. Have ready a 9-inch tart pan with a removable bottom or a 9-inch springform pan.

2. Lightly flour your fingers and press the dough about ¼ inch thick over the bottom of the pan, thinner up the sides. Press the dough to the top of the tart pan, about 1 inch high in the springform pan.

3. In a large bowl, mix the flour, sugar, and cinnamon. Add 3 cups of blueberries and stir to mix and coat. Spread the mixture evenly in the crust.

4. Bake until the crust is well browned and the filling bubbles, 50 to 60 minutes.

5. Cool the tart in the pan on a wire rack. Sprinkle with the remaining 1 cup of blueberries and the raspberries. Cool completely. • The tart can be kept at room temperature on the day it is baked, then covered and refrigerated up to 2 days.

6. To serve, remove the pan sides and put the tart on a serving plate.

Per serving with butter in the crust: 280 cal, 3 g pro, 12 g fat, 43 g car, 120 mg sod, 31 mg chol. With margarine: 140 mg sod, 0 mg chol

TART CRUSTS
A tart crust has a higher percentage of butter than a pie crust, which makes the pastry rich and crumbly.

CHERRY–CHEESE TART

Serves 8

Preparation: 20 minutes plus at least 3½ hours to chill

A delicious study in contrasts: a soft, creamy cheese layer, plus juicy cherry-pie fill-ing, atop a crunchy chocolate-cookie crust. If you don't like the combination of chocolate and cheese, graham crackers will work just as well in the crust. You'll need about 13 or 14 graham-cracker squares.

COOKIE CRUST

22 chocolate wafer cookies
½ stick (¼ cup) butter or margarine (see page 321), softened
2 tablespoons granulated sugar

CHERRY–CHEESE FILLING

1 tub (8 ounces) whipped cream cheese,
   at room temperature
1½ cups milk
2 tablespoons granulated sugar
½ teaspoon vanilla extract
¼ teaspoon almond extract (optional)
1 (4-serving) package instant vanilla-pudding mix
1 can (21 ounces) cherry-pie filling

For garnish: mint sprigs

1. Have ready an 8- or 9-inch tart pan with a removable bottom.

2. Make the crust: Put the cookies into a food processor and process until reduced to fine crumbs. (You should have 1¼ cups.) Add the butter and sugar and process until the crumbs are moistened. Press the mixture evenly over the bottom and up the sides of the pan. Refrigerate until firm, at least 30 minutes, before filling.

3. Make the filling: In a large mixer bowl, beat the cream cheese, milk, sugar, and extract(s) with an electric mixer until blended and smooth. Add the pudding mix and beat on low speed for 1 minute or until blended and slightly thickened. Spread the filling into the chilled crust. Cover with plastic wrap and refrigerate until set, at least 3 hours. • The pie can be made up to this point 1 day ahead, cov-ered, and refrigerated.

4. To serve, remove the side of the pan. (If necessary, use a small knife to loosen the crust from the pan side.) Have a serving plate ready. You can leave the tart on the pan bottom for serving or, using a spatula, loosen the tart from the pan bottom and slide it onto the plate. Shortly before serving, spoon the cherry-pie filling evenly over the cheese layer. Garnish with mint sprigs.

Per serving with butter: 410 cal, 5 g pro, 20 g fat, 54 g car, 470 mg sod, 52 mg chol.
With margarine: 37 mg chol

TART PANS
A tart pan with a flut-ed rim and removable bottom gives you not only a professional-looking tart, but a firm metal base on which to serve it.

FREE-FORM APPLE TART

Serves 6

Preparation time: 20 minutes

Baking time: 50 minutes

This rustic, French country-style tart is less formal than a fluted tart baked in a tart pan. The slices of apple are arranged over a circle of pastry dough and the tart is formed directly on a baking sheet. Because the tart is free-form, the dough can be any shape you like.

Flaky Pastry for Tarts (page 92)
4 large Golden Delicious apples (about 1½ pounds), peeled
¼ cup granulated sugar
½ teaspoon grated nutmeg
2 tablespoons butter or margarine, cut into bits (see page 321)
Confectioners' sugar (optional)

1. Heat the oven to 425°F. Have ready an ungreased cookie sheet without sides.

2. Cut each apple in half from top to bottom. Remove the core and cut out the stem and bud ends. Turn the halves cut sides down and slice thin.

3. On a lightly floured surface, roll the dough into a roughly 13-inch round. (The edges can be uneven.) Transfer to the cookie sheet. (For easy lifting, gently roll up about half the dough on the rolling pin. Lift to the cookie sheet, position carefully, and unroll.)

4. Leaving a 2-inch border, arrange the apple slices in concentric circles from the outside toward the middle. In a small cup, mix the granulated sugar and nutmeg. Sprinkle the mixture over the apples, then dot with the butter. Fold the edges of the pastry over the apples, leaving most of the apples uncovered.

5. Bake for 15 minutes. Reduce the oven temperature to 375°F and bake until the apples are tender and the pastry is golden, about 35 minutes more. Slide the tart onto a wire rack to cool. Before serving, dust with confectioners' sugar. • The tart can be kept at room temperature on the day it is baked, then covered and refrigerated up to 3 days.

Per serving with butter in the crust and filling: 350 cal, 3 g pro, 20 g fat, 43 g car, 200 mg sod, 52 mg chol. With margarine: 220 mg sod, 0 mg chol

COOK'S TIP

Remove apple cores neatly and quickly with a melon baller. Then, using a small, sharp knife, cut wedges to remove stem and bud ends.

EASY · 1 HOUR

WALNUT PEAR
UPSIDE-DOWN TARTS

Serves 9
Preparation time: 15 minutes
Cooking time: 7 minutes
Baking time: 15 minutes

Warm sautéed pears topped with a crisp, flaky square of walnut-crusted purchased puff pastry make these upside-down tarts easy, unique, and most of all, irresistible. A great dessert for guests because the puff pastry can be baked ahead of time and the fruit sautéed just before serving.

WALNUT PASTRY CRUSTS
½ cup (2 ounces) walnut pieces
¼ cup granulated sugar
1 sheet frozen puff pastry (9-inch square)
   from a 17-ounce package, thawed

PEAR FILLING
2½ pounds (about 7 medium-size) ripe pears, peeled,
   quartered, cored, and thinly sliced
¼ cup packed light brown sugar
3 tablespoons orange juice
1 teaspoon vanilla extract

For garnish: sweetened whipped cream

1. Heat the oven to 400°F.

2. Make the crusts: Put the walnuts and sugar in a food processor and process until the walnuts are finely ground. Sprinkle half the mixture over a work surface covering an area the size of the puff pastry sheet. Place the pastry over the mixture, then sprinkle the top with the remaining mixture. Roll the nut-coated pastry into a 15 x 12-inch rectangle, about ⅛ inch thick. Cut the pastry into nine 5 x 4-inch rectangles. Prick each piece several times with a fork. Place the pieces on a cookie sheet. Bake until the pastry is golden brown and crisp, 12 to 15 minutes. Remove the pastry to a wire rack and let cool. • The pastries can be frozen in an airtight freezer container or freezer bag up to 1 month. Thaw at room temperature.

3. Make the filling: Place the pears in a medium-size bowl. Add the sugar and orange juice and toss to mix. Heat a large nonstick skillet over medium-high heat. Add the pears and cook, stirring often, until tender, 5 to 7 minutes. Remove from the heat. Stir in the vanilla.

4. To serve, spoon a portion of the pear mixture onto individual serving plates. Top each one with a pastry crust and a spoonful of whipped cream. Serve right away.

Per serving: 300 cal, 3 g pro, 15 g fat, 43 g car, 70 mg sod, 0 mg chol

PUFF PASTRY
It's not the ingredients (just flour, butter, and water) that make puff pastry so unique; it's how the dough is made. The butter is worked into the dough through a series of rollings and foldings. The result is delicate layers of dough and fat. During baking the fat melts and produces steam, which causes the dough to rise to 4 or 5 times its original height.

OLD FASHIONED

MASCARPONE LEMON CREAM TARTLETS

Makes 20 tartlets
Preparation time: 30 minutes plus 30 minutes to chill
Cooking time: 10 minutes
Baking time: 15 minutes

These individual tartlets filled with a light but luscious mixture of lemon and mascarpone cheese are wonderful served as is or topped with a few fresh raspberries.

PASTRY
1½ cups all-purpose flour
¼ cup granulated sugar
½ teaspoon salt
1 stick (½ cup) cold unsalted butter or margarine (see page 321),
   cut into small pieces
2 tablespoons cream or milk
Yolk of 1 large egg

LEMON FILLING
3 large eggs
¾ cup granulated sugar
2 teaspoons freshly grated lemon peel
½ cup fresh lemon juice
8 ounces fresh mascarpone cheese or 1 package (8 ounces)
   regular or fat-free cream cheese, at room temperature

1. Lightly grease 20 muffin pan cups (2½ inches across).
2. To make the pastry in a food processor: Process the flour, sugar, and salt to blend. With the machine running, drop the butter through the feed tube and process with on/off turns until coarse crumbs form. In a small bowl, beat the cream and egg yolk with a fork until blended. With the machine running, pour this mixture through the feed tube and process until the dough leaves the sides of the bowl clean. Remove the blade, then the dough.

To make by hand: In a medium-size bowl, mix the flour, sugar, and salt. Cut in the butter with a pastry blender until the mixture resembles small peas. In a small bowl, beat the cream and egg yolk with a fork until blended. Stir this mixture into the crumb mixture until the dough holds together.

3. Gather the dough into a ball, roll into a log, wrap in waxed paper, and refrigerate for 30 minutes. ● If not using immediately, wrap with plastic and refrigerate up to 3 days or freeze up to 3 months. Thaw at room temperature 30 minutes to 1 hour.

4. Heat the oven to 375°F. Divide the dough into 20 equal pieces. Roll each piece into a ball. With lightly floured fingers, press each ball evenly over the bottom and about half an inch up the sides of the prepared muffin pan cups. Prick ▶

the bottoms with a fork. Bake until the pastry looks dry and pale golden brown, 13 to 15 minutes. Remove the pan to a wire rack and let cool completely. Carefully remove the tart shells from the cups.

5. Make the filling: Have ready a medium-size bowl of cold water. Whisk the eggs in the top of a double boiler to blend the yolks and whites. Whisk in ½ cup of the sugar, the lemon peel, and lemon juice until blended. Cook over simmering (not boiling) water, whisking constantly, for about 10 minutes, until the mixture is smooth, slightly thickened, and lightly coats the back of a spoon. Place the top of the double boiler in the bowl of cold water and stir for 1 to 2 minutes to cool the lemon mixture. Leave in the cold water, stirring occasionally, until the mixture is thoroughly chilled, 5 to 10 minutes more.

6. In a medium-size (mixer) bowl, beat the mascarpone cheese with an electric mixer until smooth, adding the remaining ¼ cup of sugar 1 tablespoon at a time. Whisk about ¼ cup of the lemon mixture into the cheese mixture, then gently stir (fold) in the remainder.

7. Just before serving, spoon about 2 tablespoons of the lemon-cheese filling into each tart shell.

Per tartlet: 190 cal, 3 g pro, 12 g fat, 18 g car, 70 mg sod, 73 mg chol. With margarine and fat-free cream cheese: 140 cal, 4 g pro, 6 g fat, 170 mg sod, 44 mg chol

---

EASY • OLD FASHIONED

BANANA CUSTARD TART

Serves 8

Preparation time: 10 minutes plus 2 hours to chill

Baking time: 12 minutes

One of America's favorite puddings can be made a little more festive by putting it in a crisp tart shell and topping it with toasted coconut.

> *Flaky or Sweet Pastry for Tarts (pages 92, 94)*
> *1 (4-serving) package instant vanilla-pudding mix*
> *2 cups milk*
> *2 medium-size bananas (1 pound), thinly sliced*
> *¼ cup sweetened flaked coconut, toasted*

1. Have ready a 9-inch tart pan with a removable bottom.

2. Press the pastry dough over the bottom and up the sides of the ungreased tart pan. Prick the bottom all over with a fork. Cover and chill 1 hour.

3. Heat the oven to 425°F.

4. Put the tart shell on a cookie sheet and bake until golden, 10 to 12 minutes. Cool the tart shell on a wire rack.

5. Prepare the pudding according to package directions, using the 2 cups of milk. Stir in the bananas. Pour the mixture into the cooled shell. Chill for 1 hour, or until slightly firm. • The tart can be made up to this point 1 day ahead, covered, and refrigerated.

C OOK'S TIP

To toast coconut: Place on a baking sheet and toast at 350° for 8 to 10 minutes, stirring once or twice, until golden.

6. Just before serving, remove the side of the pan. Sprinkle the tart with the toasted coconut.

Per serving with butter in the crust: 310 cal, 4 g pro, 15 g fat, 40 g car, 350 mg sod, 40 mg chol. With margarine: 365 mg sod, 9 mg chol

COOK'S TIP

If you do not have a thermometer, watch the egg mixture for the following visual signs to tell when it reaches 140°F. As it warms, the mixture will get thinner and a small amount of white foam will appear on the surface. Then as the mixture heats, it will thicken and the foam will disappear. If you draw the rubber spatula through the mixture at this point, it will briefly leave a path.

CLASSIC

LIME MOUSSE SCHAUMTORTE

Serves 8

Preparation time: 30 minutes plus at least 10 hours to chill

Baking time: 45 minutes

A light, delicate meringue shell serves as the base for this ethereal tart. Make it as much as 2 days ahead, so the tart lime filling mellows and softens the meringue.

MERINGUE SHELL
Whites of 3 large eggs, at room temperature
¼ teaspoon cream of tartar
⅛ teaspoon salt
¾ cup granulated sugar

LIME MOUSSE
Yolks of 4 large eggs
¾ cup granulated sugar
2 teaspoons freshly grated lime peel
⅓ cup fresh lime juice
⅔ cup heavy (whipping) cream

For garnish: unsweetened whipped cream and
* fresh raspberries or strawberries*

1. Heat the oven to 300°F. Lightly grease a round ovenproof serving dish, about 10 inches in diameter.

2. Make the meringue shell: In a medium-size (mixer) bowl, beat the egg whites with an electric mixer until frothy. Add the cream of tartar and salt and beat on high speed until soft peaks form when the beaters are lifted. Beat in 4 tablespoons of the sugar, 1 tablespoon at a time, until blended. Reduce the mixer speed to low, sprinkle the remaining sugar over the egg whites, and beat until blended. Spread the meringue over the bottom and 1 inch up the sides of the prepared pan. Bake until lightly browned, about 45 minutes. Cool the meringue in the dish on a wire rack.

3. Meanwhile, make the filling: Have ready a large-size bowl of cold water. Whisk the egg yolks and sugar in the top of a double boiler until pale and thick, 3 to 4 minutes. Whisk in the lime peel and lime juice until blended. Cook over simmering (not boiling) water, stirring constantly with a rubber spatula, for about 10 minutes, until the mixture reaches and holds 140° F for 3 minutes (see Cook's Tip). Place ▶

the top of the double boiler in the bowl of cold water and stir for 1 to 2 minutes to cool the lime mixture. Leave in the cold water, stirring occasionally, until the mixture is thoroughly chilled, 5 to 10 minutes more.

4. In a medium-size (mixer) bowl, beat the cream with an electric mixer until soft peaks form when the beaters are lifted. Stir one-fourth of the whipped cream into the cooled lime mixture until well blended. Then gently stir (fold) in the remaining whipped cream with a rubber spatula until no white streaks remain.

5. Spread the filling over the meringue base. (If the meringue is not yet cool, cover and refrigerate the filling until ready to use.) Cover the tart and refrigerate for at least 10 hours for the meringue to soften. ● The tart can be made up to 2 days ahead, covered, and refrigerated.

6. Just before serving, garnish with whipped cream and berries. To serve, spoon the meringue and filling onto plates.

Per serving: 250 cal, 3 g pro, 10 g fat, 39 g car, 70 mg sod, 134 mg chol

ALMOND TART

Serves 8 to 10
Preparation time: 20 minutes plus 1 hour to chill
Baking time: 48 minutes

A delicate tart with a subtle almond flavor, this classic, European-style dessert is the perfect finish for an elegant dinner—yet it's incredibly simple to make.

Flaky or Sweet Pastry for Tarts (pages 92, 94)

ALMOND FILLING
1 cup (4 ounces) blanched or slivered almonds
⅔ cup granulated sugar
2 large eggs
2 tablespoons lemon juice
¼ teaspoon vanilla extract

1. Grease a 9-inch tart pan with a removable bottom.

2. Lightly flour your fingertips and firmly and evenly press the dough into the bottom and up the sides of the prepared tart pan. Cover and chill for 1 hour.

3. Heat the oven to 375°F. Bake the tart shell until golden, about 18 minutes. Cool the tart shell in the pan on a wire rack. Reduce the oven temperature to 350°F.

4. Make the filling: Process the almonds and sugar until the almonds are finely ground. Add the eggs, lemon juice, and vanilla and process until blended. Pour the filling into the cooled, baked tart shell.

5. Bake the tart until the filling is set, about 30 minutes. Cool the tart in the pan on a wire rack. While still warm, gently loosen the tart from the side of the pan with a thin knife.

5. To serve, remove the side of the pan and set the tart on a serving plate. • The tart can be kept at room temperature on the day it is baked, then covered and refrigerated up to 2 days.

Per serving with butter in the crust: 310 cal, 6 g pro, 18 g fat, 31 g car, 120 mg sod, 75 mg chol. With margarine: 135 mg sod, 47 mg chol

---

EASY • CLASSIC

RASPBERRY LINZER TART

Serves 8

Preparation time: 30 minutes plus 1 hour to chill

Baking time: 50 minutes

The combination of ground almonds, spices, and raspberry jam makes this tart a sophisticated crowd-pleaser. Using almonds with skins adds a more interesting texture to the crust, but blanched, slivered, and chopped almonds will also produce nice results.

1½ sticks (¾ cup) butter, softened
½ cup granulated sugar
Yolks of 2 large eggs
½ teaspoon baking powder
¼ teaspoon ground cinnamon
⅛ teaspoon ground cloves
⅛ teaspoon salt
1 teaspoon freshly grated lemon peel
1 cup all-purpose flour
1 cup (4 ounces) almonds, finely ground
⅔ cup seedless raspberry preserves
For garnish: confectioners' sugar

1. In a medium-size (mixer) bowl, beat the butter and granulated sugar with an electric mixer until light and fluffy. Beat in the egg yolks, baking powder, cinnamon, cloves, salt, and lemon peel until blended. Add the flour and nuts and beat just until blended. Form the dough into a ball, wrap with plastic, and refrigerate for at least 30 minutes.

2. Grease a 9-inch tart pan or springform pan. With lightly floured fingers, press approximately 1½ cups of the dough over the bottom of the prepared pan. Spoon the preserves over the dough and spread evenly, leaving a ½-inch border around the edge.

3. Spoon the remaining dough into a large zipper-lock food storage bag or a large pastry bag fitted with a medium-size round plain tip. If using a zipper-lock bag, snip ½ inch from one of the bottom corners. Pipe the dough in a lattice pattern over the preserves. Chill the tart for 30 minutes.

4. Heat the oven to 350°F. Bake the tart until the preserves begin to bubble and the crust is firm and lightly golden, about 50 minutes. Cool the tart in the pan on a wire rack. ▶

VARIATION

APRICOT LINZER TART

Substitute ⅔ cup of apricot jam for the raspberry jam and proceed as directed.

Per serving: 430 cal, 6 g pro, 26 g fat, 47 g car, 260 mg sod, 100 mg chol

• EASY

5. To serve, remove the side of the pan and transfer the tart (still on its base) to a serving plate. Dust with confectioners' sugar. • The tart can be kept covered at room temperature up to 3 days.

Per serving: 430 cal, 6 g pro, 26 g fat, 47 g car, 260 mg sod, 100 mg chol

---

EASY • DECADENT

BITTERSWEET CHOCOLATE TRUFFLE TART

Serves 16

Preparation time: 20 minutes plus at least 4 hours to chill

Baking time: 20 minutes

This heavenly tart is a chocolate lover's dream come true. The filling is a simple, rich ganache—a mixture of warm melted chocolate and cream.

CHOCOLATE–HAZELNUT CRUST

⅓ cup hazelnuts, toasted and skinned (see page 321)
21 chocolate wafer cookies (6 ounces)
½ stick (¼ cup) unsalted butter, cut into small pieces

TRUFFLE FILLING

1½ cups heavy (whipping) cream
10 ounces bittersweet or semisweet chocolate, coarsely chopped

For garnish: cocoa powder, whipped cream, and chocolate shavings (see page 329)

1. Heat the oven to 350°F. Have ready a 9-inch tart pan with a removable bottom (place on a cookie sheet) or a 9-inch pie plate.

2. Make the crust: Process the hazelnuts in a food processor until finely chopped. Break up and add the cookies. Process until coarsely chopped. Add the butter and process for about 2 minutes, until the nuts and cookies are finely chopped and coated with butter. (The mixture will be in small chunks.)

3. Press the crust mixture over the bottom and up the sides of the tart pan. Bake until the edge of the crust holds together when lightly pressed, 15 to 20 minutes. Cool the crust in the pan on a wire rack.

4. Meanwhile, make the filling: In a medium-size saucepan, heat the cream over medium heat until small bubbles appear around the edges. Remove from the heat. Add the chocolate and stir until melted and smooth. Pour the filling into the cooled tart shell. Refrigerate until the filling is set, about 4 hours. • The tart can be prepared up to this point 2 days ahead, loosely covered, and refrigerated.

5. To serve, remove the side of the pan and transfer the tart (still on its base) to a serving plate. Sift 1 tablespoon of cocoa powder over the surface of the tart. Spoon the whipped cream into a pastry bag fitted with a large star tip. Pipe rosettes of whipped cream around the edges. Sprinkle chocolate shavings over the rosettes and serve.

Per serving: 250 cal, 3 g pro, 20 g fat, 19 g car, 71 mg sod, 39 mg chol

REMOVING A TART

To remove the tart from the pan:

◆ Place the tart pan on a small, sturdy bowl turned upside down. Let the pan sides fall to the counter, then slide the tart (still on the metal base) onto the serving plate.

◆ If any of the filling overflows, the crust is likely to stick to the sides. Carefully loosen any stubborn parts of the crust with the tip of a paring knife.

PUDDINGS, CUSTARDS & MOUSSES

> *"Bring on the dessert.*
> *I think I am about to die."*
> ANTHELME BRILLAT-SAVARIN
> (supposed last words)

Puddings and custards are the original comfort foods: There is something inherently soothing about them. At the same time, mousses, which are lighter (in feel, not calories!) than puddings, are among the most elegant of desserts.

Nowadays, a good homemade pudding is hard to come by, but the puddings in this chapter—from old favorites like Butterscotch Pudding and Rice Pudding to contemporary selections like Low-Fat Lemon Custard Bread Pudding—will fill that void. The Rich Chocolate and White Chocolate mousses are great for entertaining, as are the flans and crème caramels. The Chocolate Fondue is an unforgettable dessert that is also fun to serve. These "spoon foods" could very well become cornerstones of your dessert repertoire, and they're generally great kid-pleasers.

EASY

Almond French Bread
   Pudding, 142
Baked Almond Rice Pudding, 140
Cantaloupe "Mousse," 157
Chocolate Bread Pudding, 143
Chocolate Fondue, 160
Chocolate Pudding, 145
Chocolate Pudding Cake, 144
Lemon Custard Bread Pudding, 141
Lemon Sponge Pudding, 144
Low-Fat Almond French Bread
   Pudding, 142
Low-Fat Lemon Custard Bread
   Pudding, 141
Make-It-Easy Coffee Crème
   Caramel, 147
Microwave Chocolate Pudding
   Cake, 145
Rich Chocolate Mousse, 155
Strawberry-Blueberry Trifle, 159
Tropical Mango Fool, 158
White Chocolate Mousse, 155

QUICK

Chocolate Fondue, 160

1 HOUR

Chocolate Pudding Cake, 144
Lemon Sponge Pudding, 144
Microwave Chocolate Pudding
   Cake, 145

LOW FAT

Baked Almond Rice Pudding, 140
Cantaloupe "Mousse," 157
Chocolate Pudding, 145

Chocolate Pudding Cake, 144
Lemon Sponge Pudding, 144
Low-Fat Almond French Bread
　Pudding, 142
Low-Fat Lemon Custard Bread
　Pudding, 144
Mexican Mocha Flan, 153
Microwave Chocolate Pudding
　Cake, 145
Milk Chocolate Mousse, 156
Pumpkin Crunch Custard, 154
Rice Pudding, 140
Rice Pudding Brûlé, 140
Strawberry-Blueberry Trifle, 159

CLASSIC

Butterscotch Pudding, 146
Chocolate Bread Pudding, 143
Chocolate Fondue, 160
Chocolate Pudding, 145
Lemon Mousse with Raspberry
　Sauce, 157
Rice Pudding, 140
Rich Chocolate Mousse, 155
White Chocolate Mousse, 155

OLD FASHIONED

Almond French Bread Pudding, 142
Baked Almond Rice Pudding, 146
Butterscotch Pudding, 146
Chocolate Bread Pudding, 143
Chocolate Pudding, 145
Chocolate Pudding Cake, 144
Lemon Custard Bread
　Pudding, 141
Lemon Sponge Pudding, 144
Pumpkin Crunch Custard, 154
Rice Pudding, 140
Rice Pudding Brûlé, 140

DECADENT

Chocolate Bread Pudding, 143
Chocolate Fondue, 160
Chocolate Pudding Cake, 144
Coconut Flan, 141
Coffee Crème Caramel, 147
Make-It-Easy Coffee Crème
　Caramel, 147
Microwave Chocolate Pudding
　Cake, 145
Rich Chocolate Mousse, 155
White Chocolate Mousse, 155

NO-BAKE DESSERTS

Cantaloupe "Mousse," 156
Lemon Mousse with Raspberry
　Sauce, 157
Milk Chocolate Mousse, 156
Rich Chocolate Mousse, 155
Strawberry-Blueberry Trifle, 159
Tropical Mango Fool, 158
White Chocolate Mousse, 155

KID APPEAL

Butterscotch Pudding, 146
Chocolate Bread Pudding, 143
Chocolate Fondue, 160
Chocolate Pudding, 145
Chocolate Pudding Cake, 144
Rice Pudding, 140

INTERNATIONAL FLAIR

Coconut Flan, 148
Mexican Mocha Flan, 153
Strawberry-Blueberry Trifle, 159
Tropical Mango Fool, 158

ELEGANT ENTERTAINING

Chocolate Fondue, 160
Coconut Flan, 148
Coffee Crème Caramel, 147
Lemon Mousse with Raspberry
　Sauce, 157
Mexican Mocha Flan, 153
Rich Chocolate Mousse, 155
Strawberry-Blueberry Trifle, 159
White Chocolate Mousse, 155

LOW FAT • CLASSIC • OLD FASHIONED

RICE PUDDING

Serves 6

Preparation time: 5 minutes plus 1 hour to chill

Cooking time: 35 minutes

This is the quintessential rice pudding—sweet, rich, and creamy, the result of long, slow simmering and stirring on the stove.

4 cups milk

¾ cup uncooked long-grain rice (not converted)

1 large egg

⅓ cup granulated sugar

1 teaspoon vanilla extract

1. Warm the milk in a medium-size saucepan over medium-low heat. Stir in the rice. Bring to a simmer. Cook, uncovered, stirring frequently, until the rice is tender, about 30 minutes.

2. In a medium-size saucepan, whisk together the egg, sugar, and vanilla. Gradually stir in the rice mixture until blended. Return the mixture to the saucepan and stir over medium-low heat for 1 minute to cook the egg.

3. Pour the mixture into 6 custard cups or ramekins. Refrigerate for at least 1 hour. Serve chilled. ● The pudding can be covered and refrigerated up to 5 days.

Per serving: 240 cal, 8 g pro, 6 g fat, 37 g car, 90 mg sod, 58 mg chol

EASY • LOW FAT • OLD FASHIONED

BAKED ALMOND RICE PUDDING

Serves 8

Preparation time: 10 minutes

Cooking time: 20 minutes

Baking time: 1 hour

Soft, creamy, and soothing, rice pudding is a dessert you never outgrow. This version has a crunchy topping of sliced almonds, sugar, and nutmeg.

1½ cups water

¾ cup uncooked white rice (not converted)

4 large eggs

4 cups milk

⅔ cup granulated sugar

2 teaspoons vanilla extract

1 teaspoon almond extract

1 cup dark raisins

VARIATION

RICE PUDDING BRÛLÉ

● Prepare the pudding as directed and pour the mixture into six broiler-proof ramekins.

● Heat the broiler. Sprinkle ⅓ cup packed light brown sugar over the surface of the puddings. Broil 4 inches from the heat source until the sugar is melted, about 2 minutes. Serve warm or chilled.

Per serving: 290 cal, 8 g pro, 6 g fat, 49 g car, 100 mg sod, 58 mg chol

● LOW FAT

● OLD FASHIONED

ALMOND TOPPING

⅓ cup sliced almonds

1 teaspoon granulated sugar

¼ teaspoon grated nutmeg

1. In a medium-size saucepan, bring the water and rice to a boil. Reduce the heat to low. Cover and simmer for 18 to 20 minutes, or until the water is absorbed and the rice is tender. Let cool.

2. Heat the oven to 325°F. Lightly grease a shallow 2-quart baking dish.

3. In a large bowl, whisk the eggs to blend the whites and yolks. Whisk in the milk, sugar, and both extracts until well blended. Stir in the rice and raisins. Pour the batter into the prepared baking dish.

4. Make the topping: In a small bowl, mix the almonds, sugar, and nutmeg. Sprinkle the topping over the pudding.

5. Bake until a knife inserted near the center comes out clean (the center may still jiggle but will become firm on standing), 55 to 60 minutes. Remove the dish to a wire rack to cool. Serve warm, at room temperature, or chilled. • The pudding can be tightly covered and refrigerated up to 5 days.

Per serving: 330 cal, 10 g pro, 9 g fat, 53 g car, 90 mg sod, 123 mg chol

---

EASY • OLD FASHIONED

LEMON CUSTARD BREAD PUDDING

Serves 6

Preparation time: 10 minutes

Baking time: 1 hour

Here's a lemony new twist on an old favorite. Bread pudding has always been an excellent way to use up stale bread: in fact, bread that's a few days old is ideal for this kind of pudding. As the pudding bakes, it separates into two layers, both just heavenly.

6 slices firm white bread, torn into pieces

4 large eggs, yolks and whites separated,

yolks into a food processor and whites into a large bowl

2 cups milk

¾ cup granulated sugar

1 tablespoon freshly grated lemon peel

⅓ cup fresh lemon juice

2 tablespoons butter or margarine, melted

1. Heat the oven to 350°F. Have ready an 8-inch square baking dish and a large roasting pan.

2. In a food processor, process the bread, egg yolks, milk, sugar, lemon peel, lemon juice, and butter until the bread is reduced to very fine crumbs.

3. In a large (mixer) bowl, beat the egg whites with an electric mixer ▶

VARIATION

LOW-FAT LEMON CUSTARD BREAD PUDDING

For a lighter and less caloric pudding, use skim milk instead of whole milk and reduce the butter to 1 tablespoon. Proceed as directed.

Per serving: 270 cal, 9 g pro, 6 g fat, 45 g car, 260 mg sod, 144 mg chol

• EASY • LOW FAT

until stiff peaks form when the beaters are lifted. Pour the bread mixture onto the beaten whites and gently stir (fold) until no white clumps remain. Pour the mixture into the baking dish.

4. Place the dish in the roasting pan. Pour enough hot water into the pan to come halfway up the sides of the dish.

5. Bake until a knife inserted near the center comes out clean, 55 to 60 minutes. Remove the dish from the water to a wire rack to cool. Serve warm, at room temperature, or chilled. • The bread pudding can be tightly covered and refrigerated up to 5 days.

Per serving: 300 cal, 9 g pro, 11 g fat, 45 g car, 270 mg sod, 164 mg chol

---

EASY • OLD FASHIONED

ALMOND FRENCH BREAD PUDDING

Serves 6

Preparation time: 10 minutes plus 10 minutes to stand

Baking time: 1 hour

This bread pudding is special because of its deep almond flavor and occasional burst of raisins. Years ago, bread pudding was the thrifty cook's way to use up stale bread. Nowadays, though, it's worth buying a loaf of good bread just to make this delicious, comforting dessert.

9 ½-inch-thick slices French bread
¼ cup golden raisins
2 cups milk
3 large eggs
1 cup plus 2 tablespoons granulated sugar
1½ tablespoons butter or margarine, melted
½ teaspoon almond extract
3 tablespoons whole almonds with skins, finely chopped

1. Heat the oven to 350°F. Have ready a 9-inch square baking dish and a large roasting pan.

VARIATION

LOW-FAT ALMOND FRENCH BREAD PUDDING

For a lighter and less caloric pudding, use skim instead of whole milk and egg substitute instead of eggs. Reduce the butter or margarine to ¾ teaspoon and the almond extract to ¼ teaspoon. Proceed as directed.

Per serving: 190 cal, 10 g pro, 4 g fat, 30 g car, 330 mg sod, 3 mg chol

• EASY • LOW FAT

BREAD PUDDING PRIMER

◆ Almost any kind of bread can be used to make bread pudding, but firm or stale or slightly dry bread will work the best because it will soak up the custard better. To slightly dry out fresh bread, place slices in a single layer on a baking sheet and bake at 250°F for about 20 minutes.

◆ The crusts can either be left on the bread or removed. Leaving the crusts on will give the bread pudding a little more texture, and removing them will produce a lighter pudding.

◆ To give your bread pudding an extra-light consistency, try beating the egg whites separately, then gently stirring (folding) them in before adding the bread.

◆ For extra-rich pudding, use light cream or half-and-half instead of milk.

2. Line the bottom of the baking dish with the bread slices. Sprinkle the raisins over the bread.

3. In a large bowl, whisk together the milk, eggs, sugar, butter, and almond extract until blended. Pour the mixture evenly over the bread. Let stand for 10 minutes for the bread to absorb the mixture. Sprinkle the almonds over the top.

4. Place the dish in the roasting pan. Pour enough hot water into the pan to come halfway up the sides of the dish.

5. Bake until a knife inserted near the center comes out clean, 50 to 60 minutes. Remove the dish from the water to a wire rack. Serve warm, at room temperature, or chilled. • The bread pudding can be tightly covered and refrigerated up to 5 days.
Per serving: 400 cal, 10 g pro, 11 g fat, 67 g car, 330 mg sod, 125 mg chol

EASY • CLASSIC • OLD FASHIONED • DECADENT

CHOCOLATE BREAD PUDDING
Serves 6
Preparation time: 10 minutes
Baking time: 1 hour

Food philosophers like to say that bread sustains life and chocolate makes it worth living. Here's a pudding that combines the two, with delicious results.

- ¾ cup granulated sugar
- ⅓ cup unsweetened cocoa powder
- ½ teaspoon instant coffee granules
- 2 cups milk
- 2 tablespoons butter or margarine
- 3 large eggs
- 4 slices firm white bread, cut into ½-inch cubes

1. Heat the oven to 350°F. Have ready a shallow 1½-quart baking dish (about 8 inches across and 2 inches deep) and a large roasting pan.

2. In a medium-size saucepan, whisk together the sugar, cocoa, and instant coffee until blended. Whisk in 1 cup of the milk. Cook over medium heat, whisking frequently, until the mixture comes to a boil and the sugar dissolves, about 2 to 3 minutes.

3. Remove from the heat and whisk in the butter until melted. Whisk in the remaining milk, then the eggs until blended. Stir in the bread. Pour the mixture into the baking dish.

4. Place the dish in the roasting pan. Pour enough hot water into the pan to come halfway up the sides of the dish.

5. Bake until a knife inserted near the center comes out clean, 50 to 60 minutes. Remove the dish from the water to a wire rack. Serve warm, at room temperature, or chilled. • The bread pudding can be tightly covered and refrigerated up to 5 days.
Per serving: 280 cal, 8 g pro, 10 g fat, 41 g car, 210 mg sod, 128 mg chol

EASY • 1 HOUR • LOW FAT • OLD FASHIONED

LEMON SPONGE PUDDING

Serves 8

Preparation time: 15 minutes plus cooling

Baking time: 25 minutes

Sponge puddings separate into two layers as they bake—a light spongy cake forms on the top and a custardy sauce develops below. Although it can be served chilled, it is best right out of the oven.

> 1½ cups milk
> 3 large eggs, whites and yolks separated
> 1 cup sugar
> ½ cup all-purpose flour
> 2 tablespoons unsalted butter, softened
> 1 tablespoon freshly grated lemon peel
> ⅓ cup fresh lemon juice

1. Fill the bottom of a roasting pan with ½ inch of water and place the pan in the center of the oven. Heat the oven to 325°F. In a small saucepan, bring the milk just to simmer, then remove the pan from the heat.

2. In a medium bowl, whisk the egg yolks to blend. Slowly whisk in the hot milk until blended. Whisk in the sugar, flour, butter, lemon peel, and lemon juice.

3. In a medium-size bowl, beat the egg whites with an electric mixer until stiff peaks form when the beaters are lifted. Gently whisk the egg whites into the lemon mixture. Pour the mixture into eight 6-ounce custard cups.

4. Set the cups in the pan of hot water in the oven. Bake until the tops are dry and lightly golden, about 25 minutes.

5. Remove the custard cups from the water bath to a wire rack to cool. Serve at room temperature or chilled. • The puddings can be tightly covered and refrigerated up to 3 days.

Per serving: 210 cal, 5 g pro, 6 g fat, 34 g car, 50 mg sod, 94 mg chol

COOK'S TIP

This sponge pudding, which has a tart and tangy lemony flavor, can also be made with limes or oranges.

EASY • 1 HOUR • LOW FAT • OLD FASHIONED • DECADENT

CHOCOLATE PUDDING CAKE

Serves 9

Preparation time: 10 minutes

Baking time: 35 minutes

If you're not familiar with pudding cakes, they require faith: You pour hot water over the batter before it goes in the oven. Then it forms a cakelike layer on top of a thick creamy sauce as it bakes. (If using the microwave method, some of the sauce will bubble up through the cake layer.)

¾ cup all-purpose flour

⅔ cup granulated sugar

½ cup unsweetened cocoa powder

1½ teaspoons baking powder

½ teaspoon salt

½ cup milk

3 tablespoons vegetable oil

⅔ cup packed light brown sugar

¼ cup mini semisweet chocolate chips

1 teaspoon vanilla extract

1¼ cups hot water

1. Heat the oven to 350°F.

2. Put the flour, granulated sugar, ¼ cup of the cocoa, the baking powder, and salt into an ungreased 8-inch square baking pan. Stir to mix well. Add the milk and oil. Stir until well blended.

3. Sprinkle the brown sugar, the remaining ¼ cup of cocoa, and the chocolate chips over the batter. Mix the vanilla with the water and pour evenly over the top.

4. Bake until the surface looks dry and brownielike, 30 to 35 minutes.

5. Remove the dish to a wire rack to cool. Serve warm or at room temperature. To serve, spoon the cake into individual dishes. • The pudding cake can be tightly covered and refrigerated up to 3 days.

Per serving: 240 cal, 3 g pro, 7 g fat, 45 g car, 220 mg sod, 2 mg chol

EASY • LOW FAT • CLASSIC • OLD FASHIONED

CHOCOLATE PUDDING

Serves 6

Preparation time: 10 minutes plus at least 1 hour to chill

Cooking time: 15 minutes

If there is a single dessert that conjures up childhood memories, it's chocolate pudding. This version has a marvelous deep chocolatey flavor, but guess what—it's low in fat!

1 large egg

2¼ cups skim or 1%-fat milk

½ cup granulated sugar

⅛ teaspoon salt

⅔ cup unsweetened cocoa powder

2 tablespoons cornstarch

1 teaspoon vanilla extract

1. In a small bowl, lightly beat the egg to blend the white and yolk.

2. In a medium-size heavy saucepan, bring 1½ cups of the milk, ¼ cup of the sugar, and the salt to a simmer over medium heat. ▶

3. Meanwhile, in a small bowl, mix the remaining ¼ cup of sugar, the cocoa, and cornstarch. Whisk in the remaining ¾ cup of milk until blended. Whisk this mixture into the pan. Bring to a boil, whisking constantly, and boil for 2 minutes.

4. Add 1 cup of the hot mixture to the egg and whisk to blend. Return this mixture to the pan. Cook over medium-low heat, whisking constantly, for 2 minutes, or until thickened (do not let the mixture return to a boil). Whisk in the vanilla.

5. Pour the pudding into 6 individual serving dishes or 1 bowl and chill for at least 1 hour. To prevent a skin from forming, place sheets of waxed paper directly on the surface of the puddings. Serve chilled. ● The puddings can be tightly covered and refrigerated up to 5 days.

Per serving with skim milk: 140 cal, 6 g pro, 2 g fat, 29 g car, 110 mg sod, 37 mg chol

CLASSIC ● OLD FASHIONED

BUTTERSCOTCH PUDDING

Serves 6

Preparation time: 10 minutes plus at least 2 hours to chill

Cooking time: 15 minutes

This is what real butterscotch pudding tastes like—smooth and creamy, with a delicate subtle flavor that you just can't get from a mix.

3 cups milk
½ cup packed dark brown sugar
3 tablespoons butter
Yolks of 4 large eggs
¼ cup cornstarch
Pinch salt
½ teaspoon vanilla extract
For garnish: whipped cream (optional)

1. Pour 2 cups of milk into a glass measure or bowl. In a 2-quart heavy saucepan, heat the sugar and butter over medium heat until the butter is melted and the mixture begins to bubble. Stir constantly for 3 minutes, until the foam subsides and the mixture darkens and becomes smooth.

2. Immediately add the 2 cups of milk and stir until blended and smooth, about 5 minutes. (The butterscotch will harden, but as the milks heats up it will begin to dissolve.)

3. Meanwhile, in a medium-size bowl, whisk the remaining cup of milk with the egg yolks, cornstarch, and salt until smooth.

4. Add 1 cup of the butterscotch mixture to the egg-yolk mixture and whisk to blend. Return this mixture to the pan. Cook over medium heat, whisking constantly, until the pudding comes to a boil. Remove from the heat. Whisk in the vanilla.

5. Pour the pudding into 6 individual serving dishes or 1 bowl. If you want to prevent a skin from forming, lay a sheet of waxed paper or plastic wrap directly on

---

BAKING CUSTARDS IN A WATER BATH
The secret to cooking perfect custards is the hot water bath or bain-marie. While it may seem a bit of a hassle, the water bath is very important. It provides insulation from the heat so the custard can cook slowly, gently, and evenly all the way through without the edges getting overdone. When properly cooked, the texture of a baked custard will be fine and smooth. If overheated, the custard will be watery.

the surface of the pudding. Chill for 2 to 3 hours. • The puddings can be tightly covered and refrigerated up to 5 days.

6. Serve the pudding chilled and topped with whipped cream.

Per serving: 260 cal, 6 g pro, 13 g fat, 29 g car, 150 mg sod, 174 mg chol

---

COFFEE CRÈME CARAMEL

Serves 6

Preparation time: 20 minutes plus 2½ hours to steep and cool

Cooking time: 45 minutes

The rich and velvety custard for this elegant dessert gets its flavor from crushed coffee beans and whole vanilla beans. If caffeine is a problem for you or your guests, use decaffeinated beans. Look for whole vanilla beans (or pods) that are plump, soft, slightly greasy, and very aromatic. Avoid any pods that are dry or hard.

COFFEE CUSTARD

2 cups heavy (whipping) cream
½ cup milk
½ cup granulated sugar
3 tablespoons coffee beans, preferably French roast,
*   Colombian, or Kona, crushed (not ground)*
1 vanilla bean (pod), split lengthwise
Yolks of 6 large eggs

CARAMEL

1 cup sugar
¼ cup water

1. Put the cream, milk, ½ cup sugar, and the coffee beans into a small saucepan. Using the tip of a knife, scrape the seeds from the vanilla bean into the cream mixture. Bring to a boil, remove from the heat, and let steep for 1 hour for the flavor to develop and the mixture to cool to room temperature.

2. Heat the oven to 350°F. Arrange six ½-cup ramekins or custard cups in a shallow baking pan.

3. Strain the coffee mixture through a fine sieve set over a 4-cup glass measure; discard the solids. Whisk in the egg yolks until blended.

4. Pour the mixture into the ramekins, filling them almost to the top. Place the pan in the oven. Add enough hot water to the pan to come halfway up the sides of the ramekins.

5. Bake until the custards are just set but still a little wobbly and a knife inserted near the center comes out clean, 40 to 45 minutes.

6. Remove the ramekins from the water to a wire rack and cool for about 30 minutes. Refrigerate for at least 1 hour, or until well chilled. • The custards can ▶

VARIATION

MAKE-IT-EASY COFFEE CRÈME CARAMEL

• Put the 2 cups heavy cream into a medium-size bowl and set aside.

• Heat the ½ cup milk in a small saucepan or in the microwave until hot. Stir in 2 teaspoons instant coffee powder or granules and the ½ cup of sugar until dissolved. Stir in 2 teaspoons vanilla extract.

• Stir the mixture into the cream. Whisk in the egg yolks.

• Pour the mixture into the ramekins and proceed as directed.

Per serving: 540 cal, 5 g pro, 35 g fat, 54 g car, 50 mg sod, 324 mg chol

• EASY • DECADENT

COOK'S TIP

To crush coffee beans, place them in a plastic food storage bag and lightly tap with a rolling pin or mallet until broken into coarse pieces.

be made up to this point, tightly covered, and refrigerated up to 3 days.

7. When ready to serve, make the caramel: In a small heavy saucepan, cook the sugar and water over medium heat without stirring, but swirling the pan occasionally, for 10 to 12 minutes until the syrup turns golden amber. (Watch carefully that it doesn't get too dark, or it will taste burned.) Immediately pour a thin layer over each custard (you won't need all the syrup). Let cool for 5 minutes, until hard. Serve right away.

Per serving: 540 cal, 5 g pro, 35 g fat, 54 g car, 50 mg sod, 324 mg chol

COCONUT FLAN

Serves 6

Preparation time: 20 minutes plus at least 5 hours to cool

Cooking time: 10 minutes

Baking time: 1 hour

Flan—a custard with a caramel layer—is a favorite in Spain and throughout Latin America. Coconut milk can be found in markets that sell Asian or Caribbean foods.

CARAMEL
½ cup granulated sugar
2 tablespoons water

COCONUT CUSTARD
5 large eggs
1 can (about 14 ounces) coconut milk (not cream of coconut)
½ cup granulated sugar
1 cup milk

For garnish: sweetened flaked coconut, fresh or canned pineapple chunks

1. Heat the oven to 350°F. Have ready an 8-inch square baking pan and a large roasting pan.

2. Make the caramel: Put ½ cup of the sugar and the water into a small heavy saucepan. Bring to a boil over medium-high heat, swirling the pan until the sugar dissolves. Boil for about 4 minutes, until the syrup turns golden amber. (Watch carefully that it doesn't get dark or it will taste burned.)

3. Immediately pour the caramel into the baking pan. Using pot holders, tilt the pan in all directions to coat the bottom and ½ inch up the sides until the syrup solidifies (it doesn't have to look even).

4. Make the custard: In a large bowl, beat the eggs and coconut milk just until blended. Stir in the sugar and milk. Pour the mixture into the caramel-coated baking pan.

5. Set the baking pan in the roasting pan. Place in the oven. Pour enough hot water into the roasting pan to come halfway up the sides of the baking pan. ▶ *p. 153*

THE STAGES OF CARAMEL

Caramel is sugar that is cooked until it liquefies and begins to color. The sugar is dissolved in a little water and then cooked until the liquid evaporates and sugar is caramelized.

◆ Light caramel (320°F on a candy thermometer) has just a hint of a golden color and a little flavor.

◆ Medium to dark caramel (about 350°F on a candy thermometer) has a golden amber color and a strong, sweet taste.

Nothing could be simpler than this colorful, layered Strawberry-Blueberry Trifle (p.159), here garnished with puff-pastry cookies.

Puddings and custards are the original comfort foods. Whether you're a little "under the weather" or feeling just fine, there is something inherently soothing about them.

This smooth and velvety Coconut Flan (p.148), decorated with fresh pineapple and toasted coconut, is a medley of tropical flavors. Watch it disappear in a flash.

When you want a simple but impressive dessert, pull out this Rich Chocolate Mousse (p.155)—it will make you a star.

6. Bake until a knife inserted near the center comes out clean (the center will jiggle slightly), 55 to 60 minutes.

7. Remove the pan from the water to a wire rack and let cool for no more than 1 hour. Cover and refrigerate for at least 4 hours before unmolding. • The flan can be made up to this point, covered tightly, and refrigerated for up to 3 days.

8. To serve, run a thin knife around the edges of the custard. Place a serving plate with a raised edge upside down over the pan. Holding the plate and pan together, carefully turn both over. Remove the pan and let the caramel syrup run onto the plate. Garnish with coconut and pineapple.

Per serving: 350 cal, 8 g pro, 20 g fat, 38 g car, 80 mg sod, 180 mg chol

LOW FAT

MEXICAN MOCHA FLAN

Serves 12

Preparation time: 20 minutes plus at least 5 hours to cool and chill

Cooking time: 9 minutes

Baking time: 1 hour

Here's a mocha version of one of Mexico's favorite desserts. The combination of sweetened condensed milk, evaporated milk (which are both used extensively in Mexican cooking), and whole milk makes a very rich custard.

CARAMEL
½ cup granulated sugar
2 tablespoons water

MOCHA CUSTARD
1 cup milk
1 teaspoon instant coffee granules
1 tablespoon powdered chocolate-flavored drink mix
5 large eggs
1 can (14 ounces) sweetened condensed milk
1 can (12 ounces) evaporated milk
2 teaspoons vanilla extract

1. Heat the oven to 325°F. Have ready a 1½-quart soufflé dish and a baking pan large enough to hold the dish.

2. Make the caramel: Put the sugar and water into a small heavy saucepan. Bring to a boil over medium-high heat, swirling the pan until the sugar dissolves. Boil for about 4 minutes, until the syrup turns golden amber. (Watch carefully that it doesn't get dark or it will taste burned.)

3. Immediately pour the caramel syrup into the soufflé dish. Using pot holders, tilt the dish in all directions to coat the bottom and ½ inch up the sides until the syrup solidifies (it doesn't have to look even). Set aside.

▶

4. Make the custard: In a small saucepan, heat ¼ cup of the milk with the coffee and chocolate mix, stirring until smooth. Remove from the heat. In a large bowl, whisk the eggs to blend the whites and yolks. Whisk in the sweetened condensed milk, evaporated milk, vanilla, and the coffee mixture until well blended. Pour the mixture into the caramel-coated dish.

5. Set the dish in the baking pan. Place in the oven. Pour enough hot water into the baking pan to come halfway up the sides of the dish. Bake until a knife inserted near the center comes out clean (the center will jiggle slightly), about 1 hour.

6. Remove the dish from the water to a wire rack and cool for no more than 1 hour. Cover and refrigerate for at least 4 hours before unmolding. ● The flan can be made up to this point and refrigerated for up to 3 days.

7. To serve, run a thin knife between the flan and the edge of the dish to loosen. Place a serving plate with a raised edge upside down over the dish. Holding the plate and dish together, carefully turn both over. Remove the dish and let the caramel syrup run onto the plate.
Per serving: 230 cal, 8 g pro, 8 g fat, 32 g car, 110 mg sod, 112 mg chol

LOW FAT • OLD FASHIONED

PUMPKIN CRUNCH CUSTARD
Serves 8
Preparation time: 15 minutes
Baking time: 1 hour 25 minutes

This is much like pumpkin pie, but without the crust. Make it whenever you find yourself longing for the taste of Thanksgiving. Like pumpkin pie, this custard is delicious with whipped cream or vanilla ice cream.

PUMPKIN CUSTARD
3 large eggs
1 can (16 ounces) solid-pack pumpkin
1 can (12 ounces) evaporated skim milk (not sweetened condensed milk)
¾ cup packed brown sugar, or ⅓ cup each packed brown sugar and light molasses
2 teaspoons pumpkin-pie spice, or 1 teaspoon ground cinnamon
 and ½ teaspoon each ground allspice and ground ginger
1 teaspoon vanilla extract

TOPPING
3 tablespoons packed light or dark brown sugar
2 tablespoons all-purpose flour
¼ teaspoon ground cinnamon
4 teaspoons cold butter or margarine (see page 321), cut into small pieces
⅓ cup pecan pieces

1. Heat the oven to 325° F. Have ready a deep 2-quart baking dish or soufflé dish.

COOK'S TIP
When combining the milk or cream and egg yolks for a custard, be sure to whisk gently. Vigorous whisking will create air bubbles that will leave holes in the surface of the finished custard.

BAKED VS. STIRRED
There are two types of custards: baked and stirred. A baked custard is firm and will hold its shape when cut; a stirred custard is cooked on the stove and has a creamy, pourable texture.

2. In a large bowl, whisk the eggs to blend the whites and yolks. Whisk in the pumpkin, evaporated milk, sugar, spice, and vanilla until well blended.

3. Pour the mixture into the ungreased baking dish. Bake until the sides of the custard start to set, about 45 minutes.

4. Meanwhile, make the topping: In a small bowl, mix the sugar, flour, and cinnamon. Cut in the butter with two knives or a pastry blender until the mixture resembles small peas. Stir in the pecans.

5. Remove the custard from the oven and sprinkle with the topping. Return the custard to the oven and bake until a knife inserted near the center comes out clean (the center may still jiggle but will become firm on standing), 35 to 40 minutes more.

6. Remove to a wire rack to cool. Serve warm or at room temperature. • The custard can be tightly covered and refrigerated up to 5 days.

Per serving: 240 cal, 7 g pro, 7 g fat, 38 g car, 110 mg sod, 87 mg chol

---

EASY • CLASSIC • DECADENT

RICH CHOCOLATE MOUSSE

Serves 8

Preparation time: 15 minutes plus at least 1 hour to chill

This mousse is quite simple to make; there are only two steps and no egg whites to beat. It is very dense and very rich—a little goes a long way. The perfect complement would be fresh strawberries, sliced and arranged over each serving, or whole raspberries. Even a slice of fresh orange would make a nice garnish.

2 cups (12 ounces) semisweet chocolate chips
2 cups heavy (whipping) cream
3 tablespoons confectioners' sugar
2 tablespoons orange-flavored liqueur or orange juice
1 tablespoon instant espresso or coffee granules

1. In a medium-size heavy saucepan, melt the chocolate with ⅔ cup of the cream over low heat, stirring until smooth. (Or microwave the chocolate and cream in a medium-size microwave-safe bowl on High for 1 to 2 minutes, until the chocolate is shiny—it won't look melted. Let stand for 1 minute, then stir until smooth and melted. Repeat if necessary.) Scrape the mixture into a medium-size bowl and cool to room temperature.

2. Meanwhile, in a medium-size (mixer) bowl, beat the remaining cream, the confectioners' sugar, liqueur, and espresso granules until stiff peaks form when the beaters are lifted. Stir a small amount of the whipped cream into the cooled chocolate mixture. Gently stir (fold) in the remaining whipped cream with a rubber spatula until no white streaks remain.

3. Spoon the mousse into goblets or dessert dishes. Chill for at least 1 hour before serving. • The mousse can be covered with plastic wrap and refrigerated up to 2 days.

Per serving: 430 cal, 3 g pro, 34 g fat, 34 g car, 20 mg sod, 82 mg chol

---

COOLING CUSTARDS

If you cover puddings and custards before they're completely cooled (and we mean completely), you're going to create condensation and end up with a puddle on top. To avoid the problem, refrigerate the dessert uncovered for about 2 hours. After that, you can cover it normally and return it to the refrigerator until ready to serve.

VARIATION

WHITE CHOCOLATE MOUSSE

• Substitute coarsely chopped white chocolate for the semisweet chocolate, use rum or cognac for the orange liqueur, and omit the instant espresso.

• Prepare and chill the mousse as directed.

Per serving: 450 cal, 4 g pro, 35 g fat, 31 g car, 60 mg sod, 82 mg chol

• EASY • CLASSIC
• DECADENT

MILK CHOCOLATE MOUSSE

Serves 8

Preparation time: 50 minutes

plus at least 1 hour to chill

You'd never guess that this rich and chocolatey mousse is lower in fat than the traditional version. The secret comes from using whipped chilled evaporated milk and gelatin. This recipe calls for a combination of milk chocolate and semisweet chocolate chips, but you can use all semisweet chips (1 cup) if you prefer.

½ cup cool water

1 envelope (¼ ounce) unflavored gelatin

1 can (12 ounces) evaporated milk

  (not sweetened condensed)

¾ cup (4½ ounces) milk chocolate chips

¼ cup (1½ ounces) semisweet chocolate chips

2 teaspoons vanilla extract

For garnish: whipped cream, crumbled chocolate wafer cookies,

  fresh berries, and mint leaves

1. Put the water into a small bowl. Sprinkle the gelatin over the water and let stand 2 minutes to soften.

2. Meanwhile, put 1 cup of the evaporated milk in a large bowl and freeze until ice crystals form around the edge, about 35 minutes.

3. In a small saucepan, heat the remaining evaporated milk or microwave to a bare simmer. Stir in the gelatin mixture and return to a simmer. Remove from the heat, add the chocolate chips and vanilla, and whisk until blended and smooth.

4. Pour the mixture into a medium-size bowl and freeze for at least 25 minutes (no longer than 45 minutes), until the consistency of unbeaten egg whites. Whisk the mixture once or twice during chilling.

5. Remove the milk from the freezer and beat with an electric mixer until stiff peaks form when the beaters are lifted, about 5 minutes.

6. Remove the chocolate mixture from the freezer. Beat briefly with the electric mixer to blend the layers that may have formed and to incorporate any small lumps. Beat the whipped milk into the chocolate mixture.

7. Spoon the mousse into goblets or dessert dishes and refrigerate until firm, at least 1 hour. ● The mousse can be covered with plastic wrap and refrigerated up to 2 days.

8. Garnish just before serving.

Per serving: 180 cal, 4 g pro, 9 g fat, 19 g car, 60 mg sod, 14 mg chol

---

COOK'S TIP

Be sure to freeze the gelatin mixture only until the consistency of unbeaten egg whites. If the mixture becomes too cold, the gelatin will set and the mixture will be lumpy.

CLASSIC

LEMON MOUSSE WITH RASPBERRY SAUCE

Serves 6

Preparation time: 20 minutes plus at least 4 hours to chill

Cooking time: 11 minutes

This tangy mousse is a lovely dessert with which to end a richly flavored meal. Any citrus juice and grated peel or a combination of different citrus fruits may be used.

4 large eggs
Yolks of 4 large eggs
1 cup granulated sugar
1 tablespoon freshly grated lemon peel
¾ cup fresh lemon juice
10 tablespoons unsalted butter, cut into small pieces
½ cup heavy (whipping) cream
1 cup fresh or frozen raspberries
2 tablespoons granulated sugar

1. In a heavy medium-size nonaluminum saucepan, whisk the eggs and egg yolks until foamy. Whisk in the sugar, then the lemon peel and lemon juice. Cook over medium-low heat, whisking constantly, until the mixture thickens, the foam subsides, and the color deepens, 9 to 11 minutes.

2. Remove from the heat and whisk in the butter until melted and the mixture is smooth. Pour the mixture into a medium-size bowl and let cool at room temperature until very thick, stirring occasionally, about 30 minutes.

3. In a medium-size (mixer) bowl, beat the cream with an electric mixer until soft peaks form when the beaters are lifted. Gently stir (fold) the whipped cream into the lemon mixture with a rubber spatula until no white streaks remain. Spoon the mousse into individual dessert dishes or stemmed glasses. Cover and refrigerate until set, at least 4 hours. ● The mousse can be kept refrigerated up to 2 days.

4. To make the sauce, in a small bowl, mash the raspberries with a fork and stir in the sugar. Refrigerate, covered, until ready to serve. To serve, drizzle a spoonful of sauce over each serving of mousse.

Per serving: 485 cal, 7 g pro, 33 g fat, 42 g car, 60 mg sod, 362 mg chol

EASY • LOW FAT

CANTALOUPE "MOUSSE"

Serves 8

Preparation time: 15 minutes plus 1 day to drain yogurt and chill

Blueberries give this luscious cantaloupe "mousse" added texture and color. To ensure a thick, creamy mousse, the yogurt is drained for at least 24 hours. ▶

1 large container (32 ounces) low-fat vanilla yogurt
3½ cups peeled, seeded cantaloupe chunks
   (from about 1½ pounds cantaloupe)
1 tablespoon granulated sugar
¼ teaspoon ground ginger
½ pint (6 ounces) fresh blueberries,
   picked over and rinsed (1 cup)
For garnish: small, thin cantaloupe wedges
   with rind attached

1. Line a large strainer with cheesecloth or a triple layer of white paper towels. Place the strainer over a large bowl to catch the whey that will drain off. Spoon the yogurt into the strainer. Cover with plastic wrap and refrigerate at least 24 hours, until very thick. Discard the whey.

2. In a food processor or blender, process the cantaloupe with on/off turns until fairly smooth but some small chunks still remain.

3. Put the drained yogurt into a medium-size bowl. Add the cantaloupe, sugar, and ginger. Stir until well blended. Stir in the blueberries.

4. Cover and chill for at least 30 minutes. • The mousse can be made up to this point and refrigerated up to 2 days.

5. To serve, spoon the mousse into stemmed glasses. Garnish with melon wedges.
Per serving: 100 cal, 5 g pro, 2 g fat, 17 g car, 50 mg sod, 3 mg chol

TROPICAL MANGO FOOL

Serves 4

Preparation time: 20 minutes plus at least 2 hours to chill

Dessert "fools" are puréed fruit folded into softly whipped cream. They are simple, and they can be made with almost any ripe fruit that can be mashed or puréed such as raspberries, blueberries, plums, and peaches. For a streamlined version, the whipped cream can be replaced with plain low-fat yogurt or yogurt lightened with just a little whipped cream.

2 firm ripe mangoes (about 1¼ pounds each)
½ teaspoon freshly grated lime peel
1 tablespoon fresh lime juice
¼ cup granulated sugar
½ cup heavy (whipping) cream

1. Hold one mango on a cutting board and cut a slice along each side of the long flat seed so you have two halves. Holding the peel side of one half, score the flesh of the mango lengthwise, then crosswise, without cutting through the peel. Bend the scored portion backward, then cut along the peel to loosen the fruit. Cut the peel

COOK'S TIP

If you overbeat heavy (whipping) cream and it begins to turn buttery, whisk in a little additional cream, about 1 tablespoon at a time, and do not whisk any more than necessary.

off the fruit remaining on the seed. Carefully cut off the flesh. Repeat with the remaining mango. Purée the pulp in a food processor. Press the purée through a fine sieve set over a small bowl.

2. In a medium-size bowl, mix the strained purée, the lime peel, lime juice, and 3 tablespoons of the sugar until blended. Cover with plastic wrap and chill for at least 1 hour. • The fruit can be prepared up to this point, covered, and refrigerated for up to 2 days.

3. In another small bowl, beat the cream and the remaining 1 tablespoon of sugar with an electric mixer until soft peaks form when the beaters are lifted. Gently stir (fold) the whipped cream into the mango mixture, leaving streaks of mango and cream. Spoon into stemmed glasses or a glass bowl. Cover and chill for 1 hour before serving. • The fool can be covered and refrigerated up to 8 hours.

Per serving: 280 cal, 2 g pro, 12 g fat, 47 g car, 20 mg sod, 41 mg chol

---

EASY • LOW FAT

STRAWBERRY–BLUEBERRY TRIFLE

Serves 10

Preparation time: 20 minutes plus 4 hours to chill

An English trifle is an elegant dessert made with sherry-soaked sponge cake, custard, whipped cream, and jam. To show off its colorful layers, it is traditionally served from a clear glass bowl. This easy version substitutes vanilla wafers for the sponge cake. If you like, you can sprinkle some sherry or fruit liqueur on the cookies.

2 (4-serving) packages instant vanilla-pudding mix
4 cups milk
20 vanilla wafer cookies
1 pint (12 ounces) blueberries, rinsed and picked over (2½ cups)
1 pint (12 ounces) strawberries, rinsed and picked over (2½ cups)
For garnish: lightly sweetened whipped cream (optional)

1. Have ready a 2-quart glass trifle dish or bowl.

2. Prepare the two packages of pudding together, according to the package directions, using the 4 cups milk.

3. Pour half the vanilla pudding into the serving dish. Arrange the vanilla wafers on the pudding in one layer. Sprinkle on 2 cups of the blueberries. Top the blueberries with the rest of the pudding. Set aside the remaining ½ cup of blueberries. Cover the trifle and refrigerate at least 4 hours. • The trifle can be prepared to this point and refrigerated, covered, up to 24 hours.

4. Up to 1 hour before serving, hull and slice the strawberries. Toss the strawberries with the remaining blueberries, and spoon the mixed berries over the top of the trifle.

5. To serve, spoon the trifle into individual dishes, and garnish with whipped cream, if desired.

Per serving: 190 cal, 4 g pro, 5 g fat, 34 g car, 360 mg sod, 16 mg chol

CHOCOLATE FONDUE

Serves 6

Preparation time: 15 minutes
Cooking time: 10 minutes

Fondue, that convivial favorite of the Fifties, is making a comeback. And no won-der—it's fast, easy, and informal. Provide long-handled forks and let everyone dip fresh fruit, plain cake, or—as Europeans do—chunks of plain good-quality white bread into the warm chocolate.

¾ cup granulated sugar
½ cup unsweetened cocoa powder
1 can (12 ounces) evaporated milk (not sweetened condensed)
⅓ cup light corn syrup
½ stick (¼ cup) margarine
1 teaspoon vanilla extract
For dipping: assorted fruits such as grapes,
    hulled strawberries, cut-up apples and pears

1. In a medium-size saucepan, mix the sugar and cocoa. Stir in the milk and corn syrup. Stir 2 minutes over medium-low heat until boiling. Boil the mixture over medium-high heat, stirring constantly, for 1 minute.

2. Remove from the heat. Stir in the margarine and vanilla until blended. Makes 2 cups. ● The fondue can be made up to this point, covered, and refrigerated for up to 1 week. Reheat over low heat just before serving.

3. To serve, arrange the fruit on a serving platter. Ladle some of the chocolate fondue into individual bowls. (Keep the remaining chocolate fondue warm and replenish bowls as necessary.) Let each person spear fruit on a skewer and dunk into the chocolate before eating.

Per serving: 320 cal, 6 g pro, 13 g fat, 49 g car, 190 mg sod, 18 mg chol

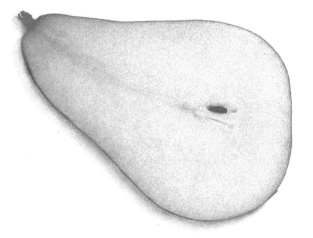

WHIPPED CREAM BASICS

◆ 1 cup of heavy (whipping) cream will yield 2 cups of whipped cream.

◆ Cream will whip faster if it is very cold and the bowl and beaters are chilled or put into the freezer for about 15 minutes before using.

◆ Cream will also whip faster in a deep, narrow bowl rather than one that is wide and shallow.

◆ To sweeten whipped cream, use about 1 tablespoon granu-lated or confection-ers' sugar per cup of cream.

CAKES

> *"Give me the luxuries of life and I will willingly do without the necessities."*
> FRANK LLOYD WRIGHT

One of the most rewarding ways to spend time in the kitchen is to bake a cake from scratch. Of course, the ultimate enjoyment comes later when you share it with family and friends. Whether you choose Lemon Poppy Seed Cake with Lemon Glaze, Spice Layer Cake with Pecan Frosting, or any of the delectable chocolate cakes, a homemade cake is the crowning finish to any meal.

There are classics like Yellow Cake with Fluffy Vanilla Buttercream and low-fat surprises like Frosted Fudge Cake Bars. If you're short on time, try the Banana Cream Cake or the Microwave Maple-Coconut Pecan Cake.

There are layer cakes, poundcakes, cheesecakes, shortcakes, and cake rolls to choose from. You are sure to find the ideal cake for any occasion, whether it's a casual family supper or an elegant gathering for guests.

EASY

Apple Upside-Down Cake, 198
Applesauce Cake with Caramel Glaze, 174
Banana Cream Cake, 210
Banana Poundcake, 196
Blueberry-Spice Coffeecake, 201
Chocolate Cheesecake, 205
Chocolate Espresso Cake, 180
Chocolate Graham Icebox Cake, 214
Chocolate-Almond Cake with Dark Chocolate Glaze, 171
Cornmeal-Honey Shortcakes with Berries, 204
German Crumb Cake, 200
Lemony Cheesecake, 208
Maple-Coconut Pecan Cake, 177
Microwave Cocoa Snack Cake, 172
Microwave Maple-Coconut Pecan Cake, 177
Microwave Peanut Butter Crumble Cake, 176
New York-Style Cheesecake, 206
No-Bake Vanilla Yogurt Cheesecake, 207
One-Bowl Chocolate Cake, 164
Peanut Butter Crumble Cake, 176
Poundcake, 194
Strawberry Shortcakes, 202
Strawberry-Peach Chocolate Chip Shortcakes, 203
Vanilla Buttermilk Bundt Cake, 181

QUICK

Microwave Cocoa Snack Cake, 172
Microwave Maple-Coconut Pecan Cake, 177
Microwave Peanut Butter Crumble Cake, 176

1 HOUR

Chocolate Mousse Roll, 210
Chocolate-Peanut Butter Cupcakes, 193
Lemon Cupcakes, 184
Maple-Coconut Pecan Cake, 177
Peanut Butter Crumble Cake, 176

LOW FAT

Berry Pavlova, 213
Boston Cream Pie, 182

Chocolate Cheesecake, 205
Chocolate Graham Icebox
  Cake, 214
Chocolate-Mocha Cherry Cake, 169
Frosted Fudge Cake Bars, 183
Gingerbread with Citrus
  Sauce, 178
Lemon Cupcakes, 184
Lemony Cheesecake, 208
No-Bake Vanilla Yogurt
  Cheesecake, 207
Orange Chiffon Cake with
  Nectarines, 208

CLASSIC

Apple Streusel Coffeecake, 199
Berry Pavlova, 213
Boston Cream Pie, 182
Carrot Cake, 175
Carrot Cake with Cream Cheese
  Frosting, 175
Chocolate Mousse Roll, 210
Gingerbread with Citrus Sauce, 178
Lemon Poppy Seed Cake with
  Lemon Glaze, 197
New York-Style Cheesecake, 206
Poundcake, 194
Strawberry Shortcakes, 202
Yellow Cake with Chocolate Cream
  Frosting, 167
Yellow Cake with Fluffy Vanilla
  Buttercream, 167

OLD FASHIONED

Apple Streusel Coffeecake, 199
Apple Upside-Down Cake, 198
Applesauce Cake with Caramel
  Glaze, 174
Banana Poundcake, 196
Blueberry-Spice Coffeecake, 201
German Crumb Cake, 200
Gingerbread with Lemon Sauce, 178
Lemon Poppy Seed Cake
  with Lemon Glaze, 197
Poundcake, 194
Sliced Almond
  Cake, 179
Spice Layer Cake
  with Pecan
  Frosting, 168
Triple-Lemon Layer
  Cake, 165
Vanilla Buttermilk Bundt Cake, 181

DECADENT

Chocolate Espresso Cake, 180
Chocolate Mousse Roll, 210
Chocolate-Almond Cake with Dark
  Chocolate Glaze, 171
Chocolate-Peanut Butter
  Cupcakes, 193
Mocha-Hazelnut Roll, 212
New York-Style Cheesecake, 206
One-Bowl Chocolate Cake, 164
Warm Chocolate Soufflé Cake, 173

SPECIAL OCCASION

Carrot Cake, 175
Carrot Cake with Cream Cheese
  Frosting, 175
Chocolate Espresso Cake, 180
Chocolate Mousse Roll, 210
Chocolate-Almond Cake with Dark
  Chocolate Glaze, 171
Chocolate-Mocha Cherry Cake, 169
New York-Style Cheesecake, 206
Spice Layer Cake with Pecan
  Frosting, 168
Triple-Lemon Layer Cake, 165
Yellow Cake with Chocolate Cream
  Frosting, 167
Yellow Cake with Fluffy Vanilla
  Buttercream, 167

SUMMERTIME FAVORITES

Berry Pavlova, 213
Chocolate Graham Icebox Cake, 214
Cornmeal-Honey Shortcakes with
  Berries, 204
No-Bake Vanilla Yogurt
  Cheesecake, 207
Orange Chiffon Cake with
  Nectarines, 208
Strawberry Shortcakes, 202
Strawberry-Peach Chocolate Chip
  Shortcakes, 203

KID APPEAL

Boston Cream Pie, 182
Chocolate Graham Icebox Cake, 214
Chocolate-Peanut Butter
  Cupcakes, 193
Frosted Fudge Cake Bars, 183
Gingerbread with Citrus Sauce, 178
Lemon Cupcakes, 184
Microwave Cocoa Snack Cake, 172
Microwave Peanut Butter Crumble
  Cake, 176
Peanut Butter Crumble Cake, 176
Yellow Cake with Chocolate Cream
  Frosting, 167

ONE-BOWL CHOCOLATE CAKE

Serves 12

Preparation time: 15 minutes plus 4 hours to chill frosting
Baking time: 30 minutes

True to its name, this rich chocolate cake requires only one bowl. The cake batter itself is made in just one step, and with only two ingredients in the frosting, you'll have a great-looking layer cake without much effort. Make the frosting about 4 hours before you plan to ice the cake, so it has time to chill to spreading consistency.

MILK CHOCOLATE FROSTING

3 cups (18 ounces) milk chocolate chips
1½ cups regular or nonfat sour cream,
  softened

CHOCOLATE CAKE

2 cups all-purpose flour
1½ cups granulated sugar
1 cup water
1½ sticks (¾ cup) butter or
  margarine (see page 321), softened
¾ cup unsweetened cocoa powder
3 large eggs, at room temperature
1½ teaspoons vanilla extract
1 teaspoon baking soda
½ teaspoon baking powder
½ teaspoon salt

1. Make the frosting: Melt the chocolate chips in the top of a double boiler set over simmering (not boiling) water, stirring until smooth. Or microwave the chocolate chips in a microwave-safe bowl or glass measure, uncovered, on Medium for 1 to 2 minutes, stirring once. Stir until melted and smooth. Repeat as necessary, microwaving for 20 seconds at a time, then stirring until melted and smooth. Immediately whisk in the sour cream. Scrape into a medium-size metal bowl. Refrigerate, stirring about every 30 minutes, until thick enough to spread (may take up to 4 hours). Makes 3¼ cups.

2. Heat the oven to 350°F. Grease and flour two 9-inch round cake pans.

3. Make the cake: Put all the cake ingredients into a large (mixer) bowl. Beat with an electric mixer on low speed just until blended. Increase the mixer speed to high and beat for 3 minutes, scraping down the sides of bowl and beater a few times. Divide the batter between the prepared pans and spread evenly.

4. Bake until the cakes pull away from the sides of the pans and a toothpick or cake tester inserted near the center comes out clean, 25 to 30 minutes. Cool the cakes in the pans on a wire rack for 10 minutes. Turn the cakes out onto the rack.

COOK'S TIP

Before icing the cake, slip strips of waxed paper underneath the bottom layer all around the edges of the cake. Frost the cake, then remove the waxed paper. This will keep the cake plate clean.

Turn right side up and cool to room temperature. • The cake layers can be wrapped well and refrigerated up to 3 days or frozen up to 3 months.

5. To assemble: Trim the top of the cake layers with a long serrated knife, cutting off any raised areas. Place 1 cake layer on a serving plate. Spread with 1 cup of frosting. Top with second cake layer. Frost the sides and top with the remaining frosting. • The cake can be kept at cool room temperature until serving time; then refrigerated, loosely covered, up to 2 days.

Per serving: 600 cal, 6 g pro, 31 g fat, 75 g car, 380 mg sod, 97 mg chol. With fat-free sour cream and margarine: 560 cal, 7 g pro, 25 g fat, 53 mg chol

OLD FASHIONED

TRIPLE–LEMON LAYER CAKE

Serves 10

Preparation time: 40 minutes plus at least 4 hours to chill

Cooking time: 20 minutes

Baking time: 40 minutes

A tart, tangy cake with luscious lemon filling and lots of creamy frosting all covered with golden toasted coconut. The texture is moist and a bit dense, more like a poundcake than most layer cakes. You may omit the Lemon Filling and use some of the frosting between the layers instead. There's more than enough.

LEMON FILLING

1 cup granulated sugar

2 large eggs, at room temperature

Yolks of 2 large eggs, at room temperature

*Peel of 1 medium lemon, removed as thin as possible
    with a vegetable peeler*

½ cup fresh lemon juice

*½ stick (¼ cup) unsalted butter or
    margarine (see page 321), cut into small pieces*

LEMON CAKE

*Peel of 3 medium lemons, removed as thin as possible
    with a vegetable peeler*

1½ cups granulated sugar

*3 sticks (1½ cups) unsalted butter or
    margarine (see page 321), softened*

1½ teaspoons baking powder

¾ teaspoon salt

1 tablespoon vanilla extract

5 large eggs, at room temperature

2¼ cups all-purpose flour

½ cup plus 1 tablespoon fresh lemon juice

▶

LEMON FROSTING

Peel of 1 medium lemon, removed as thin as possible with a vegetable peeler
⅓ cup granulated sugar
2 packages (8 ounces each) regular cream cheese, softened (do not use fat-free)
2 tablespoons fresh lemon juice
2 cups sweetened flaked coconut, toasted

For garnish: fresh berries

1. Make the filling: In a small heavy saucepan, whisk the sugar, eggs, and egg yolks until well blended. Stir in the lemon peel and juice and butter. Cook, stirring often, over low to medium-low heat for about 10 minutes. As the mixture begins to thicken, stir constantly; cook for 10 minutes more until it thickly coats the back of a metal spoon and reaches 160°F (don't boil or the mixture may curdle). Pour the filling through a strainer set over a small bowl. Lay a sheet of waxed paper or plastic wrap directly on the surface of the filling to prevent a crust from forming; chill for at least 4 hours. The filling will thicken as it cools.

2. Adjust the oven racks to divide the oven into thirds. Heat the oven to 350°F. Lightly grease three 8-inch round cake pans. Line the bottoms with waxed paper cut to fit, and lightly grease the paper. Dust the pans with flour and shake out any excess.

3. Make the cake: In a food processor or blender, process the lemon peel and sugar for 2 to 3 minutes, until the peel is finely ground, scraping down the sides of the bowl when necessary. Transfer the mixture to a large (mixer) bowl. Add the butter, baking powder, salt, and vanilla. Beat with an electric mixer until pale and fluffy. Beat in the eggs one at a time. With the mixer on low speed, beat in the flour alternately with the lemon juice. Pour the batter into the prepared pans, dividing evenly.

4. Stagger the pans on the oven racks. Bake, switching the position of the pans once to ensure even layers, until the tops spring back when gently pressed and a toothpick or cake tester inserted near the center comes out clean, about 40 minutes.

5. Cool the cakes in the pans on wire racks for 20 minutes. Turn the cakes out onto the racks and remove the waxed paper. Turn the cakes right side up and let cool completely. • The cake layers can be wrapped well and refrigerated up to 3 days or frozen up to 3 months.

6. Meanwhile, make the frosting: In a food processor or a blender, process the lemon peel and sugar for 2 to 3 minutes, until the peel is finely ground. In a medium-size (mixer) bowl, beat the cream cheese, lemon juice, and sugar mixture with an electric mixer until smooth (or process in a food processor). Cover with plastic wrap and chill for 1 hour, or until firm but spreadable. Makes 2¼ cups.

7. To assemble: Trim the top of the cake layers with a long serrated knife, cutting off any raised areas. Place 1 cake layer on a serving plate. Spread with half the filling (¾ cup). Top with another cake layer and the remaining filling. Top with the remaining cake layer. Frost the top and sides of the cake. Gently press the toasted coconut on the sides of the cake. Refrigerate until ready to serve. Just before serving, garnish with berries. • The cake can be kept loosely covered and refrigerated up to 2 days.

Per serving with butter: 960 cal, 12 g pro, 62 g fat, 92 g car, 460 mg sod, 340 mg chol.
With margarine: 880 mg sod, 241 mg chol

Cⓞook's Tip

To toast coconut: Spread flaked coconut on a cookie sheet with a rim or glass pie plate. Bake in a 350°F oven for 6 to 8 minutes, stirring once or twice, until lightly browned. Let cool before using.

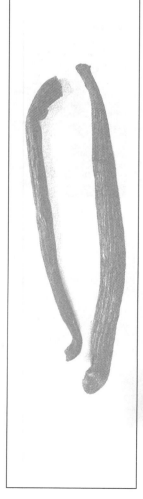

**YELLOW CAKE WITH
CHOCOLATE CREAM
FROSTING**

• Prepare and cool the
cake as directed.
• Make the frosting: Put 2
cups (12 ounces) semi-
sweet chocolate chips into
a large bowl. In a medi-
um-size saucepan, bring 2
cups heavy (whipping)
cream to a boil. Pour the
hot cream over the choco-
late chips. Let stand for 1
minute, then stir until
melted and smooth. Chill
for 2 hours, or until firm
enough to spread. Makes
2½ cups.
• Place 1 cake layer on a
serving plate. Spread ½
cup of the frosting evenly
over the layer. Top with
the remaining cake layer.
Frost the top and sides
with the remaining frost-
ing. Garnish with choco-
late curls (see page 329)
and lightly sprinkle with
confectioners' sugar.
(The cake can be kept at
cool room temperature
until serving time, then
refrigerated loosely cov-
ered up to 2 days.)

Per serving: 680 cal, 8 g
pro, 44 g fat, 69 g car, 210
mg sod, 190 mg chol

• CLASSIC

YELLOW CAKE WITH
FLUFFY VANILLA BUTTERCREAM

Serves 10

Preparation time: 45 minutes plus cooling

Baking time: 30 minutes

All home bakers need this recipe at their fingertips; it's the perfect cake for birth-
days and special celebrations and lends itself to almost any filling and frosting.

YELLOW CAKE

1½ sticks (¾ cup) unsalted butter, softened
1¼ cups granulated sugar
4 large eggs, at room temperature
2 teaspoons vanilla extract
2 teaspoons baking powder
¼ teaspoon salt
2 cups all-purpose flour
¾ cup milk

FLUFFY VANILLA BUTTERCREAM

Whites of 4 large eggs, at room temperature
¾ cup granulated sugar
⅛ teaspoon salt
2½ sticks (1¼ cups) unsalted butter, softened
1 tablespoon vanilla extract

1. Heat the oven to 350°F. Lightly grease two 8- or 9-inch round cake pans. Line
the bottoms with waxed paper, cut to fit.

2. Make the cake: In a large (mixer) bowl, beat the butter and sugar with an electric mixer until pale and fluffy. Beat in the eggs one at a time. Beat in the vanilla,
baking powder, and salt. Add the flour alternately with the milk and beat until
smooth, scraping down the sides of the bowl when necessary.

3. Pour the batter into the prepared pans, dividing evenly. Bake until the cakes
pull away from the sides of the pans and a toothpick or cake tester inserted near the
center comes out clean, 25 to 30 minutes. Cool the cakes in the pans on wire racks
for 10 minutes. Turn the cakes out onto the racks and remove the waxed paper.
Turn the cakes right side up and cool completely. • The cake layers can be wrapped
well and refrigerated up to 3 days, or frozen up to 3 months.

4. Meanwhile, make the buttercream frosting: Put the egg whites, sugar, and salt in the
top of a double boiler. Beat on low speed with an electric hand mixer (or whisk) over
simmering (not boiling) water for 15 minutes. Remove the top of the double boiler.

5. Pour the egg white mixture into a medium-size (mixer) bowl and continue to
beat with an electric mixer until thickened and cooled, about 5 minutes. Beat in
the butter, a little at a time. Beat in the vanilla until blended. Makes about 3 cups. ▶

6. To assemble: Trim the top of the cake layers with a long serrated knife, cutting off any raised areas. Place 1 cake layer on a serving plate. Spread 1 cup of the frosting evenly over the layer. Top with the remaining cake layer. Frost the top and sides with the remaining frosting. • The cake can be kept at cool room temperature until serving time; then refrigerated, loosely covered, up to 2 days.

Per serving: 630 cal, 7 g pro, 40 g fat, 61 g car, 240 mg sod, 187 mg chol

OLD FASHIONED

SPICE LAYER CAKE
WITH PECAN FROSTING

Serves 8

Preparation time: 20 minutes plus cooling

Cooking time: 7 minutes

Baking time: 40 minutes

This cinnamon-and-clove-scented layer cake with an old-fashioned boiled icing will conjure up images of a country kitchen from days gone by.

SPICE CAKE

1 stick (½ cup) unsalted butter or margarine (see page 321), softened
1¼ cups granulated sugar
1 large egg, at room temperature
½ teaspoon vanilla extract
¼ cup unsweetened cocoa powder
1 teaspoon baking soda
½ teaspoon ground cinnamon
½ teaspoon ground cloves
¼ teaspoon salt
1 ½ cups all-purpose flour
1 cup buttermilk

PECAN FROSTING

½ cup heavy (whipping) cream
1 large egg
1 cup granulated sugar
1 teaspoon vanilla extract
1 cup (4 ounces) pecans, finely chopped

1. Heat the oven to 350°F. Lightly grease two 8-inch round cake pans. Line the bottoms with waxed paper, cut to fit, and lightly grease the paper.

2. Make the cake: In a large (mixer) bowl, beat the butter and ¾ cup of the sugar until smooth. Add the egg and beat until pale and fluffy. Beat in the vanilla.

3. In a medium-size (mixer) bowl, mix the remaining ½ cup of sugar, the cocoa, baking soda, cinnamon, cloves, and salt. Add to the egg mixture and beat until blended.

COOK'S TIP

Beating the egg white and sugar mixture for a full 15 minutes over low heat assures that any harmful bacteria in the raw egg is eliminated (see Eggs, page 322).

With the mixer on low speed, beat in the flour alternately with the buttermilk. Pour the batter into the prepared pans, dividing evenly and smoothing the tops.

4. Bake until the cakes pull away from the sides of the pans and a toothpick or cake tester inserted near the center comes out clean, 35 to 40 minutes. Cool the cakes in the pans on a wire rack for 10 minutes. Turn the cakes out onto the rack and remove the waxed paper. Turn the cakes right side up and cool completely. • The cake layers can be wrapped well and refrigerated up to 3 days, or frozen up to 3 months.

5. Meanwhile, make the frosting: In a heavy medium-size saucepan, mix the cream, egg, and sugar. Cook over medium-high heat, stirring constantly, until the mixture comes to a boil. Boil for 2 minutes, stirring constantly, until the mixture thickens. Remove from the heat. Stir in the vanilla and pecans. Let cool completely. Makes about 2 cups.

6. To assemble: Trim the top of the cake layers with a long serrated knife, cutting off any raised areas. Place 1 cake layer on a serving plate. Spread about ¾ cup of frosting evenly over the layer. Top with the remaining cake layer. Frost the top and sides with the remaining frosting. • The cake can be kept at cool room temperature until serving time, then loosely covered and refrigerated up to 2 days.

Per serving with butter: 590 cal, 7 g pro, 29 g fat, 81 g car, 280 mg sod, 106 mg chol. With margarine: 415 mg sod, 75 mg chol

LOW FAT

CHOCOLATE–MOCHA CHERRY CAKE

Serves 12

Preparation time: 30 minutes plus cooling

Cooking time: 10 minutes

Baking time: 30 minutes

This cake will satisfy any chocolate lover's craving with a lot less fat.

CHOCOLATE CAKE

1 cup evaporated (not sweetened condensed) skim milk
¾ cup unsweetened cocoa powder
1 cup unsweetened applesauce
1 tablespoon vanilla extract
2 cups all-purpose flour
1½ cups granulated sugar
½ teaspoon baking powder
½ teaspoon baking soda
½ teaspoon salt
Whites of 4 large eggs, at room temperature

CHERRY FILLING

2 cans (21 ounces each) reduced-calorie cherry-pie filling
1 teaspoon almond extract

▶

COFFEE FROSTING
⅓ cup water
1 tablespoon instant coffee granules
2 cups confectioners' sugar
Whites of 2 large eggs, at room temperature
½ teaspoon cream of tartar
½ teaspoon salt
1 teaspoon vanilla extract

1. Heat the oven to 350°F. Grease three 8-inch round cake pans.

2. Make the cake: In a medium-size saucepan, heat the evaporated milk until barely simmering. Remove the pan from the heat and whisk in the cocoa until thickened and almost smooth (some tiny lumps will remain). Let stand for 2 to 3 minutes to cool slightly. Whisk in the applesauce and vanilla.

3. In a large bowl, mix the flour, 1¼ cups of the granulated sugar, the baking powder, baking soda, and salt.

4. In a medium-size bowl, beat the egg whites with an electric mixer until thick and foamy. Gradually beat in the remaining ¼ cup of granulated sugar until stiff peaks form when the beaters are lifted.

5. Pour the cocoa mixture over the flour. Stir just until blended.

6. With a rubber spatula, stir about ¼ cup of the egg whites into the flour mixture. Gently stir (fold) in the remaining egg whites until no white streaks remain. Pour the batter into the prepared pans, dividing evenly and smoothing the tops.

7. Bake until the edges of the cakes begin to pull away from the sides of the pans and a toothpick or cake tester inserted near the center comes out clean, about 25 to 30 minutes. Cool the cakes in the pans on wire racks for 10 minutes. Turn the cakes out onto the racks. Turn right side up and cool completely. • The cake layers can be wrapped well and refrigerated up to 3 days or frozen up to 3 months.

8. Meanwhile, make the filling: Drain 1 can of cherry-pie filling. Discard the liquid and pour the cherries into a medium-size bowl. Add the cherries and liquid from the second can. Stir in the almond extract. Remove 18 cherries and set aside for decoration.

9. Trim the top of the cake layers with a long serrated knife, cutting off any raised areas. Place 1 cake layer on a serving plate. Top evenly with half the cherry filling. Place a second cake layer over the filling. Top with the remaining cherry filling and the remaining cake layer.

10. Make the frosting: In a small saucepan, stir the water and coffee over low heat until the coffee has dissolved. Stir in the confectioners' sugar. Bring to a gentle boil without stirring.

11. Meanwhile, put the egg whites, cream of tartar, and salt into a large (mixer) bowl. With an electric mixer on high speed, beat in the hot coffee-sugar mixture. Beat until the mixture is light, thick, and fluffy, about 3 to 4 minutes. Beat in the vanilla.

12. As soon as possible, frost the sides and top of the cake. Decorate with the reserved cherries. • The cake can be loosely covered and refrigerated up to 1 day.
Per serving: 380 cal, 7 g pro, 1 g fat, 87 g car, 320 mg sod, 1 mg chol

CAKE PANS
Dull metal pans such as those made from aluminum, are best for baking cakes. They absorb heat quickly and retain it, giving cakes a superior texture and tender crust.

EASY • DECADENT

CHOCOLATE–ALMOND CAKE WITH DARK CHOCOLATE GLAZE

Serves 16
Preparation time: 20 minutes plus cooling
Cooking time: 5 minutes
Baking time: 35 minutes

This cake is best described as dense, rich, and oh-so-delicious. Almonds add a wonderful flavor and texture, but any nuts such as hazelnuts or walnuts can be used. Serve the slices topped with softly whipped cream.

CHOCOLATE–ALMOND CAKE

4 ounces bittersweet or semisweet chocolate, coarsely chopped
2 ounces unsweetened chocolate, coarsely chopped
3 large eggs, yolks and whites separated and at room temperature
¾ cup granulated sugar
1¼ sticks (10 tablespoons) unsalted butter, softened
2 teaspoons vanilla extract
½ cup all-purpose flour
1 cup (4 ounces) blanched almonds, finely ground

DARK CHOCOLATE GLAZE

½ cup heavy (whipping) cream
4 ounces bittersweet or semisweet chocolate, coarsely chopped
For garnish: sliced blanched almonds

1. Heat the oven to 350°F. Grease a 9-inch springform pan.

2. Make the cake: Melt both chocolates in the top of a double boiler set over simmering (not boiling) water, stirring until smooth. Remove the pan from the water and let cool. (Or microwave both chocolates in a microwave-safe bowl or glass measure, uncovered, on High for 1 to 2 minutes. Stir until melted and smooth. Repeat as necessary, microwaving for 20 seconds at a time, then stirring until melted.)

3. In a medium-size (mixer) bowl, beat the egg whites and ¼ cup of the sugar with an electric mixer until soft peaks form when the beaters are lifted.

4. In a large (mixer) bowl, beat the remaining ½ cup of sugar and the butter with an electric mixer (no need to wash beaters) until smooth and fluffy. Beat in the cooled melted chocolate, the egg yolks, and vanilla.

5. With the mixer on low, beat in the flour until blended. Stir in the ground almonds. Stir one-third of the egg whites into the chocolate batter until blended, then gently stir (fold) in the remaining egg whites with a rubber spatula until no streaks of white remain. Spoon the batter into the prepared pan, smoothing the top.

6. Bake until the cake springs back when gently pressed and a toothpick or cake tester inserted near the center comes out clean, 30 to 35 minutes.

7. Cool the cake in the pan on a wire rack for 20 minutes. Remove the ▶

C OOK'S TIP

Use the food processor to make quick work of grinding nuts, but be careful not to overprocess or you will wind up with a thick paste.

sides of the pan, turn the cake out onto the rack, and remove the pan bottom. Let the cake cool completely.

8. Meanwhile, make the glaze: In a small saucepan, heat the cream over medium heat until small bubbles appear around the edges. Remove the pan from the heat, add the chocolate, and stir until melted and smooth. Let cool to room temperature.

9. Place the cake on the rack over a cookie sheet lined with waxed paper. Spoon the glaze over the cake and spread it over the top and sides with a large metal spatula. Let stand until the glaze has set.

10. Remove the cake to a serving plate and garnish with sliced almonds. • The cake can be loosely covered and kept at cool room temperature until serving time, then loosely covered and refrigerated up to 3 days.

Per serving: 290 cal, 5 g pro, 22 g fat, 23 g car, 20 mg sod, 69 mg chol

---

EASY • QUICK

MICROWAVE COCOA SNACK CAKE

Serves 8

Preparation time: 10 minutes

Microwave cooking time: 6 minutes plus 10 minutes to stand

There is no cholesterol and virtually no saturated fat in this moist, light, and tender cake. It is delicious plain or topped with low-fat frozen yogurt.

1½ cups all-purpose flour
1 cup granulated sugar
½ cup unsweetened cocoa powder
1 teaspoon baking soda
½ teaspoon salt
1 cup water
½ cup vegetable oil
2 tablespoons distilled white vinegar or cider vinegar
2 teaspoons vanilla extract

1. In an 8- or 9-inch square microwave-safe baking dish, mix the flour, sugar, cocoa, baking soda, and salt until blended.

2. In a 4-cup measure, mix the water, oil, vinegar, and vanilla. Stir into the flour mixture until well blended.

3. Microwave, uncovered, on High for 6 to 7 minutes, rotating the dish ¼ turn twice (if there isn't a turntable), until a toothpick or cake tester inserted near the center comes out clean.

4. Place the dish on a flat heatproof surface and let stand for 10 minutes (any moist spots on the cake will dry), then place on a wire rack. Serve warm or at room temperature. • The cake can be well wrapped and kept at cool room temperature up to 3 days or refrigerated up to 1 week.

Per serving: 320 cal, 3 g pro, 15 g fat, 46 g car, 300 mg sod, 0 mg chol

DECADENT

WARM CHOCOLATE SOUFFLÉ CAKE

Serves 8

Preparation time: 15 minutes

Baking time: 1 hour

COOK'S TIP

You can make the cake ahead through step 4, freeze it, and bake it without defrosting. If you need your springform pan, remove the frozen cake, wrap it airtight in foil, and freeze for up to 1 month. Unwrap the cake, put it back in the pan, and increase the baking time to 1 hour and 45 minutes.

If you love freshly baked chocolate cakes but have never had much patience for letting them cool, here is the dessert of your dreams. The whole point is to eat this dessert right from the oven, while it is hot and rich. And if you think that sounds indulgent, try topping each serving with coffee ice cream or frozen yogurt: it will melt over the velvety soufflé for a taste, texture, and temperature combination that is indescribable.

½ cup plus 2 tablespoons granulated sugar
1 package (8 ounces) regular or fat-free cream cheese
6 ounces semisweet chocolate, coarsely chopped
½ cup whole or skim evaporated milk
   (not sweetened condensed), or whole milk
4 large eggs, whites and yolks separated
   and at room temperature
2 teaspoons cornstarch

1. Heat the oven to 300°F. Lightly butter an 8-inch springform pan and coat with 2 tablespoons of sugar. Wrap the outside of the pan with foil, molding it around the bottom of the pan to prevent the batter from seeping out.

2. Put the cream cheese and chocolate into a 1- to 1½-quart microwave-safe bowl. Microwave on High for 45 seconds. Stir, then microwave for 45 seconds more. Stir again until the chocolate and cream cheese are melted and blended. Gradually stir in the milk, then the egg yolks (the mixture may look grainy from the tiny lumps of cream cheese).

3. In a large (mixer) bowl, beat the egg whites with an electric mixer until soft peaks form when the beaters are lifted. In a small cup, mix the remaining ½ cup of sugar and the cornstarch. Gradually beat the sugar mixture into the egg whites. Beat for 5 minutes more, or until stiff peaks form when the beaters are lifted.

4. Stir about ⅓ of the beaten egg whites into the chocolate mixture. Gently stir (fold) in the remaining whites with a rubber spatula until no white streaks remain. (Don't overmix or the whites will deflate.) Pour the batter into the prepared pan.

5. Bake until the cake feels equally firm when pressed near the edge and in the center (the top of the cake may crack), about 1 hour. Cool the cake in the pan on a wire rack for 5 minutes. Remove the foil. Run a thin knife around the inside edge of cake to loosen it before removing the pan sides. Cut the cake into wedges and serve right away.

Per serving: 325 cal, 7 g pro, 20 g fat, 32 g car, 140 mg sod, 143 mg chol. With fat-free cream cheese and evaporated skim milk: 240 cal, 9 g pro, 9 g fat, 190 mg sod, 110 mg chol

APPLESAUCE CAKE WITH CARAMEL GLAZE

Serves 8

Preparation time: 20 minutes plus cooling

Cooking time: 7 minutes

Baking time: 1 hour 10 minutes

A tender, moist cake made with unsweetened applesauce: old-time bakers claim it's better the next day. The cake is coated with a caramel glaze that is poured over the cake while it is still warm and quickly broiled until bubbly.

APPLESAUCE CAKE

1½ sticks (¾ cup) unsalted butter or margarine (see page 321), softened

1½ cups granulated sugar

2 large eggs, at room temperature

1¼ cups unsweetened applesauce

½ cup regular or nonfat sour cream

2 teaspoons ground cinnamon

1½ teaspoons baking soda

1 teaspoon ground allspice

½ teaspoon ground cloves

½ teaspoon salt

1¾ cups all-purpose flour

½ cup (2 ounces) chopped walnuts

CARAMEL GLAZE

½ stick (¼ cup) butter or margarine (see page 321)

¼ cup heavy (whipping) cream

½ cup packed dark brown sugar

1. Heat the oven to 350°F. Grease a 9-inch springform pan. Dust with flour and shake out the excess.

2. In a large (mixer) bowl, beat the butter and sugar with an electric mixer until fluffy. Add the eggs one at a time, beating well after each addition. Beat in the applesauce, sour cream, cinnamon, baking soda, allspice, cloves, and salt until blended.

3. Reduce the mixer speed to low and beat in the flour and nuts until blended.

4. Spoon the batter into the prepared pan, smoothing the top. Place the pan on a cookie sheet. Bake the cake until the top springs back when gently pressed and a toothpick or cake tester inserted near the center comes out clean, about 1 hour to 1 hour and 10 minutes. Cool the cake on the baking sheet on a wire rack for 10 minutes. (The cake will pull away from the sides of the pan.)

5. Meanwhile, make the glaze: Put the butter, cream, and brown sugar into a small saucepan. Cook over medium heat, stirring often, until melted and smooth. Remove from the heat.

6. Heat the broiler. Spoon the glaze over the top of the cake, allowing the excess to drip down the sides. Broil the cake 6 inches from the heat source until the glaze is bubbly, about 30 seconds. Cool the cake in the pan on the rack for 15 minutes. Remove the pan sides. Spread over the sides of the cake any glaze that has dripped down. • The cake can be loosely covered and kept at cool room temperature up to 2 days or refrigerated up to 5 days. Bring to room temperature before serving.

Per serving: 640 cal, 6 g pro, 35 g fat, 79 g car, 470 mg sod, 132 mg chol. With margarine and nonfat sour cream: 620 cal, 7 g pro, 32 g fat, 680 mg sod, 63 mg chol

CLASSIC

CARROT CAKE

Serves 24

Preparation time: 20 minutes plus cooling

Baking time: 1 hour

A very moist, super-rich cake that keeps well. A food processor fitted with a shredding disk will make quick work of the carrots—and save your knuckles.

5 large eggs, at room temperature
3 cups granulated sugar
1 cup vegetable oil
1 cup buttermilk or plain low-fat yogurt
1 tablespoon vanilla extract
3 cups all-purpose flour
1 tablespoon baking soda
1 tablespoon ground cinnamon
½ teaspoon salt
3 packed cups shredded carrots (from 1 pound)
1 can (20 ounces) crushed pineapple in unsweetened pineapple juice, undrained
1½ cups (6 ounces) walnut pieces
1½ packed cups sweetened flaked coconut (5 ounces)

1. Heat the oven to 325°F. Grease a 13 x 9-inch baking pan.

2. In a large bowl, whisk the eggs, sugar, oil, buttermilk, and vanilla until blended. Whisk in the flour, baking soda, cinnamon, and salt. Stir in the carrots, pineapple, walnuts, and coconut.

3. Scrape the batter into the prepared pan and smooth the top. Set the pan on a cookie sheet to catch any drips.

4. Bake until the top is dark golden brown and a toothpick or cake tester inserted near the center comes out clean, about 1 hour.

5. Cool the cake in the pan on a wire rack. Cut into 24 squares. • The cake can be well wrapped and kept at cool room temperature or in the refrigerator up to 2 days or frozen up to 3 months.

Per serving: 350 cal, 5 g pro, 17 g fat, 48 g car, 250 mg sod, 45 mg chol

VARIATION

CARROT CAKE WITH CREAM CHEESE FROSTING

• Prepare and cool the cake as directed.
• To make the frosting, in a medium-size mixer bowl, beat 1 package (8 ounces) regular cream cheese (do not use fat-free), 1 stick softened unsalted butter, and 1 teaspoon vanilla extract until blended and smooth. With the mixer on low speed, beat in 4 cups confectioners' sugar until well blended. (The frosting can also made in a food processor.) Makes about 3 cups.
• Spread the frosting over the top of the cake. (The frosted cake can be kept at cool room temperature until ready to serve, then refrigerated loosely covered up to 2 days.)

Per serving: 500 cal, 5 g pro, 24 g fat, 68 g car, 280 mg sod, 65 mg chol.

• CLASSIC

PEANUT BUTTER CRUMBLE CAKE

Serves 9

Preparation time: 10 minutes plus cooling

Baking time: 30 minutes

Here's a cake that is mixed and baked in the same pan, so clean-up is a cinch. The chewy-crumbly peanut butter topping on this cake can't help but please the peanut butter fans in your house. This recipe is also well suited to the microwave (see Variation).

1¾ cups all-purpose flour

½ cup packed light brown sugar

½ cup granulated sugar

½ teaspoon ground cinnamon

1 stick (½ cup) butter or margarine (see page 321), softened

1 teaspoon baking powder

½ teaspoon baking soda

½ teaspoon salt

½ cup raisins

2½ teaspoons grated peeled fresh gingerroot,

*   or 1 tablespoon ground ginger*

¾ cup buttermilk, plain low-fat yogurt,

*   or soured milk*

1 large egg, at room temperature

½ cup chunky peanut butter

1. Heat the oven to 350°F.

2. Put the flour, both sugars, and the cinnamon into an ungreased 8- or 9-inch square baking pan. Stir with a fork to mix well. Add the butter and stir until the mixture resembles coarse crumbs. Set aside ¾ cup of the mixture in a medium-size bowl.

3. Add the baking powder, baking soda, and salt to the mixture in the pan. Stir to blend. Stir in the raisins and ginger. Add the buttermilk and egg and stir until thoroughly blended.

4. Using a rubber spatula, scrape any ingredients clinging to the sides, corners, and bottom of the pan into the batter.

5. Stir the peanut butter into the reserved crumb mixture. Sprinkle over the batter.

6. Bake until a toothpick or cake tester inserted near the center comes out clean, 25 to 30 minutes.

7. Cool the cake in the pan on a wire rack. Serve warm or at room temperature.

• The cake can be kept loosely covered at cool room temperature until serving time, then refrigerated up to 3 days.

Per serving with butter: 390 cal, 8 g pro, 18 g fat, 52 g car, 450 mg sod, 52 mg chol. With margarine: 24 mg chol

VARIATION

MICROWAVE PEANUT BUTTER CRUMBLE CAKE

• Mix the batter in an 8- or 9-inch square microwave-safe baking dish.

• Microwave on High for 6 to 8 minutes, rotating the dish ¼ turn twice (if there isn't a turntable), until a toothpick or cake tester inserted near the center comes out clean. (If using a transparent pan, lift it and check the bottom. The cake should look dry.) There will be a few moist spots on the surface of the cake. These will dry while the cake is cooling.

• Cool the cake in the pan directly on a heatproof surface for about 15 minutes, or until the edges of the cake have pulled slightly away from the sides of the pan.

Per serving with butter: 390 cal, 8 g pro, 18 g fat, 52 g car, 450 mg sod, 52 mg chol. With margarine: 24 mg chol

• EASY • QUICK

OOK'S TIP

To sour milk, put 2 teaspoons lemon juice or vinegar in a glass 1-cup measure. Add milk to the ¾-cup mark. Let stand for 5 minutes.

MICROWAVE MAPLE-COCONUT PECAN CAKE

• Mix the batter in an 8- or 9-inch square microwave-safe baking dish. (Be sure dish is also broiler-proof.)
• Microwave on High for 6 to 8 minutes, rotating the dish ¼ turn twice (if there isn't a turntable), until a toothpick or cake tester inserted near the center comes out clean. (If using a transparent pan, lift it and check the bottom. The cake should look dry.) There will be a few moist spots on the surface of the cake. These will dry while the cake is cooling.
• Cool the cake in the pan directly on a heatproof surface for about 15 minutes, or until the sides of the cake have pulled slightly away from the sides of the pan. Prepare the topping and proceed as directed.

Per serving with butter: 420 cal, 5 g pro, 20 g fat, 58 g car, 350 mg sod, 59 mg chol. With margarine: 49 mg chol

• EASY • QUICK

EASY • 1 HOUR

MAPLE–COCONUT PECAN CAKE
Serves 9
Preparation time: 10 minutes plus cooling
Baking time: 35 minutes

Whether you bake this cake in the oven or microwave, you'll need to finish it under the broiler (it works magic for the topping), so if you microwave, remember to use a pan that is also broiler-safe.

PECAN CAKE
1¾ cups all-purpose flour
¼ cup granulated sugar
1½ teaspoons baking powder
½ teaspoon salt
½ teaspoon baking soda
½ cup (2 ounces) pecans, chopped
¾ cup pure maple syrup or maple-flavored pancake syrup
⅓ cup vegetable oil
⅓ cup milk
2 large eggs, at room temperature

MAPLE-COCONUT TOPPING
3 tablespoons butter or margarine
½ cup pure maple syrup or maple-flavored pancake syrup
2 tablespoons milk
¾ cup sweetened flaked coconut

1. Heat the oven to 350°F.
2. Put the flour, sugar, baking powder, salt, baking soda, and pecans into an ungreased 8- or 9-inch square baking pan. Stir with a fork to mix well. Add the syrup, oil, milk, and eggs. Stir until well blended.
3. Using a rubber spatula, scrape any ingredients clinging to the sides, corners, and bottom of the pan into the batter.
4. Bake until a toothpick or cake tester inserted near the center comes out clean, about 35 minutes.
5. Meanwhile, make the topping: In a small saucepan, melt the butter over medium heat. Remove the pan from the heat. Stir in the syrup, milk, and coconut.
6. Remove the pan from the oven. Heat the broiler.
7. Spoon the topping over the hot cake. Broil 6 to 8 inches from the heat source for 2 to 3 minutes, watching carefully, just until the topping is golden brown.
8. Cool the cake in the pan on a wire rack. • The cake can be loosely covered and kept at cool room temperature until ready to serve, then refrigerated up to 3 days.
Per serving with butter: 420 cal, 5 g pro, 20 g fat, 58 g car, 350 mg sod, 59 mg chol.
With margarine: 49 mg chol

LOW FAT • CLASSIC • OLD FASHIONED

GINGERBREAD WITH CITRUS SAUCE

Serves 9

Preparation time: 15 minutes plus cooling

Cooking time: 4 minutes

Baking time: 1 hour

Serve this classic cake plain, with whipped cream, or with the delicious Citrus Sauce.

GINGERBREAD

1 cup dark molasses

1 cup nonfat sour cream

2 tablespoons butter or margarine (see page 321), melted

¼ cup packed light or dark brown sugar

1 tablespoon ground ginger

1 large egg, at room temperature

1 teaspoon baking soda

1 teaspoon salt

2 cups all-purpose flour

½ cup chopped candied ginger (about 2½ ounces)

CITRUS SAUCE

½ cup granulated sugar

1 teaspoon cornstarch

1 cup water

1 tablespoon butter or margarine

1½ teaspoons freshly grated lemon peel

3 tablespoons fresh lemon juice

2 navel oranges, peel and white pith removed, separated into sections

1. Heat the oven to 325°F. Lightly grease an 8- or 9-inch square baking pan.

2. In a large (mixer) bowl, beat the molasses, sour cream, butter, brown sugar, ground ginger, egg, baking soda, and salt with an electric mixer until blended.

3. With the mixer on low speed, beat in the flour just until blended. Stir in the candied ginger. Pour the batter into the prepared pan.

4. Bake until the cake is firm and a cake tester inserted into the center comes out clean, 50 to 60 minutes. Cool the cake in the pan on a wire rack. • The cake can be well wrapped and kept at cool room temperature or in the refrigerator up to 3 days or frozen up to 3 months.

5. To make the sauce, in a small saucepan mix the sugar and cornstarch. Add the water and stir over medium heat. Boil, stirring constantly, until thickened and translucent, about 1 minute. Remove from heat. Stir in butter or margarine, lemon peel and juice, and the orange sections. Serve warm over squares of warm gingerbread.

Per serving with butter: 360 cal, 5 g pro, 5 g fat, 73 g car, 470 mg sod, 35 mg chol.

With margarine: 24 mg chol

 COOK'S TIP

Dark molasses gives the cake an intense flavor and deep color. Light molasses can be used instead and will result in a less assertive gingerbread. Don't use blackstrap molasses in baking—the flavor is overwhelming and not sufficiently sweet.

OLD FASHIONED

SLICED ALMOND CAKE

Serves 8

Preparation time: 20 minutes plus cooling

Baking time: 35 minutes

This simple and delicious buttermilk cake is soaked with a hot almond-flavored syrup and adorned with sliced almonds that are quickly toasted under the broiler.

> 1 cup all-purpose flour
> ¾ cup plus 2 tablespoons granulated sugar
> ½ teaspoon baking powder
> ½ teaspoon baking soda
> ¼ teaspoon salt
> 1 large egg (cold from the refrigerator)
> ½ cup buttermilk
> ½ teaspoon vanilla extract
> 5 tablespoons plus 1 teaspoon (⅓ cup) butter or
>   margarine (see page 321), melted and cooled to room temperature
> ⅔ cup sliced almonds

HOT ALMOND SYRUP
> ¾ cup granulated sugar
> ⅓ cup water
> ½ teaspoon almond extract

1. Heat the oven to 350°F. Grease a 9-inch springform pan.

2. In a large bowl, mix the flour, ¾ cup plus 2 tablespoons sugar, the baking powder, baking soda, and salt.

3. In a medium-size bowl, whisk the egg, buttermilk, and vanilla until smooth. Whisk in the melted butter. Add to the flour mixture and mix until almost smooth. Pour the batter into the prepared cake pan.

4. Bake until the center of the cake springs back slightly when gently pressed, 30 to 35 minutes. Remove the cake to a rack and, while still hot, sprinkle with the almonds.

5. Meanwhile, make the syrup: About 10 minutes before the cake comes out of the oven, mix the sugar and water in a heavy medium-size saucepan. Bring to a boil over medium-high heat and boil until the mixture reaches 220°F on a candy thermometer. Remove from the heat and stir in the almond extract.

6. Heat the broiler. Pour the hot almond syrup over the cake, letting it soak in. Broil the cake 6 inches from the heat source until the almonds are lightly toasted, about 1 minute. Cool the cake on a rack for 15 minutes. Remove the sides of the pan and cool completely. ● The cake can be well wrapped and kept at cool room temperature or in the refrigerator up to 3 days.

Per serving with butter: 350 cal, 5 g pro, 13 g fat, 55 g car, 280 mg sod, 48 mg chol. With margarine: 27 mg chol

EASY • DECADENT

CHOCOLATE ESPRESSO CAKE

Serves 16

Preparation time: 20 minutes plus cooling

Baking time: 1 hour

This is a fine example of a simple cake that is also elegant. It can be served as is or sliced and topped with whipped cream and fresh raspberries.

6 ounces semisweet chocolate, coarsely chopped

1½ cups packed light brown sugar

1½ sticks (¾ cup) unsalted butter, softened

1¼ cups water

3 tablespoons plus 1 teaspoon instant espresso powder

3 large eggs, at room temperature

2 cups all-purpose flour

1 teaspoon baking soda

¼ teaspoon salt

1 tablespoon confectioners' sugar

1. Heat the oven to 325° F. Generously grease and flour a 10- or 12-cup Bundt or tube pan.

2. Put the chocolate, brown sugar, butter, water, and 3 tablespoons of espresso powder into a medium-size saucepan. Stir over low heat until the chocolate is melted and the mixture is smooth. Remove from the heat and let cool. Beat in the eggs.

3. In a large bowl, mix the flour, baking soda, and salt. Stir in the chocolate mixture and beat until well blended.

4. Pour the batter into the prepared pan and bake until a cake tester inserted into the thickest part comes out clean, 55 to 60 minutes. Cool the cake in the pan on a wire rack for 10 minutes. Turn the cake out onto the rack and cool completely.

5. In a small bowl, mix the remaining 1 teaspoon of espresso powder with the confectioners' sugar. Sprinkle the mixture over the top of the cake. • The cake can be well wrapped and kept at cool room temperature up to 3 days or in the refrigerator up to 5 days, or it can be frozen up to 3 months.

Per serving: 280 cal, 3 g pro, 13 g fat, 40 g car, 140 mg sod, 63 mg chol

C OOK'S TIP

To use a candy thermometer, clip it to the side of the pan with its tip immersed at least 1 inch but not touching the side of the pan.

BUNDT CAKES

These cakes take their name from the pan in which they are baked—a tube pan with fluted sides. It's important to grease Bundt pans generously, because cakes can easily stick in the ridges. Coating the pan with solid vegetable shortening or nonstick vegetable oil cooking spray is one of the easiest ways to do this.

EASY • OLD FASHIONED

VANILLA BUTTERMILK BUNDT CAKE

Serves 16

Preparation time: 15 minutes plus cooling

Baking time: 1 hour

Make this cake once, and you're likely to find yourself making it time and time again. It's moist, tender, and buttery, the perfect cake to just have around.

2½ cups all-purpose flour
1⅔ cups granulated sugar
2½ teaspoons baking powder
¾ teaspoon salt
½ cup buttermilk
⅓ cup milk
3 large eggs, at room temperature
Yolks of 2 large eggs, at room temperature
2 teaspoons vanilla extract
2½ sticks (1¼ cups) butter, softened

1. Heat the oven to 350°F. Generously grease and flour a 10- or 12-cup Bundt pan or tube pan.

2. In a large (mixer) bowl, mix the flour, sugar, baking powder, and salt.

3. In a medium-size (mixer) bowl, beat the buttermilk, milk, eggs, egg yolks, and vanilla with an electric mixer until well blended.

4. Add the butter and half the egg mixture to the flour mixture and beat until well blended. Beat on high speed for 1 minute. Add the remaining egg mixture and beat until well blended.

5. Pour the batter into the prepared pan. Bake until a cake tester inserted into the thickest part comes out clean, 50 to 60 minutes.

6. Cool the cake in the pan on a wire rack for 10 minutes. Turn the cake ▶

CAKE DECORATING 101

• It is easiest to frost and decorate a cake on a serving plate, so you don't have to move it after you've finished.
• To decorate a plain unfrosted cake quickly, place a paper doily on the cake and shake confectioners' sugar or cocoa through a strainer over the top. Carefully lift off doily.

• To make chocolate curls, draw the blade of a vegetable peeler along a room-temperature bar or square of chocolate.
• Most supermarkets carry disposable decorating bags, but if you're caught short, put icing in a clean zipper-lock plastic food bag (without pleats). Seal,

snip off a bottom corner, and squeeze the bag. Or for fancier decorating, snip off the corner and insert a piping tip.
• One cup of frosting is enough for one 8- or 9-inch round or square cake, or one 13 x 9 x 2-inch cake. Two cups will frost and fill one 8- or 9-inch layer cake or 30 cupcakes.

out onto the rack and cool completely. ● The cake can be well wrapped and kept at cool room temperature up to 3 days or in the refrigerator up to 5 days, or it can be frozen up to 3 months.

Per serving: 300 cal, 4 g pro, 16 g fat, 37 g car, 350 mg sod, 106 mg chol

LOW FAT • CLASSIC

BOSTON CREAM PIE

Serves 8

Preparation time: 22 minutes plus 3 hours to chill

Baking time: 35 minutes

Boston cream pie is not really a pie at all, but a white cake with custard filling whose origins date back in early American history. The chocolate icing was added by The Parker House Hotel in Boston, Massachusetts, and that is how it became known as Boston cream pie. Here is a reduced-fat version of this American classic.

CAKE

1⅓ cups all-purpose flour
1½ teaspoons baking powder
¼ teaspoon salt
Whites of 3 large eggs, at room temperature
½ cup granulated sugar
¼ cup extra-light vegetable oil spread,
 at room temperature
⅔ cup skim milk
2 teaspoons vanilla extract

CUSTARD FILLING

1 (4-serving) package instant vanilla-pudding mix
1½ cups skim milk

CHOCOLATE GLAZE

3 tablespoons granulated sugar
2 tablespoons unsweetened cocoa powder
1¼ teaspoons cornstarch
⅓ cup skim milk
½ teaspoon vanilla extract

1. Heat the oven to 350°F. Lightly grease a round 8- or 9-inch x 2-inch cake pan.

2. Make the cake: In a small bowl, mix the flour, baking powder, and salt.

3. In a medium-size (mixer) bowl, beat the egg whites with an electric mixer until frothy. Gradually add ¼ cup of the sugar, and continue beating until stiff peaks form.

4. In a large (mixer) bowl with the same beaters (no need to wash them), beat the remaining ¼ cup sugar with the vegetable oil spread until light and fluffy. With

BEATING EGG WHITES

Eggs beat to slightly greater volume when brought to room temperature. Bowls and beaters must be completely clean, dry, and free of any grease. The tiniest amount will prevent whites from mounding properly. Even small amounts of yolk should be removed. As a precaution, break one egg at a time, and drop the yolk into one container and the white into another before combining with other whites in a cup measure or bowl.

the mixer on low, alternately beat in the flour mixture and milk until smooth. Stir in the vanilla, then ⅓ of the egg white mixture. Gently stir (fold) in the remaining egg whites with a rubber spatula until no white streaks remain.

5. Pour the batter into the prepared pan. Bake until a toothpick or cake tester inserted near the center comes out clean, about 35 minutes.

6. Cool the cake in the pan on a wire rack for 10 minutes. Turn the cake out onto the rack and cool completely. • The cake can be well wrapped and refrigerated up to 3 days or frozen up to 3 months.

7. Meanwhile, make the filling: Prepare the pudding according to the package directions, using the 1½ cups of skim milk. Refrigerate for 30 minutes, or until thickened.

8. Make the glaze: In a small saucepan, mix the sugar, cocoa, and cornstarch. Stir in the milk and bring to a boil over medium heat. Cook for about 1 minute, stirring constantly, until slightly thickened. Stir in the vanilla. Remove the pan from the heat and let cool for 20 minutes in the refrigerator.

9. To assemble: With a serrated knife, cut the cake in half horizontally. Place the bottom layer, cut side up, on a serving plate. Spread the filling over the top. Cover with the remaining cake layer, cut side down. Spread the chocolate glaze over the top, allowing the glaze to drip down the sides. Chill the cake for 3 hours, or until the glaze sets. • The cake can be loosely wrapped and kept in the refrigerator up to 2 days.

Per serving: 260 cal, 6 g pro, 4 g fat, 50 g car, 460 mg sod, 2 mg chol

---

LOW FAT

FROSTED FUDGE CAKE BARS

Serves 12

Preparation time: 25 minutes plus 1 hour to chill

Baking time: 35 minutes

This reduced-fat fudge cake can be cut into bars for a satisfying snack. Or bring it to the table whole as a fudgy sheet cake. Either way, it's a guilt-free treat that will appease your chocolate cravings.

FUDGE CAKE

1⅓ cups all-purpose flour
½ cup unsweetened cocoa powder
Whites of 4 large eggs, at room temperature
¾ cup granulated sugar
¼ cup extra-light vegetable oil spread, softened
1½ teaspoons baking powder
¼ teaspoon salt
⅔ cup skim milk
1 tablespoon vanilla extract

▶

CHOCOLATE FROSTING

3 tablespoons unsweetened cocoa powder

1 tablespoon extra-light vegetable oil spread,
  softened

½ cup confectioners' sugar

1 tablespoon skim milk

¼ teaspoon vanilla extract

1. Heat the oven to 350°F. Lightly grease a 9-inch square baking pan with vegetable oil cooking spray.

2. Make the cake: In a small bowl, mix the flour and cocoa.

3. In a medium-size (mixer) bowl, beat the egg whites with an electric mixer until frothy. Gradually add ¼ cup of the sugar, beating until stiff peaks form when the beaters are lifted.

4. In a large (mixer) bowl with the same beaters (no need to wash), beat the remaining ½ cup of sugar with the vegetable oil spread until light and fluffy. Beat in the baking powder and salt. With the mixer on low, alternately beat in the flour mixture and the milk and vanilla until smooth. Stir in ⅓ of the egg-white mixture. Gently stir (fold) in the remaining egg whites with a rubber spatula until no white streaks remain.

5. Pour the batter into the prepared pan. Bake until the cake springs back when gently pressed and a toothpick or cake tester inserted near the center comes out clean, about 35 minutes.

6. Cool the cake in the pan on a wire rack for 10 minutes. Turn the cake out of the pan, then turn right side up. Let cool completely. • The cake can be well wrapped and refrigerated up to 3 days or frozen up to 3 months.

7. Meanwhile, make the frosting: In a medium-size bowl, beat the cocoa and vegetable oil spread with an electric mixer until smooth. Add the confectioners' sugar, milk, and vanilla and beat until smooth.

8. Put the cake on a serving plate. Spread the frosting over the top. Chill for 1 hour or until the frosting sets. To serve, cut into bars. • The cake can be kept in an airtight container in the refrigerator up to 3 days.

Per serving: 170 cal, 4 g pro, 3 g fat, 32 g car, 190 mg sod, 0 mg chol

LEMON CUPCAKES

Makes 12 cupcakes

Preparation time: 25 minutes

Baking time: 20 minutes

These "cupcakes" are a lemon-lover's temptation. Tangy, moist and dense, they don't look like traditional cupcakes because they are flat on the top; they are also richer than most cupcakes—almost like poundcake. The sweet-tart glaze is very liquid so that it soaks into the cake, leaving just a thin layer on top. ▶ *p. 193*

> ### **C**OOK'S TIP
>
> It's important to beat egg whites until stiff but not dry. Overbeaten egg whites will deflate and begin to liquefy.

This Triple-Lemon Layer Cake (p.165) makes an elegant dessert for any special occasion.

Delicious Chocolate-Mocha Cherry Cake (p.169), below, a contemporary twist on the traditional Black Forest cake, is remarkably low in fat.

Berries in a nest of crisp meringue make up the Berry Pavlova (p.213), right. It can be a showcase for any combination of fresh, sweet berries.

Have your cheesecake anyway you like it. If you're counting calories, choose the No-Bake Vanilla Yogurt Cheesecake (p.207), left; for purists, the New York-Style Cheesecake (p.206), right, will certainly fit the bill; and for chocolate lovers, the Chocolate Cheesecake (p.205), below, will be irresistible.

Whether it's baked from scratch or from a mix, or assembled from ready-made ingredients, a cake is a pleasure to make and a treat to eat.

A Boston Cream Pie (p.182), above, that isn't loaded with fat? You bet. Our guilt-free version has only 4 grams of fat per serving. So go ahead and dig in!

Rich chocolate cake layers with a delicious milk chocolate cream frosting describe the One-Bowl Chocolate Cake (p.164), right. No wonder this old favorite withstands the test of time so well.

If you love banana cream pie, then you're in for a treat with this heavenly no-bake Banana Cream Cake (p.210).

2 large eggs, at room temperature
¼ cup milk
6 tablespoons unsalted butter or margarine (see page 321), melted
  and cooled to room temperature
1 teaspoon vanilla extract
1 cup granulated sugar
1 teaspoon baking powder
¼ teaspoon salt
1 cup all-purpose flour
1 tablespoon freshly grated lemon peel

LEMON GLAZE
1 cup confectioners' sugar
2½ tablespoons fresh lemon juice

COOK'S TIP

One medium lemon will
yield about 3 tablespoons
of juice and 2 to 3
teaspoons of grated peel.

1. Heat the oven to 350°F. Generously grease twelve 2½-inch muffin pan cups or line with paper liners.

2. In a large (mixer) bowl, beat the eggs, milk, butter, and vanilla until well blended. With the mixer on low speed, beat in the sugar, baking powder, salt, and flour just until the batter is smooth. Stir in the lemon peel.

3. Spoon the batter into the prepared muffin pan cups. Bake until the cupcakes are springy to the touch and a toothpick or cake tester inserted into the center comes out clean, about 20 minutes. Cool the cupcakes in the pan on a wire rack.

4. Meanwhile, make the glaze: In a small bowl, mix the confectioners' sugar and lemon juice until well blended. With a thin wooden skewer, poke deep holes all over the surface of the slightly warm cupcakes. Spoon the glaze over each cupcake a little at a time, letting some of it be absorbed before adding more. Let the cupcakes cool completely in the pan before serving. • The cupcakes can be kept in an airtight container at cool room temperature or in the refrigerator up to 3 days or frozen up to 2 weeks.

Per cupcake with butter: 210 cal, 2 g pro, 7 g fat, 35 g car, 100 mg sod, 52 mg chol. With margarine: 170 mg sod, 36 mg chol

1 HOUR • DECADENT

CHOCOLATE–PEANUT BUTTER CUPCAKES

Makes 20 cupcakes
Preparation time: 20 minutes plus cooling
Cooking time: 3 minutes
Baking time: 18 minutes

These cupcakes will remind you of eating a chocolate-peanut butter cup candy. The recipe calls for preparing a box of devil's-food cake mix; be sure that you have the ingredients you need to prepare it.

▶

1 box (1 pound, 2.25 ounces) devil's-food cake mix

PEANUT BUTTER FILLING
1 package (3 ounces) regular or fat-free cream cheese, softened
3 tablespoons creamy peanut butter
1 tablespoon milk
½ teaspoon vanilla extract
1 cup confectioners' sugar

CHOCOLATE GLAZE
½ cup heavy (whipping) cream
4 ounces semisweet chocolate, coarsely chopped

1. Generously grease twenty 2½-inch muffin pan cups. Prepare the cake mix according to the package directions. Pour the batter into the prepared muffin cups and bake as directed.

2. Meanwhile, make the filling: In a medium-size (mixer) bowl, beat the cream cheese, peanut butter, milk, and vanilla with an electric mixer until blended and smooth. Add the sugar and beat until light and fluffy. Set aside.

3. Make the glaze: In a small saucepan, bring the cream to a simmer over medium heat. Reduce the heat to low, add the chocolate, and stir until melted and smooth. Remove from the heat and cool completely.

4. Cool the cupcakes in the pan on a wire rack for 10 minutes. Run a thin knife around the edges of the cupcakes to loosen from the pan. Remove the cupcakes to the rack and cool completely.

5. Insert a small knife into the top of each cupcake and move the tip back and forth slightly to make a small pocket. Spoon the peanut butter mixture into a pastry bag fitted with a small round tip. Insert the tip into the cupcakes from the top and squeeze in about 2 teaspoons of the peanut butter mixture.

6. Spread a thin coating of the chocolate glaze over each filled cupcake and let stand until set. • The cupcakes can be kept in an airtight container at cool room temperature until ready to serve, or refrigerated up to 3 days, or frozen well wrapped up to 1 month.

Per cupcake: 270 cal, 4 g pro, 15 g fat, 31 g car, 240 mg sod, 45 mg chol. With fat-free cream cheese: 260 cal, 14 g fat, 41 mg chol

EASY • CLASSIC • OLD FASHIONED

POUNDCAKE

Serves 12

Preparation time: 15 minutes plus cooling
Baking time: about 1 hour 15 minutes

This is dense, so serve small portions. You may get a lengthwise split down the center of the top. That's characteristic of many poundcakes.

COOK'S TIP

A quick, easy method for pitting fresh cherries: Insert a clean paper clip into the top of a stemmed cherry, twist, and pull up. The pit should pop right out. Cherry stains on fingers can be removed by rubbing with lemon juice.

2 sticks (1 cup) unsalted butter or margarine (see page 321), softened
1½ cups granulated sugar
5 large eggs, at room temperature
1½ teaspoons vanilla extract
½ teaspoon salt
2 cups cake flour (not self-rising), or 1¾ cups all-purpose flour

1. Heat the oven to 325°F. Lightly grease and flour a 9 x 5-inch loaf pan.

2. In a large (mixer) bowl, beat the butter with an electric mixer for about 30 seconds, until smooth. With the mixer on low speed, gradually add the sugar. Increase the mixer speed to high and beat until pale and fluffy.

3. With the mixer still on high, add the eggs one at a time, beating well after each addition. Continue beating, scraping down the sides of the bowl once or twice, until the mixture is smooth and very pale and has increased in volume. Beat in the vanilla and salt. (The mixture will look curdled.)

4. Gently stir (fold) in the flour with a rubber spatula, about ⅓ at a time, until the batter is smooth and no lumps remain.

5. Scrape the batter into the prepared pan and spread evenly. Bake until a toothpick or cake tester inserted near the center comes out clean, 1 hour to 1 hour 15 minutes.

6. Cool the cake in the pan on a wire rack for 20 minutes. Carefully run a thin-bladed knife around the inside edges of the cake to loosen. Turn the cake out onto the rack. Turn it right side up and cool completely. • The cake can be well wrapped and kept at cool room temperature or in the refrigerator up to 1 week or frozen up to 3 months.

Per serving with butter: 330 cal, 5 g pro, 18 g fat, 41 g car, 120 mg sod, 130 mg chol.
With margarine: 300 mg sod, 89 mg chol

POUNDCAKE SAUCES

LEMON-CHERRY SAUCE

◆ In a medium-size saucepan, bring 1 cup water and ½ cup granulated sugar to a boil. Reduce the heat and simmer, uncovered, for 15 minutes or until it forms a very thin syrup (there should be about ⅔ cup).

◆ Stir in 1 pound fresh dark, sweet cherries, rinsed, stemmed, and pitted (3⅔ cups), or one 16-ounce bag individually frozen cherries (4 cups), not thawed, and simmer for 3 to 4 minutes, or until the cherries are hot and, if fresh, not limp. Remove the pan from the heat.

◆ Stir in 1 teaspoon freshly grated lemon peel and 1 tablespoon freshly squeezed lemon juice and cool to room temperature before serving.

◆ The sauce may be refrigerated, covered, up to 5 days.

Makes 2 cups. Per 3 tablespoons: 65 cal, 1 g pro, 15 g car, 0 g fat, 0 mg chol, 0 mg sod

RUM-DATE SAUCE

◆ In a small saucepan, melt ½ stick (¼ cup) butter or margarine over low heat. Stir in ½ cup sugar and ½ cup heavy cream. Bring to a boil, stirring often. Remove the pan from the heat.

◆ Stir in ½ cup finely snipped, pitted dates (snip with scissors dipped in cold water), ¼ cup chopped pecans, 3 tablespoons dark Jamaica rum or fruit juice (pineapple, orange, or apple), and ½ teaspoon vanilla extract and bring to a simmer. Serve hot.

◆ The sauce may be refrigerated, covered, up to 2 weeks. Reheat before serving.

Makes 1½ cups. Per 2 tablespoons with butter: 140 cal, 1 g pro, 15 g car, 10 g fat, 24 mg chol, 7 mg sod. With margarine: 14 mg chol

BANANA POUNDCAKE

Serves 12

Preparation time: 18 minutes

Baking time: about 1 hour 25 minutes

A simple sprinkling of confectioners' sugar is an ideal finishing touch for this moist, flavorful cake. Or serve it topped with vanilla ice cream.

> *2 sticks (1 cup) unsalted butter or*
>   *margarine (see page 321), softened*
> *1½ cups granulated sugar*
> *4 large eggs, at room temperature*
> *1½ medium-size very ripe bananas,*
>   *mashed not too smooth with a fork (¾ cup)*
> *1 teaspoon vanilla extract*
> *1¼ teaspoons baking powder*
> *¼ teaspoon salt*
> *2½ cups cake flour (not self-rising), or*
>   *2 cups plus 3 tablespoons all-purpose flour*
> *½ cup milk*
> *1 tablespoon freshly grated orange peel*

1. Heat the oven to 350°F. Lightly grease and flour a 9 x 5-inch loaf pan.

2. In a large (mixer) bowl, beat the butter with an electric mixer for about 30 seconds, or until smooth.

3. With the mixer on low speed, gradually add the sugar. Increase the mixer speed to high and beat until pale and fluffy.

4. With the mixer still on high speed, add the eggs one at a time, beating well after each addition. Continue beating, scraping down the sides of the bowl once or twice, until the mixture is smooth and very pale and has increased in volume.

5. Beat in the bananas, vanilla, baking powder, and salt. (The mixture will look curdled.)

6. On low speed, alternately beat in the flour and milk, beating well after each addition. Stir in the orange peel.

7. Scrape the batter into the prepared pan and spread evenly. Bake until the cake pulls away slightly from the sides of the pan and a toothpick or cake tester inserted near the center comes out clean, 1 hour 15 minutes to 1 hour 25 minutes. (If the cake starts to brown too much after 1 hour of baking, cover it loosely with foil.)

8. Cool the cake in the pan on a wire rack for 20 minutes. Carefully run a thin-bladed knife around the edges of the cake to loosen. Turn the cake out onto the rack, invert, and cool completely. • The cake can be well wrapped and kept at cool room temperature or in the refrigerator up to 1 week or frozen up to 3 months.

Per serving with butter: 360 cal, 5 g pro, 18 g fat, 48 g car, 120 mg sod, 114 mg chol.
With margarine: 300 mg sod, 72 mg chol

TIPS FOR PERFECT POUNDCAKES

◆ Use very fresh eggs (they should sink when put into a bowl of cold water).

◆ Have all ingredients at room temperature (they'll blend more smoothly).

◆ Stir or fold the flour in gently by hand, not with an electric mixer, to ensure a fine texture.

◆ Bake the cake in the middle of a rack positioned in the center of the oven.

LEMON POPPY SEED CAKE WITH LEMON GLAZE

Serves 12

Preparation time: 18 minutes plus cooling

Baking time: about 1 hour 20 minutes

A cup of confectioners' sugar is all you need to transform lemon juice into a delicious glaze. Pour the glaze over the cake as soon as it comes out of the oven, while the cake is still in the pan. The warm cake absorbs the glaze.

2 sticks (1 cup) unsalted butter or
*   margarine (see page 321), softened*
1½ cups granulated sugar
5 large eggs, at room temperature
½ teaspoon vanilla extract
½ teaspoon salt
¼ cup poppy seeds
4 teaspoons freshly grated lemon peel
2 cups all-purpose flour

LEMON GLAZE
1 cup confectioners' sugar
3 tablespoons fresh lemon juice

1. Heat the oven to 350°F. Lightly grease and flour a 9 x 5-inch loaf pan.

2. In a large (mixer) bowl, beat the butter with an electric mixer for about 30 seconds, or until smooth.

3. With the mixer on low speed, gradually add the sugar. Increase the mixer speed to high and beat until pale and fluffy.

4. With the mixer still on high, add the eggs one at a time, beating well after each addition. Continue beating, scraping down the sides of the bowl twice, until the mixture is smooth and very pale and has increased in volume. Beat in the vanilla and salt, then stir in the poppy seeds and lemon peel.

5. Gently stir (fold) in the flour with a rubber spatula, about ⅓ at a time, until the batter is smooth and no lumps remain.

6. Scrape the batter into the prepared pan and spread evenly. Bake until a cake tester or toothpick inserted near the center comes out clean, 1 hour 15 minutes to 1 hour 20 minutes.

7. Meanwhile, make the glaze: In a small bowl, whisk together the confectioners' sugar and lemon juice until smooth and blended.

8. Set the cake still in its pan on a wire rack. Slowly spoon the glaze over the warm cake (some will pool in the corners of the pan). Cool the cake in the pan on the rack for 45 to 60 minutes, or until the glaze is completely absorbed.

9. Carefully run a thin-bladed knife around the edges of the cake to loosen   ▶

POPPY SEEDS
These tiny, slate-blue seeds from an annual poppy plant have a high oil content, which can make them turn rancid rather quickly. To avoid this, store them airtight in the refrigerator and use them within 6 months.

it from the pan. Turn the cake out onto the rack, then turn right side up. The sides may have moist spots from the glaze, which doesn't indicate an underbaked cake. • The cake can be well wrapped and kept at cool room temperature or in the refrigerator up to 1 week.

Per serving with butter: 400 cal, 6 g pro, 20 g fat, 53 g car, 120 mg sod, 130 mg chol. With margarine: 300 mg sod, 89 mg chol

EASY • OLD FASHIONED

APPLE UPSIDE–DOWN CAKE

Serves 8

Preparation time: 20 minutes plus 30 minutes to cool

Baking time: 45 minutes

Sweet, tart, and spicy, this upside-down cake starts on the stovetop and finishes in the oven, so be sure to use an ovenproof skillet. It's great served warm with a scoop of vanilla ice cream or low-fat frozen yogurt.

> *3 large Granny Smith or Golden Delicious apples*
> *3 tablespoons fresh lemon juice*
> *1 tablespoon apple-pie or pumpkin-pie spice,*
> *   or 1½ teaspoons ground cinnamon and*
> *   ¾ teaspoon each ground allspice and ground ginger*
> *6 tablespoons butter or margarine (see page 321)*
> *½ cup packed light brown sugar*
> *12 maraschino cherries, without stems*
> *1 box (16 ounces) poundcake mix*
> *2 teaspoons freshly grated orange or lemon peel*

1. Heat the oven to 350°F. Have ready a 10-inch cast-iron or other ovenproof skillet.

2. Cut thin slices off the top (stem end) and bottom (blossom end) of each apple. Cut each apple crosswise into 4 thick slices. Cut out the cores.

3. In a medium-size bowl, toss the apples with the lemon juice and spice until evenly coated.

4. In the skillet, melt the butter over medium heat. Remove from the heat and stir in the brown sugar until blended.

5. Place a cherry in the core hole of each apple slice. Arrange 11 slices, overlapping, around the edge of the skillet. Place the remaining slice in the middle.

6. Prepare the cake mix as directed on the package, adding the grated orange peel to the batter. Pour the batter over the apples.

7. Bake until a toothpick or cake tester inserted near the center comes out clean and the top of the cake is golden, about 45 minutes.

8. Cool the cake in the skillet on a wire rack for 30 minutes. Run a knife around the edge of the cake to loosen it from the pan. Turn the cake out onto a serving

COOK'S TIP

A skillet with a wooden or plastic handle can be used in place of an ovenproof pan, but the handle must be double-wrapped in foil to prevent scorching or melting.

plate and serve warm or at room temperature. • The cake can be well wrapped and kept in the refrigerator up to 2 days.

Per serving with butter: 450 cal, 4 g pro, 21 g fat, 63 g car, 340 mg sod, 76 mg chol. With margarine: 350 mg sod, 53 mg chol

CLASSIC • OLD FASHIONED

APPLE STREUSEL COFFEECAKE
Serves 16
Preparation time: 25 minutes plus cooling
Baking time: 1 hour 10 minutes

Rich, tender cake layered with walnut streusel and apples make this coffeecake a classic. Add a cup of hot coffee and the Sunday newspaper for a perfect combination. Unless, of course, you can't wait for Sunday!

STREUSEL TOPPING
1¼ cups packed light brown sugar
¾ cup all-purpose flour
1 stick (½ cup) cold butter or margarine (see page 321),
* cut into small pieces*
2 teaspoons ground cinnamon
1 cup (4 ounces) walnuts, coarsely chopped

COFFEECAKE
1½ sticks (¾ cup) butter or
* margarine (see page 321), softened*
1¼ cups granulated sugar
3 large eggs, at room temperature
1½ teaspoons baking powder
¾ teaspoon baking soda
2 teaspoons vanilla extract
1 container (16 ounces) plain low-fat yogurt, or
* 2 cups buttermilk*
3¼ cups all-purpose flour
2 Granny Smith or Golden Delicious apples,
* peeled, cored, and cut into ½-inch dice*

1. Heat the oven to 350°F. Grease and flour a 13 x 9-inch baking pan.

2. Make the streusel: In a medium-size bowl, stir the brown sugar, flour, butter, and cinnamon with a fork or rub together with your fingertips until the mixture is crumbly and the butter is completely incorporated. Stir in the walnuts.

To make in a food processor: Put the sugar, flour, butter, and cinnamon in a food processor and process with on/off turns until crumbly. Add the nuts and process with on/off turns to blend.

▶

3. Make the cake: In a large (mixer) bowl, beat the butter and sugar with an electric mixer until fluffy, about 2 minutes. Add the eggs one at a time, beating well after each addition. Beat in the baking powder, baking soda, vanilla, and yogurt.

4. With the mixer on low speed, beat in the flour just until blended, scraping down the bowl as necessary.

5. Spoon 3 cups of the batter into the prepared pan and spread evenly. Sprinkle with ¼ cup of the streusel, the apples, then ½ cup of streusel. Spoon on the remaining batter and spread evenly. Sprinkle with the remaining streusel, pressing down lightly so it sticks to the batter.

6. Bake until the top is lightly browned and the cake springs back when gently pressed in the center, 1 hour to 1 hour 10 minutes. Cool the cake in the pan on a wire rack for 15 minutes. Place a cookie sheet over the pan, and holding both, carefully turn upside down. Remove the pan and let stand to cool.

7. To serve, turn the cake right side up onto a serving plate. Serve warm or at room temperature. • The cake can be loosely covered and kept at cool room temperature up to 3 days or well wrapped and frozen up to 1 month.
Per serving with butter: 460 cal, 7 g pro, 20 g fat, 63 g car, 290 mg sod, 80 mg chol. With margarine: 320 mg sod, 42 mg chol

EASY • OLD FASHIONED

GERMAN CRUMB CAKE
Serves 10
Preparation time: 15 minutes plus cooling
Baking time: 50 minutes

Quick to put together, this coffeecake made with walnuts and raisins has a wonderful texture. The spiced crumb mixture is used both in the batter and as a topping. It's the perfect treat for breakfast, brunch, or with a cup of afternoon tea.

2 cups all-purpose flour
1½ cups granulated sugar
¼ teaspoon salt
1 teaspoon ground cinnamon
1 teaspoon grated nutmeg
¼ teaspoon ground allspice
¼ teaspoon ground cloves
1 stick (½ cup) unsalted butter or margarine
  (see page 321), softened
1 cup dark raisins
1 cup chopped walnuts
1 large egg
½ teaspoon vanilla extract
1 teaspoon baking soda
1 cup buttermilk

NUTMEG
For the best flavor and aroma, buy whole nutmeg and grate it yourself. Small nutmeg graters are sold in kitchenware shops. Traditional graters have compartments for storing nutmegs.

1. Heat the oven to 350°F. Grease a 9-inch square baking pan.

2. In a large bowl, mix the flour, sugar, salt, cinnamon, nutmeg, allspice, and cloves. Cut in the butter with a pastry blender until the mixture resembles small peas.

To make in a food processor: Put the flour, sugar, salt, cinnamon, nutmeg, allspice, and cloves in a food processor and process with on/off turns to blend. Add the butter and process with on/off turns until crumbly.

3. Remove 1 cup of the mixture and set aside. Scrape the remaining mixture into a large bowl.

4. Stir the raisins and walnuts into the crumb mixture. In a small bowl, beat the egg with the vanilla. Stir the baking soda into the buttermilk.

5. Add the buttermilk mixture and egg mixture to the crumb mixture and stir until well blended. Pour the batter into the prepared pan and spread evenly.

6. Sprinkle the reserved crumb mixture evenly over the top. Bake until the cake springs back when lightly pressed in the center and a toothpick or cake tester inserted near the center comes out clean, 40 to 50 minutes.

7. Cool the cake in the pan on a wire rack. Cut into squares and serve warm or at room temperature. ● The cake can be well wrapped and kept at cool room temperature up to 3 days, or frozen up to 1 month.

Per serving with butter: 430 cal, 6 g pro, 18 g fat, 64 g car, 220 mg sod, 47 mg chol.
With margarine: 320 mg sod, 22 mg chol

EGG SUBSTITUTES
You can use egg substitutes in any recipe calling for whole eggs, but you're out of luck if it calls for separated eggs.

EASY ● OLD FASHIONED

BLUEBERRY-SPICE COFFEECAKE

Serves 8

Preparation time: 10 minutes plus cooling

Baking time: 55 minutes

If you remember eating a delicious coffeecake, it was probably made with sour cream. Here, sour cream cake is topped with fresh blueberries and a crunchy brown sugar and pecan mixture. Nothing beats it for ease, dependability, and old-fashioned goodness. Keep fresh blueberries unwrapped in the refrigerator in an open basket and they will last up to 1 week. They are high in vitamin C and have plenty of fiber.

TOPPING
½ cup all-purpose flour
½ cup packed light brown sugar
½ teaspoon ground cinnamon
¼ teaspoon grated nutmeg
½ stick (¼ cup) cold butter or margarine (see page 321),
   cut into small pieces
⅓ cup pecans, chopped

▶

CAKE

½ stick (¼ cup) butter or margarine (see page 321), softened

½ cup granulated sugar

1 large egg

½ cup regular or nonfat sour cream

1 teaspoon vanilla extract

1 teaspoon baking powder

¼ teaspoon baking soda

1 cup all-purpose flour

1½ cups (¾ pint) fresh blueberries, picked over and rinsed

1. Heat the oven to 350°F. Lightly grease an 8-inch square baking pan.

2. To make the topping in a food processor: Put the flour, sugar, cinnamon, and nutmeg in a food processor and process with on/off turns to blend. Add the butter and process with on/off turns until crumbly. Add the nuts and process with on/off turns to blend.

To make by hand: In a medium-size bowl, mix the flour, sugar, cinnamon, and nutmeg. Add the butter and cut in with a pastry blender until the mixture resembles coarse crumbs. Stir in the chopped pecans.

3. Make the cake: In a large (mixer) bowl, beat the butter and sugar with an electric mixer until pale and fluffy. Beat in the egg, sour cream, vanilla, baking powder, and baking soda until blended. Stir in the flour until blended.

4. Spread the batter in the prepared pan. Scatter the blueberries over the top, then cover with the topping.

5. Bake until the topping is lightly browned and a toothpick or cake tester inserted near the center of the cake comes out clean, 50 to 55 minutes. Cool the cake in the pan on a wire rack for at least 20 minutes before cutting. Serve slightly warm or at room temperature. ● The cake can be loosely covered and kept at cool room temperature up to 4 days or well wrapped and frozen up to 1 month.

Per serving: 380 cal, 4 g pro, 19 g fat, 50 g car, 240 mg sod, 64 mg chol. With margarine and nonfat sour cream: 355 cal, 15 g fat, 260 mg sod, 27 mg chol

---

EASY • CLASSIC

STRAWBERRY SHORTCAKES

Serves 6

Preparation time: 10 minutes plus 1 hour to stand

Baking time: 15 minutes plus 10 minutes to cool

Most biscuits require cutting fat into flour with a pastry blender or your fingers. Here, the ingredients are simply stirred together with a fork. Then you need only roll out the dough into a log, slice, and bake.

2 pints (1½ pounds) ripe strawberries, rinsed

3 tablespoons granulated sugar, or to taste

COOK'S TIP

These super-easy biscuits taste best if eaten within 6 hours of baking, but if you really want to make the biscuits ahead, cool them completely, then wrap airtight and freeze up to 1 month. Reheat the biscuits on a cookie sheet in a 350°F oven.

VARIATION

STRAWBERRY-PEACH CHOCOLATE CHIP SHORTCAKES

• Add ⅓ cup semisweet mini chocolate chips to the flour mixture in step 3, then prepare the biscuits as directed.
• While the biscuits cool, hull and slice 1 pint (12 ounces) strawberries and thinly slice 2 medium-size ripe peaches (1½ cups). In a medium-size bowl, toss the berries and peaches with 1 tablespoon granulated sugar. Let stand at room temperature for about 20 minutes, stirring once or twice, until juicy.
• Proceed as directed from step 5.

Per serving: 550 cal, 7 g pro, 33 g fat, 60 g car, 460 mg sod, 109 mg chol

• **EASY**

CREAM BISCUITS
2 cups all-purpose flour
¼ cup granulated sugar
1 tablespoon baking powder
½ teaspoon salt
1 cup heavy (whipping) cream

1 cup heavy (whipping) cream
2 teaspoons granulated sugar (optional)

1. Hull and slice the strawberries. Put 1 cup of berries into a medium-size nonreactive bowl. Sprinkle with the 3 tablespoons sugar and mash lightly with a fork until juicy. Gently stir in the remaining berries. Let stand for 1 hour at room temperature. ● The berries can also be refrigerated, covered, up to 12 hours; bring to room temperature before serving.

2. Heat the oven to 400°F. Lightly grease a cookie sheet.

3. Make the biscuits: In a large bowl, mix the flour, sugar, baking powder, and salt. Gradually add the cream, tossing the mixture with a fork until clumps form. Press the clumps into a fairly smooth ball (with a motion similar to kneading, but don't overwork the dough). Shape the dough into a 6-inch log. Cut into 6 even slices and place on the prepared cookie sheet.

4. Bake until the tops and bottoms are light golden brown, about 15 minutes. Remove to a wire rack and cover with a kitchen towel. Cool at least 10 minutes before filling.

5. To serve, in a chilled medium-size bowl, whip the cream and sugar until soft peaks form when the beaters are lifted. With a serrated knife, cut the biscuits in half. Put the bottom halves on serving plates. Spoon about ¼ cup of the berries and juice, then ¼ cup of the whipped cream over each. Replace the tops. Spoon over the remaining whipped cream and berries. Serve right away.

Per serving: 520 cal, 6 g pro, 30 g fat, 57 g car, 460 mg sod, 110 mg chol

PERFECT CAKES

◆ Always, always preheat the oven.
◆ Be sure all ingredients are at room temperature, especially eggs. (If eggs are cold, immerse them in warm water before you crack them.)
◆ To distribute spices and flavorings evenly in a batter, beat them in with the butter and sugar.
◆ To avoid disasters and infinite frustrations, don't experiment with pan sizes. Use what the recipe calls for.

◆ Add nuts to the batter at the last moment and they'll keep their texture.
◆ Batter should fill the pan ½ to ¾ full, depending on the cake.
◆ Bake cakes in the center of the oven on one rack unless directed otherwise. Allow at least 2 inches of space around the sides of the oven for good heat circulation.
◆ Keep freshly baked cakes from sticking to wire cooling racks by

spraying the racks with vegetable oil cooking spray.
◆ If your cake has a "hump," cut it off with a long serrated knife.
◆ To keep cake crumbs from ruining your frosting, spread the cake with a thin layer of frosting, let it set for a few minutes, then frost as usual.
◆ Arrange garnishes on cakes so they'll be in the middle of individual servings after the cake is cut.

EASY

CORNMEAL–HONEY SHORTCAKES WITH BERRIES

Serves 8

Preparation time: 20 minutes plus 1 hour to stand

Baking time: 12 minutes

Cornmeal and honey give these easy-to-make shortcake biscuits a slightly different flavor. They're best used within 8 hours of baking.

1 pint (12 ounces) ripe strawberries, rinsed, hulled, and sliced (2½ cups)

2 tablespoons granulated sugar, or to taste

½ pint (6 ounces) red raspberries, picked over and rinsed (1¼ cups)

½ pint (6 ounces) blueberries, picked over and rinsed (1 cup)

CORNMEAL–HONEY SHORTCAKES

1½ cups all-purpose flour

½ cup yellow cornmeal

2 teaspoons baking powder

½ teaspoon salt

¼ teaspoon baking soda

¾ cup heavy (whipping) cream

¼ cup honey

1 cup heavy (whipping) cream

2 tablespoons granulated sugar

½ teaspoon vanilla extract

1. Heat the oven to 425°F. Have ready an ungreased cookie sheet.

2. In a medium-size bowl, mash ½ cup of the strawberries with the sugar. Stir in the remaining sliced strawberries, the raspberries, and blueberries. Let stand for 1 hour at room temperature. • The berries can be refrigerated, covered, up to 12 hours; bring to room temperature before serving.

3. Meanwhile, make the shortcakes: In a large bowl, mix the flour, cornmeal, baking powder, salt, and baking soda. Mix the cream and honey until well blended. Pour into the flour mixture and stir with a fork just until a soft dough forms. Scrape onto waxed paper or plastic wrap and shape into a 10-inch log. Cut into 8 equal slices and place, evenly spaced, on the cookie sheet.

4. Bake until pale golden brown, 10 to 12 minutes. Remove to a wire rack to cool.

5. To serve, in a chilled medium-size bowl, beat the cream, sugar, and vanilla with an electric mixer until soft peaks form when the beaters are lifted. Cut the biscuits in half. Put the bottom halves on serving plates. Spoon about ⅓ cup of the berries with juice and ¼ cup of the whipped cream on each. Replace the tops. Spoon the remaining berries over the tops. Serve right away.

Per serving: 390 cal, 5 g pro, 20 g fat, 50 g car, 320 mg sod, 71 mg chol

CHOCOLATE CHEESECAKE

Serves 10

Preparation time: 25 minutes plus at least 3 hours to cool and chill

Baking time: 35 minutes

This cocoa-flavored creation is the perfect compromise when cheesecake lovers dine with chocoholics. And absolutely no one will guess that it's low-fat.

CRUST

14 honey-cinnamon graham-cracker squares (2¼ x 2¼ inches)

2 tablespoons granulated sugar

2 tablespoons margarine, melted

FILLING

Whites of 3 large eggs, at room temperature

1 container (15 ounces) reduced-fat or nonfat ricotta cheese

⅓ cup reduced-fat sour cream

¾ cup granulated sugar

¼ cup unsweetened cocoa powder

1 teaspoon vanilla extract

For decoration: vanilla-milk chips

1. Lightly grease the bottom and sides of an 8-inch springform pan.

2. Make the crust: Put the graham crackers into a food processor and process until fine crumbs. Add the sugar and margarine and process with on/off turns just until crumbs are evenly moistened. Press the mixture evenly over the bottom and 1¼ inches up the sides of the prepared pan.

3. Heat the oven to 350°F. Make the filling: Put all the filling ingredients in a food processor or blender and process until thick and smooth, scraping down the sides two or three times, about 2 minutes.

4. Pour the batter into the prepared pan. Bake until the filling is just set (the center will jiggle slightly), 30 to 35 minutes. Turn the oven off but leave the cake in for 5 minutes longer.

5. Cool the cake in the pan on a wire rack for no more than 1 hour. Refrigerate, uncovered, until chilled, then loosely cover and refrigerate at least 2 hours.

6. To serve, run a knife around the cake to loosen it from the sides of the pan. Remove the pan sides. Serve the cake on the pan base, or run a long metal spatula under the bottom crust to loosen it from the pan bottom. With the spatula, carefully ease the cake onto a serving plate. Decorate with a ring of vanilla-milk chips.

• Store the cheesecake well wrapped in the refrigerator up to 3 days, or freeze undecorated up to 3 months.

Per serving: 190 cal, 6 g pro, 6 g fat, 29 g car, 140 mg sod, 13 mg chol. With nonfat ricotta cheese: 9 g pro, 5 g fat, 160 mg sod, 3 mg chol

COOK'S TIP

You can also crush the graham crackers in a plastic bag with a rolling pin or the bottom of a saucepan until the crumbs are fine.

EASY • CLASSIC • DECADENT

NEW YORK–STYLE CHEESECAKE
Serves 12
Preparation time: 10 minutes plus at least 8 hours to chill
Baking time: 1 hour

In New York, "real" cheesecake is dense and super-rich, made with cream cheese, and unadorned. But you'll love this fruit topping, even if it's not strictly authentic. Don't despair if the cake cracks while baking (as cheesecakes often do). The glazed peach and berry topping will cover any flaws. The thick batter may strain the motor on some portable mixers; use a heavy-duty standing mixer if possible.

½ cup graham-cracker crumbs
  (about 7 graham-cracker squares)
1 cup granulated sugar
2 tablespoons cornstarch
5 packages (8 ounces each) cream cheese, softened
2 large eggs, at room temperature
2 teaspoons vanilla extract
½ cup heavy (whipping) cream
2 medium-size ripe peaches, halved, pitted,
  cut into wedges, and wedges cut in half
¾ cup fresh or frozen blueberries,
  thawed if frozen
⅓ cup apricot preserves

1. Heat the oven to 350°F. Grease an 8-inch springform pan. Sprinkle the bottom with the cracker crumbs.

2. In a large (mixer) bowl, mix the granulated sugar and cornstarch. Add the cream cheese and beat with a heavy-duty electric mixer on medium speed until smooth. Beat in the eggs and vanilla until blended. Reduce the mixer speed to low, add the cream, and beat until blended. Pour the batter into the prepared pan and spread smooth.

3. Bake until a toothpick or cake tester inserted near the center comes out clean but the center of the cake is still jiggly, about 1 hour. Cool the cake in the pan on a wire rack for no more than 1 hour. Refrigerate, uncovered, until completely chilled. The cake will set completely as it cools. Loosely cover and refrigerate overnight. • The cheesecake can be well wrapped and refrigerated up to 3 days or frozen up to 3 months.

4. Up to 1 hour before serving, run a knife around the edge of the cake and remove the pan sides. Mound the peaches in a border over the top of the cake and fill the center with the blueberries.

5. In a small saucepan, melt the preserves over low heat, stirring often. Press the preserves through a fine strainer set over a small bowl. Brush the preserves over the fruit.
Per serving: 500 cal, 9 g pro, 38 g fat, 34 g car, 330 mg sod, 153 mg chol

COOK'S TIP
To cut fat by more than 33 grams per serving, use bricks (not tubs) of fat-free cream cheese.

FREEZING CHEESECAKE
To freeze cheesecake, remove from the pan, place on a tray, and freeze until firm. Wrap in plastic, then in foil, and freeze up to 3 months. Thaw in the wrapping in the refrigerator.

NO–BAKE VANILLA YOGURT CHEESECAKE

Serves 8

Preparation time: 20 minutes plus 1 day to drain yogurt and chill

The creamy cheese layer is made of drained low-fat yogurt—significantly lower in fat, cholesterol, and calories than the traditional cream-cheese and sour-cream version. The method of draining yogurt in a strainer layered with cheesecloth or paper towels so it becomes very thick works very well. There are also yogurt drainers available in specialty kitchenware shops.

FILLING

2 containers (32 ounces each) low-fat vanilla yogurt
1 cup confectioners' sugar

CRUST

¾ cup graham-cracker crumbs (about 10½ graham-cracker squares)
1 tablespoon granulated sugar
2 tablespoons butter or margarine, melted

TOPPING

2 medium-size ripe peaches, halved,
  pitted, and thinly sliced
3 tablespoons apricot preserves
½ pint (6 ounces) fresh raspberries,
  picked over and rinsed (1¼ cups)

1. Make the filling: Line a large strainer with three layers of white paper towels. Place the strainer over a large bowl. Scrape the yogurt into the strainer. Cover and refrigerate for at least 24 hours. The yogurt will become very thick.

2. Make the crust: In a medium-size bowl, mix the cracker crumbs and sugar. Add the butter and toss with a fork to moisten evenly. Press the mixture over the bottom of an ungreased 8- or 9-inch springform pan. Cover and refrigerate until firm, at least 1 hour.

3. In a medium-size bowl, mix the drained yogurt and confectioners' sugar. Spoon the filling into the chilled crust. Smooth the surface with a rubber spatula. Cover and chill for at least 2 hours, or overnight if possible. ● The cheesecake can be made up to this point, covered, and refrigerated up to 2 days.

4. To serve, run a knife between the cheesecake and the pan sides to loosen. Remove the pan sides. Leave the cheesecake on the base. Arrange the peach slices over the top in a circle around the edge. Melt the preserves and brush over the peaches. Mound the raspberries in the center.

Per serving: 240 cal, 6 g pro, 6 g fat, 42 g car, 140 mg sod, 11 mg chol.
With margarine: 3 mg chol

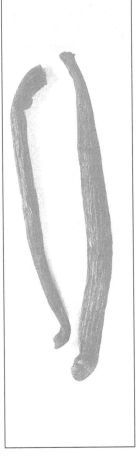

COOK'S TIP

If you have trouble cutting cheesecake, try using dental floss or fishing line. Simply stretch a length across the top of the cake and, holding it taut, bring it down to the bottom of the cake. Let go of one end and pull the floss out with the other. You may want to do this before guests arrive.

LEMONY CHEESECAKE
Serves 8
Preparation time: 10 minutes plus 2 hours to chill
Baking time: 55 minutes

No sacrifices here. The combination of fat-free cream cheese and low- or no-fat condensed milk makes a deliciously rich, creamy cheesecake that's low in fat.

¼ cup graham-cracker crumbs (about 3½ graham-cracker squares)
2 packages (8 ounces each) fat-free cream cheese (in bricks, not tubs)
1 can (14 ounces) nonfat sweetened condensed milk (not evaporated milk)
Whites of 4 large eggs, at room temperature
1 large egg, at room temperature
⅓ cup fresh lemon juice
1 teaspoon vanilla extract
⅓ cup all-purpose flour
1 cup assorted fresh fruit

1. Heat the oven to 300°F. Coat the bottom of an 8-inch springform pan with vegetable oil cooking spray. Sprinkle the graham-cracker crumbs over the bottom of the pan.

2. In a large (mixer) bowl, beat the cream cheese with an electric mixer until fluffy. Gradually beat in the condensed milk until smooth. Beat in the egg whites, whole egg, lemon juice, and vanilla until well blended. Stir in the flour. Pour the batter into the prepared pan.

3. Bake until the center is set, 50 to 55 minutes. Cool the cake in the pan on a wire rack for 30 minutes. Refrigerate, uncovered, until thoroughly chilled, then loosely cover and refrigerate for at least 2 hours.

4. To serve, run a knife around the cake to loosen it from the sides of the pan. Remove the pan sides. Cut the cake into wedges and serve with fresh fruit. • Store the cheesecake well wrapped in the refrigerator up to 3 days or freeze up to 3 months.
Per serving: 260 cal, 15 g pro, 1 g fat, 45 g car, 380 mg sod, 36 mg chol

CHEESECAKE TIPS
◆ If your cheesecakes always crack, try this: Before heating the oven, place a baking pan half-filled with hot tap water on the bottom rack. Bake the cake on the middle rack above the pan and don't peek.
◆ Cheesecake is done when the edges are slightly puffed and an area the size of a silver dollar in the center is moist and soft. The center will firm as the cake cools.

ORANGE CHIFFON CAKE WITH NECTARINES
Serves 8
Preparation time: 20 minutes plus cooling
Baking time: 40 minutes

This easy way to decorate a cake is low-cost and low-calorie too: Cut strips of waxed paper and lay them across the cake. Sift confectioners' sugar or cocoa between the strips, then lift them off.

3 large eggs, whites and yolks separated
and at room temperature
¾ cup granulated sugar
1 cup all-purpose flour
1½ teaspoons baking powder
½ teaspoon salt
¼ cup vegetable oil
1 teaspoon freshly grated orange peel
¼ cup fresh orange juice
2 tablespoons water
¼ cup strawberry jelly

TOPPING
3 medium-size ripe nectarines (about 1 pound),
halved, pitted, and sliced into ½-inch wedges
1 tablespoon confectioners' sugar

1. Heat the oven to 325°F. Lightly grease an 8-inch round cake pan. Line the bottom with waxed paper, cut to fit.

2. Make the cake: In a large (mixer) bowl, beat the egg whites with an electric mixer until foamy. Add ¼ cup of the sugar and beat until stiff peaks form when the beaters are lifted.

3. In another large (mixer) bowl, mix the flour, the remaining ½ cup of sugar, the baking powder, and salt. Add the oil, orange peel, orange juice, water, and egg yolks. Beat with an electric mixer on medium speed (no need to clean the beaters) until blended and smooth.

4. Stir ¼ of the beaten egg whites into the flour mixture. Gently stir (fold) in the remaining whites with a rubber spatula just until no white streaks remain.

5. Pour the batter into the prepared pan and spread evenly. Bake until a toothpick or cake tester inserted near the center comes out clean, 35 to 40 minutes. Cool the cake in the pan on a wire rack for 10 minutes. Turn the cake out onto the rack and remove the waxed paper. Turn the cake right side up and cool completely. • The cake may be well wrapped and frozen up to 3 months. Thaw before assembling.

6. To assemble: Using a long serrated knife, slice the cake in half horizontally to form 2 layers. Lift off the top layer and set aside.

7. Put the jelly into a small bowl and stir with a fork until syrupy. Brush or spread 3 tablespoons of the jelly over the bottom cake layer. Reserve 10 of the most attractive nectarine slices and arrange the rest over the jelly. Cover with the top layer of cake.

8. To decorate: Cut 3 strips of waxed paper, each 1 inch wide and 10 inches long. Place 1 inch apart on top of the cake. Put confectioners' sugar in a small strainer and sift over the top of the cake. Gently lift off the paper. Brush the remaining jelly between the bands of sugar.

9. Just before serving, place the reserved nectarine slices in rows on the bands of jelly. Serve right away.

Per serving: 280 cal, 5 g pro, 9 g fat, 46 g car, 260 mg sod, 80 mg chol

EASY

BANANA CREAM CAKE

Serves 8

Preparation time: 30 minutes plus 3 hours to chill

Cooking time: 5 minutes

This fast, make-ahead dessert will fool your guests into thinking you spent all day in the kitchen. Fill and frost the cake up to 8 hours ahead. Top with sliced bananas and coconut just before serving.

BANANA FILLING
1 (4-serving) package vanilla-pudding mix
1½ cups milk
4 small bananas (about 1 pound), thinly sliced (2½ cups)

1 (8- to 9-inch) purchased sponge-cake layer
1½ cups heavy (whipping) cream
¼ cup confectioners' sugar
For garnish: sliced bananas, toasted coconut (see page 326)

1. Make the filling: Cook the pudding according to package directions, using the 1½ cups milk. Remove the pan from the heat and cool slightly. Cover the pudding with plastic wrap laid directly on the surface to keep a skin from forming. Refrigerate until cool, then stir in the bananas.

2. To assemble: Using a long serrated knife, cut the cake horizontally into 3 even layers. Place 1 layer on a serving plate and spread with about 1½ cups of filling. Top with the second cake layer, spread with the remaining filling, then cover with the remaining cake layer.

3. In a medium-size (mixer) bowl, beat the cream and sugar with an electric mixer until stiff peaks form when the beaters are lifted. Spread the whipped cream over the top and sides of the cake.

4. Just before serving, slice the banana over the top of the cake and sprinkle with toasted coconut. Serve right away.

Per serving: 370 cal, 5 g pro, 20 g fat, 44 g car, 180 mg sod, 112 mg chol

1 HOUR • CLASSIC • DECADENT

CHOCOLATE MOUSSE ROLL

Serves 8

Preparation time: 35 minutes

Baking time: 10 minutes

This elegant dessert is a variation of the old-fashioned jelly roll, but instead of jelly, it's filled with an easy-to-make light chocolate mousse.

COCOA CAKE
⅔ cup all-purpose flour
¼ cup plus 2 tablespoons unsweetened cocoa powder
¾ teaspoon baking powder
Whites of 3 large eggs, at room temperature
2 large eggs, at room temperature
⅔ cup granulated sugar

MOUSSE FILLING
1 cup heavy (whipping) cream
½ cup confectioners' sugar
¼ cup unsweetened cocoa powder

For garnish: ¼ cup vanilla-milk chips, strawberries

1. Heat the oven to 375°F. Grease the bottom and sides of a 15½ x 10½-inch jelly roll pan. Line the bottom with waxed paper, cut to fit. Lightly grease the paper.

2. Make the cake: On a sheet of waxed paper, mix the flour, ¼ cup of the cocoa, and the baking powder.

3. In a large (mixer) bowl, beat the egg whites, whole eggs, and sugar with an electric mixer on high speed for 8 to 10 minutes, until thick and tripled in volume. Sprinkle the flour mixture over the top. Stir gently (fold) with a rubber spatula just until blended. Spread the mixture evenly in the prepared pan.

4. Bake until the cake springs back when lightly pressed in the center, about 10 minutes. Cool the cake in the pan on a wire rack for 10 minutes. Meanwhile, spread a clean kitchen towel (cotton or woven linen) on a countertop. Using a small strainer, sift the remaining 2 tablespoons of cocoa over the towel, covering an area the size of the cake.

5. Turn the cake in the pan onto the towel. Remove the pan and peel off the waxed paper. Starting at a narrow end, roll up the cake and the towel. Cool the rolled cake completely on a wire rack. ● The cake can be wrapped in plastic and refrigerated up to 1 week.

6. Meanwhile, make the filling: In a large (mixer) bowl, beat the cream, confectioners' sugar, and cocoa with an electric mixer until stiff peaks form when the beaters are lifted.

7. Gently unroll the cake and the towel. Spread the mousse filling over the cake to within 1 inch of all the edges. Reroll the cake gently without the towel, starting at the same end as before. Transfer the filled cake, seam side down, to a serving platter. ● The cake roll can be covered and refrigerated undecorated up to 1 day.

8. Up to 8 hours before serving, put the vanilla chips in a small saucepan and stir over very low heat until melted. (Or microwave in a small microwave-safe bowl, uncovered, on medium for 30 seconds to 1 minute. Stir until melted and smooth.) Scrape into a sandwich-size plastic food storage bag (without pleats). Snip off a small corner and drizzle over the cake. Refrigerate until ready to serve. Garnish with strawberries just before serving.

Per serving: 280 cal, 6 g pro, 13 g fat, 37 g car, 100 mg sod, 94 mg chol

---

COOK'S TIP

The success of a cake roll depends on many things, but it is essential that the cake still be warm when it is first rolled.

MOCHA–HAZELNUT ROLL

Serves 10

Preparation time: 30 minutes plus cooling

Baking time: 20 minutes

The many steps of making a cake roll are drastically reduced with this streamlined recipe. The cake bakes right on top of the filling, which is then rolled up inside.

HAZELNUT FILLING

1½ bricks (12 ounces) light cream cheese (Neufchâtel), softened

½ cup granulated sugar

1 large egg, at room temperature

3 tablespoons hazelnut liqueur or milk

1 cup (4 ounces) hazelnuts, toasted, skinned, and finely ground
  (see page 325)

MOCHA CAKE

⅔ cup all-purpose flour

¼ cup unsweetened cocoa powder

½ teaspoon baking powder

4 large eggs, at room temperature

1 tablespoon instant coffee granules

¾ cup granulated sugar

1 teaspoon vanilla extract

For garnish: hazelnuts, chocolate leaves, whipped cream

1. Heat the oven to 375°F. Lightly grease a 15½ x 10½-inch jelly roll pan. Line the bottom with waxed paper, cut to fit, and lightly grease the paper.

2. Make the filling: In a medium-size (mixer) bowl, beat the cream cheese and sugar with an electric mixer until smooth. Beat in the egg and liqueur until blended. Stir in the hazelnuts. Spread the filling evenly in the prepared pan.

3. Make the cake: In a small bowl, mix the flour, 2 tablespoons of the cocoa, and the baking powder. Put the eggs and coffee granules into a large (mixer) bowl. Beat with an electric mixer on high speed, gradually adding the sugar, for 8 to 10 minutes, until thick and at least doubled in volume. Beat in the vanilla. Sprinkle the flour mixture over the top. Gently stir (fold) with a rubber spatula just until blended. Spread the batter evenly over the filling in the pan.

4. Bake until the cake springs back when lightly pressed in the center, about 20 minutes. Cool the cake in the pan on a wire rack for 10 minutes. Meanwhile, spread a clean kitchen towel (cotton or woven linen) on a countertop. Sift the remaining 2 tablespoons of cocoa through a small strainer over the towel, covering an area the size of the cake.

5. Turn the warm cake out onto the towel. Remove the pan and carefully peel off

COOK'S TIP

To make chocolate leaves: Wash, rinse, and dry rose or lemon leaves (from florist). Melt ⅓ cup semisweet chocolate chips. Brush a generous layer on the undersides of the leaves. Arrange on a waxed-paper-lined cookie sheet and refrigerate until the chocolate sets. Gently but quickly peel off the leaves. Store the chocolate leaves in a cool place with waxed paper between layers.

the paper. Starting at a narrow end, neatly roll up the cake, using the towel as a guide. Cool the cake completely on a wire rack. • The cake can be well wrapped and refrigerated up to 1 week.

6. To serve, arrange nuts and chocolate leaves on the roll. Top each serving with a spoonful of whipped cream.

Per serving: 330 cal, 9 g pro, 15 g fat, 38 g car, 220 mg sod, 122 mg chol

---

LOW FAT • CLASSIC

BERRY PAVLOVA

Serves 8

Preparation time: 15 minutes plus at least 3 hours to cool

Baking time: 2½ hours

This dessert was created in Australia in honor of the great Russian ballerina Anna Pavlova. Choose a dry day to make the meringue since it tends to absorb moisture from the air, which makes it soggy.

MERINGUE
Whites of 4 large eggs, at room temperature
¼ teaspoon cream of tartar
2½ teaspoons cornstarch
¾ cup superfine granulated sugar (not confectioners')
½ teaspoon vanilla extract

1½ cups regular, reduced-fat, or nonfat sour cream
1 pint (12 ounces) small ripe strawberries, rinsed and hulled if desired (2 cups)
½ pint (6 ounces) fresh raspberries, picked over and rinsed (1¼ cups)
½ pint (6 ounces) fresh blueberries, picked over and rinsed (1 cup)

For garnish: additional fresh berries

1. Heat the oven to 250°F. Cover a cookie sheet with waxed paper. Draw an 8-inch circle on the waxed paper or use a meringue pattern (see How to Make a Meringue Pattern).

2. Make the meringue: In a large bowl, beat the egg whites with an electric mixer until frothy. Add the cream of tartar and continue beating until soft peaks form when the beaters are lifted.

3. Stir the cornstarch into the sugar. Very gradually add the sugar mixture to the egg whites, beating until stiff and glossy peaks form when the beaters are lifted. Beat in the vanilla until blended.

4. Spread the meringue with the back of a spoon over the outlined circle to cover, building up the edge to form a rim about 2 inches high and 2 inches wide.

5. Bake until the meringue is firm and dry to the touch but not browned, 2 to 2½ hours. Turn off the oven. Prop the door open with the handle of a wooden spoon ▶

HOW TO MAKE A MERINGUE PATTERN
Use an 8-inch salad plate or cake pan to draw a circle on plain paper. Slip the paper between the waxed paper and the cookie sheet to use as a guide in spreading the meringue. Put dots of meringue under each of the corners of waxed paper to keep it from slipping. Remove the paper with the outline before baking. Save the pattern for the next time you make Pavlova.

and let the meringue cool completely, at least 3 hours. • The meringue can be kept loosely covered at room temperature up to 3 days or frozen airtight up to 2 months.

6. Carefully peel off the waxed paper. Transfer the meringue to a serving plate. Fill the center with the sour cream. In a medium-size bowl, gently mix the strawberries, raspberries, and blueberries and spoon over the sour cream. Garnish with additional berries. Serve right away.

Per serving: 210 cal, 4 g pro, 9 g fat, 30 g car, 50 mg sod, 19 mg chol. With nonfat sour cream: 150 cal, 5 g pro, 0 g fat, 0 mg chol

CHOCOLATE GRAHAM ICEBOX CAKE

Serves 12

Preparation time: 20 minutes plus at least 7 hours to chill

This simple treat is just layers of graham crackers and cocoa-flavored whipped topping.

FILLING

½ cup unsweetened cocoa powder
¼ cup granulated sugar
¼ cup water
1 teaspoon vanilla extract
1 container (12 ounces) frozen light nondairy whipped topping, thawed

18 whole honey-cinnamon graham crackers (5 x 2½ inches each)
For decoration: 2 tablespoons each confectioners' sugar and unsweetened cocoa powder

1. In a large bowl, whisk the cocoa, sugar, water, and vanilla until blended and smooth. Stir in a large spoonful of the whipped topping, then gently stir (fold) in the remaining whipped topping with a rubber spatula until blended.

2. Line a small cookie sheet with waxed paper. Arrange 3 graham crackers side by side (long sides touching) in the middle of the cookie sheet. Spread a heaping ½ cup of the filling evenly to the edges. Repeat with 5 more layers of crackers and filling. Spread the sides with the remaining filling.

3. Refrigerate for 3 hours, or until the cake is soft enough to insert a toothpick into each corner. Carefully cover with plastic (the toothpicks will keep the plastic from sticking to the cake). Refrigerate for at least 4 more hours or up to 12 hours.

4. Using 2 spatulas, transfer the cake to a serving plate.

5. To decorate: Cut 3 strips of waxed paper each 12 inches long and 1½ inches wide. Lay the strips diagonally on the cake, leaving 1-inch spaces between the strips. Sift the confectioners' sugar between the strips. Carefully lift the paper. Repeat by "crisscrossing" the strips in the opposite direction (over the confectioners' sugar), clean side down. Sift the cocoa powder between the strips. Lift the paper.

6. To serve, slice the cake with a serrated knife.

Per serving: 190 cal, 2 g pro, 6 g fat, 30 g car, 130 mg sod, 0 mg chol

COOK'S TIP

Superfine granulated sugar is perfect for making meringues because it dissolves almost instantly. To make your own superfine sugar, simply process regular granulated sugar in a food processor until powdery.

REVEREND GRAHAM

The graham cracker is named after the Reverend Sylvester Graham, a persistent advocate of nutrition and healthy baking using whole-wheat flour containing the bran of the wheat kernel (also known as "graham flour" after him). He began his crusade in 1830 and attracted many followers. But it wasn't until 1882 that a flat, slightly sweet cookie made with the flour and called the graham cracker became known.

FRUIT
DESSERTS

> *"All millionaires love a baked apple."*
> RONALD FIRBANK

Fruits and berries were humankind's first sweets, and they are still the basis for some of our favorite desserts. Fruit is also the most tempting resource when it comes to making low-fat desserts. In the summertime when fruits and berries are at their peak, all they need is a simple sauce or topping to transform them. Tropical Fruit Salad, Raspberries with Amaretti Cream, Gingered Plums and Mango, and Fruit Melba all testify to that.

In the fall, nothing compares to the homespun quality of baked fruit desserts like Orange-Glazed Baked Apples and Pear Granola Crisp. For the colder months, Dried Fruit Compote is easy to make, warm, and nourishing.

From fresh and macerated to cooked and baked, fruits and berries offer the dessert cook seasonal variety, incomparable taste, vibrant colors, and wholesome goodness.

EASY

Apples with Custard Sauce, 236
Chilled Pineapple-Mango Soup, 235
Cranberry-Raspberry-Orange
  Gelatin, 233
Dried Fruit Compote, 231
Fragrant Fruit with Raspberry
  Sherbet, 222
Fruit Melba, 234
Gingered Plums and Mango, 222
Melon and Berries with
  Strawberry Sauce, 221
Melon Compote, 230
Nectarines in Wine, 229
Nectarines with Rum Cream, 218
Peach Passion, 219
Pineapple-Poached Pears, 234
Plum and Walnut Compote, 229
Raspberries with Amaretti
  Cream, 220
Strawberries Brûlé, 236
Strawberries-and-Cream Gelatin, 232
Strawberry Shortcake Parfaits, 232
Summer Fruit with Brown Sugar
  Cream, 221
Watermelon-Berry Cassis, 219

QUICK

Fruit Melba, 234
Melon and Berries with
  Strawberry Sauce, 221
Pineapple-Poached Pears, 234
Plum and Walnut Compote, 229
Raspberries with Amaretti
  Cream, 220
Strawberries Brûlé, 236
Strawberry Shortcake Parfaits, 232
Summer Fruit with Brown Sugar
  Cream, 221
Watermelon-Berry Cassis, 219

1 HOUR

Apple Walnut Crisp, 244
Apples with Custard Sauce, 236
Blueberry-Plum Crisp, 245
Dried Fruit Compote, 231
Layered Fresh Fruit with Raspberry
  Sauce, 230
Melon Compote, 230
Nectarine Crisp, 242
Orange-Glazed Baked Apples, 237
Pear Granola Crisp, 244

Plum Oatmeal Crumble, 242
Tropical Fruit Salad, 223

LOW FAT

Ambrosia, 218
Apple Brown Betty, 238
Apples with Custard Sauce, 236
Chilled Pineapple-Mango Soup, 235
Cranberry-Raspberry-Orange
   Gelatin, 233
Dried Fruit Compote, 231
Fragrant Fruit with Raspberry
   Sherbet, 222
Fresh Fruit Terrine, 224
Fruit Melba, 234
Gingered Plums and
   Mango, 222
Layered Fresh Fruit with Raspberry
   Sauce, 230
Melon and Berries with Strawberry
   Sauce, 221
Melon Compote, 230
Nectarines in Wine, 229
Nectarines with Rum Cream, 218
Orange-Glazed Baked Apples, 237
Peach-Blueberry Cobbler, 239
Peach Cobbler, 239
Peach Passion, 219
Pear Granola Crisp, 244
Pineapple-Poached Pears, 234
Plum and Walnut Compote, 229
Plum Oatmeal Crumble, 242
Strawberries Brûlé, 236
Strawberries-and-Cream
   Gelatin, 232
Summer Fruit with Brown Sugar
   Cream, 221
Tropical Fruit Salad, 223
Watermelon-Berry Cassis, 219

CLASSIC

Ambrosia, 218
Apple Brown Betty, 238
Apple Walnut Crisp, 244
Blueberry-Plum Crisp, 245
Nectarine Crisp, 242
Peach-Blueberry Cobbler, 239
Peach Cobbler, 239

OLD FASHIONED

Ambrosia, 218
Apple Brown Betty, 238
Apple Walnut Crisp, 244
Blueberry-Plum Crisp, 245
Cherry-Pear Cobbler, 240
Dried Fruit Compote, 231
Nectarine Crisp, 242
Orange-Glazed Baked Apples, 237
Peach-Blueberry Cobbler, 239
Peach Cobbler, 239
Pear Granola Crisp, 244
Pineapple-Macadamia Cobbler, 241
Plum Oatmeal Crumble, 242

FALL FAVORITES

Apple Brown Betty, 238
Apple Walnut Crisp, 244
Apples with Custard Sauce, 238
Cherry-Pear Cobbler, 240

Dried Fruit Compote, 231
Orange-Glazed Baked Apples, 237
Pear Granola Crisp, 244
Pineapple-Poached Pears, 234

CROWD PLEASERS

Ambrosia, 218
Fresh Fruit Terrine, 224
Nectarine Crisp, 242
Strawberries-and-Cream Gelatin, 232
Tropical Fruit Salad, 223

BERRIED TREASURES

Blueberry-Plum Crisp, 245
Melon and Berries with Strawberry
   Sauce, 221
Peach-Blueberry Cobbler, 239
Raspberries with Amaretti
   Cream, 220
Strawberry Shortcake Parfaits, 232
Watermelon-Berry Cassis, 219

NECTARINES WITH RUM CREAM

Serves 8

Preparation time: 20 minutes plus at least 2 hours to chill

Ricotta cheese, sugar, and rum make a delectable topping for sliced ripe nectarines. Served over slices of poundcake, this is an easy and elegant dessert for guests.

RUM CREAM
1 container (15 ounces) part-skim ricotta cheese
⅓ cup confectioners' sugar
3 tablespoons dark rum, or ½ teaspoon rum extract

6 large ripe nectarines (about 2¼ pounds), halved, pitted, and sliced (6 cups)
2 tablespoons granulated sugar
1 tablespoon fresh lemon juice
8 (½-inch-thick) slices fat-free chocolate-chip poundcake
  (from a 15-ounce loaf)

For garnish: semisweet chocolate shavings (see page 329)

1. Make the rum cream: In a blender, purée the ricotta until smooth. (You can use a food processor but the ricotta won't be as smooth.) Add the confectioners' sugar and rum and process until well blended. Pour into a small bowl, cover, and refrigerate for at least 2 hours to allow the ricotta to thicken and the flavor to mellow. • The rum cream can be covered and refrigerated up to 5 days.

2. Put the nectarines into a medium-size glass bowl. Sprinkle with the granulated sugar and lemon juice and stir gently to coat. Cover and let stand at room temperature until the juices are released, about 1 hour. • The fruit can be covered and refrigerated up to 1 day.

3. To serve, put a slice of cake on each dessert plate. Top with nectarines and juices from the bowl, and some rum cream. Garnish with shaved semisweet chocolate.

Per serving: 240 cal, 9 g pro, 5 g fat, 41 g car, 180 mg sod, 16 mg chol

---

LOW FAT • CLASSIC • OLD FASHIONED

AMBROSIA

Serves 12

Preparation time: 30 minutes plus at least 4 hours to chill

Coconut is the key ingredient in ambrosia, an American fruit dessert that was first enjoyed in the South during the nineteenth century. Packaged flaked coconut works well, but for optimum flavor, try using fresh coconut.

ORANGES AND GRAPEFRUIT

Choose oranges not for color but for feel. Pick firm, heavy ones with smooth skins. Navels are seedless and peel easily. Valencias are thin-skinned. Both are good eating oranges. For juicing, choose Valencia, Hamlin, Parson Brown, or Pineapple oranges. Look for grapefruit that is thin-skinned and heavy. Avoid puffy ones. Pink and white grapefruit have the same flavor, and both are available with seeds or without.

OOK'S TIP

Peeled and cored pineapple is now available in most supermarkets.

*1 ripe pineapple (about 4 pounds), peeled, cored,
  and cut into bite-size pieces (5 cups)*
*6 navel oranges, peeled and white pith removed,
  thinly sliced*
¼ cup granulated sugar
⅓ cup shredded coconut, packaged sweetened flaked or fresh
For garnish: maraschino cherries

1. In a large bowl, mix the pineapple, oranges, and sugar. Cover and refrigerate for at least 4 hours to release the juices and develop flavor. • The fruit mixture can be covered and refrigerated up to 3 days.
2. Just before serving, sprinkle the fruit with the coconut and cherries.
Per serving: 100 cal, 1 g pro, 1 g fat, 23 g car, 10 mg sod, 0 mg chol

EASY • QUICK • LOW FAT

WATERMELON–BERRY CASSIS
Serves 4
Preparation time: 10 minutes

Cassis is the French term for black currants, and it was the French who introduced crème de cassis, the sweet, syrupy black-currant liqueur. This recipe uses melted currant preserves instead of liqueur.

4 cups watermelon chunks, seeded
½ pint (6 ounces) fresh black raspberries, picked over and rinsed (1¼ cups)
½ pint (6 ounces) fresh red raspberries, picked over and rinsed (1¼ cups)
⅓ cup black-currant preserves

1. Put the watermelon and raspberries into a medium-size bowl.
2. In a small saucepan, stir the preserves over low heat until melted. Stir the melted preserves through a fine strainer over the fruit. Stir the fruit gently to coat. Serve right away, or cover and refrigerate up to 8 hours.
Per serving: 160 cal, 2 g pro, 1 g fat, 38 g car, 10 mg sod, 0 mg chol

EASY • LOW FAT

PEACH PASSION
Serves 6
Preparation time: 10 minutes plus 1 hour to chill

Passion fruit looks like a purple-skinned egg with yellow pulp. When ripe, the skin is wrinkled and the inside sloshes around when shaken. The intense flavor and fragrance are reminiscent of lemon, peach, honey, and jasmine. ▶

3 large ripe peaches, halved, pitted,
and cut into thin wedges (3 cups)
2 tablespoons granulated sugar
1 tablespoon fresh lemon juice
2 ripe passion fruit
1 pint coconut or pineapple sherbet

1. In a large bowl, mix the peaches, sugar, and lemon juice.

2. Halve the passion fruit and scoop the pulp onto the peach mixture. Stir gently to break up and coat all the fruit. Cover and refrigerate for 1 hour. • The fruit mixture can be covered and refrigerated up to 2 days.

3. To serve, scoop the sherbet into 6 individual dessert dishes and top with the fruit mixture.

Per serving: 150 cal, 1 g pro, 1 g fat, 35 g car, 30 mg sod, 3 mg chol

EASY • QUICK

RASPBERRIES WITH AMARETTI CREAM

Serves 4

Preparation time: 10 minutes

Amaretti—the crisp almond meringue cookies—are an Italian invention. Here they are crushed and folded into whipped cream for a topping that is wonderful over raspberries or any other berries. Amaretti are available at supermarkets and Italian markets, usually wrapped in pairs in paper and sold in decorative canisters. We have a recipe for homemade amaretti on page 286.

AMARETTI CREAM
3/4 cup heavy (whipping) cream
1/4 cup coarsely crushed amaretti cookies or other crisp,
dry almond cookies
1 tablespoon granulated sugar
2 teaspoons almond-flavored liqueur,
or 1/4 teaspoon almond extract

1 pint fresh raspberries, picked over
and rinsed (2 1/2 cups)

1. Make the cream: In a medium-size bowl, beat the cream with an electric mixer until soft peaks form when the beaters are lifted. Add the crushed cookies, sugar, and liqueur and beat just until blended.

2. To serve, divide the raspberries among 4 individual dessert dishes. Top with the cream mixture. Serve right away.

Per serving: 210 cal, 1 g pro, 17 g fat, 11 g car, 20 mg sod, 61 mg chol

PEACHES
Choose peaches that have a cream or yellow background instead of a red blush. A green undertone indicates that the fruit was picked too early and the flavor will never fully develop. To ripen peaches, leave them at room temperature or put them into a paper bag with an apple or banana, whose natural ethylene gas will hasten ripening.

EASY • QUICK • LOW FAT

SUMMER FRUIT WITH BROWN SUGAR CREAM

Serves 6

Preparation time: 10 minutes

Mixing sour cream with brown sugar is a simple and easy topping for fresh fruit. Here we call for honeydew melon and raspberries, but any cut-up fruit can be used.

BROWN SUGAR CREAM

½ cup nonfat sour cream
3 tablespoons packed light brown sugar

4 cups bite-size chunks honeydew melon (about half a medium-size melon)
1 pint fresh raspberries, picked over and rinsed (2½ cups)

For garnish: grated nutmeg

1. Make the cream: In a small bowl, mix the sour cream and brown sugar. • The cream can be covered and refrigerated up to 5 days.

2. To serve, divide the melon chunks and raspberries among 6 individual dessert dishes. Top with the sour cream mixture and sprinkle with nutmeg.

Per serving: 100 cal, 2 g pro, 0 g fat, 24 g car, 30 mg sod, 0 mg chol

EASY • QUICK • LOW FAT

MELON AND BERRIES WITH STRAWBERRY SAUCE

Serves 6

Preparation time: 12 minutes

Pure and simple, this dessert combines watermelon and blueberries with puréed strawberries. Serve with your favorite crisp cookies.

1 package (10 ounces) frozen strawberries in light syrup, thawed
6 cups bite-size chunks watermelon (from a 4-pound piece of melon)
½ pint (6 ounces) fresh blueberries, picked over and rinsed (1 cup)

1. In a blender or food processor, purée the strawberries with their syrup until smooth. Pour into a large bowl.

2. Add the watermelon and blueberries and mix gently.

3. Spoon into 6 individual dessert dishes. Serve right away, or cover and refrigerate up to 30 minutes.

Per serving: 110 cal, 1 g pro, 1 g fat, 28 g car, 10 mg sod, 0 mg chol

FRAGRANT FRUIT WITH RASPBERRY SHERBET

Serves 6

Preparation time: 5 minutes plus at least 4 hours to chill

Here's a great way to use the aromatic leaves of rose-scented geraniums. They impart a delicate rose fragrance to the berries. If unavailable, use mint sprigs instead.

1 pint (12 ounces) fresh blackberries, picked over
    and rinsed (about 3 cups)
8 rose-geranium leaves, or four 3-inch mint sprigs,
    rinsed and lightly crushed
1½ tablespoons packed light brown sugar
1 pint raspberry sherbet
2 ripe kiwifruit, peeled, quartered, and thinly sliced

1. In a medium-size glass bowl, layer the blackberries, geranium leaves, and brown sugar. Cover and refrigerate for about 4 hours to release the juices and develop the flavor.

2. To serve, remove and discard the leaves. Scoop the sherbet into 6 individual dessert dishes. Top with the berries and kiwifruit. Drizzle the juices over the fruit. Serve right away.

Per serving: 150 cal, 1 g pro, 2 g fat, 34 g car, 32 mg sod, 3 mg chol

GINGERED PLUMS AND MANGO

Serves 6

Preparation time: 8 minutes plus 1 hour to chill

Crystallized ginger is bits of gingerroot preserved in sugar syrup and then coated with granulated sugar. Look for it in jars in the spice section of the supermarket or in specialty food shops or Asian markets, where it may be sold in bulk.

1 firm ripe mango (about 1¼ pounds)
6 ripe plums (about 1½ pounds), halved, pitted,
    and cut into thin wedges (3 cups)
2 tablespoons finely chopped crystallized ginger
1 pint lime sherbet

1. Hold the mango on a cutting board and cut a slice along each side of the long flat seed so you have two halves. Holding the peel side of one half, score the flesh of

---

SCENTED GERANIUM LEAVES

◆ There are more than 200 varieties of scented geraniums, including apple, lemon, nutmeg, and peppermint, but the rose geranium is by far the most popular to use in cooking, scenting cakes, cookies, ice creams, fruits, and beverages. Sometimes the leaves can be purchased at gourmet food shops and local herb farms.

◆ Don't confuse scented geraniums with the garden geraniums that are popular houseplants. The leaves of garden geraniums are not edible.

the mango lengthwise, then crosswise, without cutting through the peel. Bend the scored portion backward, then cut along the peel to loosen the fruit. Cut the peel off the fruit remaining on the seed. Carefully cut off the flesh.

2. In a large bowl, mix the mango chunks, plums, and ginger. Cover and chill about 1 hour. ● The fruit mixture can be covered and refrigerated up to 1 day.

3. To serve, scoop the sherbet into 6 individual dessert dishes and top with the fruit mixture. Serve right away.

Per serving: 210 cal, 2 g pro, 2 g fat, 49 g car, 30 mg sod, 3 mg chol

---

1 HOUR • LOW FAT

TROPICAL FRUIT SALAD

Serves 12

Preparation time: 30 minutes plus 30 minutes to freeze

This dessert combines familiar and exotic fruits in a creamy mixture of sour cream, pineapple juice, brown sugar, and vanilla. Served in hollowed-out pineapple shells, it makes a truly festive presentation.

DRESSING
2 cups nonfat sour cream
½ cup pineapple juice
2 tablespoons light brown sugar
1 teaspoon vanilla extract

1 large ripe pineapple (about 5 pounds)
1 ripe papaya (about 1 pound), peeled, seeded, and cut into thin slices (2 cups)
1 firm ripe mango (about 14 ounces), cut into ½-inch chunks (see page 222)
1 cup bite-size pieces watermelon
1 cup bite-size pieces honeydew melon
1 cup green or red seedless grapes
2 ripe nectarines, pitted and cut into thin wedges
½ pint (6 ounces) ripe fresh strawberries, rinsed, hulled, and sliced
2 ripe apricots, pitted and cut into thin wedges
1 ripe kiwifruit, peeled and thinly sliced
1 ripe star fruit (carambola), thinly sliced
½ cup (2 ounces) macadamia nuts, toasted and chopped (see page 325)

1. Make the dressing: In a small bowl, mix the sour cream, pineapple juice, brown sugar, and vanilla until well blended. Cover and refrigerate until ready to use.

2. Cut the pineapple in half lengthwise. Remove the core by cutting a V-shaped wedge. Cut the fruit from each half with a small serrated knife, leaving ¼-inch-thick shells.

3. Freeze the shells for about 30 minutes. (This will help keep the fruit salad chilled.) ▶

4. Cut the pineapple fruit into bite-size pieces (you'll have about 6 cups).

5. In a large bowl, gently mix the pineapple chunks, papaya, mango, watermelon, honeydew, grapes, nectarines, strawberries, apricots, kiwifruit, and star fruit.

6. To serve, place the pineapple shells on a serving platter. Spoon the fruit in and around the shells. Sprinkle with the macadamia nuts. Serve the dressing separately.

Per serving with dressing: 190 cal, 4 g pro, 4 g fat, 36 g car, 30 mg sod, 0 mg chol

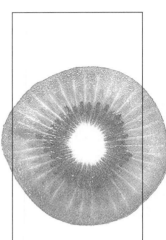

FRESH FRUIT TERRINE

Serves 12

Preparation time: 30 minutes plus at least 8 hours to chill

Cooking time: 1 minute

Kiwifruit looks delightful on this no-fat dessert, but don't be tempted to put it in the terrine. An enzyme in fresh kiwi breaks down gelatin.

1 cup orange, pineapple, or white grape juice
2 envelopes (1 ounce each) unflavored gelatin
2 cans (16 ounces each) pear halves in light syrup, well drained
2 tablespoons fresh lemon juice
½ pint (6 ounces) fresh raspberries, picked over and rinsed (1¼ cups)
3 small navel oranges, peel and white pith removed,
*   sectioned, and drained on paper towels*
1 pint ripe fresh strawberries, rinsed, hulled, and sliced (2½ cups)
For garnish: peeled kiwifruit slices

1. Line an 8 x 4-inch loaf pan with plastic wrap.

2. Put the juice into a small saucepan. Sprinkle with the gelatin. Let stand for 2 minutes to soften the gelatin. Heat almost to a simmer, stirring often, to dissolve the gelatin completely.

3. In blender or food processor, puree the pears with the lemon juice until smooth. Pour in the gelatin mixture and process to blend.

4. Arrange the raspberries in a single row down each long side of the prepared pan. Arrange the orange sections, slightly overlapping, down the center of the pan.

5. Pour about ⅓ of the puréed pears carefully and evenly over the fruit. Smooth with a rubber spatula to cover completely. Arrange ½ the strawberry slices in one layer over the purée. Cover evenly with another ⅓ of the purée. Repeat with the remaining strawberries and purée. Tap the pan gently on a work surface to get rid of air bubbles.

6. Cover and refrigerate for at least 8 hours, until firm. ● The terrine can be covered and refrigerated up to 1 day.

7. To serve, turn the terrine over onto a serving plate, then remove the pan and the plastic wrap. Garnish with sliced kiwifruit. Slice the terrine with a thin, sharp knife.

Per serving: 90 cal, 2 g pro, 0 g fat, 21 g car, 10 mg sod, 0 mg chol

KIWIFRUIT
Choose fairly firm kiwis and let them ripen at room temperature for several days. Do not buy soft kiwis, which lack flavor and could have a mushy texture. When the fruit yields slightly to gentle pressure, it is ready to use. Store ripe kiwis in the refrigerator in a plastic bag for up to several weeks.

Strawberries Brûlé (p.236) defines quick and easy for dessert: It uses only three ingredients and is ready to eat in under 15 minutes.

Nectarines in Wine (p. 229), above, is a simple yet sophisticated dessert suitable for any festive occasion. The fruit can also be marinated in non-alcoholic wine.

These three treats, Plum Oatmeal Crumble (p.242), Pear Granola Crisp (p.244), and Apple Walnut Crisp (p.244), are easier than pie. While it's traditional to top them with vanilla ice cream, whipped cream, or plain heavy cream if served warm, the extra calories aren't essential. Whether you call them crisps, crumbles, or cobblers, crunch-topped fruit desserts are great on their own.

Fragrant Fruit with Raspberry Sherbet (p.222) is a lusciously low-fat, easy-to-prepare dessert. What more could you ask?

NECTARINES IN WINE

Serves 6

Preparation time: 12 minutes plus 2 hours to chill

Light and refreshing, fruit macerated in wine is a simple dessert, yet appealing enough for company. Fruity wines such as rosé or white zinfandel are good choices, and nonalcoholic wine can also be used.

1¾ cups rosé, white zinfandel, or nonalcoholic wine
¼ cup granulated sugar
6 large ripe nectarines (about 2¼ pounds), halved, pitted,
    and cut into thin wedges (6 cups)
For garnish: tiny fresh basil leaves

1. In a large bowl, mix the wine and sugar until the sugar dissolves.
2. Stir in the nectarines. Cover and let stand for at least 2 hours at room temperature. • The fruit can be covered and refrigerated up to 6 hours. Bring to room temperature before serving.
3. To serve, spoon the fruit into 6 individual serving cups or bowls. Pour the wine mixture over the fruit and garnish with basil leaves.

Per serving: 160 cal, 2 g pro, 1 g fat, 28 g car, 4 mg sod, 0 mg chol

PLUM AND WALNUT COMPOTE

Serves 6

Preparation time: 15 minutes

This compote also makes an excellent cereal topping or fruit dish for Sunday brunch.

½ cup damson plum preserves
1 tablespoon fresh lemon juice
6 ripe plums (about 1½ pounds), halved, pitted, and cut into thin wedges (3 cups)
½ cup coarsely chopped walnuts
½ cup low-fat or nonfat vanilla yogurt
For garnish: coarsely chopped walnuts

1. In a medium-size bowl, mix the preserves and the lemon juice.
2. Add the plums and walnuts. Toss gently to mix and coat. • The fruit mixture can be covered and refrigerated up to 1 day. Bring to room temperature before serving.
3. To serve, spoon the fruit mixture into dessert dishes. Stir the yogurt until smooth. Top the fruit with a spoonful of yogurt and some chopped nuts.

Per serving: 200 cal, 3 g pro, 7 g fat, 36 g car, 20 mg sod, 1 mg chol

COOK'S TIP

The most flavorful plums will have slightly soft tips. The cloudy-gray "bloom" you sometimes see on the skin is completely natural and doesn't affect the taste.

MELON COMPOTE

Serves 6

Preparation time: 15 minutes plus 30 minutes to chill

America's most popular melons are cantaloupe and honeydew. But because melons are easy to crossbreed, new varieties are appearing in supermarkets all the time. Although this compote is delicious and looks beautiful with honeydew and cantaloupe, try some other varieties such as casaba, crenshaw, or Persian.

½ medium-size ripe honeydew (about
  1½ pounds), cut into bite-size chunks
½ medium-size ripe cantaloupe (about
  1⅓ pounds), cut into bite-size chunks
¼ cup thawed frozen orange juice concentrate
1 tablespoon light rum or lemon juice
6 tablespoons sweetened flaked coconut
For garnish: sprigs of fresh mint

1. In a large bowl, gently mix the melon chunks, orange juice, and rum. Cover and refrigerate until chilled, about 30 minutes. • The fruit mixture can be covered and refrigerated up to 1 day.

2. To serve, spoon the fruit into 6 individual dessert glasses. Sprinkle with coconut and garnish with mint.

Per serving: 80 cal, 1 g pro, 2 g fat, 16 g car, 20 mg sod, 0 mg chol

LAYERED FRESH FRUIT WITH RASPBERRY SAUCE

Serves 8

Preparation time: 30 minutes

Vary the kinds of fruits you use for this salad based on what's available and looks good.

½ fresh pineapple, peeled, cored, and cut into 1-inch pieces (3½ cups)
3 ripe purple plums, halved, pitted, and thickly sliced
1 medium-size ripe banana, sliced
1 cup (5 ounces) red or green seedless grapes
1 large ripe nectarine, halved, pitted, and thickly sliced
1 pint (12 ounces) ripe fresh strawberries, rinsed, hulled,
  and sliced (2½ cups)
1 large ripe peach, halved, pitted, and thickly sliced
⅔ cup fresh orange juice

KUDOS FOR CANTALOUPE

They're sweet, juicy, and nutrient-dense, which means loads of nutrition in a fairly small package. Half a 2-pound cantaloupe contains: 100% of the RDA of vitamin A (beta-carotene), 100% of the RDA of vitamin C, and almost half of the RDA of heart-smart potassium—all for just 90 calories.

RASPBERRY SAUCE

½ pint (6 ounces) fresh raspberries, picked over and rinsed (1¼ cups),
*   or 1 box (10 ounces) thawed frozen sweetened red raspberries*
1 to 2 tablespoons cherry brandy or raspberry liqueur (optional)
Granulated sugar to taste

1. Have ready a 3-quart container, preferably clear glass or plastic with a wide mouth, or a deep 3-quart bowl.

2. Layer the fruit in the container in the order listed above. Pour the orange juice over the fruit. Cover and refrigerate until ready to serve.

3. Make the sauce: In a blender or food processor, purée the raspberries. Pour into a very fine mesh strainer and stir with a rubber spatula to strain out the seeds. Discard the seeds. Stir in the brandy or liqueur and sugar to taste. • Cover and refrigerate until ready to serve, or up to 8 hours.

4. To serve, spoon the fruit into 8 individual dessert bowls and drizzle each serving with the sauce.

Per serving: 120 cal, 2 g pro, 1 g fat, 30 g car, 0 mg sod, 0 mg chol

EASY • 1 HOUR • LOW FAT • OLD FASHIONED

DRIED FRUIT COMPOTE

Serves 6
Preparation time: 15 minutes
Cooking time: 40 minutes

You can buy a package of mixed dried fruit (whole, not diced), or you can select your own mixture from bulk jars. This recipe is also a great way to use up hard dried fruit that has been in your pantry too long. Try this compote warm or at room temperature, plain for breakfast, or with a small scoop of vanilla ice cream for dessert.

1 cup water
1 cup orange juice
¼ to ½ cup granulated sugar
1 cinnamon stick, about 3 inches long
2 whole cloves
3 cups (about 1 pound) mixed dried fruit (such as apricots, prunes,
*   peaches, figs, apple slices, pears, cranberries, cherries, raisins)*
¼ cup cognac or bourbon (optional)

1. In a medium-size saucepan, bring the water, juice, ¼ cup of the sugar, the cinnamon stick, and cloves to a boil over medium-high heat.

2. Meanwhile, halve the apricots, quarter the prunes, peaches, figs, and apple slices, and cut the dried pears into about 4 strips.

3. Add all the dried fruit to the boiling liquid. Cover and return to a boil. Reduce the heat to low and simmer until the fruit is very tender, about 30 minutes, ▶

stirring 2 or 3 times. Taste after 15 minutes and add the remaining sugar if you wish and a little more water or orange juice if all the liquid is absorbed.

4. Remove the pan from the heat. Stir in the cognac. Serve warm or at room temperature. ● Store the cooled compote airtight in the refrigerator up to 2 months.
Per serving: 290 cal, 2 g pro, 0 g fat, 68 g car, 10 mg sod, 0 mg chol

STRAWBERRY SHORTCAKE PARFAITS

Serves 6

Preparation time: 20 minutes

This smooth, creamy dessert laced with fresh strawberries looks difficult, but it is simple to make.

> *1 quart (2 pounds) ripe fresh strawberries, rinsed (6 cups)*
> *3 tablespoons granulated sugar, or to taste*
> *2 tablespoons water*
> *1 container (8 ounces) frozen regular or*
> *reduced-calorie nondairy whipped topping, thawed*
> *12 unfilled ladyfingers*

1. Reserve 6 whole strawberries with stems for garnish. Hull the remaining strawberries.

2. In a food processor or blender, process about half the strawberries with the sugar and water until almost puréed but still chunky. Scrape into a large bowl.

3. Thinly slice the remaining hulled strawberries and stir into the purée. Gently stir in the whipped topping.

4. Spoon the mixture into 6 individual serving dishes. Cut the ladyfingers in half crosswise and place, cut ends down, into the strawberry cream around the edges of each bowl. Garnish with the reserved berries. Serve right away.
Per serving: 270 cal, 4 g pro, 12 g fat, 38 g car, 43 mg sod, 80 mg chol. With reduced-calorie topping: 240 cal, 7 g fat, 30 mg sod

STRAWBERRIES–AND–CREAM GELATIN

Serves 12

Preparation time: 15 minutes plus at least 8 hours to chill

Cooking time: 5 minutes

Anyone who loves strawberries will find this dessert irresistible. It contains strawberry ice cream, strawberry gelatin, and fresh strawberries. Serve it with whipped cream or nondairy whipped topping for a refreshing finale.

STRAWBERRIES
Look for fresh strawberries that are plump, bright red, and topped with caps of tiny green leaves. Don't rinse the berries until you are ready to use them. Strawberries can be stored in an airtight container in the refrigerator up to 3 days. Once rinsed, they'll spoil much more rapidly.

3 pints strawberry ice cream or strawberry frozen yogurt
  (regular or nonfat)
3 cups water
3 (4-serving) packages (3 ounces each) strawberry gelatin
For garnish: whipped cream, fresh strawberries, and raspberries

1. Refrigerate the ice cream for 30 to 40 minutes to soften. Lightly coat an 8-cup metal ring mold with nonstick cooking spray.

2. Bring the water to a boil in a large saucepan. Remove from the heat, add the gelatin, and stir with a rubber spatula until completely dissolved.

3. Stir in the softened ice cream until well blended and smooth. Pour into the mold and refrigerate until firm, at least 8 hours. • The gelatin can be covered tightly and refrigerated up to 3 days.

4. Up to 3 hours before serving, unmold the gelatin. Dip the mold up to the rim in warm (not hot) water, for about 10 seconds. Lift from the water and gently shake to loosen gelatin. Dampen a serving plate with cold water (this allows the gelatin to be moved on the plate after unmolding). Place the moistened plate upside down over the mold. Turn the mold and plate over, shake gently, then carefully remove the mold. (If the gelatin doesn't release easily, dip the mold in warm water again for a few seconds.) Garnish with whipped cream and berries.

Per serving with ice cream: 210 cal, 4 g pro, 6 g fat, 37 g car, 90 mg sod, 19 mg chol.
With nonfat frozen yogurt: 180 cal, 42 g car, 0 g fat, 0 mg chol

EASY • LOW FAT

CRANBERRY–RASPBERRY–ORANGE GELATIN

Serves 6

Preparation time: 15 minutes plus at least 5 hours to chill

Easy, light, and refreshing, here is a dessert perfect for a hot summer's day when you don't want to turn on your oven.

1 (4-serving) package raspberry gelatin
¾ cup boiling water
1 cup cranberry-juice cocktail
4 navel oranges, peel and white pith removed,
  coarsely chopped

1. In a 1-quart bowl, completely dissolve the gelatin in the boiling water. Stir in the cranberry juice. Refrigerate until slightly thickened, about 1 hour.

2. Gently stir in the oranges. Refrigerate until firm, about 4 hours. • The gelatin can be covered tightly and refrigerated up to 3 days.

3. To serve, spoon the gelatin into 6 individual dessert dishes.

Per serving: 120 cal, 2 g pro, 0 g fat, 30 g car, 40 mg sod, 0 mg chol

FRUIT MELBA

Serves 4

Preparation time: 20 minutes

A quick and easy raspberry purée is mixed with diced honeydew melon and fresh blueberries. A splash of seltzer and a sprig of fresh cilantro add a unique twist. It all combines for a colorful and cool dessert—and without any fat.

1 package (10 ounces) frozen raspberries in light syrup, thawed
3½ cups diced honeydew (from about half a medium-size melon)
½ pint (6 ounces) fresh blueberries, picked over and rinsed (1 cup)
¼ teaspoon ground cinnamon
Plain seltzer water
For garnish: chopped fresh cilantro leaves

1. In a blender or food processor, purée the raspberries with the syrup. Pour into a very fine mesh strainer set over a large bowl and stir with a rubber spatula to strain out the seeds. Scrape the purée from outside the strainer into the bowl. Discard the seeds. (You'll have about 1 cup of purée.)

2. Stir in the melon, blueberries, and cinnamon. • The fruit mixture can be covered and refrigerated up to 1 day.

3. To serve, spoon the mixture into 4 individual dessert dishes. Top each with a splash of seltzer and garnish with cilantro.

Per serving: 150 cal, 1 g pro, 0 g fat, 38 g car, 20 mg sod, 0 mg chol

PINEAPPLE–POACHED PEARS

Serves 4

Preparation time: 10 minutes

Cooking time: 15 minutes

Pears of one kind or another are available all year, but they are at their peak during the chilly winter months, when their sweetness is especially welcome. Simple poached pears make a great breakfast dish as well as a wonderful year-round dessert.

2 medium-size firm ripe pears, peeled, halved, and cored
1 cup pineapple juice
2 tablespoons orange marmalade
2 tablespoons golden raisins

1. Put the pears cut side down in a single layer in a 3-quart saucepan. Add the juice, marmalade, and raisins. Bring to a boil over medium-high heat. Reduce the

---

HONEYDEW

◆ Buy honeydew melons that have a yellowish-white to creamy rind, are softening slightly at the blossom end and have a faint, pleasant aroma.

◆ Store at room temperature for a few days or refrigerate, but only if the melon is too ripe to last at room temperature.

heat to low. Cover and simmer for 12 to 15 minutes, until the pears are fork-tender.

2. Serve warm, at room temperature, or chilled, with poaching liquid and raisins spooned over top.

Per serving: 120 cal, 1 g pro, 0 g fat, 31 g car, 10 mg sod, 0 mg chol

---

EASY • LOW FAT

CHILLED PINEAPPLE–MANGO SOUP

Serves 6

Preparation time: 20 minutes plus at least 4 hours to chill

Besides making an unusual and elegant dessert, a cup of this chilled soup makes a perfect starter to a spicy meal or a dinner of simple grilled meat, chicken, or fish. It's also a quick and terrific afternoon pick-me-up.

> 2 firm ripe mangoes (about 1 pound each)
> 1 ripe pineapple (about 3 pounds), peeled, cored,
>   and cut into small pieces (4 cups)
> 2 tablespoons fresh lime juice
> 2 cups cold milk
> 2 to 3 tablespoons light brown sugar, as needed
> For garnish: plain low-fat or nonfat yogurt

1. Hold one mango on a cutting board and cut a slice along each side of the long flat seed so you have two halves. Holding the peel side of one half, score the flesh of the mango lengthwise, then crosswise, without cutting through to the peel. Bend the scored portion backward, then cut along the peel to loosen the fruit. Cut the peel of the fruit remaining on the seed. Carefully cut off the flesh. Repeat with the remaining mango.

2. In a food processor or blender (in batches), purée the mango chunks, pineapple, and lime juice until smooth. Pour the mixture into a medium-size bowl. • The fruit mixture can be covered and refrigerated up to 2 days.

3. Stir in the milk until blended. Taste and add brown sugar if needed. Cover and refrigerate until well chilled, at least 4 hours (but no more than 6 hours).

4. To serve, stir the soup and ladle it into cups. Garnish with a spoonful of yogurt.

Per serving: 200 cal, 4 g pro, 3 g fat, 42 g car, 50 mg sod, 11 mg chol

---

MANGOES

Out of the more than 40 varieties of mangoes, there are about six readily available in American markets. The skin of an unripe mango is green; splashes of yellow, orange, and red appear as the mango ripens. A mango can be stored at room temperature up to 1 week to ripen, then refrigerated for several days. Soft spots or wrinkled skin indicate the fruit is overripe.

STRAWBERRIES BRÛLÉ

Serves 4

Preparation time: 10 minutes

Cooking time: 2½ minutes

Brûlé is French for "burned" and refers to the caramelized sugar atop this dish. Place the dishes no farther than 2 to 3 inches from the heat source when broiling, so the sugar will caramelize quickly while the strawberries remain cool.

1 pint (12 ounces) ripe fresh strawberries, rinsed,
*   hulled, and cut in half*
½ cup regular or reduced-fat sour cream
¼ cup packed light brown sugar

1. Heat the broiler. Have ready four 6-ounce ramekins or shallow custard cups and a baking pan with sides or a jelly roll pan.

2. In each ramekin, arrange about ½ cup of strawberries, cut sides down, in a fairly even layer. Top with 2 tablespoons of sour cream and spread to the edges. Crumble 1 tablespoon of brown sugar evenly over the surface to completely cover the sour cream.

3. Place the ramekins on the baking sheet. Broil 2 to 3 inches from the heat source just until the sugar melts, 1½ to 2½ minutes. Serve right away.

Per serving: 140 cal, 1 g pro, 6 g fat, 20 g car, 20 mg sod, 13 mg chol. With reduced-fat sour cream: 4 g fat, 10 mg chol

APPLES WITH CUSTARD SAUCE

Serves 8

Preparation time: 15 minutes

Baking time: 35 minutes

Richly flavored baked apples topped with a quick custard sauce made with instant vanilla pudding make a warm and comforting conclusion to almost any meal.

4 medium-size baking apples (such as Rome or Winesap),
*   peeled, halved, and cored*
¼ cup water
¼ cup packed light or dark brown sugar
1 (4-serving) package instant vanilla-pudding mix
2½ cups skim milk
¼ teaspoon rum extract (optional)

1. Heat the oven to 350°F. Arrange the apples, cut sides down, in a 13 x 9-inch baking dish. Pour in the water. Cover and bake until the apples are tender, 25 to 30 minutes. Remove from the oven.

2. Heat the broiler. Turn the apples cut side up. Sprinkle with the brown sugar. Broil 6 inches from the heat source until the sugar is bubbly, 4 to 5 minutes.

3. Meanwhile, make the sauce: Prepare the pudding mix using the skim milk according to package directions. Stir in the rum extract. Serve the sauce separately to pour over each serving.

Per serving: 140 cal, 3 g pro, 1 g fat, 33 g car, 240 mg sod, 2 mg chol

1 HOUR • LOW FAT • OLD FASHIONED

ORANGE–GLAZED BAKED APPLES

Serves 5
Preparation time: 10 minutes
Baking time: 45 minutes

Who doesn't enjoy the satisfaction of eating a warm baked apple, a beloved comfort food. Here, the apples are baked in a spicy orange juice mixture that accents their tartness wonderfully. Rome, Winesap, Stayman, and Idared are all good baking apples because they're firm, juicy, and slightly tart. Each apple is adorned with a cinnamon stick. Try to buy stick cinnamon from a store with a fairly quick turnover, as it loses much of its flavor with long storage. Without the whipped cream, baked apples are also wonderful for breakfast.

1 can (6 ounces) frozen orange juice concentrate, thawed
½ teaspoon pumpkin-pie spice, or
    ¼ teaspoon ground cinnamon and
    ⅛ teaspoon each ground allspice and ground ginger
5 medium-size baking apples,
    such as Rome or Winesap
5 3-inch cinnamon sticks
For garnish: whipped cream

1. Heat the oven to 350°F. In a small bowl, mix the orange juice concentrate and pumpkin-pie spice.

2. Core the apples, but don't cut through the bottoms. Arrange the apples upright in a shallow baking dish. Put a cinnamon stick and 1 tablespoon of the orange juice mixture into each hole. Cover the dish loosely with foil.

3. Bake until tender, about 45 minutes, brushing the apples 2 or 3 times with the remaining orange juice mixture.

4. Serve warm or at room temperature in shallow bowls accompanied by the pan juices and whipped cream.

Per serving: 150 cal, 1 g pro, 1 g fat, 38 g car, 0 mg sod, 0 mg chol

CINNAMON STICKS
Cinnamon comes from the inner bark of a tropical evergreen tree. When the bark is left in the sun to dry, it rolls up into tight curls, making cinnamon sticks.

WHAT'S IN A NAME?

Crisps, grunts, slumps, cobblers, crumbles—these are some of the names of early American cooked fruit desserts, all of which take advantage of the bounty of seasonal fruits and all of which include a crust of some sort.

◆ Cobblers are baked fruit topped with a biscuit dough, which can be dropped over the fruit in pieces for a "cobbled"

effect, or pressed into one single layer. Grunts and slumps resemble cobblers in that they are topped with biscuit dough, but they are steamed on top of the stove instead of baked. The result is a topping that is more like dumplings than crisp, golden biscuits.

◆ Crisps, crumbles, and crunches all feature buttery crumb toppings. Typically the crumb mixture is made from flour,

sugar, and butter, but bread crumbs, oatmeal, and nuts are also used. If the crumbs are layered between the fruit, the result is a Brown Betty.

◆ A pandowdy, much like a pie, is made of a fruit filling encased in two flaky pie crusts. During the last minutes of baking, the top crust is cut up and pressed back into the fruit. This technique is referred to as "dowdying."

LOW FAT • CLASSIC • OLD FASHIONED

APPLE BROWN BETTY

Serves 6

Preparation time: 20 minutes

Baking time: 55 minutes

This layered dessert of apples and buttered bread crumbs is an American classic that dates back to 1864. Granny Smith apples are a good choice because they don't fall apart during baking. Serve warm, with whipped cream, topping, or ice cream.

3 slices firm white or whole-wheat bread
¾ cup packed light brown sugar
½ teaspoon ground cinnamon
6 medium-size Granny Smith apples (about 2 pounds),
  peeled, quartered, cored, and thinly sliced (8 cups)
½ stick (¼ cup) butter or margarine (see page 321),
  cut into small pieces
¼ cup water

1. Heat the oven to 375°F. Have ready an ungreased 1-quart baking dish.
2. In a food processor, process the bread slices with on/off turns until finely ground. Add the brown sugar and cinnamon, and process with on/off turns until blended.
3. Arrange half the apple slices over the bottom of the baking dish. Sprinkle with half the crumb mixture and dot with half the butter.
4. Repeat with the remaining apple slices, crumb mixture, and butter. Drizzle with the water.
5. Cover with foil and bake until the apples in the center are tender, 45 to 55 minutes. Set the dish on a wire rack to cool. Serve warm or at room temperature.
Per serving with butter: 280 cal, 1 g pro, 9 g fat, 52 g car, 160 mg sod, 21 mg chol.
With margarine: 170 mg sod, 0 mg chol

COOK'S TIP

To make fresh (sometimes called soft) bread crumbs without a food processor, use firm white or whole-wheat bread or bread that has dried out a bit. Leave the crusts on. Crumble the bread by rubbing small pieces between your fingers. The average slice of bread yields ⅓ to ½ cup coarse crumbs.

PEACH COBBLER

Serves 8

Preparation time: 20 minutes

Baking time: 45 minutes

This may be the quintessential summer dessert. Fresh ripe peaches need little enhancement in the way of flavor—just a little lemon juice and sugar—for a luscious dessert that tastes as fresh as the fruit itself. When cobbler is served warm, cream is its traditional accompaniment.

9 medium-size ripe peaches (3 pounds)

2 tablespoons fresh lemon juice

½ cup granulated sugar

BISCUIT TOPPING

1⅓ cups all-purpose flour

3 tablespoons granulated sugar

1½ teaspoons baking powder

½ teaspoon baking soda

½ stick (¼ cup) cold butter or margarine see (see page 321),
*   cut into small pieces*

⅔ cup buttermilk, or plain low-fat yogurt

2 teaspoons granulated sugar

¼ teaspoon grated nutmeg

1. Heat the oven to 400°F. Have ready a 2-inch-deep, 2-quart baking dish or a deep 10-inch pie plate.

2. To peel the peaches: Immerse them in boiling water for 1 minute. Remove with a slotted spoon. Cool under cold running water, then slip off the skins.

3. Slice the peaches into wedges directly into the baking dish (give the knife a twist to release the slices). Toss the peaches with the lemon juice and sugar. Cover with foil and bake for 15 minutes, until the peaches are hot and the juices bubble.

4. Meanwhile, make the topping: In a large bowl, mix the flour, sugar, baking powder, and baking soda. Cut in the butter with a pastry blender, or rub with your fingertips, until the mixture resembles small peas. Pour the buttermilk over the top. Toss with a fork until the mixture clumps together.

5. Using two spoons, drop heaping tablespoonfuls of the dough over the peaches. In a small cup, mix the 2 teaspoons sugar and the nutmeg. Sprinkle over the biscuits.

6. Bake until the biscuits are golden brown and a toothpick inserted into them comes out clean, about 30 minutes. Set the dish on a wire rack to cool slightly before serving.

Per serving with butter: 260 cal, 4 g pro, 6 g fat, 50 g car, 250 mg sod, 16 mg chol.

With margarine: 1 mg chol

VARIATION

PEACH-BLUEBERRY COBBLER

• Prepare and bake 5 medium-size ripe peaches as directed through step 3. Gently stir in 1 pint (2 cups) rinsed blueberries.

• Proceed as directed from step 4.

Per serving: with butter: 280 cal, 4 g pro, 6 g fat, 55 g car, 250 mg sod, 16 mg chol. With margarine: 1 mg chol

• LOW FAT
• CLASSIC
• OLD FASHIONED

OLD FASHIONED

CHERRY–PEAR COBBLER

Serves 8

Preparation time: 20 minutes

Baking time: 55 minutes

If the midwinter blues are getting to you, brighten up with a delicious (and very red) cherry-pear cobbler. Since it's made with cherry-pie filling and a simple biscuit dough, it's even a breeze to make. Vanilla ice cream or plain heavy cream poured over it makes this simple cobbler irresistible. You could also substitute chopped tart apples, such as Granny Smith, for the pears.

2 cans (21 ounces each) cherry-pie filling

3 large firm ripe pears (1½ pounds), peeled, cored, and

   cut into ½-inch chunks (3 cups)

BISCUIT DOUGH

1¼ cups all-purpose flour

¼ cup plus 1 tablespoon granulated sugar

1½ teaspoons baking powder

¼ teaspoon salt

1 cup heavy (whipping) cream

2 tablespoons sliced almonds

1. Heat the oven to 400°F.

2. In a deep 2½-quart baking dish or casserole (at least 10½ inches across), gently mix the cherry-pie filling and pears. Place the dish on a baking sheet (to catch drips) and bake for 15 minutes to heat through.

3. Meanwhile, make the biscuit dough: In a medium-size bowl, mix the flour, ¼ cup sugar, the baking powder, and salt. Gradually stir in the cream with a fork until the mixture forms a thick, sticky batter.

4. Remove the baking dish from the oven. Using two spoons, drop clumps of the dough evenly over the fruit mixture. Sprinkle the dough with the remaining 1 tablespoon sugar and the almonds.

5. Bake until the biscuits are golden brown and a toothpick inserted into them comes out clean, about 40 minutes.

6. Set the dish on a wire rack to cool. Serve warm or at room temperature. Spoon into deep plates or bowls.

Per serving: 430 cal, 4 g pro, 13 g fat, 79 g car, 180 mg sod, 41 mg chol

PEARS

Choose firm pears that yield to gentle pressure at the stem end. Finish ripening at home in a paper bag. For cooking, pick yellow and red Bartletts or Bosc pears; for eating, any of those plus Anjou and Comice are good. Pears are a good source of fiber and potassium.

OLD FASHIONED

PINEAPPLE–MACADAMIA COBBLER

Serves 9

Preparation time: 25 minutes

Baking time: 1 hour

This cobbler, a new take on an old favorite, uses a macadamia nut crust and fresh pineapple filling to offer a taste of Hawaii.

PINEAPPLE FILLING

1/3 cup granulated sugar

1/4 cup buttermilk baking mix

4 cups bite-size pieces fresh pineapple
   (from a 3 1/4-pound pineapple), or 2 cans (20 ounces each)
   pineapple chunks in juice, well drained

1 teaspoon freshly grated lemon peel

TOPPING

1/2 cup sweetened flaked coconut

2 large eggs

1/2 cup granulated sugar

1/2 stick (1/4 cup) butter or margarine
   (see page 321), melted

1 1/2 cups buttermilk baking mix

1/2 cup (2 ounces) macadamia nuts,
   coarsely chopped

1. Heat the oven to 350°F. Grease an 8-inch square baking dish.

2. Make the filling: In a large bowl, mix the sugar and 1/4 cup of baking mix. Add the pineapple and lemon peel and toss to mix and coat. Scrape the filling into the prepared dish.

3. Make the topping: Spread the coconut on an ungreased cookie sheet. Bake until golden, stirring occasionally, 8 to 10 minutes. Remove to a wire rack to cool.

4. In a medium-size bowl, whisk the eggs, sugar, and butter until well blended and smooth. Stir in the 1 1/2 cups of baking mix and 1/4 cup of the coconut. Spread the mixture evenly over the filling to cover completely. Sprinkle with the remaining coconut and the macadamia nuts.

5. Bake until the topping is puffed and golden, and a toothpick inserted into the topping comes out clean, about 50 to 60 minutes. (If the topping begins to get too brown, cover loosely with foil during the last 5 to 10 minutes of baking.)

6. Set the dish on a wire rack to cool. Serve warm or at room temperature. Spoon into deep plates or bowls.

Per serving with butter: 330 cal, 4 g pro, 16 g fat, 45 g car, 360 mg sod, 60 mg chol.

With margarine: 47 mg chol

1 HOUR • CLASSIC • OLD FASHIONED

NECTARINE CRISP

Serves 10

Preparation time: 20 minutes

Baking time: 35 minutes

Nectarines don't need peeling: the skins soften as they bake. Assemble the crisp ahead of time, then pop it into the oven just as you sit down to dinner.

4½ pounds ripe nectarines (about 12), halved, pitted, and sliced (12 cups)

TOPPING

1¼ cups packed light brown sugar

⅔ cup all-purpose flour

10 tablespoons plus 2 teaspoons (⅔ cup) cold butter
  or margarine (see page 321), cut into small pieces

2 cups uncooked old-fashioned or quick-cooking oats

⅛ teaspoon ground cinnamon

1. Heat the oven to 350°F. Lightly grease a 13 x 9-inch baking pan or dish.

2. Arrange the sliced nectarines in the prepared pan.

3. To make the topping in a food processor: Process the brown sugar and flour to blend. Add the butter and process with on/off turns until coarse crumbs form. Remove to a medium-size bowl and stir in the oats with a fork.

To make by hand: In a medium-size bowl, mix the brown sugar and flour. Cut in the butter with two knives or a pastry blender, or rub in with your fingertips until the mixture resembles coarse crumbs. Stir in the oats with a fork.

4. Sprinkle the topping evenly over the fruit. Dust with cinnamon.

5. Bake until the fruit is soft and the topping is crisp and browned, 30 to 35 minutes. Set the dish on a wire rack to cool. Serve warm or at room temperature. Spoon into deep plates or bowls.

Per serving with butter: 400 cal, 5 g pro, 14 g fat, 66 g car, 140 mg sod, 33 mg chol. With margarine: 155 mg sod, 0 mg chol

1 HOUR • LOW FAT • OLD FASHIONED

PLUM OATMEAL CRUMBLE

Serves 10

Preparation time: 20 minutes

Baking time: 40 minutes

In this topping, rolled oats add a hearty, chewy texture that makes a good contrast to the softness of the baked plums. Using old-fashioned oats makes a sturdier topping than the quick-cooking variety, although either will work.

COOK'S TIP

If a recipe calls for light brown sugar and all you have is dark brown sugar, you can use a combination of half dark brown sugar and half granulated sugar as a replacement.

3 pounds ripe plums (about 15 medium-size),
  halved, pitted, and cut into ½-inch-thick wedges (10 cups)
3 tablespoons granulated sugar
⅛ teaspoon grated nutmeg

TOPPING
¾ cup packed light brown sugar
⅔ cup all-purpose flour
6 tablespoons cold butter or margarine (see page 321),
  cut into small pieces
¾ cup uncooked old-fashioned or quick-cooking oats

COOK'S TIP

When making the topping, be sure the butter (or margarine) is cold, or the topping will not come out crumbly.

1. Heat the oven to 400°F. Have ready a 13 x 9-inch baking pan or dish.

2. Make the filling: Put the plums, sugar, and nutmeg into the baking pan and stir to mix well. Spread the mixture evenly in the pan.

3. To make the topping in a food processor: Process the brown sugar and flour to blend. Add the butter and process with on/off turns until coarse crumbs form. Remove to a medium-size bowl and stir in the oats with a fork.

To make by hand: In a medium-size bowl, mix the brown sugar and flour. Cut in the butter with two knives or a pastry blender, or rub in with your fingertips until the mixture resembles coarse crumbs. Stir in the oats with a fork.

4. Sprinkle the topping evenly over the fruit filling.

5. Bake until the fruit is tender and the topping is crisp and lightly browned, 35 to 40 minutes.

6. Set the dish on a wire rack to cool. Serve warm or at room temperature. Spoon into deep plates or bowls.

Per serving with butter: 260 cal, 3 g pro, 8 g fat, 47 g car, 80 mg sod, 19 mg chol. With margarine: 88 mg sod, 0 mg chol

OAT NOTES

Oats have an affinity for fruit flavors and spicy-sweet flavors, making them a natural in desserts. They are sold in many forms. Make sure to use the specific oat called for in a recipe.

◆ Steel-cut (Scotch) oats are hulled whole oats that have been sliced with a steel blade. They take the longest to cook and have a chewy, firm texture. Look for steel-cut oats in specialty food shops or health food stores, where the price is usually lower.

◆ Rolled or old-fashioned oats are steamed, then flattened into flakes. They take about 15 minutes to cook and have a firm texture.

◆ Instant oats are cut into very small pieces and precooked, then dried. They don't require any cooking, just the addition of boiling water. They cannot be substituted in any recipes calling for old-fashioned or quick-cooking oats.

◆ Quick-cooking oats are cut into several pieces before steaming and flattening. They cook in about 5 minutes and have a tender texture.

1 HOUR • LOW FAT • OLD FASHIONED

PEAR GRANOLA CRISP

Serves 8

Preparation time: 20 minutes

Baking time: 40 minutes

This dessert takes its name from the crumbly mixture that bakes over the fruit into a crisp topping. Granola makes the topping extra-crunchy in this fast from-scratch dessert.

4½ pounds firm ripe pears, preferably Bosc (8 to 9 large),
   peeled, cored, and cut into 1-inch chunks (10 cups)
3 tablespoons granulated sugar
3 tablespoons fresh lemon juice
½ teaspoon ground ginger

GRANOLA TOPPING
3 cups low-fat granola without raisins
3 tablespoons all-purpose flour
½ stick (¼ cup) cold butter or margarine (see page 321), softened

1. Heat the oven to 400°F. Have ready a 13 x 9-inch baking pan or dish.

2. Put the pears, sugar, lemon juice, and ginger into the baking pan and stir to mix well. Spread the mixture evenly in the pan.

3. To make the topping in a food processor: Process the granola and flour to blend. Add the butter and process with on/off turns until coarse crumbs form.

To make by hand: In a medium-size bowl, mix the granola and flour. Cut in the butter with a pastry blender, or rub in with your fingertips until the mixture resembles coarse crumbs.

4. Sprinkle the topping evenly over the fruit filling.

5. Bake until the fruit is tender and the topping is crisp and lightly browned, 35 to 40 minutes.

6. Set the pan on a wire rack to cool. Serve warm or at room temperature. Spoon into deep plates or bowls.

Per serving with butter: 340 cal, 4 g pro, 8 g fat, 67 g car, 16 mg chol, 0 chol.
With margarine: 135 mg sod

VARIATION

APPLE WALNUT CRISP

• Heat the oven and prepare the baking dish as in step 1.

• Peel and core 3½ pounds (6 to 7 large) Granny Smith apples, then cut into ½-inch-thick wedges (10 cups). Prepare the recipe as in step 2, using the apples instead of the pears and omitting the ginger.

• Make the topping: In a medium-size bowl, mix ¾ cup all-purpose flour, ¾ cup packed light brown sugar, ½ teaspoon ground cinnamon, 1 stick (½ cup) cold butter or margarine, cut into small pieces, and ½ cup walnuts, chopped. Rub together with your fingers or stir with a fork until the mixture resembles coarse crumbs. Proceed as directed from step 4.

Per serving with butter: 390 cal, 3 g pro, 17 g fat, 61 g car, 130 mg sod, 31 mg chol. With margarine: 143 mg sod, 0 mg chol

• 1 HOUR • CLASSIC
• OLD FASHIONED

BLUEBERRY–PLUM CRISP

Serves 8
Preparation time: 20 minutes
Baking time: 40 minutes

Blueberries and plums baked together are a wonderful flavor combination and a beautiful color. Red and purple plums all work well, and so do the small Italian "prune" plums that appear late in the season—you'll just need more. The crispy and crunchy topping is made with oatmeal, which adds a nice whole-grain flavor. This old-fashioned favorite is best served warm or at room temperature. For a special treat, top it with vanilla ice cream or lightly sweetened whipped cream.

1 pint (12 ounces) fresh blueberries,
  rinsed and picked over (2 cups)
2 pounds ripe plums, halved, pitted, and
  cut into ½-inch-thick slices (about 7 cups)
2 tablespoons granulated sugar
1 tablespoon all-purpose flour
1 tablespoon fresh lemon juice
½ teaspoon ground cinnamon

TOPPING
¾ cup packed light brown sugar
⅔ cup all-purpose flour
6 tablespoons cold butter or margarine (see page 321),
  cut into small pieces
¾ cup uncooked old-fashioned or quick-cooking oats

1. Heat the oven to 375°F. Have ready a 9-inch pie plate.

2. Put the blueberries, plums, granulated sugar, flour, lemon juice, and cinnamon into the pie plate. Mix, then spread evenly.

3. To make the topping in a food processor: Combine the brown sugar and flour in the food processor and process to blend. Add the butter and process with on/off turns until coarse crumbs form. Transfer to a medium-size bowl and stir in the oats with a fork.

To make by hand: In a medium-size bowl, mix the brown sugar and flour. Cut in the butter with a pastry blender until the mixture resembles coarse crumbs. Stir in the oats with a fork.

4. Sprinkle the topping evenly over the fruit, then press down gently.

5. Bake until the plums are tender when pierced, the juices bubble, and the topping is crisp and lightly browned, 35 to 40 minutes. Set the pan on a wire rack to cool. Serve warm or at room temperature.

Per serving with butter: 320 cal, 4 g pro, 10 g fat, 57 g car, 100 mg sod, 23 mg chol.
With margarine: 110 mg sod, 0 mg chol

QUICK FRUIT FIXES

Here are more than 20 easy solutions for a quick and delicious dessert or snack in a pinch. All use fresh fruit, so they're packed with nutrition and are low- or no-fat as well.

◆ **DUNKING APPLES:** Slice half an apple. Dip in 2 teaspoons honey or pure maple syrup, then in 2 teaspoons chopped toasted walnuts.

◆ **QUICK-FIX CARAMEL APPLES:** Slice half an apple and dip into 1 tablespoon caramel ice cream topping.

◆ **SAUCY RAISIN-TOAST TRIANGLES:** Spread 2 tablespoons applesauce on a slice of toasted raisin bread. Sprinkle with cinnamon and pop under the broiler until bubbly. Cut into triangles.

◆ **DESSERT À LA WALDORF:** Chop 2 apples and 8 dates and toss them with ¼ cup low-fat or nonfat lemon yogurt. Sprinkle some grated nutmeg over the top.

◆ **FROZEN YOGURT BANANA TREAT:** Insert a popsicle stick into a medium-size peeled, firm ripe banana and coat with 2 tablespoons strawberry yogurt. Freeze on a square of foil. Spread with 2 more tablespoons yogurt, then roll in about 2 tablespoons toasted coconut. Freeze until the coating is firm. Wrap tightly and freeze up to 2 weeks.

◆ **CINNAMON-SCENTED BANANAS IN HONEY YOGURT:** Slice 1 medium-size ripe banana. Stir into 1 cup low-fat honey yogurt. Sprinkle with cinnamon.

◆ **BLUEBERRY-BANANA LICKETY SPLIT:** Halve a small banana lengthwise and top with 2 small scoops vanilla frozen yogurt (about ½ cup) and 2 tablespoons bottled blueberry pourable fruit (look for it near the jams or ice cream syrups in the supermarket).

◆ **TROPICAL SMOOTHIE:** Process 1 cut-up medium-size ripe banana, 1 cup frozen unsweetened strawberries, and 1 cup pineapple juice in a blender or food processor until smooth. Pour into a tall glass and serve.

◆ **WELL-DRESSED MELON:** Thin honey

with orange juice and pour over chilled cantaloupe or honeydew melon chunks.

◆ **CHERRY DIP:** Serve sweet cherries (leave stems on) from a large bowl of crushed ice. Dip into low-fat vanilla yogurt, stirred until smooth.

◆ **IN-THE-PINK GRAPEFRUIT:** Peel and section a grapefruit (or buy sections in jars) and divide between 2 dessert dishes. Pour ¼ cup chilled raspberry-cranberry drink over each and serve.

◆ **SOUR GRAPES:** Mix seedless red and green grapes with nonfat sour cream sweetened with brown sugar.

◆ **NECTARINE SUNDAE:** Arrange nectarine slices around scoops of low-fat coffee yogurt. Sprinkle with a mixture of sugar and cinnamon.

◆ **MELON TOSS:** Toss watermelon chunks with blueberry pourable fruit.

◆ **BROILED BROWN-SUGARED ORANGES:** Peel an orange, cut it into chunks, and put them into 2 small broilerproof dishes. Sprinkle each with ½ tablespoon brown sugar and a little ground ginger. Broil for 5 to 6 minutes until the sugar is melted and bubbly. Serve as is or spoon the hot oranges over vanilla frozen yogurt.

◆ **CREAMY HAWAIIAN FRUIT CUPS:** Peel, seed, and cut 1 medium-size papaya into chunks. Mix with ½ cup halved seedless

green grapes, ½ cup plain low-fat yogurt, and 3 tablespoons orange marmalade. Let stand at room temperature for 30 minutes for the flavor to develop. Stir gently before serving.

◆ **DESERT DELIGHT:** Drizzle sliced fresh figs with honey.

◆ **HONEY-TOPPED PAPAYA FANS:** Peel and seed a medium-size papaya. Save some of the soft peppery black seeds for garnish. Cut the papaya lengthwise into quarters. Slice and fan out onto 4 plates. Mix 2 tablespoons honey and 1 tablespoon fresh lime juice. Drizzle over the papaya and scatter the seeds on top.

◆ **ALMOND PEACH PARFAIT:** Stir mashed, peeled ripe peaches and a few drops of almond extract into thawed light nondairy whipped topping. Layer in parfait glasses with sliced ripe peaches.

◆ **PEARS JUBILEE:** Cut pears in half. Core and fill each half with 1 tablespoon bottled black-cherry pourable fruit.

◆ **PEARS MELBA:** Fan thinly sliced pears on dessert plates. Spoon low-fat lemon yogurt in the center of each plate and top with fresh raspberries.

◆ **FAST AND FRESH PINEAPPLE SHERBET:** Peel and core a medium-size ripe pineapple. Cut it into chunks and freeze until firm. Purée in a blender or food processor with ½ cup skim milk. Serve right away or cover airtight and return to the freezer to eat anytime.

◆ **ALMOST-MARGARITA PINEAPPLE:** Dip pineapple spears in lime juice, then in granulated sugar. To make Margarita Pineapple, add tequila to the lime juice.

◆ **BROILED PINEAPPLE ROUNDS:** Cut peeled pineapple into ¾-inch rounds and arrange on a broilerproof dish. Sprinkle ½ teaspoon brown sugar over each slice. Broil for 3 to 4 minutes, until hot and bubbly.

SILLY CAKES

As a dessert for a special occasion, a decorated "silly" cake will steal the show. They are a lot easier to make than you might think—many use cake mixes or frozen cakes and ready-to-spread frosting, and store-bought cookies, candies, and snacks for decoration.

Cutting undecorated cakes into shapes is one way to produce an impressive design, and the technique is used here for Hot Dog, What a Cake!, Jolly Wally Walrus, and the Box of Crayons Cake. Other equally delightful designs involve stacking cakes, some of different shapes, as with the Big Maccake and the Stack-of-Gifts Cake. And you'll be amazed to discover what clever creations can be made using only a Bundt pan—cakes like the Jack-O'-Lantern Cake, Tomato-in-the-Sun Cake, and Gloria Glowworm. Any one of these is a sure-fire hit at a child's birthday celebration, but there are plenty of options for holiday parties, bridal showers, or simple summer get-togethers.

Also featured here are instructions for making sugared flowers and using a pastry bag, plus many more cake decorating tips for the novice as well as the experienced dessert chef.

THE SILLY CAKES...

Big Maccake, 252
Box of Crayons Cake, 254
Bunny Cake, 269
Buttercream Bow Cake, 274
Carlyle the Crocodile, 253
Frosty, 270
Gloria Glowworm, 253
Hot Dog, What a Cake!, 257
Jack-O'-Lantern Cake, 270
Jolly Wally Walrus, 250
Keep on Truckin' Cake, 255
Make-it-Easy Bunny Cake, 270
Make-it-Easy Jack-O'-Lantern
    Cake, 271
Make-it-Easy Watermelon Cake, 260
Stack-of-Gifts Cake, 273
Sunflower Cake, 256
Tomato-in-the-Sun Cake, 258
Watermelon Cake, 260

SUMMER PARTIES

Hot Dog, What a Cake!, 257
Make-it-Easy Watermelon
    Cake, 260
Sunflower Cake, 256
Tomato-in-the-Sun
    Cake, 258
Watermelon Cake, 260

NO-BAKE CAKES

Keep on Truckin' Cake, 255
Hot Dog, What a Cake!, 256

SHOWER TIME

Buttercream Bow Cake, 274
Stack-of-Gifts Cake, 273
Sunflower Cake, 256

CAKES FOR A CROWD

A Whale of a Cake, 251
Big Maccake, 252
Carlyle the Crocodile, 253
Jolly Wally Walrus, 250

HOLIDAY CAKES

Bunny Cake, 269
Frosty, 270
Jack-O'-Lantern Cake, 270
Make-it-Easy Bunny Cake, 270
Make-it-Easy Jack-O'-Lantern
    Cake, 271

FOR BEGINNERS

Box of Crayons Cake, 254
Gloria Glowworm, 250
Keep on Truckin' Cake, 255
Sunflower Cake, 256

SILLY CAKE

JOLLY WALLY WALRUS

Serves 24

Preparation time: 10 minutes
plus at least 30 minutes to decorate
Baking time: 1 hour

Jolly Wally is a stack of three cakes: two baked in round cake pans, topped with one baked in a bowl. Set on a sheet of crystal-blue plastic wrap and surrounded by rock candy, he'll look as if he just broke through the ocean's ice (see photo, page 268).

> 2 boxes (about 18 ounces each) cake mix,
>   any flavor
> 2 cans (16 ounces each) ready-to-spread
>   chocolate frosting

FOR DECORATION
1 container (3½ ounces) chocolate sprinkles
1 tube white ready-to-pipe icing
2 large marshmallows
3 thin pretzel sticks
2 brown M&M's candies
1 large orange gumdrop
2 cherry fruit rolls

1. Heat the oven to 350°F. Grease and flour two 8-inch round cake pans and one 2-quart, 8-inch (across the top) metal or ovenproof glass mixing bowl with a rounded bottom.

2. Prepare both boxes of cake mix together according to the package directions. Fill the prepared pans and bowl ⅔ full. (You can make cupcakes with any remaining batter.) If necessary, set the bowl in a custard cup in the oven to keep it level.

3. Bake until a toothpick or cake tester inserted near the center of the cakes comes out clean, about 35 minutes for the pans and 60 minutes for the bowl. Cool the cakes on wire racks: the pans for 15 minutes and the bowl for 25 minutes. Turn the cakes out onto the racks and cool completely.

4. Reserve ⅓ cup of the chocolate frosting.

5. Using a serrated knife, trim the tops of the cake layers level. Place one layer on a plate. Tuck strips of

waxed paper under the edges of the cake to keep the plate clean while frosting. Spread the top of the cake with frosting. Top with the second cake and spread with frosting. Place the bowl cake on top. Frost it and the sides of the cake layers. These three cakes together create a single round mound: Wally's head.

6. Draw an outline of the walrus' oval-shaped tusk area (as in photo) on a sheet of waxed paper or foil. Cut out and press in position on the side of the cake where Wally's face will be. Press the chocolate sprinkles all over the cake except in the area covered with the waxed paper. Pull off the waxed paper.

7. Mix the reserved chocolate frosting with the white ready-to-pipe icing. Spread the mixture smoothly over the area left free of sprinkles.

8. Press the marshmallows to flatten slightly. Use pretzel sticks to attach them to the cake as eyes by inserting one end of each pretzel into a marshmallow and the other all the way into the cake. Use a dab of frosting to glue an M&M's candy on each eye.

9. Attach the gumdrop as a nose with the remaining pretzel stick.

10. Unroll the fruit rolls. Reroll, tapering one end of each to a point, or simply cut one end of each to a point to create tusks. Attach them to the face, evenly spaced in Wally's tusk area, pointed ends drooping down (as in photo). • The completed cake can be loosely covered and refrigerated up to 1 day. Bring to room temperature before serving.

Per serving: 360 cal, 2 g pro, 11 g fat, 67 g car, 340 mg sod, 0 mg chol

SILLY CAKE

GLORIA GLOWWORM

Serves 12

Preparation time: 10 minutes
plus at least 30 minutes to decorate
Baking time: 45 minutes

She's made from a mix, and her slinky body is a cinch. Just cut a Bundt cake in three pieces and reassemble. Put Gloria in her element by lining a tray with artificial grass that's topped with green doilies for easy serving (see photo, page 262).

1 box (about 18 ounces) cake mix, any flavor
⅓ cup water
3¾ cups (1 pound) confectioners' sugar
Yellow and red liquid food coloring

FOR DECORATION
1 orange fruit roll
1 cherry fruit roll
2 coconut-covered marshmallow cookies
2 brown M&M's candies
2 (2- to 3-inch) pieces peppermint-stick candies
or 2 candy canes with handles broken off
2 large red gumdrops

1. Heat the oven to 350°F. Grease and flour a 12-cup Bundt pan.

2. Prepare the cake mix according to the package directions. Pour into the prepared pan. Bake until a toothpick or cake tester inserted near the center comes out clean, about 45 minutes. Cool the cake in the pan on a wire rack for 15 minutes. Turn the cake out onto the rack and cool completely.

3. Cut the cake in half crosswise to create 2 semicircles. Cut one half in half crosswise again, creating 2 quarter-circles. Put all 3 pieces on a wire rack set over a sheet of waxed paper.

4. In a medium-size bowl, stir the water into the confectioners' sugar. Stir in 9 drops of yellow food coloring and 1 drop of red, adding more color if needed.

5. Reserve about ⅓ cup of the colored icing; cover with plastic wrap to prevent drying. Spoon the remaining icing over the cake, reusing any that drips off. Leave on the rack until the icing dries, about 1 hour.

6. Transfer the 2 small sections of the cake to a serving platter. Assemble by turning one around and joining with other to form an S shape (see diagram). Lift the remaining half of the cake and place at one end of the S. (Once arranged, the pieces should be touching.)

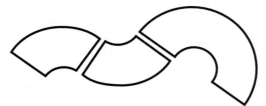

7. Spoon some of the reserved icing over the joined pieces to cover the seams.

8. Cut 1- to 1½-inch circles from the fruit rolls. Press in place all over the glowworm, using a dab of leftover icing as glue if needed.

9. Press the marshmallow cookies, coconut side out, onto one end for eyes (as in photo). Use icing to glue an M&M's candy to each for the pupils.

10. Push 1 peppermint stick into each gumdrop. Insert the other end of each peppermint stick in the cake just behind the eyes to create antennae. • The completed cake can be loosely covered and refrigerated for up to 1 day. Bring to room temperature before serving.
Per serving: 400 cal, 4 g pro, 11 g fat, 74 g car, 280 mg sod, 53 mg chol

SILLY CAKE

A WHALE OF A CAKE
Serves 20

Preparation time: 10 minutes plus at least 45 minutes to assemble and decorate
Baking time: 1 hour 5 minutes

Thar he blows! This big blue whale-shaped cake, made from a mix, will delight every child (and adult, too) at the party (see photo, page 264).

2 boxes (16 ounces each) poundcake mix
2 cans (16 ounces each) ready-to-spread vanilla frosting
Blue liquid or paste food coloring

FOR DECORATION
5 large marshmallows
3 or 4 strands dried fusilli pasta
2 red M&M's candies
2 starlight peppermint candies

1. Heat the oven to 350°F. Grease a 9 x 5 x 3-inch loaf pan and one 8-inch square baking pan.

2. Prepare both boxes of cake mix together according to the package directions. Divide the batter among the pans. Bake until a toothpick or ▶

cake tester inserted near the centers of the cakes comes out clean, about 50 minutes for the square pan and 1 hour and 5 minutes for the loaf pan. Cool the cakes in the pans on wire racks for 15 minutes. Turn the cakes out onto the racks and cool completely.

3. Scrape the frosting into a bowl. Stir in the blue food coloring, a little at a time, until pale blue.

4. To make the whale's head: With the loaf cake standing right side up, use a serrated knife to cut off a slice from the long side of the cake. This slice should be wider at the right edge, about 1½ inches, than at the left edge, about ¾ inch (see diagram, top view).

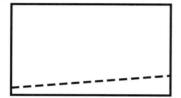

5. Turn the small wedge around so that the wider part is to the left (see diagram). This creates a triangular gap between the wedge and the loaf: the whale's mouth. Lay the cake to the right side of a serving platter.

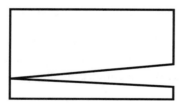

6. Cover the wedge with frosting, including the inside of the mouth. Stick a row of marshmallows into the bottom of the mouth, cutting one marshmallow in half to fit in the narrowest part of the mouth. (You can pull the loaf part of the head away from the wedge to make it easier to insert the teeth.) Cover the rest of the loaf with frosting (and reconnect to wedge). Stick fusilli strands into the top of the whale's head as spouting water (as in the photo). Glue 1 M&M's candy in the middle of each mint with a dab of icing. Press into place for the eyes.

7. To make the whale's tail: Trim the square cake to 7 inches. Cut in half diagonally. Place the halves on top of each other, lining up the edges. Along one side of the double-decker triangle, cut out a shallow

V that runs from corner to corner, cutting through both layers (as in photo).

8. Attach the corner of the tail opposite the V to the base of the whale's head. Cover with frosting.

● The completed cake can be loosely covered and refrigerated for up to 1 day. Bring to room temperature before serving.

Per serving: 420 cal, 3 g pro, 17 g fat, 63 g car, 240 mg sod, 43 mg chol

SILLY CAKE

BIG MACCAKE

Serves 20

Preparation time: 20 minutes plus 1 hour to decorate

Baking time: 1 hour 35 minutes

Our most asked-for recipe ever! There have been more than 6,000 requests for this recipe since we first published it. If you know a burger fanatic, run—don't walk—to your kitchen. It's a lot easier to make than you might think (see photo, page 262).

> *3 boxes (16 ounces each) poundcake mix*
> *6 plain, flat, round cookies*
> *(each 3½ to 4 inches in diameter)*
> *2 cans (16 ounces each) ready-to-spread vanilla frosting*
> *Red and yellow liquid or paste food coloring*

FOR DECORATION
> *2 brown M&M's candies*
> *2 large marshmallows*
> *¼ cup granulated sugar*
> *20 or more spearmint jelly-candy leaves*
> *1 can (16 ounces) ready-to-spread milk chocolate frosting*
> *1 can (16 ounces) ready-to-spread (dark) chocolate fudge frosting*
> *1 box (2½ ounces) chocolate-snap cookies, coarsely crushed*
> *About 30 pine nuts (pignoli)*

1. Heat the oven to 350°F. Grease two 8-inch round cake pans and one 2½- to 3-quart metal or

ovenproof glass mixing bowl with a rounded bottom.

2. Prepare 2 boxes of cake mix together according to package directions. Then prepare 1 single batch. Fill each cake pan ⅔ full. Scrape the remaining batter into the prepared bowl.

3. Bake until a toothpick or cake tester inserted near the centers comes out clean, 30 to 35 minutes for the pans and 55 to 60 minutes for the bowl. Cool the cakes on wire racks, about 15 minutes for the pans and 30 minutes for the bowl. Turn the cakes out onto the racks and cool completely.

4. Place the plain cookies on a wire rack set over a sheet of waxed paper. Put ½ cup of vanilla frosting into a small saucepan. Stir over low heat until melted and smooth. Remove from the heat and stir in the red food color (and a bit of yellow if needed) until the frosting is tomato-colored. Brush or spoon over the top and sides of the cookies. Let stand for at least 30 minutes, until firm to the touch. These will be the burger's tomato slices.

5. Spoon 1 cup of vanilla frosting into a medium-size bowl. Stir in the milk chocolate frosting and red and yellow food coloring, a little at a time, until the frosting is the color of a hamburger bun. Trim the top of the cake layers with a long serrated knife, cutting off any raised areas. Place 1 cake layer on a serving plate. Cover with bun-colored frosting. This is the bottom half of the hamburger bun.

6. Sprinkle granulated sugar on a work surface. Working with 1 at a time, place a spearmint leaf on the sugar and roll with a rolling pin until flattened and the edges are jagged. This is the burger's lettuce. Arrange the lettuce over the top and around the edges of the bun (as in photo).

7. Place the remaining cake layer on a sheet of waxed paper. Cover with the chocolate fudge frosting. Press the crushed chocolate-snap cookies into the frosting to make the cake layer look like a hamburger patty. Using a broad spatula, lift the patty onto the lettuce-lined bun.

8. Spoon the remaining ½ cup of vanilla frosting into a small bowl. Stir in the yellow food color until mustard-colored. Spoon this mustard about 1 inch from the edge of the top of the burger, letting some run down the sides. Top with the tomato slices.

9. Trim the hump (where the cake has risen) off

the bowl cake. Place the cake trimmed side down on a sheet of waxed paper and frost with the remaining bun-colored frosting. Lift onto the tomato-topped burger.

10. To create eyes for the burger, press the marshmallows to flatten slightly and use a dab of frosting to glue the brown M&M's candies as pupils on the marshmallows. Glue the eyes in position with a dab of frosting. Press the pine nuts in place on the top of the bun as sesame seeds. ● The completed cake can be loosely covered and refrigerated for up to 1 day. Bring to room temperature before serving.

Per serving: 820 cal, 6 g pro, 32 g fat, 130 g car, 480 mg sod, 65 mg chol

---

SILLY CAKE

CARLYLE THE CROCODILE

Serves 24

Preparation time: 10 minutes

plus at least 1 hour to decorate

Baking time: 30 minutes

This is what you might call a transformer cake—it's baked in a teddy bear cake pan, then transformed into a cute crocodile (see photo, page 264).

2 boxes (about 18 ounces each) cake mix, any flavor
3 cans (16 ounces each) ready-to-spread vanilla frosting
Green paste food coloring

FOR DECORATION
12 mini marshmallows
2 large marshmallows
2 round black licorice Allsorts candies
2 black jelly beans
20 candy corn kernels

1. Heat the oven to 350°F. Grease a 13 x 9-inch baking pan and a teddy bear cake pan (see Cook's Tip, page 254) about 13½ x 12¼ x 2 inches. Have ready a serving surface at least 27 x 13 inches.

2. Prepare both boxes of cake mix together ▶

according to package directions. Divide the batter between the prepared cake pans. Bake until a toothpick or cake tester inserted near the center of the cakes comes out clean, 25 to 30 minutes. Cool the cakes in the pans on wire racks for 15 minutes. Turn the cakes out onto the racks and cool completely.

3. Cut the teddy bear cake (see diagram A), cutting off and saving the bear's ears and trimming away a bit of the bear's feet. The ears will be used for Carlyle's front feet.

A

4. Cut five differently shaped pieces from the 13 x 9-inch cake (see diagram B). The tongue-shaped piece will be Carlyle's mouth; the other four are for his tail.

B

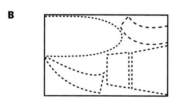

5. Arrange the pieces into the shape of a crocodile (see diagram C).

C

6. Reserve ¼ cup of the frosting. Tint the remaining frosting green (the color will deepen slightly as it stands).

7. Use dabs of green frosting to glue the mouth and feet onto the body. Glue the tail sections together, and glue to the body.

8. Using a long knife, cut out a narrow wedge of cake from the front of the head for the mouth (see diagram D).

D

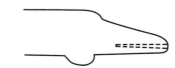

9. Carefully holding the mouth open, spread inside the bottom with most of the plain frosting, then insert the mini marshmallows as teeth, spacing them evenly (as in photo). Spread the cake with the remaining green frosting, building the frosting up slightly over the back. Score the back with a knife to resemble crocodile skin.

10. Glue the licorice Allsorts to the marshmallows with a dab of the remaining plain frosting to create eyes. Glue the eyes to the head. Use 2 jelly beans for the nose, and gently press the candy corn kernels into the feet as toenails. • The completed cake can be loosely covered and refrigerated for up to 1 day. Bring to room temperature before serving.

Per serving: 490 cal, 4 g pro, 21 g fat, 76 g car, 340 mg sod, 53 mg chol

COOK'S TIP

The Huggable Teddy Bear Cake Pan can be found in discount, cookware, craft, and party supply stores.

SILLY CAKE

BOX OF CRAYONS CAKE

Serves 12
Preparation time: 10 minutes
plus at least 30 minutes to decorate
Baking time: 30 minutes

This clever creation will make any child's eyes light up with delight (see photo, page 266). Luckily for Mom, it's a lot easier than it looks.

1 box (about 18 ounces) cake mix, any flavor
2½ cans (16 ounces each) ready-to-spread
*   vanilla frosting*
Purple, red, blue, yellow, green, and
*   orange paste food coloring*

FOR DECORATION
Purchased candy cake-decoration letters to spell
*   C-R-A-Y-O-N-S or a name*
Candles (optional)
Candy star-shaped candleholders (optional)

1. Heat the oven to 350°F. Grease a 13 x 9-inch baking pan. Have ready a serving surface at least 13½ x 9 inches.

2. Prepare the cake mix and bake in prepared pan following the package directions. Cool the cake in the pan on a wire rack for 15 minutes. Turn the cake out onto the rack and cool completely.

3. Cut the cake into the shape of a carton of crayons (see diagram).

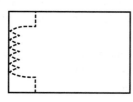

4. Spoon ¾ cup plus 2 tablespoons of the frosting into a small bowl. Tint purple (the color will deepen slightly as it stands) and set aside. Spoon 2 tablespoons of frosting into each of 5 custard cups. Leave 1 batch plain; tint the remaining batches red, blue, yellow, and green. These will be the colors for the crayons. Scrape the remaining frosting into a bowl and tint it orange.

5. Using a small metal spatula, decorate the cake (as in photo): Spread the colors on the crayons, including the plain (white) frosting and the purple. Cover the crayon box with the orange frosting. Spread some of the remaining purple frosting on the lower corners of the front of the box. Spoon the left-over purple frosting into a pastry bag fitted with a small writing tip. Pipe outlines of the crayons, box, and purple corners. Gently press the candy letters into the frosting on the box. • The completed cake can be loosely covered and refrigerated for up to 1 day. Bring to room temperature before serving.

6. If desired, just before serving, insert the candles into the stars and press into the frosting.

Per serving: 650 cal, 4 g pro, 27 g fat, 102 g car, 370 mg sod, 53 mg chol

SILLY CAKE

KEEP ON TRUCKIN' CAKE

Serves 12

Preparation time: 45 minutes

This cake was designed and sent to us by a reader, Pam Bolz of Palmyra, Nebraska. Incredibly, it can be made from start to finish in under an hour. We use candy corn for the cargo, but any candy or an assortment of candies can be used (see photo, page 264).

> *2 frozen poundcakes (10.75 ounces each), thawed*
> *2 cans (16 ounces each) ready-to-spread vanilla frosting*
> *Blue paste food coloring*

FOR DECORATION
5 whole graham crackers
4 round chocolate-sandwich cookies
Assorted licorice Allsorts candies
1 black licorice lace
Candy corn

1. Have ready a serving surface at least 11 x 5½ inches.

2. Cut 1 cake in half crosswise. Set half of this cake and the remaining whole cake end to end. Stack the remaining half-cake on top of the two others at the seam where they meet (see diagram).

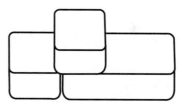

3. Reserve ¾ cup of plain frosting. Scrape the remaining frosting into a bowl and tint a deep blue (the color will deepen slightly as it stands). Reserve ½ cup of the blue frosting to use as glue and spoon ¼ cup into a pastry bag fitted with a small writing tip.

4. Break 1 whole graham cracker in half crosswise. Sandwich 2 whole crackers and halved crackers ▶

with frosting. Line up the crackers in the middle of the serving surface to create a long rectangle. Top the crackers with dabs of reserved frosting.

5. Use some reserved blue frosting to glue the three blocks of cake in place. Set the truck on the stacked crackers to elevate it (the frosting will hold it in place). With a small spatula, use white frosting to paint windows on the 4 sides of the cab. Spread the truck with the remaining blue frosting.

6. Cut 1 whole graham cracker in half lengthwise. Press half into the frosting on each side of the cargo bed for the side rails (as in photo). Cut the remaining whole graham cracker in half lengthwise, then trim to a 3½-inch-wide rectangle and press in place for the tailgate. Glue the cookie wheels in place with dabs of frosting. Glue on Allsorts candy headlights, license plate, and door handles.

7. With the frosting in the pastry bag, outline the fenders, cab, windows, doors, and side rails. Write TRUCK (or the child's name) on the license plate. Place a licorice outline around the windshield. Fill the cargo bed with candy corn. • The completed cake can be loosely covered and refrigerated for up to 1 day. Bring to room temperature before serving.

Per serving: 510 cal, 3 g pro, 23 g fat, 77 g car, 270 mg sod, 112 mg chol

SUNFLOWER CAKE

Serves 12

Preparation time: 5 minutes plus 10 minutes to decorate
Baking time: 40 minutes

All this sensational cake requires is 4 ingredients and 1 hour of your time. To boost your confidence, pipe a few trial petals onto a sheet of waxed paper before decorating the cake (see photo, page 261).

> *2 boxes (16 ounces each) poundcake mix*
> *2 cans (16 ounces each) ready-to-spread*
>   *vanilla frosting*
> *Yellow liquid or paste food coloring*
> *⅔ cup milk chocolate chips (4 ounces)*

1. Heat the oven to 350°F. Grease and lightly flour two 9-inch round cake pans. Have ready a large piping bag fitted with a large rosette (star) piping tip.

2. Prepare both boxes of cake mix together according to package directions. Divide the batter evenly between the prepared pans.

3. Bake until a toothpick or cake tester inserted near the centers comes out clean, 35 to 40 minutes.

4. Cool the cakes in the pans on a wire rack for 10 minutes. Turn the cakes out onto the rack. Turn right side up and cool completely.

5. Trim the top of the cake layers with a long serrated knife, cutting off any raised areas. Place 1 cake layer on a serving plate. Using the frosting from one

CAKE DECORATING TIPS

◆ Bake the cake the day before and leave loosely wrapped at room temperature so the outside can dry slightly. Freeze the cake partially for even easier frosting.

◆ To avoid getting crumbs mixed in the frosting, brush the cake with a pastry brush to remove the loose crumbs and try not to let the spatula touch the cake as you ice it. You can also apply a thin coat of frosting to the cake and let it dry (this is called a "crumb coat"). Then spread the cake with a heavier second coat of frosting.

◆ If you don't have a large platter or serving tray for the cake, cut a large piece of cardboard or a sheet of plastic foam to size and cover with foil or wrap as the recipe directs.

◆ To keep the serving tray free of frosting, tuck 3-inch-wide strips of waxed paper around the cake edge before frosting. Pull the strips away when finished.

◆ For deepest color use paste food coloring (available in cake-decorating and party-supply shops and some cookware stores). Liquid food coloring is OK, but the selection of colors is limited and they will be much paler.

of the cans, spread ⅓ cup over the top. Top with the remaining cake layer and frost the sides and top with the remaining frosting.

6. Scrape the frosting from the remaining can into a bowl. Stir in the yellow food coloring, a few drops at a time (you may need as many as 25), until bright yellow.

7. Spoon the frosting into the prepared pastry bag. Starting 1½ inches from the edge of cake, pipe sunflower petals by squeezing the frosting from the bag while slowly pulling past the edge of the cake, gradually releasing pressure, so that the petals extend down the side (as in photo). Run a layer of petals all around the cake, and another, overlapping layer in the seams between the petals of the first layer. Fill the center with chocolate chips. • The completed cake can be covered loosely and refrigerated for up to 1 day. Bring to room temperature before serving.
Per serving: 760 cal, 6 g pro, 32 g fat, 113 g car, 400 mg sod, 71 mg chol

HOT DOG, WHAT A CAKE!

Serves 10

Preparation time: 1½ hours

Use purchased poundcakes for this fast-food treat because they're firm enough to shape without crumbling (see photo, page 263).

> *2 frozen poundcakes (16 ounces each), thawed*
> *3 1.4-ounce sponge cakes with creamy filling,*
>   *such as Twinkies*
> *1 can (16 ounces) ready-to-spread vanilla frosting*
> *Red, green, and yellow paste food coloring*

FOR DECORATION
Green gumdrops or spearmint jelly-candy leaves
1 green Life Savers candy
1 flexible drinking straw

1. In 1 of the poundcakes, cut a lengthwise trench 1 inch deep and 1 inch from each of the cake edges (see diagram A). Slide knife under cut piece and lift out; save to make French fries. Trim a thin wedge off

each long side of the loaf, slightly tapering from top to bottom. This is the hot dog bun.

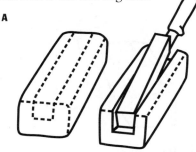

2. Cut and line up sponge cakes (see diagram B). This is the hot dog. Run a skewer through all three sponge cakes (this makes them easier to lift to the bun).

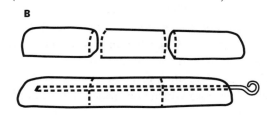

3. Spoon about 1¾ cups of the vanilla frosting into a bowl. Stir in water, ½ teaspoonful at a time, until thinned to the consistency of mayonnaise. Spoon 1 cup of the thinned frosting into a small bowl. Stir in the red food coloring until deep pink. Spoon about half into a cup and reserve for French fries carton. Add green and yellow food coloring, a little at a time, to the remaining pink frosting until the reddish color of frankfurters.

4. Spread frankfurter-colored frosting over the top and sides of the hot dog. Place the bun on a serving platter. Holding the end of a skewer, lift the hot dog into the bun. Remove the skewer. With an oiled sharp knife, cut the gumdrops into small dice. Place at the sides of the hot dog as relish.

5. Put ¼ cup of the thinned vanilla frosting into a cup. Stir in the yellow food coloring until mustard-colored. Scrape into a sandwich-size plastic food storage bag. Snip off a small corner and pipe the mustard over the hot dog

6. Cut a 3-inch slice off one end of the second poundcake. On the larger portion of the loaf, score the outline of a soda bottle with the tip of a knife (or draw bottle on paper, cut out, place on cake, and use as a guide). Cut out bottle shape (see diagram C). ▶

Reserve trimmings for French fries. Stand bottle up and sculpt shape by shaving off pieces of cake with a sharp knife.

7. Stir the green food coloring into the remaining thinned vanilla frosting until the color of a cola bottle. With the bottle upright, frost all sides. For the bottle label, roll one gumdrop with a rolling pin until flattened. Cut in the shape of a label and press on the bottle. Set the Life Saver on top of the bottle as the opening. Cut a few inches off the straw and insert through the hole in the candy.

8. Lay the 3-inch piece of poundcake (from the same loaf from which you made the soda bottle) on its side and trim its edges slightly so they taper in (see diagram D). Stand piece up with the narrow side down. On top, make a cut ½ inch from the outer edges and 1½ inches deep all the way around. Carefully scoop out the center with a grapefruit knife or small spoon. This is the French fries carton.

9. Cut cake scraps in 2- to 3-inch-long French fries. Heat the broiler. Spread the French fries in a single layer in a baking pan and broil 5 to 6 inches from the heat source for 1 to 2 minutes, turning the pieces once, until lightly toasted. Let cool.

10. Add more red food coloring to the reserved thinned pink frosting until a deep shade of red. With the French fries carton upright, frost the top edge and all the sides. Place the carton on a platter. Fill with the French fries and scatter a few more on the platter. • The completed cake can be loosely covered and refrigerated for up to 1 day. Bring to room temperature before serving.

Per serving: 590 cal, 5 g pro, 27 g fat, 83 g car, 460 mg sod, 206 mg chol

---

TOMATO-IN-THE-SUN CAKE

Serves 16

Preparation time: 12 minutes
plus at least 30 minutes to decorate
Baking time: 1½ hours

This cake makes a fun and whimsical finale for a summer party (see photo, page 268).

> 2 boxes (16 ounces each) poundcake mix
> 2 cans (16 ounces each) ready-to-spread
>   vanilla frosting
> Yellow, red, and orange paste food coloring

FOR DECORATION

> 10 large green gumdrops or spearmint jelly-candy
>   leaves
> About ¼ cup granulated sugar
> Mini banana candies and jelly-candy fruit slices,
>   cut into 1-inch pieces
> 7 green jelly-candy fruit slices
> 1 yellow jelly-candy fruit slice

1. Heat the oven to 350°F. Grease and flour a 6-cup Bundt pan and one 6-ounce custard cup.

2. Prepare 1 box of cake mix according to package directions. Pour ½ cup of the batter into the custard cup. Pour the remaining batter into the Bundt pan. Bake both until a toothpick or cake tester inserted near the centers of the cakes comes out clean, about 20 minutes for the custard cup and 45 minutes for the Bundt pan.

3. Cool the cakes on a wire rack, 5 minutes for the custard cup and 15 minutes for the Bundt cake. Turn the cakes out onto the racks and cool completely.

4. Wash, grease, and flour the Bundt pan. Prepare the second box of cake mix according to package directions. Bake and cool as above.

5. Trim the bottoms of the cakes with a serrated knife until flat. Place 1 Bundt cake flat side up on a serving plate. Tuck strips of waxed paper under the edges of the cake to keep the plate clean while frosting. Place the other cake flat side down over the first cake, lining up the ridges.

6. Mix ½ cup of the frosting with yellow food coloring. Scrape the remaining frosting into a large bowl and stir in orange and red food coloring until the frosting is tomato red (color will darken on standing). With a small spatula, spread the tomato-colored frosting over the cake from bottom to top, using vertical strokes.

7. Spread the yellow frosting over the sides and top of the custard cup cake. This will be the tomato's hat.

8. To make the leaves for the top of the tomato's head (as in the photo): Heat the oven to 300°F. Put the green jelly candies into a custard cup and heat in the oven for 6 minutes, until warm and soft. Press the candies together until they stick to each other and form a clump. Sprinkle 2 tablespoons of granulated sugar on a work surface. Place the clump on the sugar and turn until completely coated. Knead, turning constantly to coat with sugar, until most lumps are gone. Sprinkle extra sugar on the clump and roll out with a rolling pin to a 6 x 4-inch rectangle. Trim the sides evenly and cut 7 long, narrow wedges (leaves) from the rectangle. Press the leaves into the icing around the hole in the cake, so their points droop over the sides of the cake.

9. Set the hat over the hole. Place the banana candies around the base of the hat.

10. Create each of the 2 sunglass lenses for the tomato's face by pressing 2 green jelly-candy fruit slices in position on the side of the cake, touching them together so as to make a full circle (as in photo). Trim the "rind" from the remaining 3 green slices. Use 2 rinds for earpieces and the third for the bridge over the nose. Use the rind from the yellow slice for the tomato's mouth. • The completed cake can be loosely covered and refrigerated for up to 1 day. Bring to room temperature before serving.

11. To serve, cut wedges first from the top of the cake, then from the bottom.

Per serving: 530 cal, 4 g pro, 22 g fat, 80 g car, 300 mg sod, 53 mg chol

EDIBLE CAKE FLOWERS

A cake decorated with flowers makes a truly dazzling centerpiece. Using edible flowers either au naturel or sugared is an easy way to make any cake (store-bought or homemade) gorgeous.

SELECTING EDIBLE FLOWERS:
◆ Be sure that the flowers you are using are edible (when in doubt, leave them out) and pesticide-free. Your best bet is to avoid flowers from florists (they're usually sprayed) and to use only flowers you grow yourself, or those that can be bought in specialty produce markets.
◆ Some common flowers that may be eaten: Bachelors' buttons, carnations, daisies, dianthus, forget-me-nots, gardenias, honeysuckle, lilacs, marigolds, nasturtiums, pansies, impatiens, rose petals, scented geraniums, and violets. Stamens and styles found in the flower's center may cause an allergic reaction. To be on the safe side, remove them before using.

TO MAKE SUGARED FLOWERS:
◆ Mix meringue powder or packaged powdered egg whites following package directions. Using your fingers, gently dab the mixture evenly on both sides of the edible flowers. Don't dip the flowers or the coating will be too thick.
◆ Sprinkle superfine granulated sugar over both sides of the flowers until evenly coated. Place on a wire rack to dry for at least 8 hours.
◆ Gently press the sugared flowers into the frosting of a layer cake, or use a dab of frosting to glue them in place.

SILLY CAKE

WATERMELON CAKE

Serves 12

Preparation time: 45 minutes

Baking time: 1 hour 10 minutes

Even the inside of this bright pink watermelon cake (tinted with raspberry or cherry gelatin) is studded with chocolate seeds (see photo, page 262). If you make this with a cake mix (see Variation), be warned that the chocolate chips may sink to the bottom.

RED RASPBERRY CAKE

2¼ cups all-purpose flour

1 tablespoon plus ½ teaspoon baking powder

1 (4-serving) package raspberry or cherry gelatin

1 teaspoon vanilla extract

1 cup milk

1⅓ cups granulated sugar

½ cup solid vegetable shortening

Whites of 4 large eggs, whisked until frothy

¼ cup plus 3 tablespoons mini semisweet chocolate chips

1 can (16 ounces) ready-to-spread vanilla frosting

Green and red liquid or paste food coloring

1 can (16 ounces) ready-to-spread raspberry or strawberry frosting

1. Heat the oven to 350°F. Lightly grease and flour an 8- or 9-inch springform pan.

2. In a medium-size bowl, mix the flour, baking powder, and gelatin. In a separate bowl, add the vanilla to the milk.

3. In a large (mixer) bowl, beat the sugar and shortening with an electric mixer until blended. Beat in the egg whites until fluffy. With the mixer on low speed, alternately beat in the flour mixture and milk mixture just until blended. Stir in ¼ cup of mini chocolate chips.

4. Scrape the batter into the prepared pan. Bake until a toothpick or cake tester inserted near the center comes out clean, about 1 hour and 10 minutes. Cool the cake in the pan set on a wire rack for 15 minutes. Remove the sides of pan, turn the cake over onto

the rack, and remove the bottom. Cool the cake completely.

5. Meanwhile, spoon ¼ cup of vanilla frosting into a bowl and reserve. Spoon the remaining vanilla frosting into a small bowl and stir in green food coloring until the frosting is as green as watermelon rind. Stir the red food coloring into the raspberry or strawberry frosting until a deep watermelon pink. Spoon ½ cup of pink frosting into a cup and reserve for the ends of the cake.

6. Using a long serrated knife, cut the cake horizontally into 2 even layers. Cut the layers in half crosswise to form 4 semicircles.

7. Spread one side at a time of each of 3 of the semicircles with a thin layer of pink frosting. Stand the semicircles up on their flat edge, arch sides up, in a row on a tray or rectangular platter, pressing the semicircles together (so each pink-frosted side touches an unfrosted side) and leaving both ends unfrosted. This is the watermelon.

8. Spread the reserved pink frosting over the ends of the cake, leaving a ¾-inch-wide arch-shaped border unfrosted. Frost the border (the watermelon's rind) with the reserved uncolored frosting.

9. Spread the green frosting over the top of the cake to cover completely. Stick the remaining mini chips into the pink frosting at the ends as watermelon seeds. • The completed cake can be loosely covered and refrigerated for up to 1 day. Bring to room temperature before serving.

10. To serve in wedge-shaped portions, make 2 score lines to divide the cake lengthwise in thirds. Use a long knife and cut through the score lines down to a point at the center of the cake, then make 3 crosswise cuts to get 12 wedge-shaped servings.

Per serving: 640 cal, 5 g pro, 24 g fat, 105 g car, 250 mg sod, 3 mg chol

Variation
MAKE-IT-EASY WATERMELON CAKE

• Grease and flour a springform pan as directed. Prepare 1 box (about 18 ounces) raspberry or strawberry cake mix as directed on the package. Stir in ¼ cup mini chocolate chips.

• Scrape the batter into the prepared pan and bake until a toothpick or cake tester inserted near the center comes out clean, about 55 minutes. Cool and assemble the cake as directed.

Per serving: 600 cal, 4 g pro, 26 g fat, 93 g car, 360 mg sod, 53 mg chol

This Sunflower Cake (p.256) is truly dazzling and easy enough even for a novice.

A slice of Watermelon Cake (p.260), below, tastes as good as it looks and is perfect for a summertime celebration.

Gloria Glowworm (p.250), above, looks elaborate but is quite simple to assemble—a Bundt cake cut into three pieces is all it takes.

Hot Dog, What a Cake! (p.257), right. Just follow our step-by-step instructions to make this professional-looking cake "lunch."

If you know a burger fanatic from 6 to 96, this Big Maccake (p.252), below, is the perfect treat.

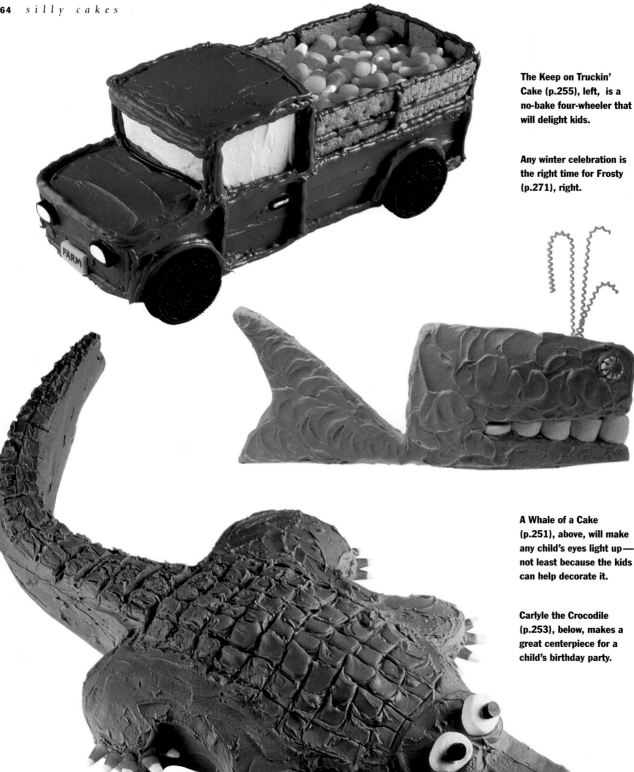

The Keep on Truckin' Cake (p.255), left, is a no-bake four-wheeler that will delight kids.

Any winter celebration is the right time for Frosty (p.271), right.

A Whale of a Cake (p.251), above, will make any child's eyes light up— not least because the kids can help decorate it.

Carlyle the Crocodile (p.253), below, makes a great centerpiece for a child's birthday party.

It's child's play to transform a 13 x 9-inch cake into this colorful Box of Crayons (p.254).

Create a Stack-of-Gifts Cake (p.273) for an anniversary party or bridal or baby shower, and you'll be showered with compliments.

This Bunny Cake (p.269) is tailor-made for an Easter celebration.

Tomato-in-the Sun Cake (p.258) is perfect for summer.

Jolly Wally Walrus (p.250) is a cinch to make with a pair of round cake pans and a bowl.

The Jack-O'-Lantern Cake (p.270) is a Halloween treat.

BUNNY CAKE

Serves 16

Preparation time: 20 minutes
plus at least 30 minutes to decorate
Baking time: 1 hour 10 minutes

Peter Cottontail makes an adorable Easter center-piece (see photo, page 268). Made with a mix and ready-to-spread frosting (see Variation), it's even easier.

CAKE

2½ sticks (1¼ cups) unsalted butter or margarine
  (see page 321), softened
2¼ cups granulated sugar
3 large eggs, at room temperature
1½ teaspoons vanilla extract
1½ teaspoons baking powder
⅛ teaspoon salt
3 cups plus 3 tablespoons all-purpose flour
1¼ cups milk

2¼ cups sweetened flaked coconut
Green and red liquid food coloring

FROSTING

1½ sticks (¾ cup) unsalted butter or margarine
  (see page 321), softened
⅛ teaspoon salt
1 tablespoon vanilla extract
5¾ cups (1 pound plus 2 cups) confectioners' sugar
⅓ cup milk
Yellow liquid or paste food coloring

FOR DECORATION

3 thin pretzel sticks, each broken in half
1 oval sandwich cookie
2 slices from a mini marshmallow
1 green jelly bean, cut in half
1 pink jelly bean
1 tube chocolate ready-to-pipe icing
M&M's candies
Candy flowers
Egg-shaped cookie (see Cut-out Cookies, page 283)
Jelly beans, Jordan almonds, Easter candies

1. Heat the oven to 350°F. Lightly grease and flour two 8- or 9-inch round cake pans, one 2-cup oven-proof glass measuring cup, and one 6-ounce oven-proof custard cup.

2. In a large (mixer) bowl, beat the butter and sugar with an electric mixer on medium speed until creamy. Add the eggs one at a time, beating well after each addition. Beat in the vanilla, baking powder, and salt.

3. With the mixer on low speed, add the flour alternately with the milk and beat just until blended, beginning and ending with the flour.

4. Spoon the batter into the prepared measuring cup to the 1⅓-cup line; fill the custard cup ⅔ full. Set aside. Divide the remaining batter evenly between the prepared cake pans.

5. Bake the cake pans until a toothpick or cake tester inserted near the centers comes out clean, about 30 minutes. Cool the cakes in the pans set on a wire rack for 15 minutes. Turn the cakes out on the rack and cool completely. Meanwhile, place the measuring cup and custard cup on a cookie sheet (for easier handling). Place in the oven and bake until a toothpick or cake tester inserted near the centers comes out clean, about 30 minutes for the custard cup and 40 minutes for the measuring cup. Cool the cakes set on a wire rack 10 minutes. Turn the cakes out on the rack and cool completely.

6. Meanwhile, put 1 cup of the coconut in a zipper-lock food storage bag. Squeeze 3 drops of green food coloring on the coconut, seal the bag, and shake until the coconut is evenly tinted. Using a fresh bag, repeat with ¼ cup of coconut and 1 drop of red food coloring. Leave the remaining coconut white.

7. In a medium-size (mixer) bowl, beat the butter, salt, and vanilla with an electric mixer on medium speed until creamy. With the mixer on low speed, gradually beat in the sugar and milk until blended. Increase the mixer speed to high and beat until the frosting is fluffy and spreadable (you'll have 3⅓ cups). Spoon 1⅓ cups of frosting into a separate bowl for the bunny. Add 10 drops of yellow food coloring to the remaining frosting and beat until thoroughly blended.

8. Trim the top of the cake layers with a long serrated knife, cutting off any raised areas. Place 1 cake layer on a serving plate. Spread some of the yellow frosting over the top of the cake. Top with ▶

the second cake layer. Spread the top and sides with the remaining yellow frosting.

9. To form the bunny: Trim the "hump" off the wide surface of the measuring-cup cake and place trimmed side down on a plate. This will be the bunny's body. Trim an arc off 1 side of the custard-cup cake to make the side flat (see diagram). This will be the bunny's head. Stick 2 pretzel pieces into the trimmed side of the head. Gently connect the head to the body by pressing the pretzels into the top of the body.

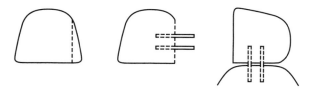

10. To make the ears, separate the halves of the sandwich cookie, scrape off the filling, and spread both sides with the white frosting. Press 1 side in the pink coconut, the other in the white coconut. Frost the bunny with the remaining frosting. Pat the remaining white coconut all over the bunny. To position the ears, make 2 shallow cuts on each side of the bunny's head and gently press the ears into the openings. Insert pretzel pieces at the side of ears if needed to keep the ears in position. • The cake can be made to this point, loosely covered, and refrigerated for up to 1 day.

11. No more than 4 hours before serving, place the green coconut on top of the layer cake as grass. Using a broad spatula, gently lift the bunny and place it on the grass in the center of the cake.

12. Press the green jelly bean halves into the mini marshmallows to create eyes and press into position on the bunny's face (as in photo). Use the pink jelly beans as a nose and draw on a mouth with the ready-to-pipe icing. M&M's candies serve as buttons down the front and a candy flower makes a nice bowtie. Scatter candy flowers, jelly beans, Jordan almonds, and other Easter candies on the grass.

13. To serve, remove the bunny from the cake and place on its side on a plate. Slice crosswise. Cut the cake into wedges.

Per serving with butter in the cake and frosting: 660 cal, 5 g pro, 28 g fat, 98 g car, 130 mg sod, 105 mg chol. With margarine: 400 mg sod, 43 mg chol

Variation
MAKE-IT-EASY BUNNY CAKE

• Use three 16-ounce boxes poundcake mix. Prepare 2 boxes at one time (as directed on box) and bake them in the round cake pans. Prepare the third box to bake in the measuring cup and custard cup (bake cupcakes with leftover batter).
• Frost the cake and bunny using 2 cans (16 ounces each) ready-to-spread lemon frosting. Assemble and decorate as directed.

Per serving: 670 cal, 5 g pro, 28 g fat, 99 g car, 420 mg sod, 80 mg chol

---

SILLY CAKE

JACK-O'-LANTERN CAKE
Serves 16
Preparation time: 10 minutes
plus at least 45 minutes to decorate
Baking time: 45 minutes per cake

This grinning pumpkin (see photo, page 268) can also be made with a mix (see Variation).

CAKE
2¼ cups granulated sugar
1½ cups buttermilk
1 cup vegetable oil
6 large eggs, at room temperature
1 tablespoon vanilla extract
1 tablespoon baking powder
¾ teaspoon baking soda
½ teaspoon salt
5¼ cups all-purpose flour

*2 cans (16 ounces each) ready-to-spread vanilla
  frosting*
2 tablespoons unsweetened cocoa powder
1 teaspoon milk
1½ teaspoons orange paste food coloring

FOR DECORATION
1 bar (4 ounces) milk chocolate
1 brown M&M's candy
*Bear-shaped graham-cracker cookies
  (optional)*

1. Heat the oven to 350°F. Grease and flour one

10¾-ounce clean soup can (label removed) and a 6-cup Bundt pan.

2. In a large bowl, beat the sugar, buttermilk, oil, eggs, vanilla, baking powder, baking soda, and salt with an electric mixer or wooden spoon until blended. Gradually add the flour and beat until thick and smooth.

3. Pour ¾ cup of the batter into the soup can. Pour half the remaining batter (about 3¼ cups) into the prepared Bundt pan. Bake until a toothpick inserted near the centers of the cakes comes out clean, about 30 minutes for the soup can and 45 minutes for the Bundt pan.

4. Cool the cakes in the pans on wire racks, the soup can for 5 minutes and the Bundt pan for 15 minutes. Turn the cakes out onto the racks and cool completely.

5. Wash, grease, and flour the Bundt pan. Add the remaining batter. Bake and cool as directed above.

6. Using a serrated knife, trim the bottoms of the Bundt cakes until flat. Place one cake flat side up on a serving plate. Tuck strips of waxed paper under the edges of the cake to keep the plate clean while frosting. Place the other cake flat side down over the first cake, lining up the ridges. This double-Bundt construction is the pumpkin.

7. In a cup, mix ⅓ cup of the vanilla frosting, the cocoa powder, and the milk. Scrape the remaining vanilla frosting into a large bowl. Stir in the food coloring (the color will darken upon standing).

8. Cut a 1½-inch-thick slice from one end of the soup-can cake. Push the slice gently into the hole in the pumpkin to block the hole. Top with a dab of cocoa frosting. Using a small serrated knife, carve the rest of the can cake into the pumpkin's stem. Press gently onto the dab of frosting. Frost the stem with the remaining cocoa frosting. For the look of a fresh-cut stem, cut a thin diagonal slice off the top.

9. With a small spatula, spread the orange frosting on the pumpkin from the top to bottom with vertical strokes.

10. Cut 2 large triangles from the chocolate bar for the eyes and 7 small triangles for the teeth. Press into the frosting. Use the brown M&M's candy for the nose. Arrange bear-shaped cookies on cake, if using.

• The completed cake can be loosely covered and refrigerated for up to 1 day. Bring to room temperature before serving. To serve, cut wedges first from the top cake, then from the bottom.

Per serving: 670 cal, 8 g pro, 26 g fat, 102 g car, 320 mg sod, 80 mg chol

Variation
MAKE-IT-EASY JACK-O'-LANTERN CAKE

• **Instead of making the cake from scratch, you can use 2 boxes (16 ounces each) poundcake mix. Prepare both boxes of cake mix together according to package directions.**
• **Bake as directed, baking the soup-can cake for 20 minutes and each Bundt cake for 35 minutes. Cool and assemble as directed.**

Per serving: 540 cal, 4 g pro, 22 g fat, 81 g car, 300 mg sod, 53 mg chol

---

SILLY CAKE

FROSTY

Serves 16
Preparation time: 10 minutes
plus at least 30 minutes to decorate
Baking time: 1 hour

Frosty is just the cake to bring you out of the winter doldrums, and he's surprisingly easy to make (see photo, page 265).

3 boxes (16 ounces each) poundcake mix
3 cans (16 ounces each) ready-to-spread vanilla or white-chocolate frosting
Black paste food coloring or green and red liquid food coloring, and orange paste or yellow and red liquid food coloring

FOR DECORATION
3 large gumdrops or spearmint jelly-candy leaves
Granulated sugar
2 yellow M&M's candies
1 ice cream sugar cone
12 each red and yellow sugar-coated jelly rings, each ring cut in half
2 mini chocolate-sandwich cookies
1 red licorice twist, cut in ¾-inch pieces

1. Heat the oven to 350°F. Grease and flour a 6-cup Bundt pan, an 8-inch round cake pan, and ▶

6 standard-size muffin cups. (You'll only be using one muffin-size cake for Frosty. Enjoy the rest.)

2. Prepare 1 box of cake mix according to package directions. Pour the batter into the Bundt pan. Bake until a toothpick or cake tester inserted near the center of the cake comes out clean, about 40 minutes.

3. Cool the cake in the pan on a wire rack for 15 minutes. Turn the cake out onto the rack and cool completely.

4. Wash, grease, and flour the Bundt pan. Prepare a second box of cake mix according to package directions. Bake and cool as directed.

5. Prepare the third box of cake mix. Pour 1 inch of batter into the prepared 8-inch cake pan and the remainder into the muffin cups. Bake until a toothpick or cake tester inserted near the center of the cake comes out clean, about 20 minutes for the pan and 15 minutes for the muffins. Cool the cakes on wire racks, 10 minutes for the pan and 5 minutes for the muffins. Turn out onto the racks and cool completely.

6. Trim the bottom of the Bundt cakes and the top of 1 muffin with a long serrated knife until flat. Place 1 Bundt cake flat side up on a serving plate. Tuck strips of waxed paper under the edges of the cake to keep the plate clean while frosting. Place a second cake flat side down over the first, lining up the ridges.

7. Trim the 8-inch round cake to a 6-inch round, creating the brim for Frosty's hat. Glue the muffin to the brim as the crown of the hat with a dab of frosting. In a small bowl, mix 1 cup of the frosting with black paste food coloring or mixed green and red liquid food coloring until the frosting is dark (the color will darken on standing). With a small spatula, spread over the top and sides of the hat.

8. To make the hatband: Heat the oven to 300°F. Put the gumdrops into a custard cup and heat in the oven until warm and soft, 4 minutes. Press them together until they form a clump. Sprinkle a few tablespoons of granulated sugar on a work surface. Place the clump on the sugar and turn to coat. Roll out with rolling pin to a 12-inch-long strip. Trim evenly to ½ inch wide. Carefully wrap this strip around the base of the crown, cut off and reserve the excess, and pinch the ends of the band together. Use frosting to glue the hatband ends together, and glue on the yellow M&M's candies at that spot as well. The extra gumdrop

material can also be attached here as tassels (as in photo). Let the hat stand for at least 20 minutes, until the frosting is dry and firm to the touch.

9. To make the nose: Using a serrated knife, trim about 1½ inches off the wide end of the ice cream cone. Mix about 2 tablespoons of frosting with orange paste coloring or a few drops each of red and yellow liquid food coloring until carrot-colored. Spread over the cone. Let stand for at least 20 minutes or until firm (or you can use a real baby carrot).

10. With a small spatula, spread the remaining uncolored frosting over the snowman from top to bottom with vertical strokes. Remove the strips of waxed paper. Arrange the jelly-candy rings around the base as a muffler. Set the hat over the hole in the top of the cake. Gently press the cookies in place for eyes, the ice cream cone in place for the nose, and a line of the red licorice pieces in place for a smiling mouth. • The completed cake can be loosely covered and refrigerated for up to 1 day. Bring to room temperature before serving.

11. To serve, cut wedges first from the top of the cake, then from the bottom.

Per serving: 790 cal, 5 g pro, 32 g fat, 119 g car, 440 mg sod, 80 mg chol

---

PASTRY BAG TIPS

◆ There are several sizes of pastry bags. The 12-inch bag is the best size to use for most cake decorating.

◆ Look for reusable polyester pastry bags or disposable plastic bags, which are used once then thrown away.

◆ Don't fill a pastry bag more than 2/3 full. This will give you more control over the pressure as you pipe. It will also prevent the icing from coming out of the top of the bag as you pipe.

◆ Fold down the end of the bag to form a cuff when you fill the bag. Unfold the cuff and push down the frosting toward the tip.

◆ Squeeze a little frosting into a bowl to force out air bubbles.

◆ The piping effect depends on the amount of pressure applied and on the angle of the bag. The bag is usually held at an angle between 45 and 90 degrees. For fine piping, exert minimum but steady pressure. For a heavy, bold decoration, apply more pressure on the bag.

SILLY CAKE

STACK–OF–GIFTS CAKE

Serves 12

Preparation time: 15 minutes plus 1½ hours to decorate

Baking time: 35 minutes

By changing the color of the ribbons and using different candy decorations, you can suit this charming cake to all sorts of occasions. You don't even need a special pan (see photo, page 267). The "ribbons" can be made with buttercream, instead of marzipan, if you prefer (see Variation).

CHOCOLATE CAKE

1 cup water

¾ cup unsweetened cocoa powder

2 sticks (1 cup) butter or margarine (see page 321), softened

2 cups all-purpose flour

2 cups granulated sugar

1½ teaspoons baking soda

½ cup buttermilk or plain low-fat or nonfat yogurt

2 large eggs, at room temperature

1 teaspoon vanilla extract

½ teaspoon almond extract (optional)

BUTTERCREAM FROSTING

2 sticks (1 cup) butter or margarine (see page 321), softened

2 pounds (about 8 cups) confectioners' sugar

6 tablespoons milk

2 teaspoons vanilla extract

FOR DECORATION

Multicolored candy stars, from baking section of supermarket

2 rolls (7 ounces each) marzipan (not almond paste) (see page 333)

Confectioners' sugar

Green, yellow, blue, pink, and purple paste food coloring

1. Heat the oven to 350°F. Grease a 13 x 9-inch baking pan. Line the bottom with waxed paper, cut to fit.

2. Make the cake: In a medium-size saucepan, bring the water to a boil. Stir in the cocoa and butter until well blended.

3. In a large (mixer) bowl, beat the flour, sugar, and baking soda with an electric mixer on low speed until blended. Gradually pour in the butter mixture. Increase the mixer speed to medium and beat until well blended. Beat in the buttermilk, eggs, and extract(s) until blended. Pour the batter into the prepared pan.

4. Bake until a toothpick or cake tester inserted near the center of the cake comes out clean, 30 to 35 minutes. Cool the cake in the pan on a wire rack for 15 minutes. Turn the cake out onto the rack and peel off the paper. Turn right side up and cool completely.

5. In a medium-size (mixer) bowl, beat the butter, sugar, milk, and vanilla with an electric mixer until well blended, fluffy, and spreadable. (Makes 4½ cups of frosting.)

6. Line 2 large cookie sheets or a large area on a countertop with waxed paper. Put the cake right side up on a cutting board. If the center is higher than sides, slice off the raised part with a serrated knife. Cut the cake in half crosswise (see diagram). Remove one half to waxed paper. Cut the remaining piece in half crosswise and remove one of those pieces to waxed paper. (Leave a space in between the pieces for easier frosting.) Again, cut the remaining piece in half crosswise and remove one of those pieces to waxed paper. Repeat this procedure two more times, so you end up with 6 pieces (though you only need 5, so do what you wish with one of the 2 smallest pieces). Frost the sides, then the top of each piece, decorating each piece with candy stars before frosting the next. These are the gift boxes. • The cakes can be prepared up to this point 3 days ahead. Store at room temperature, covered with inverted bowls or anything that covers the cake without touching the frosting.

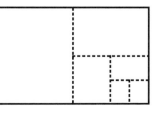

7. To make the ribbons and bows for each gift: Cut one roll of marzipan in half (these are for the ▶

two largest layers). Cut the other roll in thirds. (When not actually working with marzipan, keep the pieces wrapped airtight to prevent drying.) Sprinkle a work surface with confectioners' sugar. Tint each piece of marzipan by kneading in a small amount of food coloring (add a little at a time and continue kneading until evenly colored). Pat each piece into a disk. Place one of the two largest disks on a large square of plastic wrap.

Ribbon: With a rolling pin, roll out one disk to a strip ⅛-inch thick and at least 8 inches long. With a fluted pastry wheel or sharp knife, cut two 8 x 1-inch strips. Peel from the plastic wrap and drape over the opposite corners of the largest gift, tucking the ends under (as in photo).

Bow: Cut a 7½ x 1¼-inch strip. Peel from the plastic wrap and slightly moisten the center with water. Bring the ends to the middle and press gently to adhere. Next cut a 2½ x 1-inch strip. Loop the strip around the middle of the bow and press the ends together in the back. Cut 2 triangular strips, each 3 inches long and 1¼ inches wide at the wide end. Cut a V from each of the wide ends. Press the narrow ends onto the back of the bow, with the wide ends fanning outward (as in photo). Set the bow aside.

8. Repeat with the remaining pieces of marzipan, cutting each tie and ribbon a little narrower and shorter for each layer (the two smallest bows are just narrow strips looped to resemble string ties). Scraps may be kneaded together and rerolled.

9. When all the gifts have their ribbons in place, lift each with one or two spatulas to a serving platter, stacking them artfully on top of one another. Put the bows in place upon the ribbons. Scatter more candy stars on the platter around the cake. • The cake can be completed and kept at cool room temperature for up to 8 hours.

10. To serve, lift the top gift from the stack to a plate. Cut in half. Remove the remaining gifts one at a time and cut into serving-size portions.

Per serving with butter in the cake and frosting: 810 cal, 5 g pro, 33 g fat, 129 g car, 500 mg sod, 120 mg chol. With margarine: 540 mg sod, 37 mg chol

Variation
BUTTERCREAM BOW CAKE

• Prepare the cake and frosting as directed through step 6.
• Make an additional half-recipe of buttercream frosting. Divide the half-recipe of frosting into 5 equal portions. Tint each portion with green, yellow, blue, pink, and purple paste food coloring (liquid food coloring may be used but colors won't be as vibrant). Spoon the tinted frosting into 5 piping bags fitted with tips (we used a #47 ribbon tip for purple ribbon, #46 ribbon tip for green, #98 shell tip for pink, #16 star tip for blue, and #3 round tip for yellow).
• Pipe all except the pink and purple bows. Stack the layers, then pipe the remaining bows by piping loops from the center out, then back to the center. (Practice on a sheet of waxed paper.)
• The completed cake can be kept at cool room temperature for up to 24 hours.

Per serving: 810 cal, 5 g pro, 33 g fat, 129 g car, 500 mg sod, 120 mg chol. With margarine: 540 mg sod, 37 mg chol

WHAT TO DO WITH CAKE SCRAPS

◆ Petits fours: Cut out small cakes with cookie cutters. Heat ready-to-spread canned frosting until melted. Spoon over the cakes. Chill until set.

◆ Parfaits: Cut the scraps into small pieces and layer with pudding or fruit in goblets.

◆ "Mud" cups: Press the tops of frosted cupcakes into crumbled cake. Tuck a gummy worm or two into each.

◆ Mini ice cream sandwiches: Cut bite-size pieces into 2 layers. Fill with ice cream, wrap, and freeze.

◆ Banana splits: Surround dessert-size pieces with sliced bananas. Top the cake with hot fudge or butterscotch ice cream topping, whipped cream, nuts, and a cherry.

◆ "Dirty" snowballs: Roll scoops of frozen yogurt in finely crumbled cake until coated. Wrap and freeze. Serve with chocolate syrup.

HOLIDAY DESSERTS

> *"Everyone has something secret they like to eat."*
> M.F.K. FISHER

Holidays are popular times for entertaining, and they inspire us to make special desserts to mark the occasion. We've created a collection of show-stoppers—including cakes, pies, cookies, and confections—all sure to dazzle friends and family.

For Valentine's Day, there is a luscious tiered chocolate heart cake. For Easter, there is a light and airy orange chiffon cake decorated with sponge cookies to resemble an Easter basket. For a post-barbecue dessert to enjoy with Fourth of July fireworks, try the Lemon Cheesecake Flag Bars.

For Thanksgiving and Christmas, we offer an assortment of traditional pies and cookies—plus some variations that may well begin new traditions in your family.

Food makes everyone happy, and a gift from the kitchen is always appreciated. Our recipes for food gifts are easy to prepare and a joy to receive.

VALENTINE'S DAY

Chocolate-Raspberry Heart Cake, 278
Chocolate-Covered Cherries, 279
Marbled Truffles, 280

EASTER

Chocolate Ribbon Coconut Cream Pie, 282
Coconut Nest Egg Cookies, 284
Cut-Out Cookies, 283
Orange Chiffon Easter Basket Cake, 280

PASSOVER

Amaretti, 286
Chocolate-Orange Sponge Cake, 285
Nut Cake with Fruit Sauce, 284

FOURTH OF JULY

Big Bang Cupcake Cake, 286
Individual Cheesecake Flags, 288
Lemon Cheesecake Flag Bars, 287
Starry Shortcake, 288

HALLOWEEN

Caramel Apples, 291
Popcorn Balls, 291
Pumpkin-Chocolate Cake, 289

THANKSGIVING

Apple, Date, and Pecan Pie, 295
Cold Pumpkin Soufflé, 295
Crimson Pie, 293
Gingerbread-Pumpkin Ice Cream Roll, 296
Holiday Pecan Cake, 292
Honey Pumpkin Pie with Orange Whipped Cream, 292

HANUKKAH

Apple Fritters, 297
Butter Strips with Honey-Almond
    Glaze, 298
Orange-Poppy Seed Cookies, 297

CHRISTMAS

Austrian Linzer Cookies, 307
Chocolate-Dipped Fruit
    and Cookie Wreath, 300
Chocolate-Orange
    Cups, 308
Cinnamon Triangles, 310
Cocoa-Mint Wafers, 310
Coconut Crispies, 306
Cranberry Icebox
    Cookies, 309
Fruitcake Squares, 311
No-Bake Petits Fours, 305
Pine Cone Cake, 299
Spice Cookie Cutouts, 308
Spiral Cookies, 306

GIFTS FROM THE KITCHEN

Almond Chocolate-Covered
    Toffee, 311
Cranberry Pecan Loaves, 314
Double-Dipped Chocolate
    Caramel Apple, 316
Easy Triple-Chocolate Fudge, 312
Peanut Butter and Banana
    Fudge, 312
Pear Quick Breads, 315
Peppermint Stick Fudge, 312
Petite Gingerbreads, 313
Sea Glass Candy, 312
Tropical Fruit Cakes, 314

THE CANDY DISH

Almond Chocolate-Covered
    Toffee, 311
Chocolate-Covered Cherries, 279
Easy Triple-Chocolate Fudge, 312
Marbled Truffles, 280
Peanut Butter and Banana
    Fudge, 312
Peppermint Stick Fudge, 312
Sea Glass Candy, 312

GREAT CAKES

Big Bang Cupcake Cake, 286
Chocolate Raspberry Heart
    Cake, 278
Holiday Pecan Cake, 292
Orange Chiffon Easter Basket
    Cake, 280
Pine Cone Cake, 299
Pumpkin-Chocolate Cake, 289

GREAT COOKIES

Amaretti, 286
Austrian Linzer Cookies, 307
Butter Strips with Honey-Almond
    Glaze, 298
Cinnamon Triangles, 310
Cocoa-Mint Wafers, 310

Coconut Crispies, 306
Coconut Nest Egg Cookies, 284
Cranberry Icebox Cookies, 309
Cut-Out Cookies, 283
Orange-Poppy Seed Cookies, 297
Spice Cookie Cutouts, 308
Spiral Cookies, 306

CHOCOLATE INDULGENCES

Almond Chocolate-Covered
    Toffee, 311
Chocolate-Raspberry Heart
    Cake, 278
Chocolate Ribbon Coconut Cream
    Pie, 282
Chocolate-Covered Cherries, 279
Chocolate-Dipped Fruit and
    Cookie Wreath, 300
Chocolate-Orange Cups, 308
Double-Dipped Chocolate Caramel
    Apple, 316
Easy Triple-Chocolate Fudge, 312
Marbled Truffles, 280
Pine Cone Cake, 299
Pumpkin-Chocolate Cake, 289
Spiral Cookies, 306

Whether you're celebrating with your sweetheart or your whole family, nothing says Valentine's Day more than chocolate, and rich, sweet chocolate is what's featured in these three decadent treats.

VALENTINE'S DAY

CHOCOLATE–RASPBERRY HEART CAKE

Serves 12

Preparation time: 45 minutes plus cooling

Baking time: 25 minutes

Roses may be red, and candy may be dandy, but if you really want to impress your loved ones on Valentine's Day, try this heart-shaped chocolate cake, iced with a bittersweet chocolate frosting.

CHOCOLATE CAKE

5 ounces unsweetened chocolate

1 stick (½ cup) butter or margarine (see page 321), softened

1¾ cups granulated sugar

3 large eggs, at room temperature

1 teaspoon baking soda

1 teaspoon vanilla extract

2 cups all-purpose flour

1 cup milk, at room temperature

RASPBERRY SYRUP

3 tablespoons seedless red-raspberry jam

3 tablespoons very hot water

CHOCOLATE FROSTING

12 ounces bittersweet or semisweet chocolate, finely chopped

2 tablespoons butter, softened

1 cup heavy (whipping) cream

2 tablespoons corn syrup

For garnish: fresh raspberries

1. Heat the oven to 350°F. Grease a 15½ x 10½-inch jelly roll pan. Line the bottom of the pan with waxed paper, cut to fit. Grease and lightly flour the paper.

2. Make the cake: Melt the chocolate in the top of a double boiler set over simmering (not boiling) water, stirring until smooth. (Or microwave the chocolate in a microwave-safe bowl or glass measure, uncovered, on High for 1 minute; stir until smooth and melted. Repeat as necessary, microwaving for 20 seconds at a time, then stirring until smooth.) Cool slightly.

3. In a large (mixer) bowl, beat the butter and sugar with an electric mixer until smooth. Add the eggs one at a time, beating well after each addition. Beat in the cooled chocolate, baking soda, and vanilla. With the mixer on low speed, alternately add the flour and milk in 3 additions, beginning and ending with the flour (don't overmix). Spread the batter evenly in the prepared pan.

4. Bake until a toothpick or cake tester inserted into the center comes out clean, about 25 minutes. Cool the cake in the pan on a wire rack.

5. Run a knife around the edges of the cake. Turn the cake out onto a cutting board. Peel off the waxed paper. To make the two heart-shaped layers, cut the cake in half crosswise. From one half, cut a heart shape the full length and width of the piece. From the other half, cut a slightly smaller heart (see diagram). Place the large cake heart on a serving plate. Place the small heart on a sheet of waxed paper.

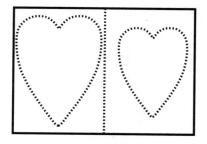

6. Make the syrup: In a small bowl, whisk the jam and hot water until blended. Using a pastry brush, dab the syrup over the tops of both hearts.

7. Make the frosting: Put the chocolate and butter into a medium-size bowl. In a small saucepan, bring

the cream and corn syrup to a boil. Whisk to blend, then pour over the chocolate. Whisk occasionally until blended and smooth. Set the bowl into a larger bowl of ice water. Gently whisk the frosting until thick enough to spread, 3 to 4 minutes. (If the mixture thickens too quickly, remove the bowl from the ice water and whisk until smooth, returning to the ice water as necessary.)

8. Spread the top and sides of the large cake heart with frosting. Center the small heart on top and frost (you will have about ¾ cup frosting left).

9. Fit a pastry bag with a medium-size star tip. Whisk the remaining frosting until smooth. Spoon into the bag and pipe a simple border around the bottom edges of each heart. • The frosted cake can be made 1 day ahead. Refrigerate in a cake keeper or covered with a large bowl. Let stand at room temperature for 1 hour before serving.

10. Before serving, scatter the berries over the cake.

Per serving with butter: 600 cal, 8 g pro, 36 g fat, 72 g car, 240 mg sod, 109 mg chol. With margarine in the cake: 88 mg chol

VALENTINE'S DAY

CHOCOLATE–COVERED CHERRIES

Makes 96 pieces
Preparation time: 1½ hours plus 4½ hours to stand and chill

Ever wonder how the liquid that surrounds the cherries gets inside the chocolate coating? Now you'll know the secret. Allow about a week for the "fondant" around the cherries to liquefy. If you use nonfat sweetened condensed milk, the "fondant" will not liquefy as much as with regular, but the taste will still be scrumptious.

> *4 jars (16 ounces each) maraschino cherries with stems*
> *¼ cup dark rum or maraschino liqueur*

EASY FONDANT

> *1 can (14 ounces) regular or nonfat sweetened condensed milk (not evaporated milk)*
> *2 tablespoons plus 2 teaspoons light corn syrup*
> *½ teaspoon almond extract*
> *2 pounds confectioners' sugar (7½ cups)*

> *1½ pounds dark, milk, or white coating chocolate or ½ pound of each (see Cook's Tip, page 280)*

1. Remove 1 tablespoon of liquid from each jar of cherries and add 1 tablespoon of rum to each jar. Cover, shake gently, and let stand for at least 4 hours to flavor the cherries.

2. Drain the cherries in a colander, then on paper towels. (Cherries are easier to work with if well dried.) Discard the liquid.

3. Make the fondant: In a large bowl, mix the sweetened condensed milk, corn syrup, and almond extract. Gradually stir in the sugar with a wooden spoon until blended. (You may need to work in the last bit with your hands as the mixture will be very stiff.)

4. Line 4 cookie sheets and/or jelly roll pans with waxed paper.

5. Holding a rounded teaspoon of fondant in your hand, press it into a 2-inch circle with your fingertips. Place a cherry in the center and wrap it completely, leaving the stem bare. Place on a prepared cookie sheet.

6. Repeat with the remaining cherries. Refrigerate each sheet for at least 20 minutes, or up to 2 hours, until the fondant is firm.

7. Melt the chocolate in the top of a double boiler set over simmering (not boiling) water, stirring until smooth. (Or microwave the chocolate in a microwave-safe bowl or glass measure, uncovered, on High for 1½ minutes; stir until melted and smooth. Repeat as necessary, microwaving for 20 seconds at a time, then stirring until melted.) Pour some of the chocolate into a small bowl or custard cup. Holding a cherry by the stem, dip it into the chocolate to coat. Return to the lined cookie sheet. Repeat with the remaining cherries, remelting the chocolate as needed. Refrigerate for 10 minutes, or until the coating is firm. ▶

8. Remove from the refrigerator, cover loosely, and store the candies at room temperature for 1 week to allow the centers to liquefy; then refrigerate in airtight containers up to 1 month.

Per piece: 110 cal, 1 g pro, 3 g fat, 22 g car, 20 mg sod, 1 mg chol. With nonfat sweetened condensed milk: 2 g fat, 0 mg chol

COOK'S TIP

Look for chocolate-coating wafers in the baking or produce section of your market or in stores with a cake-decorating department.

VALENTINE'S DAY

MARBLED TRUFFLES

Makes 72 pieces

Preparation time: 20 minutes plus at least 4 hours to chill

These truffles are surprisingly easy and will look as if a professional made them.

*½ cup white chocolate chips or
 3 ounces white chocolate, chopped
⅔ cup heavy (whipping) cream
1 stick (½ cup) butter or margarine (see page 321),
 cut into small pieces
4 cups (24 ounces) semisweet chocolate chips
For decoration: unsweetened cocoa powder
 and/or confectioners' sugar*

1. Line an 8-inch square pan with foil, letting the foil extend above the pan on two sides.
2. Melt the white chocolate in a sealed small zipper-lock food storage bag (without pleats) in a pan of very hot tap water.
3. In a medium-size saucepan, heat the cream and butter over medium heat (or in a microwave-safe bowl in the microwave on High) until the cream simmers and the butter melts. Reduce the heat to low, add the chocolate chips, and stir until melted and smooth. Pour into the prepared pan.
4. Snip the tip off 1 corner of the bag containing the melted white chocolate. Squeeze the bag and drizzle the white chocolate over the warm truffle mixture. Run a skewer through the mixture to create a marbled effect. Tap the pan on a counter to settle the mixture. Let stand for 10 minutes, then refrigerate until firm, at least 4 hours.

5. Lift the foil by the ends onto a cutting board. Trim the edges of the truffle block, then cut into nine ¾-inch-wide strips. Cut each strip into 8 squares. Dip the sides and bottoms (not tops) of each square in confectioners' sugar or cocoa powder.
● The truffles can be kept airtight with waxed paper between layers in the refrigerator up to 1 month, or frozen well wrapped up to 6 months.

Per piece with butter: 70 cal, 1 g pro, 5 g fat, 7 g car, 20 mg sod, 7 mg chol. With margarine: 3 mg chol

EASTER

Celebrate Easter with these special desserts decorated just for the holiday. Not only will they get noticed, but they'll get many compliments as well. The Bunny Cake on page 269 also makes a splendid Easter dinner centerpiece.

EASTER

ORANGE CHIFFON EASTER BASKET CAKE

Serves 12

*Preparation time: 20 minutes plus
30 minutes to decorate
Baking time: 1 hour*

You can serve this cake simply frosted or you can make the flight-of-fancy Easter basket. With the easy-to-follow directions, you won't be a basket case making our basket cake.

CAKE

1 cup egg whites (from 7 or 8 large eggs),
*   at room temperature*
1⅓ cups plus 2 tablespoons granulated sugar
1 tablespoon freshly grated orange peel
¾ cup fresh orange juice
⅓ cup vegetable oil
Yolks of 4 large eggs
1 teaspoon orange extract
2¼ cups cake flour (not self-rising) or
*   2 cups all-purpose flour*
1 tablespoon baking powder
½ teaspoon salt

FROSTING

3¾ cups (1 pound) confectioners' sugar
1 stick (½ cup) butter or margarine (see page 321),
*   softened*
¼ cup water
¾ teaspoon orange extract
4 drops yellow food coloring and 2 drops red
*   food coloring*

FOR DECORATION

24 anisette sponge cookies (not anisette toast)
18 red (strawberry) licorice twists
*   (each at least 5 inches long)*
Wire clothes hanger, straightened and cut to
*   25 inches long*
One 32-inch length and two 15-inch lengths of
*   ribbon about ¾ inch wide*
1 cup sweetened flaked coconut
1 drop green food coloring
Pastel-colored jelly beans
1 candy-coated chocolate egg

1. Heat the oven to 325°F. Have ready a 9- to 10-inch tube pan. If the pan has a removable bottom, do nothing to it. If it does not, lightly grease and line the bottom with waxed paper, cut to fit. Lightly grease the paper (don't grease the pan sides).

2. Make the cake: In a large (mixer) bowl, beat the egg whites with an electric mixer on medium speed until frothy. Increase the mixer speed to high, gradually adding the 2 tablespoons of sugar. Beat until the whites form stiff peaks when the beaters are lifted.

3. In another large (mixer) bowl, with the electric mixer on medium speed (no need to wash the beaters), beat the remaining 1⅓ cups of sugar, the orange peel and juice, oil, egg yolks, and orange extract until well blended. With the mixer on low speed, gradually beat in the flour, then the baking powder and salt.

4. Stir about ⅓ of the egg whites into the batter. Pour the batter over the remaining whites and gently stir (fold) with a rubber spatula until just blended.

5. Scrape the batter into the prepared tube pan and smooth the top. Bake until the cake springs back when gently pressed and a toothpick or cake tester inserted near the center of the cake comes out clean, about 1 hour. Turn the tube pan over onto its "feet" (if it has them) or hang it upside down on the neck of a glass bottle. Let cool completely.

6. Run a knife around the edges and tube and remove the pan. Loosen and remove the bottom, or peel off the waxed paper. ● The cake can be covered and refrigerated for up to 3 days or wrapped airtight and frozen for up to 1 month. Place the cake right side up on serving plate.

7. Make the frosting: In a medium-size bowl, beat the confectioners' sugar, butter, water, and orange extract with an electric mixer on medium speed for 1 minute until fluffy. Beat in the food coloring, 1 drop at a time. Spread the frosting evenly over the cake, including the inside of the tube hole.

8. To make the Easter basket: Cut each sponge cookie lengthwise in half. Cut the curved crust from each slice to a thickness of ⅜ inch. You will use the curved crust for the basketwork. Trim ½ inch from each end of the curve (you'll have 48 curves).

9. Trim 15 licorice twists until they are ½ inch higher than the cake. To make the basket, press 1 licorice twist (post) against the frosting. Starting at the base of the cake, place 3 sponge-cookie-arches evenly spaced over the post, gently pressing the ends into the frosting. Add a second post. Repeat with 2 cookie-arches, creating a woven effect. Repeat around the cake, trimming the last arches to fit if necessary.

10. To make the handle, bend the wire hanger in a curve until the ends are 8 inches apart. Cut both ends off the remaining 3 licorice twists. Thread the twists onto the hanger, leaving 3½ inches of hanger ▶

exposed on both ends. Stick the ends into the cake.

11. Weave the long ribbon through the tops of licorice posts. Tie the shorter pieces in bows around the ends of the handle.

12. Put the coconut into a zipper-lock food storage bag. Add the green food coloring and shake until the coconut is evenly tinted. Sprinkle a border around the top of the cake. Fill the center hole of the cake and the coconut border with jelly beans. Set the candy-coated egg in the middle. ● The frosted and decorated cake can be refrigerated, loosely covered, up to 1 day ahead. *Per serving with butter in the frosting: 610 cal, 5 g pro, 31 g fat, 80 g car, 480 mg sod, 133 mg chol. With margarine: 520 mg sod, 71 mg chol. With canned frosting: 580 cal, 95 g car, 21 g fat, 320 mg sod, 71 mg chol*

COOK'S TIP

To save time, you can use 2 cans (16 ounces each) ready-to-spread vanilla frosting. Scrape the frosting into a medium-size bowl. Stir in 1¼ teaspoons of orange extract and the food coloring until smooth and evenly tinted a pale orange. Proceed as directed.

EASTER

CHOCOLATE RIBBON COCONUT CREAM PIE

Serves 8

Preparation time: 40 minutes
plus at least 3 hours to chill
Cooking time: 13 minutes
Baking time: 40 minutes

Here is a delicious and pretty finale to the Easter holiday—it will remind you of chocolate-covered coconut Easter eggs. Without the decorations, it's perfect for any special occasion.

Pastry for a Single-Crust Pie (page 92)

CHOCOLATE LAYER
⅔ cup semisweet chocolate chips or 4 ounces
semisweet chocolate, chopped
⅓ cup heavy (whipping) cream

COCONUT CREAM
⅔ cup granulated sugar
½ cup all-purpose flour
¼ teaspoon salt
3 cups milk
Yolks of 3 large eggs
1½ cups sweetened flaked coconut
2 tablespoons butter or margarine
(see page 321)
1 teaspoon vanilla extract
½ teaspoon almond extract

1 cup sweetened flaked coconut
⅔ cup heavy (whipping) cream
1 tablespoon granulated sugar

For decoration: Jordan almonds

1. Have ready a 9-inch pie plate.

2. Roll out the dough on a lightly floured surface with a lightly floured rolling pin into a 12-inch circle. Trim the ragged edges. Line the pie plate with the dough. Trim the overhang of the pastry to ¾ inch. Fold the overhang under to form a rim. Trim and crimp the rim. Freeze for 30 minutes until firm.

3. Heat the oven to 375°F. Line the pastry with a double thickness of foil. Bake until the crust is set and just beginning to brown, 25 to 30 minutes. Remove the foil and bake until the crust is golden brown, 5 to 10 minutes more. Cool the pie shell on a wire rack.

4. Meanwhile, make the chocolate layer: In a small saucepan, heat the chocolate and cream over low heat, stirring constantly. (Or microwave the chocolate and cream in a small microwave-safe bowl on High for 1½ to 2 minutes, stirring twice, until the chocolate melts and the mixture is smooth.) Pour into the cooled pie shell and spread evenly.

5. Make the coconut cream: In a medium-size saucepan, mix the sugar, flour, and salt. Whisk in 1 cup of milk until smooth.(Make sure the whisk reaches the inside edges of the pan.) Whisk in the remaining 2 cups of milk.

6. Whisking constantly, bring the mixture to a boil, reduce the heat, and simmer for 9 to 10 minutes, until thick as pudding. Remove from the heat.

7. Whisk the yolks in a medium-size bowl. Grad-

ually whisk in about 2 cups of the hot milk mixture. Return this mixture to the pan and simmer, whisking constantly, until slightly thicker, 2 to 3 minutes. Remove from the heat.

8. Stir in the coconut, butter, and extracts. Place a sheet of waxed paper or plastic wrap directly on the surface of the mixture to prevent a skin from forming. Let cool for 10 minutes, then refrigerate until the mixture mounds when dropped from a spoon, about 30 minutes.

9. Stir the mixture and pour it over the chocolate layer. Again, place a sheet of waxed paper or plastic wrap directly on the surface; refrigerate until set, at least 2 hours. ● The pie can be covered and refrigerated up to 2 days.

10. To toast the coconut: Heat the oven to 350°F. Spread the coconut on an ungreased jelly roll pan or cookie sheet with a rim. Bake until golden, stirring occasionally, 8 to 10 minutes. Cool on a wire rack.

11. Up to 1 hour before serving, beat the cream and sugar in a medium-size bowl with an electric mixer until stiff peaks form when the beaters are lifted. Spread the whipped cream over the pie and decorate with the toasted coconut and Jordan almonds.

Per serving with butter in the crust and filling: 630 cal, 9 g pro, 39 g fat, 66 g car, 270 mg sod, 147 mg chol. With margarine: 133 mg chol

EASTER

CUT–OUT COOKIES

Makes 72 cookies

Preparation time: 30 minutes plus at least 1 hour to chill

Baking time: 8 minutes per batch

With one versatile dough you can make these festive cut-out cookies or Coconut Nest-Egg Cookies (see Variation). The royal icing calls for fresh egg whites. If you are concerned about the small but real chance of salmonella contamination from raw eggs (especially dangerous for children and the elderly), we recommend that you make this icing with meringue powder or powdered egg whites, available in the cake decorating section of large supermarkets as well as craft, party supply, and cookware stores.

COOKIE DOUGH

1½ sticks (¾ cup) unsalted butter or
*   margarine (see page 321), softened*
½ cup granulated sugar
1 large egg, at room temperature
1 teaspoon vanilla extract
¼ teaspoon salt
2½ cups all-purpose flour

ROYAL ICING

Whites of 3 large eggs, at room temperature
½ teaspoon cream of tartar
3¾ cups (1 pound) confectioners' sugar
Paste food coloring

For decoration: assorted sprinkles (jimmies)
*   and colored coarse sugar*

1. Make the cookie dough: In a large (mixer) bowl, beat the butter, sugar, egg, vanilla, and salt with an electric mixer until pale and fluffy. With the mixer on low speed, gradually beat in the flour, half at a time, just until blended.

2. Divide the dough in half. Shape each into a ball and flatten to a disk. Wrap individually in plastic wrap and refrigerate for at least 1 hour or until firm enough to roll out. ● The dough can be well wrapped and refrigerated up to 3 days.

3. Heat the oven to 350°F. Have ready one or more ungreased cookie sheets.

4. On a well-floured surface, roll out one disk of dough at a time with a rolling pin to ¹⁄₁₆-inch thickness. Cut out cookies with 3- to 3½-inch cookie cutters. Using a small metal spatula, carefully lift the cookies and place them 1 inch apart on the cookie sheet(s). Reroll and cut out scraps.

5. Bake until the edges are golden, about 8 minutes. Cool the cookies on the sheet set on a wire rack for 2 to 3 minutes, then remove the cookies to the rack to cool completely.

6. Meanwhile, make the icing: In a large (mixer) bowl, beat the egg whites and cream of tartar with an electric mixer until frothy. Gradually add the confectioners' sugar and beat until glossy stiff peaks form when the beaters are lifted, 5 to 7 minutes. (Makes 2½ cups.)

▶

7. To color the icing, spoon small portions into cups. With a toothpick or cake tester, add paste food color (don't forget to leave some icing white), a small amount at a time, mixing well after each addition, until you get the shade you want. Cover with plastic wrap.

8. To thin icing for spreading, stir a few drops of water into the remaining icing until it's thin enough to apply with a brush.

9. Place the cookies, icing, brushes, decorating bag(s) and tip(s), and a glass of water (for cleaning brushes between colors) on a work surface.

10. Dip the paintbrush in the thinned icing and spread over the cookies. Add sprinkles while still wet. To prevent colors from bleeding, don't apply a second color until the first color is dry. Pipe details around the edges of the cookies. Let dry overnight.

• The cookies can be kept in an airtight container between sheets of waxed paper at cool room temperature for up to 2 weeks.

Per cookie with butter: 70 cal, 1 g pro, 2 g fat, 11 g car, 10 mg sod, 8 mg chol. With margarine: 33 mg sod, 3 mg chol

Variation
COCONUT NEST-EGG COOKIES

• Prepare the cookie dough as directed, adding 1 cup sweetened flaked coconut after adding the flour.
• In a small bowl, slightly beat 1 egg white with a fork. Roll tablespoonfuls of the dough into balls. Dip in the egg white to coat, let the excess drip off, then roll in a bowl filled with 1 cup sweetened flaked coconut.
• Place the balls 2 inches apart on a lightly greased cookie sheet. Gently press a Jordan almond in the center of each. Bake at 350°F. until the cookies are firm and the coconut is golden, about 18 minutes. Cool the cookies on the sheet on wire rack for 2 to 3 minutes, then remove to the rack to cool completely. (The cookies can be kept in an airtight container between sheets of waxed paper at cool room temperature for up to 1 week.)

Per cookie with butter: 50 cal, 1 g pro, 3 g fat, 7 g car, 10 mg sod, 8 mg chol. With margarine: 30 mg sod, 3 mg chol

PASSOVER

One of the most important holidays on the Jewish calendar, Passover celebrates the exodus of the Israelites from slavery in Egypt. During their flight, the Israelites had to eat unleavened bread, since there was no time to allow dough to rise before baking. In commemoration, there are strict prohibitions against eating foods with leavening or yeast during the eight-day celebration. The festive meal is the centerpiece of the celebration of Passover, but finding appropriate desserts is a challenge. As well as being simple and elegant, these desserts all meet Passover requirements.

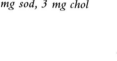

PASSOVER

NUT CAKE WITH FRUIT SAUCE

Serves 8
Preparation time: 30 minutes plus cooling
Baking time: 45 minutes

This airy cake made with ground walnuts and topped with a sauce made from oranges and strawberries provides a special ending to a Passover meal.

NUT CAKE
1½ cups (6 ounces) walnuts
1 cup granulated sugar
¼ cup matzo meal
5 large eggs, yolks and whites separated: yolks into a large bowl, whites into a medium bowl
1½ teaspoons freshly grated orange peel

FRUIT SAUCE
4 medium-size oranges, peel and white membrane removed, separated into sections
1 pint (12 ounces) ripe strawberries, rinsed, hulled, and sliced (2½ cups)
1 tablespoon granulated sugar

1. Heat the oven to 350°F. Grease an 8- or 9-inch springform pan.

2. Make the cake: Put the nuts, ¼ cup of the sugar,

and the matzo meal into a food processor. Process with on/off turns until the nuts are finely ground (about the size of sesame seeds).

3. In a large (mixer) bowl, beat the egg yolks, ½ cup of the sugar, and the orange peel with an electric mixer on high speed until very thick, pale, and doubled in volume, 3 to 4 minutes.

4. Wash the beaters and dry well. In a medium-size (mixer) bowl, beat the egg whites on medium speed until foamy. Increase the mixer speed to high and gradually add the remaining ¼ cup sugar. Continue beating until stiff glossy peaks form when the beaters are lifted.

5. Gently stir (fold) the nut mixture into the yolk mixture with a rubber spatula (the mixture will be thick). Stir in about one-fourth of the beaten whites, then gently stir (fold) in the remaining egg whites until no white streaks remain. Scrape the batter into the prepared pan and spread evenly.

6. Bake until a toothpick or cake tester inserted near the center of the cake comes out clean and the top is lightly browned and crusty, 35 to 45 minutes. Cool the cake in the pan on a wire rack for 10 minutes (the cake will sink about 1 inch). Run a knife around the edge of the pan, remove the pan sides, and cool completely. • The cake can be well wrapped and kept at room temperature or in the refrigerator for up to 2 days.

7. Make the fruit sauce: In a medium-size bowl or serving bowl, mix the oranges, strawberries, and sugar. Chill or leave at room temperature until ready to serve. (The sauce should be prepared at least 30 minutes before serving so the sugar has time to draw out the fruit's juice.) Serve the sauce with the cake.

Per serving: 350 cal, 8 g pro, 17 g fat, 46 g car, 40 mg sod, 133 mg chol

ⒸOOK'S TIP

It's easier to separate egg yolks from whites when the eggs are cold, but for best volume egg whites should be brought to room temperature before beating.

CHOCOLATE–ORANGE SPONGE CAKE

Serves 16

Preparation time: 20 minutes plus cooling

Baking time: 50 minutes

Although made from flour and water, meal made from Passover matzo is permissible because it is made under close supervision to ensure that no rising takes place. In this light and delectable cake, beaten egg whites act as a leavening, adding lightness and volume.

> *16 blanched whole almonds*
> *8 large eggs, whites and yolks separated and at room temperature*
> *1½ cups granulated sugar*
> *1 tablespoon freshly grated orange peel*
> *¼ cup fresh orange juice*
> *¼ cup sweet Concord grape wine or sweetened grape juice*
> *1 cup matzo cake meal*
> *2 tablespoons unsweetened cocoa powder*

1. Heat the oven to 350°F. Have ready a 10-inch tube pan. (Do not grease or line it with waxed paper.) Arrange the almonds around the bottom of the pan at the outer edge.

2. In a large (mixer) bowl, beat the egg whites with an electric mixer until foamy. Add 2 tablespoons of the sugar one at a time, beating after each addition. Increase the mixer speed to high and add 2 more tablespoons of sugar one at a time, beating until stiff glossy peaks form when the beaters are lifted.

3. In a medium-size (mixer) bowl, beat the egg yolks, the remaining 1¼ cups of sugar, and the orange peel with an electric mixer (no need to wash the beaters) at high speed until the yolks are thick and pale, 2 to 3 minutes.

4. Reduce the mixer speed to low and beat in the orange juice and wine just until blended. Beat in the matzo meal and cocoa just until blended, stopping the mixer once to scrape down the sides of the bowl with a rubber spatula.

▶

5. Stir about one-fourth of the egg whites into the yolk mixture. Gently stir (fold) in the remaining egg whites with a rubber spatula until no white streaks remain. Pour the batter into the tube pan, being careful not to dislodge the almonds. Smooth the top with a rubber spatula.

6. Bake until the cake springs back when gently pressed, 45 to 50 minutes. Turn the cake in the pan over onto a wire rack and let cool completely.

7. Run a thin knife around the edges of the cake pan and tube. Top the cake with a plate, turn over, shake firmly, and remove the pan. ● The cake can be covered and kept at room temperature or in the refrigerator for up to 2 days, or well wrapped and frozen up to 3 months.

Per serving: 150 cal, 4 g pro, 3 g fat, 27 g car, 30 mg sod, 106 mg chol

PASSOVER

AMARETTI

Makes 75
Preparation time: 12 minutes
plus 2 hours to stand
Baking time: 30 minutes per batch

For a change of pace from the traditional almond macaroons served on Passover, try these flourless light-as-air, almond-scented meringue cookies. They are delicious served alongside a fruit salad or cooked fruit compote, both excellent finishes to a substantial holiday dinner.

> *4 cups (1 pound) slivered almonds*
> *2 cups granulated sugar*
> *Whites of 4 large eggs, at room temperature*
> *1 teaspoon almond extract*
> *Superfine sugar, for dusting*

1. Lightly grease 1 or more cookie sheets.

2. In a food processor or blender, process the almonds and sugar (in batches if necessary) until finely ground.

3. In a large (mixer) bowl, beat the egg whites with an electric mixer until stiff peaks form when the beaters are lifted. Beat in the almond extract. Gently stir (fold) the almond mixture into the egg whites with a rubber spatula (the result will be a thick, sticky paste).

4. Drop rounded teaspoonfuls of the batter 1½ inches apart on the prepared cookie sheet(s) or foil. Dust the tops with a sprinkling of superfine sugar. Let stand uncovered at room temperature until the tops dry, about 2 hours. (This will help the cookies retain their shape.)

5. Heat the oven to 300°F. Bake the cookies, one sheet at a time, until golden brown, 27 to 30 minutes.

6. Cool the cookies on the sheet set on a wire rack for 1 minute, then remove the cookies to the rack to cool completely. Dust with superfine sugar. ● Store the amaretti loosely wrapped at cool room temperature for up to 2 weeks, or freeze airtight for up to 6 months.

Per cookie: 60 cal, 1 g pro, 3 g fat, 7 g car, 0 mg sod, 0 mg chol

COOK'S TIP

Be sure that the amaretti are completely cool and dry before storing, or they will become soggy.

FOURTH OF JULY

These make-ahead patriotic desserts are the perfect way to celebrate our nation's Independence Day — and independence from the kitchen.

FOURTH OF JULY

BIG BANG CUPCAKE CAKE

Serves 8
Preparation time: 30 minutes

Talk about American ingenuity, this easy-to-make giant cupcake serves eight—a bang-up finish for any Fourth of July celebration. And the best part is, you don't have to turn on your oven to make it.

1 purchased angel-food cake (13 to 16 ounces)

Freezer paper or parchment paper

1½ cups fresh blueberries, picked over and rinsed

3 tablespoons granulated sugar

2 cups ripe strawberries, rinsed and hulled

1 cup (8 ounces) frozen nondairy whipped topping, thawed

For decoration: Red, blue, and gold sticky-back stars (from stationery store); strawberries, blueberries, raspberries; red and blue sprinkles (jimmies); miniature paper American flags (from party supply shop)

1. Measure the circumference of the cake. Multiply the number of inches by 3. Cut a piece of freezer paper of that length. (If the cake measures 21 inches around, you'll need to cut a 63-inch length of freezer paper.) Measure the height of the cake and add 1 inch. Trim the freezer paper to that width. (If the cake is 4 inches high, you'll need to trim the strip of freezer paper to a 5-inch width.) Fold the trimmed paper into ½-inch-wide pleats.

2. Cut the cake horizontally into 3 equal layers. Place the bottom layer of the cake cut side up on a serving platter.

3. In a small bowl, mash 1 cup of the blueberries with 1 tablespoon of sugar. Spoon evenly over the bottom cake layer. Top with the middle cake layer.

4. Mash 1 cup of the strawberries with 1 tablespoon of sugar. Spoon over the middle cake layer. Add the remaining cake layer, cut side down.

5. In a medium-size bowl, slice the remaining strawberries. Stir in the remaining blueberries and 1 tablespoon of sugar. Spoon the berry mixture into the opening in the center of the cake.

6. Frost the sides of the cake with the whipped topping from the bottom to the top, gradually increasing the thickness of frosting toward the top. Frost the top of the cake. Wrap the pleated paper around the cake, flaring the pleats toward the top to resemble a cupcake paper. Tape the ends together.

7. To decorate, stick stars on the paper. Decorate the cake with sprinkles, berries, and flags. Serve right away or refrigerate up to 1 hour.

Per serving: 270 cal, 4 g pro, 8 g fat, 47 g car, 394 mg sod, 0 mg chol

---

FOURTH OF JULY

LEMON CHEESECAKE FLAG BARS

Makes 48 bars

Preparation time: 20 minutes plus at least 4 hours to chill

Baking time: 50 minutes

Whether arranged as one big flag or individually decorated as in the variation, these bars are great for a picnic. Tart, tangy, creamy, and heavenly—what's not to love? Plus, they freeze well.

CRUST

1½ sticks (¾ cup) unsalted butter or margarine (see page 321), softened

1½ cups all-purpose flour

½ cup confectioners' sugar

LEMON FILLING

1 package (8 ounces) light cream cheese (Neufchâtel), softened

⅔ cup granulated sugar

2 large eggs

2 teaspoons freshly grated lemon peel

⅓ cup fresh lemon juice

TOPPING

1½ cups reduced-fat sour cream

⅓ cup granulated sugar

½ teaspoon vanilla extract

For garnish: fresh blueberries, tube of red piping gel

1. Heat the oven to 350°F. Line a 13 x 9–inch baking pan with foil, letting the foil extend above both ends of the pan.

2. Make the crust: In a food processor or with an electric mixer, process or beat the butter, flour, and confectioners' sugar until the mixture holds together and forms a dough. Press evenly over the bottom of the prepared pan. Bake until lightly golden and firm when gently pressed, 15 to 20 minutes.

3. Make the filling: In a large (mixer) bowl, beat the cream cheese and sugar with an electric mixer on high speed until smooth. Reduce mixer speed to ▶

medium and beat in the eggs, lemon peel and juice just until blended. Pour the mixture over the crust and spread evenly. Bake until the top is almost set, about 20 minutes.

4. Make the topping: In a small bowl, mix the sour cream, sugar, and vanilla until well blended. Carefully pour the mixture over the filling and spread evenly. Bake for 10 minutes more. Put the pan on a wire rack to cool completely, then refrigerate for at least 4 hours before cutting. ● The bars can be kept in an airtight container in the refrigerator for up to 3 days or frozen well wrapped up to 3 months.

5. To decorate, lift the foil by the ends onto a cutting board. Cut into 48 bars. Arrange the bars on a serving tray in a 13 x 9-inch rectangle (the same shape as the pan). Pile blueberries in the top left corner, then pipe 7 horizontal red stripes with the piping gel.
Per bar with butter: 170 cal, 3 g pro, 9 g fat, 18 g car, 50 mg sod, 35 mg chol. With margarine: 120 mg sod, 10 mg chol

Variation
INDIVIDUAL CHEESECAKE FLAGS
Cut into 24 bars. Place a few blueberries on the upper left-hand corner of each bar and pipe 3 or 4 stripes with the red piping gel.

Per bar with butter: 340 cal, 6 g pro, 18 g fat, 36 g car, 100 mg sod, 70 mg chol. With margarine: 240 mg sod, 20 mg chol

FOURTH OF JULY

STARRY SHORTCAKE

Serves 8

Preparation time: 20 minutes plus 30 minutes to stand
Baking time: 15 minutes

Although it looks as if you spent hours making this, this dazzling dessert is really easy and sure to be the "star" attraction at any Fourth of July celebration.

1 sheet frozen puff pastry (from a 17¼-ounce box), thawed according to package directions

BERRY FILLING
1 pint (12 ounces) blueberries, picked over, rinsed, and patted dry (2 cups)
2 pints (1½ pounds) ripe strawberries, rinsed, hulled, and sliced (about 5 cups)
2 tablespoons granulated sugar
2 tablespoons water

WHIPPED CREAM
1 cup heavy (whipping) cream
2 tablespoons granulated sugar
½ teaspoon vanilla extract

GLAZE
½ cup confectioners' sugar
1 tablespoon milk

1. Heat the oven to 400°F. Have ready an ungreased 17 x 14-inch cookie sheet.

2. On a 12½-inch square of lightweight cardboard, trace a star that measures 10¼ inches from the top to the bottom down the center. Cut out the star pattern.

3. On a lightly floured surface, with a lightly floured rolling pin, roll the puff pastry out to a 12½-inch square. Place the pattern on top and cut around it with the tip of a sharp knife. Transfer the pastry to the ungreased cookie sheet. With a 1½-inch star-shaped cookie cutter, cut out 16 stars from the puff pastry scrap. Place on the cookie sheet about ½ inch from each other and the large star.

4. Bake until golden brown, about 15 minutes. Remove the stars to a wire rack to cool completely. ● The pastry stars can be loosely covered and kept at room temperature up to 1 day.

5. Make the berry filling: Reserve about 10 blueberries for garnish. In a medium-size bowl, gently mix the strawberries, the remaining blueberries, sugar, and water. Let stand at room temperature for about 30 minutes to release the juices.

6. Make the whipped cream: In a medium-size bowl, beat the cream, sugar, and vanilla with an electric mixer on high speed until soft peaks form when the beaters are lifted.

7. Make the glaze: In a small bowl, mix the confectioners' sugar and milk until smooth.

8. With a long sharp knife, carefully cut the large

star in half horizontally. Place the bottom half on a serving platter. Spoon over the whipped cream, then the berry filling. Gently brush the glaze over the top half of the star. With a large spatula, place the top half over the berries. Garnish with the reserved blueberries and the small stars.

Per serving: 380 cal, 4 g pro, 23 g fat, 42 g car, 92 mg sod, 41 mg chol

H A L L O W E E N

Here's a collection of bewitching treats sure to please Halloween fans of all ages. The spectacular Jack-o'-Lantern Cake on page 270 would also be terrific for a kids' Halloween party.

HALLOWEEN

PUMPKIN–CHOCOLATE CAKE

Serves 16

Preparation time: 45 minutes plus 45 minutes to decorate

Baking time: 1 hour

Without the decorations, this marbled cake would make a great Halloween treat for adults and kids too old for tricks. Decorated (see page 290), it's home sweet home for a holiday witch.

PUMPKIN BATTER

1 cup plus 2 tablespoons cake flour (not self-rising)
¾ cup granulated sugar
1½ teaspoons baking powder
1¼ teaspoons pumpkin-pie spice, or ¾ teaspoon ground cinnamon and ¼ teaspoon each ground allspice and ground ginger
⅛ teaspoon salt
½ cup canned solid-pack pumpkin
⅓ cup vegetable oil
2 teaspoons freshly grated orange peel
3 tablespoons orange juice

CHOCOLATE BATTER

1 cup plus 2 tablespoons cake flour (not self-rising)
1 cup granulated sugar
1½ teaspoons baking powder
¼ cup unsweetened cocoa powder
½ cup very hot water
⅓ cup vegetable oil
1 teaspoon vanilla extract
Whites of 10 large eggs,
*   at room temperature*
½ cup confectioners' sugar

ORANGE–CREAM CHEESE FROSTING

2 packages (8 ounces each) cream cheese or light cream cheese (Neufchâtel), softened
3¾ cups (1 pound) confectioners' sugar
2 tablespoons freshly grated orange peel
2 tablespoons orange juice
Red and yellow food coloring

1. Heat the oven to 350°F. Grease and flour a 12-cup Bundt or tube pan.

2. Make the pumpkin batter: In a large bowl, mix the flour, sugar, baking powder, pumpkin-pie spice, and salt. In a small bowl, mix the pumpkin, oil, orange peel, and juice until blended. Add to the flour mixture and whisk to make a smooth batter.

3. Make the chocolate batter: In a large bowl, mix the flour, sugar, and baking powder. In a small bowl, mix the cocoa, hot water, oil, and vanilla until blended. Add to the flour mixture and whisk to make a smooth batter.

4. In a large (mixer) bowl, beat the egg whites with an electric mixer until soft peaks form when the beaters are lifted. Continue beating, gradually adding the confectioners' sugar, until stiff (but not dry) peaks form when the beaters are lifted. Stir a large spoonful of the whites into each bowl of batter. Divide the remaining whites in half (level the whites in the bowl, then "cut" through the middle). Gently stir (fold) one-half of the whites into each bowl of batter with a rubber spatula.

5. Place alternating spoonfuls of the pumpkin and chocolate batters into the prepared pan until all is used.

6. Bake until a toothpick or cake tester inserted near the center of the cake comes out clean, ▶

about 1 hour. Cool the cake in pan on a wire rack for 10 minutes. Loosen the edges with a blunt knife and turn the cake out onto the wire rack to cool completely. • The cake can be covered and kept at room temperature or in the refrigerator for up to 3 days, or well wrapped and frozen up to 3 months.

7. Make the frosting: In a large (mixer) bowl, beat the cream cheese with an electric mixer until smooth. Add the confectioners' sugar, about 1 cup at a time, beating well after each addition. Beat in the orange peel and juice, then the food coloring, a small amount at a time, until orange. (Color will darken on stand-

ing.) Refrigerate until firm enough to spread, about 30 minutes. (Makes 3⅓ cups of frosting.)

8. Place the cake on a serving plate. Tuck strips of waxed paper under the edges of the cake to keep the plate clean while frosting. With a small spatula, spread the frosting on the cake from the top to the bottom with vertical strokes. Remove the waxed paper.

9. Serve as is or decorate according to directions in box below.

Per serving: 470 cal, 6 g pro, 19 g fat, 70 g car, 230 mg sod, 31 mg chol. With light cream cheese: 423 cal, 14 g fat, 277 mg sod, 13 mg chol

DECORATING THE PUMPKIN–CHOCOLATE CAKE

Follow these steps carefully to make a spectacular Halloween party centerpiece (see photo, page 304).

WHAT YOU'LL NEED:

CATS: large black gumdrops (bodies); licorice lace (whiskers); sugar dots (noses)

WITCH: 1 sugar-type ice cream cone (hat and skirt); 2 chocolate-covered candies (shoes); 2 to 3 tablespoons canned chocolate frosting (hat and skirt); 1 flavored large marshmallow (head); 1 chocolate wafer cookie (hat brim); 5 sugar dots (eyes, buttons); licorice lace (hair, mouth)

LEAVES: marzipan (from can or roll); green food coloring

OTHER DECORATIONS: small black gumdrops (candleholders); birthday candles; candy corn

TO MAKE THE DECORATIONS:

• **CATS:** Cut large black gumdrops in thirds horizontally and arrange the slices on waxed paper. The large slice will be the body, the small piece will be the head; cut ears and a tail from the middle piece, as in photo. Cut licorice-lace whiskers. Attach sugar-dot noses and whiskers to the face with frosting.

• **WITCH:** With a sharp knife, saw off about 2 inches of the pointed end of an ice cream cone. (The end will be the hat; larger piece, the skirt.) Cut about ⅓ off the chocolate-covered candies. For the skirt: If necessary, break pieces off the wide end of the cone to even the edge. Spread the skirt with the canned chocolate frosting. Press the cut sides of the chocolate-covered candies in place for the shoes. For the head: Hold the marshmallow at the ends and spread a thick line of frosting, about ½ inch wide, on one side of the marshmallow. Press the frosted side on top of the skirt. For the hat brim: Put about 1 teaspoon frosting in the middle of the top and bottom of the wafer cookie. Press the bottom on top of the head. Frost the pointed end of the cone. Press lightly into the frosting on the brim. (If necessary, support the witch while the frosting dries by leaning her against a can or sturdy box.) For the details: Dab frosting on the sugar dots

with a toothpick or cake tester and stick them on for eyes and buttons. Smear the frosting on both sides of the head. Cut short lengths of licorice lace and press into the frosting for hair. Stick on a short piece for the mouth. Let dry for at least 1 hour at room temperature.

• **LEAVES:** Put about half the marzipan in a zipper-lock food storage bag. Add a small amount of green food coloring and knead until blended, adding more color as needed. Place the green marzipan between sheets of plastic wrap and roll out to about ⅛-inch thickness. Cut into leaf shapes. Mark veins with a knife.

TO DECORATE THE CAKE:

Lift the witch onto the cake plate or set on the center of the cake. Assemble the cats by lightly pressing pieces into the frosting on the sides of the cake. Cut a slit in each small black gumdrop and insert a candle. Place the candles on the cake. Arrange the leaves and candy corn on or around the cake.

HALLOWEEN

CARAMEL APPLES

Makes 4 apples
Preparation time: 20 minutes
Cooking time: 5 minutes

Caramel apples are almost as easy to make as they are to buy. The recipe is easily expandable to serve more "ghosts" and "goblins."

> *4 medium-size apples*
> *Wooden sticks*
> *1 package (14 ounces) individually wrapped*
>   *caramels, unwrapped*
> *2 tablespoons water*
> *Finely chopped nuts: almonds, peanuts, or pecans*
>   *(optional)*

1. Wash and dry the apples. Insert a stick into the stem end of each apple. Place a sheet of waxed paper on a counter and grease it lightly.

2. Put the caramels and water into a small saucepan. Cook over low heat, stirring frequently, until the caramels are melted and the mixture is smooth. (Or put the caramels and water into a small microwave-safe bowl. Microwave on High for 2½ to 3½ minutes or until smooth, stirring every minute.) If the sauce is too thin, let it stand for 2 minutes before dipping the apples.

3. Spread the nuts on an additional sheet of waxed paper. Dip the apples into the hot sauce and turn until coated. Scrape the excess sauce from the bottom of the apples. Roll the apples in the nuts. Place them on the greased waxed paper. Let stand for 15 minutes before serving. • The caramel apples can be tightly wrapped and kept in the refrigerator for up to 2 days.
Per apple: 460 cal, 5 g pro, 9 g fat, 97 g car, 240 mg sod, 7 mg chol

HALLOWEEN

POPCORN BALLS

Makes 16 pieces
Preparation time: 20 minutes
Cooking time: 10 minutes

These are a traditional Halloween treat and are great to serve at a spooky bash with the Caramel Apples and apple cider.

> *6 cups air-popped popcorn*
> *1 cup mixed nuts, coarsely chopped*
> *1 package (14 ounces) individually wrapped*
>   *caramels, unwrapped*
> *¼ cup light corn syrup*
> *2 tablespoons water*

1. Heat the oven to 250°F. Evenly spread the popcorn and nuts on a cookie sheet and keep them warm in the oven until ready to use.

2. Melt the caramels in the top of a double boiler set over simmering (not boiling) water. (Or microwave in a medium-size microwave-safe bowl, uncovered, for 2 to 4 minutes; stir until smooth and melted.) Stir in the corn syrup and water until smooth.

3. Put the warm popcorn and nuts into a large oiled bowl and gradually add the caramel mixture, stirring to coat well. Oil a ¼ cup measure and a rubber spatula. Using the measure and spatula, scoop quarter-cupfuls of the mixture onto a sheet of waxed paper or a cookie sheet. Let cool slightly, then with oiled hands shape the mounds into balls. Remove the popcorn balls to a wire rack to cool and dry completely. • The popcorn balls can be wrapped in plastic and kept at cool room temperature for up to 1 week.
Per piece: 180 cal, 3 g pro, 8 g fat, 27 g car, 70 mg sod, 2 mg chol

THANKSGIVING

You might say these delectable desserts are a little untraditional for a holiday steeped in tradition, but they were created using customary ingredients, such as pumpkin, apples, and pecans. They're different enough to keep your Thanksgiving dessert table fresh, but they shouldn't upset the traditionalists in your family.

THANKSGIVING

HONEY PUMPKIN PIE WITH ORANGE WHIPPED CREAM

Serves 8

Preparation time: 20 minutes

Baking time: 55 minutes

For many, Thanksgiving just wouldn't be the same without a homemade pumpkin pie. Honey makes a marvelous addition to this American classic, and so does the orange-flavored whipped cream.

Pastry for a Single-Crust Pie (page 92)

2 large eggs
1 can (16 ounces) solid-pack pumpkin
1 can (12 ounces) evaporated milk (not sweetened condensed milk)
⅔ cup honey
1½ teaspoons ground cinnamon
1½ teaspoons ground allspice

ORANGE WHIPPED CREAM
¾ cup heavy (whipping) cream
3 tablespoons orange-flavored liqueur, or
* 3 tablespoons orange juice and 1 tablespoon granulated sugar*

1. Have ready a 9-inch pie plate.
2. Roll out the dough on a lightly floured surface with a lightly floured rolling pin into a 12-inch circle. Trim the ragged edges. Line the pie plate with the dough. Trim the overhang of the pastry to ¾ inch. Fold the overhang under to form a rim. Trim and crimp the rim.

3. Adjust the oven rack to the lowest position. Heat the oven to 375°F.

4. In a large bowl, whisk the eggs to blend the yolks and whites. Brush about 1 teaspoon of the eggs around the rim of the dough.

5. Add the pumpkin, milk, honey, cinnamon, and allspice to the remaining eggs. Whisk until well blended. Pour into the pie shell.

6. Bake until the filling is set, 45 to 55 minutes. (If the edges become too dark during baking, carefully cover with 2-inch-wide foil strips.) Set the pie on a wire rack to cool completely. • The pie can be covered and refrigerated for up to 3 days.

7. Just before serving, make the whipped cream: In a medium-size (mixer) bowl, beat the cream and liqueur with an electric mixer until soft peaks form when the beaters are lifted. Serve the pie chilled or at room temperature with the whipped cream.

Per serving: 430 cal, 8 g pro, 22 g fat, 52 g car, 140 mg sod, 103 mg chol

THANKSGIVING

HOLIDAY PECAN CAKE

Serves 12

Preparation time: 45 minutes plus 30 minutes to cool

Baking time: 1 hour 5 minutes

This delectable dessert is sure to become a holiday favorite along with the usual roster of pies.

PECAN CAKE
2 cups (8 ounces) pecans
6 large eggs, yolks and whites separated and at room temperature
¾ cup granulated sugar
1½ teaspoons vanilla extract
1½ teaspoons dark rum or bourbon

CHOCOLATE FROSTING
6 ounces bittersweet or semisweet chocolate, chopped
¾ cup heavy (whipping) cream

WHIPPED CREAM
2 cups heavy (whipping) cream
3 tablespoons confectioners' sugar
1 teaspoon vanilla extract

For garnish: 10 pecan halves

1. Heat the oven to 325°F. Grease an 8-inch springform pan.

2. Make the cake: Coarsely chop ½ cup of the pecans and put into a large bowl. Very finely chop the remaining pecans. Stir the finely chopped pecans into the coarsely chopped pecans until blended.

3. In a large (mixer) bowl, beat the egg yolks with all but 2 tablespoons of the sugar until thick and pale. Beat in the vanilla and rum. Stir in the pecans (the mixture will be a thick paste).

4. Wash and dry the beaters. In a medium-size (mixer) bowl, beat the egg whites with an electric mixer until soft peaks form when the beaters are lifted. Gradually beat in the remaining 2 tablespoons sugar and continue beating until stiff shiny peaks form when the beaters are lifted. Stir about one-third of the beaten whites into the nut mixture, then gently stir (fold) in the remaining whites with a rubber spatula until no white streaks remain. Spread the batter in the prepared pan. Tap the pan lightly on the counter, then smooth the top with the spatula.

5. Bake until the cake rises slightly above the sides of the pan, is golden brown, and springs back when lightly pressed in the center, about 1 hour and 5 minutes. Cool the cake in the pan on a wire rack for 5 minutes (the cake will start to sink; if the sides hang over the edge of pan, gently push them back into the pan). Let the cake cool completely.

6. Meanwhile, make the frosting: In a small saucepan, stir the chocolate and cream over very low heat until the chocolate melts and the mixture is smooth. Scrape into a medium-size bowl. (Or in a medium-size microwave-safe bowl, microwave the chocolate and ¾ cup of cream on High until the cream is steaming hot, 45 seconds to 1 minute. Let stand for 1 minute, then stir until smooth.) Cool slightly and refrigerate, stirring occasionally, until firm enough to spread, 30 minutes.

7. Run a knife around the cake and remove the

sides of the pan. Spread the chocolate frosting over the sides and top of the cake. Refrigerate until firm.
• The frosted cake can be loosely wrapped and refrigerated up to 3 days or wrapped airtight and frozen up to 3 weeks. If frozen, thaw for 1 day in the refrigerator before proceeding.

8. Up to 4 hours before serving, remove the cake from the pan bottom to a serving plate. In a medium-size (mixer) bowl, beat the 2 cups heavy cream, confectioners' sugar, and vanilla with an electric mixer until stiff peaks form when the beaters are lifted. Spread the frosting over the sides and top. Garnish with pecans. Refrigerate until serving.
Per serving: 480 cal, 7 g pro, 40 g fat, 28 g car, 50 mg sod, 181 mg chol

COOK'S TIP

Take extra care not to overbeat the egg whites. If they become dry and grainy-looking, they won't incorporate easily into the cake batter.

THANKSGIVING

CRIMSON PIE
Serves 8
Preparation time: 20 minutes
Cooking time: 11 minutes
Baking time: 45 minutes

This fabulous lattice-top pie gets its color from cranberries; their tartness is mellowed by raisins. Serve it as part of a Thanksgiving pie buffet along with your favorite heirloom recipes.

Pastry for a Double-Crust Pie (page 92)
1 bag (12 ounces) fresh or frozen cranberries
  (3⅔ cups)
1½ cups plus 2 teaspoons granulated sugar
¾ cup water
⅔ cup raisins
2 teaspoons freshly grated orange peel
1 tablespoon heavy cream or milk

1. Have ready a 9-inch pie plate. Adjust the oven rack to the lowest position. Heat the oven to 375°F. ▶

2. In a large saucepan, bring the cranberries, 1½ cups of the sugar, and the water to a boil. Reduce the heat and boil gently for 6 minutes, stirring often, until the mixture thickens. Stir in the raisins and orange peel. Remove from the heat and let cool slightly.

3. On a lightly floured surface with a lightly floured rolling pin, roll out half the dough to a 12-inch circle. Trim the ragged edges. Line the pie plate with the dough.

4. Spoon the cranberry mixture into the pie shell.

5. Roll the remaining dough out into a 12-inch circle. Cut with a pastry wheel or sharp knife into twelve ¾-inch-wide strips. Arrange 6 strips across the filling, using the longest in the center. Lay the remaining strips over the top in the opposite direction, weaving them under the bottom strips, if desired. Trim the ends to the inner edge of the pie plate. Press the ends to the edge of the bottom crust. Roll the overhang of the bottom crust up over the edges of the strips to form an even rim. Flute or crimp the edge. Brush the lattice and rim with the cream, then sprinkle with the remaining 2 teaspoons of sugar.

6. Bake the pie until the pastry is golden brown, 40 to 45 minutes. Cool on a wire rack before serving. ● The pie can be kept at room temperature on the day it is baked, then wrapped and refrigerated for up to 3 days.

Per serving with butter in the crust and cream: 480 cal, 4 g pro, 16 g fat, 82 g car, 90 mg sod, 8 mg chol. With margarine and milk: 0 mg chol

TWELVE WAYS TO DRESS UP DESSERT

◆ Keep a sugar shaker (from a cookware store) filled with confectioners' sugar at the ready in the kitchen. A snowy dusting of white is the fastest way to give a pretty finish to plain cakes, pies, or cookies—any dessert that has a dry surface.

◆ Cut snowflake shapes out of paper doilies and arrange them on an unfrosted dark cake (such as chocolate or gingerbread). Sift confectioners' sugar over the cake, then carefully lift off the doilies.

◆ Do as pastry chefs do and lightly sift confectioners' sugar over the food and the rim of the plate. Or sprinkle a light trail of cocoa around the edge of the plate before dusting with sugar.

◆ Add squeeze bottles (former mustard and ketchup bottles are fine) to your box of tricks. Fill them with chocolate and caramel sauce, lemon curd (look in your supermarket jam section), or raspberry sauce, and drizzle or zigzag one or more flavors across dessert plates. Or pipe a line and draw the tip of a knife through it a few times for a feathered effect.

◆ Fill your sugar bowl with unusual sugars: colored crystals (also called decorating and coarse sugar), rock candy, or brown raw sugar granules or cubes.

◆ Add elegance to even the simplest spoonable dessert by serving it in stemmed glasses.

◆ Arrange spearmint jelly-candy leaves and cinnamon red-hots or halved red jelly beans on top of a simple frosted cake to make holly and berries.

◆ For a fun nibble to serve with after-dinner coffee, dip the tips of salted pretzel rods into melted chocolate, then in colored sprinkles. When the chocolate has set, stand the pretzels upright in a small straight-sided container.

◆ Shape marzipan (from a can or tube) into small fruit shapes, then paint with food coloring. For apples and pears, use whole cloves for the stems. To give oranges texture, roll the ball gently on a fine grater, then push a clove almost all the way into one side to resemble a stem.

◆ For a relaxed and festive (and as-easy-as-they-come) dessert, put out a big bowl of nuts in the shell (with a nutcracker or two) and a box of fine chocolates. Pour sweet champagne, port, or dessert wine, and let everyone enjoy dessert at their own pace.

◆ If you don't have time to bake but feel the urge to decorate, buy packaged gingerbread cookies and decorate them with canned or tube icing.

◆ Fresh berries, such as raspberries, are a simple way to decorate cakes or individual servings of almost any dessert.

THANKSGIVING

APPLE, DATE, AND PECAN PIE

Serves 8

Preparation time: 20 minutes plus 30 minutes to freeze

Baking time: 40 minutes

This hearty, down-home pie is delicious the day it's made but even better the next, when the flavor of the dates has had time to develop. Serve with softly whipped cream.

> *Pastry for a Single-Crust Pie (page 92)*
> *2 large eggs*
> *1 tablespoon vanilla extract*
> *⅔ cup packed light brown sugar*
> *½ cup all-purpose flour*
> *½ teaspoon baking powder*
> *1 pound (about 3 medium-size) Granny Smith*
>   *apples, peeled, quartered, cored, and chopped*
>   *into ½-inch pieces (3 cups)*
> *⅔ cup (3½ ounces) pitted dates,*
>   *snipped into small pieces*
> *⅔ cup pecans, about half coarsely chopped*

1. Have ready a 9-inch pie plate.

2. Roll out the dough on a lightly floured surface with a lightly floured rolling pin into a 12-inch circle. Trim the ragged edges. Line the pie plate with the dough. Trim the overhang of the pastry to ¾ inch. Fold the overhang under to form a rim. Trim and crimp the rim. Freeze for 30 minutes until firm.

3. Adjust the oven rack to the lowest position. Heat the oven to 375°F.

4. In a large bowl, whisk the eggs to blend the yolks and whites. Brush about 1 teaspoon of the beaten egg over the rim of the dough.

5. Add the vanilla, brown sugar, flour, and baking powder to the eggs. Stir until well blended. Stir in the apples, dates, and pecans. Spread the mixture in the prepared pie shell.

6. Bake until lightly browned and a toothpick or cake tester inserted near the center comes out clean, 35 to 40 minutes.

7. Cool the pie on a wire rack. Serve at room tem-

perature. • The pie can be covered and kept at cool room temperature or in the refrigerator up to 3 days.

Per serving with butter in the crust: 390 cal, 5 g pro, 16 g fat, 58 g car, 110 mg sod, 59 mg chol. With margarine: 53 mg chol

THANKSGIVING

COLD PUMPKIN SOUFFLÉ

Serves 12

Preparation time: 20 minutes plus at least 4 hours to chill

An ideal dessert for entertaining, this easy-to-make no-bake soufflé can be made up to 2 days in advance. It will look spectacular on any holiday table or autumn dinner party buffet.

> *2 cups heavy (whipping) cream*
> *1 can (30 ounces) pumpkin-pie filling*
> *2 envelopes (1 ounce each) plus 1 teaspoon*
>   *unflavored gelatin*
> *¼ cup bourbon whiskey, or*
>   *1 tablespoon vanilla extract*
> *For garnish: lightly sweetened whipped cream,*
>   *ground cinnamon, chopped pistachio nuts*

1. Have ready a 1½-quart soufflé dish or a 2- to 3-quart serving bowl.

2. If using a soufflé dish: Tear off a piece of foil or waxed paper 4 inches longer than the circumference of the soufflé dish. Fold in thirds lengthwise. Fit around the outside of the dish so a 2-inch collar extends above the dish. Fasten the overlapping ends to each other with cellophane tape or paper clips.

3. In a large (mixer) bowl, beat the cream with an electric mixer just until soft peaks form when the beaters are lifted.

4. Put ½ cup of the pumpkin-pie filling into a small saucepan. Stir in the gelatin. Place over low heat and stir until the mixture is almost boiling and the gelatin is completely dissolved, 3 to 4 minutes. Remove from the heat.

5. Put the remaining pumpkin-pie filling into a large bowl. Stir in the hot gelatin mixture, then the bourbon and ½ cup of the whipped cream. ▶

Gently stir (fold) in the remaining whipped cream with a rubber spatula until blended.

6. Pour into the prepared dish or serving bowl. Cover with plastic wrap and refrigerate for at least 4 hours. • The soufflé can be covered and refrigerated for up to 2 days.

7. To serve, remove the foil or waxed paper collar. Spread the top of the soufflé with whipped cream. Score lightly with a knife and sprinkle with cinnamon. Press pistachio nuts into the sides of the soufflé or, if serving from a bowl, sprinkle them over the whipped cream.

Per serving: 210 cal, 3 g pro, 15 g fat, 20 g car, 160 mg sod, 54 mg chol

THANKSGIVING

GINGERBREAD–PUMPKIN ICE CREAM ROLL

Serves 12

Preparation time: 25 minutes plus 10 hours to freeze

Baking time: 13 minutes

For Thanksgiving, no flavor combination could be better than the pairing of gingerbread and pumpkin. The pumpkin ice cream is so easy to make and would be wonderful served on its own or with a slice of pecan pie.

PUMPKIN ICE CREAM

1½ pints regular or nonfat vanilla ice cream (3 cups)

1 cup canned solid-pack pumpkin

1 teaspoon pumpkin-pie spice, or ½ teaspoon ground cinnamon and ¼ teaspoon each ground allspice and ground ginger

GINGERBREAD

1 box (14 ounces) gingerbread mix

1 cup water

2 tablespoons confectioners' sugar

For garnish: grapes, nuts in shells, confectioners' sugar

1. Make the ice cream: Put the ice cream, pumpkin, and spice into a large bowl. Beat with a wooden spoon until blended. Cover and freeze until firm, at least 4 hours.

2. Heat the oven to 350°F. Lightly grease the bottom and sides of a 15½ x 10½-inch jelly roll pan. Line with waxed paper.

3. Make the gingerbread: In a medium-size bowl, stir the gingerbread mix and water together until blended and smooth. Pour the batter into the prepared pan.

4. Bake until the cake springs back when lightly touched in the center, 10 to 13 minutes. Cool the cake in the pan on a wire rack for 10 minutes.

5. Meanwhile, spread a clean, cloth towel (cotton or woven linen) on a countertop. Using a small strainer, sift the 2 tablespoons of confectioners' sugar over the towel, covering an area the size of the cake.

6. Turn the cake over onto the towel. Remove the pan and peel off the waxed paper. Starting at a narrow end, roll up the cake and the towel. Cool the rolled cake completely on a wire rack. (The cake must be at room temperature before unrolling and filling.)

7. To fill, let the ice cream soften until spreadable but still firm. Gently unroll the cake and the towel. Spoon on the ice cream, then spread to within 1 inch of all the edges. Reroll the cake gently without the towel but using it as a guide (the cake may crack).

8. Put a sheet of plastic wrap on a cookie sheet. Put the cake onto the plastic, then use the plastic to wrap the cake. Freeze on the cookie sheet until hard, about 6 hours, before removing from the sheet. • The cake roll can be made to this point, wrapped in foil, and frozen up to 1 month.

9. To serve, trim the ends of the cake with a serrated knife. Place the cake seam-side down on a serving platter and leave at room temperature for about 10 minutes for the filling to soften. Garnish with grapes and nuts. Dust with confectioners' sugar.

Per serving: 230 cal, 3 g pro, 8 g fat, 36 g car, 270 mg, sod, 15 mg chol. With nonfat ice cream: 210 cal, 5 g fat, 39 g car, 0 mg chol

HANUKKAH

Hanukkah is a favorite time for family and friends to gather. These tasty treats are equally terrific for a family dinner or to serve to a crowd after potato pancakes!

HANUKKAH

ORANGE–POPPY SEED COOKIES

Makes 64 cookies

Preparation time: 30 minutes plus 4 hours to chill

Baking time: 16 minutes per batch

Poppy seeds come primarily from poppies grown in Central Europe, which is why they are an ingredient in many traditional Jewish baked goods. The colored sugar gives these cookies a festive gilded edge.

> 1 stick (½ cup) butter or margarine (see page 321), softened
> ¾ cup granulated sugar
> 1 large egg, at room temperature
> 1½ tablespoons freshly grated orange peel
> 1½ teaspoons baking powder
> ⅛ teaspoon salt
> ¼ cup poppy seeds
> 2 cups all-purpose flour
> ¼ cup colored sugar (orange or yellow)
> For decoration: candied orange peel, cut into diamonds (optional)

1. In a large (mixer) bowl, beat the butter and sugar with an electric mixer until fluffy. Beat in the egg, orange peel, baking powder, salt, and poppy seeds. With the mixer on low speed, gradually beat in the flour just until blended.

2. Divide the dough in half. Shape each half into an 8-inch log. Spread the colored sugar on sheets of waxed paper. Roll the logs in the sugar to coat them. Wrap in plastic or waxed paper, transfer to a cookie sheet, and chill until firm, at least 4 hours. • The dough can be made up to this point and refrigerated for up to 3 days, or wrapped in foil and frozen for up to 3 months. If frozen, transfer to the refrigerator 2 hours before baking.

3. Heat the oven to 350°F. Lightly grease 1 or more cookie sheets.

4. Cut 1 log at a time (keep the remainder in the refrigerator) into 32 slices. Place 1 inch apart on the prepared cookie sheet(s).

5. Bake until the cookies feel firm and the bottoms are lightly browned, 14 to 16 minutes. Cool the cookies on the sheet on a wire rack for 2 to 3 minutes, then remove to the rack to cool completely. (Decorate with the orange peel, if using, while cookies are still warm.) • The cookies can be kept in an airtight container or plastic bag at cool room temperature for up to 1 week, or frozen for up to 1 month.

Per cookie with butter: 40 cal, 1 g pro, 2 g fat, 6 g car, 30 mg sod, 7 mg chol. With margarine: 3 mg chol

---

HANUKKAH

APPLE FRITTERS

Serves 10

Preparation time: 15 minutes

Cooking time: 20 minutes

Though potato pancakes are the one food that Americans associate with Hanukkah, any food cooked in oil is traditional and appropriate for the Festival of Lights—which celebrates a miracle involving a supply of lamp oil.

> 8 cups vegetable oil
> 1⅓ cups all-purpose flour
> 1 can (12 ounces) beer (regular or nonalcoholic)
> ¼ cup granulated sugar
> 4 medium-size tart apples, such as Granny Smith or Braeburn (1½ pounds)
> Confectioners' sugar, for dusting

1. Heat the oil in a Dutch oven or electric deep fryer to 380°F.

2. In a medium-size bowl, mix the flour, beer, and granulated sugar. ▶

3. Core and peel the apples. Cut crosswise into ½-inch-thick rings. Pat dry with paper towels.

4. Using a fork, dip the apple rings in the batter, letting the excess drip back into the bowl. Carefully slip about 4 dipped slices into the hot oil. Fry for about 4 minutes, turning once, until golden brown. Remove with a slotted spoon and drain well on paper towels. Repeat with the remaining slices.

5. Dust with confectioners' sugar and serve right away.

Per serving: 160 cal, 2 g pro, 4 g fat, 28 g car, 0 mg sod, 0 mg chol

COOK'S TIP

For crisp fried foods that don't soak up too much oil, use a deep-fat or candy thermometer, maintain the heat, and fry only a few pieces of food at a time. (Too many pieces lowers the oil's temperature.) For safety, keep children and pets well away from the hot oil.

HANUKKAH

BUTTER STRIPS WITH HONEY–ALMOND GLAZE

Makes 70 cookies
Preparation time: 12 minutes
Baking time: 25 minutes

The golden honey-almond topping gives these cookies an Old World feel. This recipe makes plenty for company or to share with friends and neighbors, and while the directions say one week, the cookies will keep just fine for eight nights.

HONEY–ALMOND GLAZE
5 tablespoons plus 1 teaspoon (⅓ cup) butter or margarine (see page 321)
1 cup (4 ounces) blanched almonds, chopped
¼ cup granulated sugar
¼ cup brandy, or ¼ cup water and 1 teaspoon brandy extract
2 tablespoons honey
¾ teaspoon almond extract

CRUST
1¼ cups all-purpose flour
½ cup granulated sugar
¼ teaspoon salt
1 stick (½ cup) butter or margarine (see page 321), chilled
1 large egg, lightly beaten

1. Heat the oven to 350°F. Lightly grease a 15½ x 10½-inch jelly-roll pan.

2. Make the glaze: In a small saucepan, melt the butter over medium-low heat. Add the almonds, sugar, brandy, honey, and almond extract. Increase the heat to medium-high and stir until the mixture comes to a boil. Remove from the heat and let the mixture cool slightly.

3. Meanwhile, make the crust: In a large bowl, mix the flour, sugar, and salt. Cut in the butter with a pastry blender until the mixture resembles fine crumbs. Stir in the egg until blended. Press the dough evenly over the bottom of the prepared pan.

4. Pour the warm glaze over the top and spread evenly to cover the entire surface.

5. Bake until the top is lightly brown, 20 to 25 minutes. Cool completely in the pan on a wire rack. Cut into 2 x 1-inch strips. • The bars can be kept in an airtight container between layers of waxed paper at cool room temperature for up to 1 week.

Per cookie with butter: 50 cal, 1 g pro, 3 g fat, 5 g car, 30 mg sod, 9 mg chol. With margarine: 3 mg chol

COOK'S TIP

These cookies look great cut in strips, but you can also cut them into small diamond or triangle shapes.

'Tis the season to entertain family and friends, and these superb, easy-to-make desserts will help you do it perfectly. Kids will also enjoy the Frosty cake on page 271.

CHRISTMAS

PINE CONE CAKE

Serves 12

Preparation time: 1 hour 15 minutes

Baking time: 35 minutes

This lovely holiday cake is easier to make than you might think. To save time, prepare it in stages. Make the cake layers ahead and freeze them (you can also use a cake mix that makes a two-layer cake).

CHOCOLATE CAKE

1 cup water

2 sticks (1 cup) butter or margarine (see page 321), cut into small pieces

¾ cup unsweetened cocoa powder

2 cups all-purpose flour

2 cups granulated sugar

1½ teaspoons baking soda

½ cup buttermilk or plain low-fat or nonfat yogurt

2 large eggs, at room temperature

1 teaspoon vanilla extract

½ teaspoon almond extract (optional)

BUTTERCREAM FROSTING

1 stick (½ cup) butter or margarine (see page 321), softened

3¾ cups (1 pound) confectioners' sugar

3 tablespoons milk

1 teaspoon vanilla extract

▶

DECORATING THE PINE CONE CAKE

These simple and elegant decorations (see photo, page 304) make this cake a holiday showpiece.

WHAT YOU'LL NEED:

Lemon leaves (from a florist's shop), washed, rinsed, and patted dry

⅔ cup (4 ounces) semisweet chocolate chips, melted

½ cup sliced almonds

Reserved buttercream frosting

Red paste food coloring

Chocolate frosting ovals

1 box (4.3 ounces) chocolate twigs

10-inch-long piece narrow green ribbon

TO MAKE THE DECORATIONS:

• CHOCOLATE LEAVES: Brush the underside of the lemon leaves with a thick layer of melted chocolate. Refrigerate on a cookie sheet until set. Peel off the leaves. (You can refrigerate

chocolate leaves in an airtight container with waxed paper between the layers for up to 1 week.)

• BERRIES: Uncover the reserved 1 tablespoon buttercream. Mix in red food coloring to the desired shade. Cover and refrigerate or freeze until firm enough to shape. Roll small bits into balls. Refrigerate until needed.

• PINE CONES: Heat the oven to 350°F. Spread the almonds in a single layer in a baking pan. Bake for 8 minutes,

stirring twice, or until browned. Cool in the pan. Insert the almonds into the chocolate frosting ovals, starting at the base and overlapping slices until the ovals are covered. Reserve 6 almond slices for decoration. Chill until firm.

TO DECORATE THE CAKE:

Using a metal spatula, lift the pine cones onto the cake. Press 3 almond slices onto the side of the cake and put 3 almond slices on the edge of the serving plate. Press the berries onto 1 chocolate twig. Use the ribbon to tie a bundle of twigs, keeping the "berry" twig on top. Place on the cake. Arrange the chocolate leaves and remaining twigs around the cake.

CHOCOLATE FROSTING

2/3 cup heavy (whipping) cream
1 1/3 cups (8 ounces) semisweet chocolate chips

1. Heat the oven to 350°F. Lightly grease two 9-inch round cake pans. Line the bottoms with waxed paper, cut to fit.

2. Make the cake: In a medium-size saucepan, bring the water to a boil. Stir in the butter and cocoa until the butter is melted and the mixture is blended.

3. In a large (mixer) bowl, beat the flour, granulated sugar, and baking soda with an electric mixer on low speed. Gradually pour in the cocoa mixture. Increase the speed to medium and beat until well blended. Beat in the buttermilk, eggs, and extract(s) until blended and smooth. Divide the batter between the prepared pans and spread evenly.

4. Bake until a toothpick or cake tester inserted near the centers comes out clean, 30 to 35 minutes. Cool the cakes in the pans on a wire rack for 10 to 15 minutes. Turn the cakes out of the pans and remove the waxed paper. Turn the cakes right side up and cool completely. ● The cake layers can be well wrapped and refrigerated for up to 3 days or frozen for up to 3 months.

5. Make the buttercream: In a medium-size (mixer) bowl, beat the butter, confectioners' sugar, milk, and vanilla with an electric mixer until well blended, fluffy, and spreadable. (Makes 2 1/4 cups.) Remove 1 tablespoon of the buttercream to a small bowl, cover with plastic wrap, and set aside for decoration.

6. Make the chocolate frosting: In a small saucepan, heat the cream just until steaming. Stir in the chocolate chips until smooth. Pour into a medium-size metal bowl and refrigerate, stirring often, until cooled but not firm. (If firm, stir over low heat.) Beat with an electric mixer on high speed until lighter in color and spreadable, about 1 minute. Using an oval serving spoon, drop 3 mounds of chocolate frosting onto a sheet of wax paper. Gently pat the mounds into ovals. Refrigerate until firm but not hard, 5 minutes. Set aside for decoration.

7. To assemble: Trim the top of the cake layers with a long serrated knife, cutting off any raised areas. Place 1 cake layer on a serving plate. Tuck strips of waxed paper under the edges of the cake to keep the plate clean while frosting. Spread evenly with half the buttercream. Top with the remaining cake layer. Spread the remaining buttercream over the top (not on the sides). Frost the sides of cake with the remaining chocolate frosting. Remove the waxed paper. To decorate, see box, page 299.

Per serving with butter: 720 cal, 6 g pro, 35 g fat, 104 g car, 420 mg sod, 117 mg chol. With margarine: 460 mg sod, 55 mg chol

CHRISTMAS

CHOCOLATE–DIPPED FRUIT AND COOKIE WREATH

Serves 12

Preparation time: 30 minutes plus about 1 hour to stand

This easy decorative fruit and cookie wreath is the perfect thing to set out for a holiday open house or as a cocktail party sweet. It can be made in advance—just don't expect any leftovers. You'll need a flat, round plate at least 12 inches across to hold it.

1 cup (6 ounces) semisweet chocolate chips
2 tablespoons solid vegetable shortening
2 pints (1 1/2 pounds) ripe strawberries with hulls and/or stems, rinsed, patted dry, and chilled
2 small ripe star fruit (carambola), chilled, each cut into 6 slices
1 cup (6 ounces) white chocolate or vanilla-milk chips
1 pound store-bought leaf-shaped sandwich cookies

1. Line 2 cookie sheets with waxed paper.

2. In a small microwave-safe bowl or glass measure, melt the semisweet chocolate chips and 1 tablespoon of the shortening, uncovered, on High for 1 minute. Stir until melted and smooth. If necessary, microwave again, 20 seconds at a time, until melted. (Or melt the chocolate and shortening in a small heatproof bowl set over pan of simmering—not boiling—water, stirring until smooth.)

3. Dip half the strawberries and half the star fruit slices about 2/3 into the chocolate mixture. ▶ *p.305*

Candy may be dandy, but this Valentine's Day, indulge in our Chocolate-Raspberry Heart Cake (p.278).

Add Cold Pumpkin Soufflé (p.295), above, to your Thanksgiving dessert repertoire. It's a new idea even traditionalists will love.

An embarrassment of riches? Perhaps. But cookies make us wild about the holidays. So pull out the flour, the sugar, and all the stops. Featured here are some particular holiday favorites, including

Orange-Poppy Seed Cookies (p.297), Coconut Crispies, Spiral Cookies, Cocoa-Mint Wafers, Cinnamon Triangles, Fruitcake Squares, Spice Cookie Cutouts, and Austrian Linzer Cookies (pp.306–311), among others.

It might seem that only a professional pastry chef could turn out a showstopper like the Pine Cone Cake (p.299), above. In fact, the decorations are remarkably easy, and the cake tastes divine.

A marble cake is the base for this fabulous Pumpkin-Chocolate Cake (p.289), left, which is equally tasty without the elaborate decorations. Make it the centerpiece for a haunted Halloween party.

Shake gently to remove the excess. Set the dipped fruit on one of the prepared cookie sheets. Let stand at room temperature for about 45 minutes, until the chocolate is set.

4. Melt the white chocolate chips and the remaining 1 tablespoon of shortening over simmering water as directed above (not in the microwave). Dip the remaining berries and star fruit about ⅔ into the melted mixture. Set the dipped fruit on one of the prepared cookie sheets. Let stand at room temperature for about 45 minutes, until set.

5. To assemble, arrange the leaf cookies in a circle on a large round serving platter, overlapping slightly. Arrange the dipped fruit in a circle around the cookies, stacking the smaller fruit on top to give the wreath height. Refrigerate until ready to serve. • The completed wreath can be loosely covered and refrigerated for up to 8 hours.

Per serving: 370 cal, 4 g pro, 18 g fat, 51 g car, 150 mg sod, 0 mg chol

COOK'S TIP

Have the fruit well chilled before dipping so the coating will quickly harden at room temperature.

CHRISTMAS

N O – B A K E
P E T I T S   F O U R S

Makes 24

Preparation time: 45 minutes
plus 1½ hours to stand

These miniature cakes will make a festive and colorful addition to your Christmas table. They are also wonderful served with tea or wrapped in a pretty box and given as a gift. Don't defrost the poundcake; it's easier to cut while it's still almost frozen.

1 frozen poundcake (16 ounces)

COATING ICING

5¼ cups (1½ pounds) confectioners' sugar
½ cup water
3 tablespoons light corn syrup
2 teaspoons almond extract

DECORATING ICING

1¾ cups (½ pound) confectioners' sugar
1 tablespoon light corn syrup
2 tablespoons water
Liquid or paste food coloring

1. With a long, sharp knife, trim the rounded hump off the poundcake so the top is flat. Trim the crust off the sides. Slice the cake in half horizontally. Cut each half in half lengthwise, then crosswise to make 12 squares (or cut with cookie cutters in rounds, stars, or other simple shapes).

2. Set the cake squares 1 to 1½ inches apart on a wire rack. Place the rack on a cookie sheet with sides to catch the drips.

3. Make the coating icing: In a medium-size bowl, mix the confectioners' sugar, water, corn syrup, and almond extract until smooth. (The icing should be somewhat thinner than pancake syrup.) Spoon about ¾ of the icing over the cakes, completely covering the tops and sides. Scrape up any drips on the cookie sheet and stir back into the icing in the bowl. Cover the bowl airtight. Let the icing on the cakes set for 20 to 30 minutes. If needed, thin the icing with 1 or 2 teaspoons of water, then give the petits fours a second coat. Let stand until firm, about 1 hour.

4. Make the decorating icing: In a small bowl, mix the confectioners' sugar, corn syrup, and 1 tablespoon of water. Add the second tablespoon of water a bit at a time, stirring until the mixture is smooth but stiff enough to pipe. Spoon into small bowls. Stir a different food coloring into each (paste colors will be more intense). Spoon the icing into pastry bags fitted with plain round number-1 or -2 tips. Decorate the petits fours as desired. • The petits fours can be refrigerated in an airtight container up to 1 week, or frozen up to 3 months. Thaw uncovered at room temperature.

Per piece: 230 cal, 1 g pro, 4 g fat, 49 g car, 80 mg sod, 39 mg chol

COCONUT CRISPIES

Makes 36

Preparation time: 20 minutes plus cooling
Baking time: 9 minutes per batch

Made with coconut, whole-wheat flour, and oats, these wholesome cookies have a crisp exterior and chewy texture.

1½ cups sweetened flaked coconut
1 stick (½ cup) butter or margarine (see page 321), softened
½ cup packed dark brown sugar
1 large egg
1 teaspoon vanilla extract
½ teaspoon baking powder
½ teaspoon baking soda
¼ teaspoon salt
1 cup whole-wheat flour
1 cup uncooked quick-cooking oats
½ cup raisins

1. Heat the oven to 350°F. Spread the coconut on an ungreased cookie sheet. Bake until golden, stirring occasionally, 8 to 10 minutes. Place the cookie sheet on a wire rack to cool.

2. Lightly grease 1 or more cookie sheets.

3. In a large (mixer) bowl, beat the butter and sugar with an electric mixer until fluffy. Beat in the egg, vanilla, baking powder, baking soda, and salt.

4. With the mixer on low speed, gradually beat in the flour just until blended. Stir in the coconut, oats, and raisins.

5. Shape the dough by level tablespoonfuls into balls. Place 1 inch apart on the prepared cookie sheet(s). Flatten slightly with the back of a fork. Bake until golden brown around the edges, 7 to 9 minutes. Cool the cookies on the sheet on a wire rack for 5 minutes, then remove to the rack to cool completely.

• The cookies can be kept in an airtight container or plastic bag at cool room temperature up to 1 week or frozen up to 1 month.

Per cookie with butter: 80 cal, 1 g pro, 4 g fat, 10 g car, 80 mg sod, 13 mg chol. With margarine: 6 mg chol

SPIRAL COOKIES

Makes 72

Preparation time: 30 minutes plus 10 hours to chill
Baking time: 12 minutes per batch

You don't have to wait until Christmas to make these fun patterned cookies. They take an extra step or two to prepare but are convenient to make ahead of time.

1 stick (½ cup) butter or margarine (see page 321), softened
¾ cup granulated sugar
1 large egg, at room temperature
1 teaspoon vanilla extract
¼ teaspoon baking powder
¼ teaspoon salt
1¼ cups all-purpose flour
1 ounce unsweetened chocolate, melted

1. In a large (mixer) bowl, beat the butter and sugar with an electric mixer until pale and fluffy. Beat in the egg, vanilla, baking powder, and salt. With the mixer at low speed, gradually beat in the flour just until blended.

2. Remove half of the dough. Mix the melted chocolate into the remaining half. Wrap each half in plastic. Chill until firm enough to roll, at least 2 hours.

3. Dampen a flat surface with water and cover with an 18-inch-long sheet of plastic wrap. Lightly flour the wrap. Roll the plain dough out onto the plastic to form a 16 x 6-inch rectangle. Repeat with the chocolate dough, using another sheet of plastic.

4. Turn the chocolate dough over on top of the plain dough. Peel off the plastic. Press down on the dough gently with a rolling pin. Roll up one long side into an even log, peeling the plastic away from the plain dough as you go, making sure the center is tight. Cut the log in half. Wrap the halves in plastic and chill for 8 hours or overnight. • The dough can be made up to this point and refrigerated for up to 3 days, or wrapped in foil and frozen for up to 3 months. If frozen, transfer to the refrigerator 2 hours before baking.

5. Heat the oven to 350°F. Grease 1 or more cookie sheets.

6. Cut each log into 36 slices. Place 1 inch apart on prepared cookie sheets. Bake until lightly browned around the edges, about 12 minutes. Cool the cookies on the sheet set on a wire rack for 2 to 3 minutes, then remove to the rack to cool completely.
• The cookies can be kept in an airtight container or plastic bag at cool room temperature for up to 1 week or frozen up to 1 month.

Per cookie with butter: 30 cal, 0 g pro, 2 g fat, 4 g car, 20 mg sod, 6 mg chol. With margarine: 3 mg chol

CHRISTMAS

AUSTRIAN LINZER COOKIES
Makes 60
Preparation time: 1 hour plus 1 hour to chill
Baking time: 15 minutes per batch

Buttery, rich almond pastry filled with raspberry jam makes a festive Christmas cookie (or a romantic offering for Valentine's Day).

1 stick (½ cup) butter or margarine (see page 321), softened
½ cup granulated sugar
1 large egg, yolk and white separated and at room temperature
2 teaspoons vanilla extract
1 tablespoon unsweetened cocoa powder
½ teaspoon ground cinnamon
¼ teaspoon ground cloves
1 cup all-purpose flour
1 cup (4 ounces) blanched almonds, finely ground
1 tablespoon water
¼ cup confectioners' sugar
¼ cup seedless red-raspberry jam

1. In a large (mixer) bowl, beat the butter, granulated sugar, and egg yolk until pale and fluffy. Beat in the vanilla, cocoa, cinnamon, and cloves. With the mixer on low speed, gradually beat in the flour and nuts just until blended. Press together to form a dough. Wrap in plastic and chill for 1 hour, or until the dough is firm enough to handle.

2. Heat the oven to 350°F. Lightly grease 1 or more cookie sheets.

3. On a lightly floured surface with a lightly floured rolling pin, roll the dough out to ⅛-inch thickness. Cut the dough with a 1½-inch round cookie cutter. Place half the rounds ½ inch apart on the prepared cookie sheets. With a ¾-inch shaped cookie cutter (such as bell, Christmas tree or star), cut out the centers of the remaining rounds.

4. In a small bowl, beat the egg white and water with a fork until foamy. Brush the solid rounds with the egg white mixture. Top with rounds that have cutouts in the center. Brush the tops and sides of the cookies with egg white. Reroll the scraps and cut the remaining dough as directed.

5. Bake until the cookies are firm and light brown around the edges, 12 to 15 minutes. Cool the cookies on the sheet on a wire rack for 2 to 3 minutes, then remove to the rack to cool completely.

6. Just before serving, dust with confectioners' sugar. Stir the jam until runny, then carefully spoon into the cutouts. • The cookies can be kept in an airtight container between sheets of waxed paper at cool room temperature for up to 1 week or frozen for up to 1 month.

Per cookie with butter: 50 cal, 1 g pro, 3 g fat, 5 g car, 20 mg sod, 8 mg chol. With margarine: 4 mg chol

PACKAGING COOKIES AND OTHER FOOD GIFTS
Homemade food gifts are always welcome, and you can double the appeal of these gifts by placing them in attractive tins, boxes, and bottles. Long after their contents are gone, the containers will almost certainly find other uses. When it comes to finding the right packaging, be resourceful: Specialty paper shops carry sturdy decorative boxes covered with textured paper; fabric stores and Christmas shops have a wide array of ribbons; housewares stores stock glass and plastic jars and bottles; flea markets and consignment shops are good places to find unusual tins and glass jars; and surgical supply stores sell handsome stainless steel tins and heatproof glass jars.

CHRISTMAS

CHOCOLATE–ORANGE CUPS

Makes 20 pieces

Preparation time: 15 minutes plus cooling

Baking time: 16 minutes per batch

These flourless treats, baked in small foil baking cups, are somewhere between a cake and a confection. Topped with a chocolate glaze and chopped almonds, they are as elegant as they are simple to make.

1 cup (4 ounces) blanched almonds, finely chopped
¾ cup confectioners' sugar
¼ cup unsweetened cocoa powder
2 teaspoons freshly grated orange peel
6 tablespoons butter or margarine (see page 321), softened
Whites of 3 large eggs, at room temperature (keep 1 egg white separate)
1 tablespoon granulated sugar

GLAZE
2 ounces semisweet chocolate, melted and cooled
2 tablespoons butter or margarine (see page 321), softened
1 teaspoon vegetable oil

For garnish: 2 tablespoons coarsely chopped almonds

1. Heat the oven to 350°F. Arrange twenty 1½-inch foil baking cups on a cookie sheet.

2. In a small bowl, mix the almonds, confectioners' sugar, cocoa, and orange peel. Stir in the butter and 1 egg white.

3. In a medium-size (mixer) bowl, beat the remaining egg whites with an electric mixer until foamy. Add the granulated sugar. Beat just until stiff peaks form when the beaters are lifted. Gently stir (fold) the egg white mixture into the almond mixture with a rubber spatula.

4. Spoon the batter into the baking cups, filling them ¾ full. Bake until the tops look dry, 13 to 16 minutes. Cool the cookies on the sheet set on a wire rack for 2 to 3 minutes, then remove to the rack to cool completely.

5. Meanwhile, make the glaze: In a small bowl, mix the melted chocolate and butter until well blended. Stir in the oil. Spread the mixture over the cups and sprinkle with the chopped almonds. • The cookies can be kept in an airtight container in the refrigerator for up to 3 weeks.

Per piece with butter: 120 cal, 2 g pro, 9 g fat, 9 g car, 60 mg sod, 12 mg chol. With margarine: 0 mg chol

CHRISTMAS

SPICE COOKIE CUTOUTS

Makes 50 cookies

Preparation time: 30 minutes plus 1 hour to chill and 2 hours to set

Baking time: 12 minutes per batch

Rolling out and cutting this spiced and fragrant dough into shapes is not only a time-honored way of making cookies but also a good way of enlisting helpers.

3 sticks (1½ cups) butter or margarine (see page 321), softened
1 cup granulated sugar
1 large egg, at room temperature
1 teaspoon vanilla extract
1½ teaspoons ground cinnamon
1 teaspoon ground ginger
½ teaspoon grated nutmeg
¼ teaspoon ground allspice
¼ teaspoon ground cloves
½ teaspoon salt
4 cups all-purpose flour
For decoration: colored ready-to-pipe icing

1. In a large (mixer) bowl, beat the butter and sugar with an electric mixer until pale and fluffy. Beat in the egg, vanilla, cinnamon, ginger, nutmeg, allspice, cloves, and salt. With the mixer on low speed, gradually beat in the flour just until blended.

2. Divide the dough into 3 balls. Flatten each into a 1-inch-thick round. Wrap in plastic and chill until firm enough to roll, 1 hour.

3. Heat the oven to 375°F. Have ready 1 or more ungreased cookie sheet(s).

4. On a lightly floured surface, with a lightly floured rolling pin, roll the dough, one piece at a time (keep the remainder in the refrigerator), to ¼-inch thickness. Cut out desired shapes with floured 3-inch cookie cutters. Place 1 inch apart on the cookie sheet(s). Bake until the bottoms and edges are just brown, about 12 minutes. Cool the cookies on the sheet on a wire rack for 2 to 3 minutes, then remove to the rack to cool completely.

5. Decorate the cooled cookies with colored icing as desired. Let them stand for about 2 hours for the icing to set. ● The cookies can be kept in an airtight container between sheets of waxed paper for up to 2 weeks or frozen for up to 1 month.

Per cookie with butter: 100 cal, 1 g pro, 6 g fat, 12 g car, 80 mg sod, 19 mg chol. With margarine: 90 mg sod, 4 mg chol

CHRISTMAS

CRANBERRY ICEBOX COOKIES

Makes 64 cookies
Preparation time: 30 minutes plus
3½ hours to chill
Baking time: 14 minutes per batch

Adding cranberries, almonds, and lemon peel turns a simple icebox cookie dough into a festive and sophisticated treat.

1 stick (½ cup) butter or margarine (see page 321), softened
1 cup packed light brown sugar
1 large egg, at room temperature
1 teaspoon vanilla extract
½ teaspoon baking soda
½ teaspoon cream of tartar
½ teaspoon salt
2½ cups all-purpose flour
½ cup (2 ounces) blanched almonds, finely chopped
½ cup fresh or frozen cranberries, coarsely chopped
1 teaspoon freshly grated lemon peel
For decoration: halved fresh cranberries, granulated sugar

1. In a large (mixer) bowl, beat the butter and brown sugar with an electric mixer until fluffy. Beat in the egg, vanilla, baking soda, cream of tartar, and salt. With the mixer on low speed, gradually beat in the flour just until blended. Gently stir in the almonds, chopped cranberries, and lemon peel.

2. Divide the dough in half. Wrap each half separately and chill for about 30 minutes or until firm enough to handle.

3. Shape each half into an 8-inch-long roll. Wrap and chill about 3 hours until hard. ● The dough can be made up to this point and refrigerated up to 3 days, or wrapped in foil and frozen up to 3 months. If frozen, thaw in the refrigerator 2 hours before baking.

4. Heat the oven to 350°F. Lightly grease 1 or more cookie sheet(s).

5. With a serrated knife, cut one roll at a time (keep the remainder in the refrigerator) into 32 ¼-inch-thick slices. Place 1 inch apart on the prepared cookie sheets. Press a cranberry half, cut side down, into the center of each cookie. Sprinkle with granulated sugar.

6. Bake until the edges are golden brown, 12 to 14 minutes. Cool the cookies on the sheet on a wire rack for 2 to 3 minutes, then remove to the rack to cool completely. ● The cookies can be kept in an airtight container at cool room temperature for up to 1 week or frozen for up to 3 months.

Per cookie with butter: 50 cal, 1 g pro, 2 g fat, 7 g car, 40 mg sod, 7 mg chol. With margarine: 3 mg chol

CRANBERRIES
Grown mostly in New England and Canada, cranberries are harvested from September to December, November being the peak month. Since they store well, fresh cranberries are often available in supermarkets for up to 2 months after the harvest or longer. Cranberries contain benzoic acid, a natural preservative, and even after prolonged storage will remain very nutritious (they are very high in vitamin C). Enjoy fresh cranberries year-round by purchasing extra bags of fresh cranberries when they are in season and freezing them airtight. They will keep frozen up to 1 year.

CHRISTMAS

CINNAMON TRIANGLES

Makes 70 cookies
Preparation time. 15 minutes
Baking time: 30 minutes

A mixture of granulated sugar, cinnamon, and chopped walnuts sprinkled over these cookies before baking gives them a sparkling and crunchy finish. The triangle shapes will add variety to your cookie tray.

2 sticks (1 cup) butter or margarine (see page 321),
*   softened*
1 cup packed light brown sugar
1 large egg, yolk and white separated and
*   at room temperature*
2 cups all-purpose flour
1½ teaspoons ground cinnamon
1 cup (4 ounces) walnuts, chopped
2 tablespoons granulated sugar

1. Heat the oven to 350°F. Line a 15½- x 10½-inch jelly-roll pan with foil, letting the foil extend a few inches above the ends of the pan.

2. In a large (mixer) bowl, beat the butter and brown sugar with an electric mixer until fluffy. Beat in the egg yolk, flour, and 1 teaspoon of the cinnamon until blended, then beat in ½ cup of the walnuts. Press the dough evenly over the bottom of the prepared pan.

3. In a small bowl, beat the egg white with a fork until frothy. Brush over the dough. In another small bowl, mix the granulated sugar with the remaining cinnamon and walnuts. Sprinkle the mixture evenly over the dough.

4. Bake until lightly browned, 25 to 30 minutes. Cool slightly in the pan on a wire rack. Lift the foil by the ends onto a cutting board. Trim the "sheet cookie" to a 14 x 10-inch rectangle, then cut into 2-inch squares. Cut each square diagonally into 2 triangles. • The cookies can be kept in an airtight container at cool room temperature for up to 2 weeks or frozen up to 3 months.

Per cookie with butter: 60 cal, 1 g pro, 4 g fat, 6 g car, 30 mg sod, 10 mg chol. With margarine: 30 mg sod, 3 mg chol

CHRISTMAS

COCOA–MINT WAFERS

Makes 64 cookies
Preparation time: 20 minutes plus 4 hours to chill
Baking time: 12 minutes per batch

Enjoy these crisp treats on their own or with ice cream or mousse.

1½ sticks (¾ cup) butter or margarine (see page
*   321), softened*
1¼ cups granulated sugar
1 large egg, at room temperature
1¼ teaspoons baking powder
⅛ teaspoon salt
¾ cup unsweetened cocoa powder
1½ cups all-purpose flour
24 rectangular chocolate mint parfait wafers

1. In a large (mixer) bowl, beat the butter and sugar with an electric mixer until fluffy. Beat in the egg, baking powder, and salt. With the mixer on low speed, gradually beat in the cocoa, then the flour just until blended.

2. Divide the dough in half. Shape each half into an 8-inch log. Wrap with plastic or waxed paper and refrigerate until firm, about 4 hours. • The dough can be made up to this point and refrigerated for up to 3 days, or wrapped in foil and frozen for up to 3 months. If frozen, transfer to the refrigerator 2 hours before baking.

3. Heat the oven to 350°F. Lightly grease 1 or more cookie sheets.

4. Cut each log into 32 ¼-inch-thick slices. Place 1 inch apart on the prepared cookie sheet(s). Bake until the cookies look dry, 10 to 12 minutes. Cool the cookies on the sheet on a wire rack for 2 to 3 minutes, then remove to the rack to cool completely.

5. Meanwhile, in a small saucepan, melt the mints over low heat. With a small spoon, drizzle the melted mints over the cooled cookies. • The cookies can be kept in an airtight container at cool room temperature for up to 1 week or frozen for up to 3 months.

Per cookie with butter: 50 cal, 1 g pro, 2 g fat, 7 g car, 40 mg sod, 9 mg chol. With margarine: 3 mg chol

FRUITCAKE SQUARES

Makes 24 squares

Preparation time: 8 minutes plus cooling

Baking time: 30 minutes

Perfect for the holiday season. Candied fruit adds texture and color to these bar cookies, which will look great on a tray with other Christmas sweets.

2 sticks (1 cup) butter or margarine (see page 321), softened
¾ cup granulated sugar
1 large egg, at room temperature
1 teaspoon vanilla extract
1 teaspoon freshly grated lemon or orange peel
2 cups all-purpose flour
1 cup chopped mixed candied fruit
½ cup confectioners' sugar
For decoration: green and red candied cherries, cut up

1. Heat the oven to 325°F. Line a 13 x 9 x 2-inch baking pan with foil. Lightly grease the foil.

2. In a large (mixer) bowl, beat the butter and sugar with an electric mixer until pale and fluffy. Beat in the egg, vanilla, and lemon peel. Gradually stir in the flour just until blended, then the chopped fruit. Spread evenly in the prepared pan.

3. Bake until set and lightly golden around the edges, about 30 minutes. Cool completely in the pan on a wire rack.

4. Sprinkle generously with confectioners' sugar. Cut into 2-inch squares. Decorate the tops with cherry pieces. ● The fruitcake squares can be kept in an airtight container between sheets of waxed paper at cool room temperature for up to 2 weeks or frozen for up to 3 months.

Per piece with butter: 180 cal, 1 g pro, 8 g fat, 25 g car, 110 mg sod, 30 mg chol. With margarine: 123 mg sod, 9 mg chol

GIFTS FROM KITCHEN

During the holidays, the simplicity of a gi[...] is really appreciated. The only problem with [...] homemade food presents is finding time to make them. That's why we've selected these recipes for speed and ease of preparation.

ALMOND CHOCOLATE–COVERED TOFFEE

Makes 2¼ pounds

Preparation time: 10 minutes plus chilling

Cooking time: 15 minutes

The combination of chocolate, almonds, and toffee is unbeatable. Easy to make and elegant to give, this confection is a sure bet for anyone with a sweet tooth.

1 cup (4 ounces) unblanched (natural) almonds
1½ cups granulated sugar
2 sticks (1 cup) butter or margarine (see page 321)
3 tablespoons water
1 tablespoon light corn syrup
1 teaspoon vanilla extract
2 cups (12 ounces) semisweet chocolate chips

1. Heat the oven to 350°F. Spread the almonds in a single layer on a jelly roll pan or cookie sheet with a rim and toast until they are lightly browned, 8 to 10 minutes. Remove to a plate or cool baking sheet and cool completely. Coarsely chop and set aside.

2. Lightly grease a 13 x 9-inch baking pan.

3. In a medium-size saucepan, bring the sugar, butter, water, and corn syrup to a boil over medium heat. Boil without stirring until a candy thermometer registers between 300° and 310°F. (Or test by dropping a small amount into ice water. When the mixture forms a brittle mass that snaps easily when pressed between fingers, it is ready.) Remove from the heat. Stir in the vanilla.

4. Pour the mixture into the prepared pan. Wait 2 minutes, then sprinkle evenly with the chocolate ▶

ps. When the chips are shiny, in about 2 minutes, spread over the toffee. Sprinkle the almonds over the top, pressing them gently into the chocolate.

5. Refrigerate the candy until cold. Break into bite-size pieces. ● The toffee can be kept in an air-tight container in the refrigerator or at cool room temperature for up to 1 month.

GIFTS FROM THE KITCHEN

EASY TRIPLE-CHOCOLATE FUDGE

Makes 81 pieces
Preparation time: 15 minutes plus 8 hours to chill

Whether you're looking for an indulgence for your-self or a quick and tasty gift, try your hand at fudge. For presentation, put the squares of fudge in paper or foil candy cups, available at cake decorating and candy supply stores and some supermarkets, and package them in a shallow basket.

> *1 can (14 ounces) sweetened condensed milk*
> *(not evaporated milk)*
> *2 tablespoons butter or margarine*
> *2⅔ cups (16 ounces) milk chocolate chips*
> *3 ounces bittersweet or semisweet chocolate,*
> *coarsely chopped*
> *½ cup white chocolate chips, or 3 ounces white*
> *chocolate, coarsely chopped*
> *½ cup (2 ounces) walnuts, toasted and coarsely*
> *chopped (see page 321)*

1. Line an 8- or 9-inch square pan with foil or waxed paper, letting the foil extend a few inches above the pan on 2 sides.

2. In a medium-size saucepan, stir the sweetened condensed milk and butter over low heat until the butter melts. Remove from the heat, add the choco-late chips and bittersweet chocolate, and stir until the chocolate is melted and the mixture is smooth. Stir in the white chocolate and walnuts. Spread in the prepared pan and refrigerate until firm enough to cut, 8 hours.

3. Lift the foil by the ends onto a cutting board. Cut

the fudge into 1-inch squares. ● The fudge can be kept in an airtight container with waxed paper between the layers in the refrigerator for up to 1 month.

Variation
PEPPERMINT STICK FUDGE

Use 2⅔ cups (16 ounces) vanilla chips instead of the chocolate chips. Omit the chopped chocolate and nuts. Add ½ teaspoon peppermint extract with the butter. Add a few drops of red or green food coloring and stir just until swirled, like a peppermint stick. Proceed as directed.

Variation
PEANUT BUTTER AND BANANA FUDGE

Use 2⅓ cups (14 ounces) peanut butter chips instead of the chocolate chips. Omit the chopped chocolate and nuts. Instead stir in 2 cups (5 ounces) dried banana chips and ½ cup unsalted peanuts. Proceed as directed. When the fudge is firm, melt 3 tablespoons semisweet chocolate chips and drizzle over the fudge.

GIFTS FROM THE KITCHEN

SEA GLASS CANDY

Makes 1 pound 6 ounces (4 cups)
Preparation time: 2 minutes plus cooling
Cooking time: 15 minutes

Make an assortment of fruit or spice flavors in a vari-ety of colors. A candy thermometer is very helpful, but not essential. Flavoring oils are available at most cake decorating and candy supply stores.

> *2 cups granulated sugar*
> *¾ cup light corn syrup*
> *¾ cup water*
> *¼ to 1 teaspoon flavoring oil,*
> *depending on strength of flavor*
> *Liquid or paste food coloring*
> *(paste colors are more intense)*
> *Confectioners' sugar, for dusting*

1. Lightly grease a cookie sheet. Place the sheet on a wire rack.

2. In a medium-size heavy saucepan, stir the sugar, corn syrup, and water over medium-high heat just until the sugar dissolves.

3. Bring to a boil and cook without stirring until

a candy thermometer registers between 300°F and 310°F. (Or test by dropping a small amount into ice water; the syrup should separate into threads that are hard and brittle.) Immediately remove from the heat and wait 1 to 2 minutes for the boiling to subside.

4. With a wooden spoon, stir in the flavoring oil and the food coloring until blended. Immediately pour onto the prepared cookie sheet. Let cool completely, about 20 minutes.

5. Lightly dust the slab of candy on both sides with confectioners' sugar, brushing off the excess sugar. Break into small pieces. (Store in an airtight container at cool room temperature for up to 1 year.)

ⒸOOK'S TIP

Flavoring oils, available at baking supply shops, are similar to extracts, but they deliver even more flavor from an even smaller dose. They will keep indefinitely if stored airtight in a cool, dry place.

CANDY-MAKING TIPS

◆ Proper equipment is essential to candy-making. When boiling candy, use a heavy-bottomed saucepan; it will conduct heat evenly. A thin-bottomed pan can get too hot in spots, scorching the syrup.

◆ Use an accurate clip-on candy thermometer marked in increments of 1 or 2 degrees. (A few degrees can produce completely different results.) Never plunge a cold candy thermometer into a boiling-hot candy mixture. If it is very cold, warm it in hot water until you are ready to use it.

◆ Be sure the sugar in the candy mixture is completely dissolved before boiling. To test for this, cool a small amount, then rub it between your fingers; it should feel smooth without any trace of granules.

PETITE GINGERBREADS

Makes 10 gingerbreads
Preparation time: 30 minutes
Baking time: 45 minutes

You rarely find gingerbread in a bakery, so this is an ideal treat to make for friends and family. Your treat will be the warm, spicy aroma that will fill your kitchen while the gingerbread bakes.

> *2 sticks (1 cup) butter or margarine (see page 321), softened*
> *½ cup packed light or dark brown sugar*
> *3 large eggs, at room temperature*
> *1½ cups (18 ounces) light or dark molasses (not blackstrap)*
> *1 cup low-fat or nonfat plain yogurt, or light sour cream*
> *2 tablespoons ground ginger*
> *2 teaspoons baking soda*
> *1½ teaspoons salt*
> *4 cups all-purpose flour*
> *8 ounces pitted dates, snipped into small pieces (1¾ cups)*
> *For decoration: red and green candied cherries and sliced almonds*

1. Heat the oven to 325°F. Lightly grease ten 1-cup custard cups or miniature loaf pans (see Cook's Tip).

2. In a large (mixer) bowl, beat the butter and sugar with an electric mixer on high speed until pale and fluffy. Add the eggs one at a time, beating well after each addition. Beat for 2 to 3 minutes longer, scraping down the sides of the bowl once or twice, until the mixture has increased slightly in volume. With the mixer on low speed, beat in the molasses, yogurt, ginger, baking soda, and salt (the mixture will look curdled). Gradually beat in the flour just until blended. Stir in the dates.

3. Spoon ¾ cup of the batter into each of the prepared cups. Smooth the tops. Decorate with cherries and almonds.

4. Bake until a toothpick inserted near the center comes out clean, 40 to 45 minutes. ▶

5. Cool the gingerbreads in the cups set on a wire rack for 10 minutes. Turn out onto the rack and cool completely. • The gingerbreads can be kept airtight in the refrigerator for up to 1 month or frozen for up to 3 months.

ⒸOOK'S TIP

If you have fewer than 10 custard cups or loaf pans, the breads may be baked in batches. The covered batter will hold up at room temperature for at least 4 hours. Wash and regrease the cups or pans between batches.

TROPICAL FRUITCAKES

Makes 18 cupcakes
Preparation time: 20 minutes
Baking time: 25 minutes

These individual fruitcakes don't taste anything at all like the traditional variety. Coconut, dried bananas, pineapple, dates, and pecans all combine for a sensational island flavor. And using a box of poundcake mix as the base makes preparation time a snap.

1 cup sweetened flaked coconut
1 cup dried banana chips
¼ cup dark rum or orange juice
1 can (8 ounces) crushed pineapple in juice
1 box (16 ounces) poundcake mix
½ stick (¼ cup) butter or margarine (see page 321), melted
2 teaspoons freshly grated orange peel
2 large eggs, at room temperature
½ cup pitted dates, snipped into small pieces
¼ cup (1 ounce) pecans, chopped

1. Heat the oven to 350°F. Line 18 regular-size muffin cups with paper liners.
2. Reserve ¼ cup of coconut. Spread the remaining coconut on a cookie sheet with a rim and toast in the oven until golden, 8 to 10 minutes.
3. Place the banana chips in a zipper-lock food storage bag and coarsely crush with a rolling pin. Place in a small bowl, add the rum or orange juice,

and let soak for 15 minutes.
4. Drain the pineapple, reserving ¼ cup of juice.
5. In a medium-size (mixer) bowl, beat the poundcake mix with the butter, orange peel, eggs, and reserved pineapple juice until moistened. Beat on medium speed for 2 minutes. Stir in the toasted coconut, bananas and any liquid, the pineapple, and dates. Spoon ⅓ cup of batter into each muffin cup. In a small bowl, mix the reserved coconut and pecans. Sprinkle over the batter.
6. Bake until a toothpick or cake tester inserted into the center of a cake comes out clean, about 25 minutes. Cool the cakes in the pan set on a wire rack for 10 minutes, then remove from the pan to the rack to cool completely. • The cakes can be kept in airtight containers at cool room temperature for up to 3 days or frozen for up to 3 months.

CRANBERRY PECAN LOAVES

Makes 2 loaves (24 servings)
Preparation time: 15 minutes plus cooling
Baking time: 1 hour 10 minutes

Tart, tangy cranberries and toasted pecans make a complementary pairing in these moist loaves that taste like poundcake.

2 sticks (1 cup) butter or margarine (see page 321), softened
2 cups granulated sugar
5 large eggs, at room temperature
½ cup plain low-fat or nonfat yogurt
2 teaspoons vanilla extract
1 teaspoon freshly grated orange peel
2½ cups all-purpose flour
1 cup (4 ounces) pecans, toasted and chopped (see page 325)
1 cup fresh or thawed frozen cranberries, chopped

1. Heat the oven to 350°F. Grease and flour two 8 x 4-inch loaf pans.
2. In a large (mixer) bowl, beat the butter and

sugar with an electric mixer until well blended. Add the eggs one at a time, beating well after each addition. Beat in the yogurt, vanilla, and orange peel.

3. With the mixer on low speed, beat in the flour just until blended. Stir in the pecans and cranberries.

4. Divide the batter evenly between the pans and smooth the tops. Bake until the edges have pulled away from the sides of the pans, the top is lightly golden, and a cake tester inserted near the center comes out clean, about 1 hour and 10 minutes. Cool the loaves in the pans on a wire rack for 10 minutes. Turn the loaves out onto the rack. Turn right side up and cool completely. • The cakes can be wrapped tightly and kept at cool room temperature for up to 3 days or frozen for up to 3 months.

GIFTS FROM THE KITCHEN

PEAR QUICK BREADS

Makes 3 loaves
Preparation time: 20 minutes
Baking time: 1 hour

This quick bread combines the taste and texture of fresh and dried pears. It's delicious served in plain thin slices or spread with Honey-Maple Spice Butter (see box). The mini-loaf size makes it perfect for gift-giving.

3 firm-ripe red Bartlett pears
1½ cups plus 1 tablespoon granulated sugar
½ cup vegetable oil
1 stick (½ cup) butter or margarine
   (see page 321), melted
2 teaspoons freshly grated lemon peel
2 teaspoons vanilla extract
1½ teaspoons baking powder
½ teaspoon baking soda
½ teaspoon salt
4 large eggs, at room temperature
½ cup chopped dried pears
4 cups all-purpose flour

1. Heat the oven to 350°F. Grease three 7½ x 3½ x 2¼-inch loaf pans (3½-cup capacity).

2. Halve and core the fresh pears. Set aside 1 pear half. Dice the remaining pears.

3. In a large (mixer) bowl, beat 1½ cups of the sugar, the oil, butter, lemon peel, vanilla, baking powder, baking soda, and salt with an electric mixer until blended. Add the eggs one at a time, beating well after each addition. Beat for 1 minute longer. With a wooden spoon, stir in the chopped fresh and dried pears, then the flour until blended (the batter will be thick).

4. Divide the batter among the prepared pans, spreading evenly. Thinly slice the remaining pear half into 12 slices. Place 4 slices on the batter in each pan. Sprinkle the slices with the remaining tablespoon of sugar.

5. Bake until a toothpick or cake tester inserted near the centers comes out clean, about 1 hour. Cool the breads in the pans set on a wire rack for 15 minutes. Turn the breads out onto the racks. Turn right side up and cool completely. • Store wrapped airtight at cool room temperature for up to 4 days, or freeze, double-wrapped in foil, for up to 6 months.

FLAVORED BUTTERS

Flavored butters are a wonderful accompaniment to quick breads, tea cakes, and muffins. Follow these suggestions, then invent some flavored butters of your own.

Beat 1 stick softened butter or margarine with an electric mixer until fluffy, then choose one of the following flavorings:

◆ For Honey-Maple Spice Butter: Gradually beat in 6 tablespoons honey, ¼ cup maple syrup, ¼ teaspoon ground cinnamon and ⅛ teaspoon grated nutmeg until thoroughly blended. (Makes about 1 cup.)

◆ For Citrus Butter: Gradually beat in ¼ cup orange juice and 1 teaspoon grated orange peel until thoroughly blended. (Makes about ¾ cup.)

◆ For Raspberry Butter: Gradually beat in ¼ cup seedless raspberry jam until thoroughly blended. (Makes about ¾ cup.)

Store butters in an airtight container in the refrigerator up to 1 month.

DOUBLE–DIPPED CHOCOLATE CARAMEL APPLE

Makes 1 apple
Preparation time: 10 minutes
plus 2 hours to chill
Cooking time: 5 minutes

Using colorful plastic wrap and a bow of striped ribbon to wrap this splendid treat will make it fun to give and to receive. A wooden chopstick makes a great handle and will make coating the apple easy.

1 large Red Delicious or Granny Smith apple, washed and dried

1 wooden chopstick or thin wooden dowel, about 8 inches long

25 individually wrapped caramels (from a 14-ounce package), unwrapped

4 ounces good-quality bittersweet or semisweet chocolate, chopped

3 tablespoons heavy (whipping) cream

¾ cup (3 ounces) toasted chopped pecans, walnuts, or almonds (see page 325)

1. Grease a 5-inch square of waxed paper. Place on a small plate.

2. Insert the chopstick into the stem end of the apple, being careful not to go all the way through.

3. In a medium-size microwave-safe bowl, microwave 15 of the caramels and 1 tablespoon of water on High for 1 to 1½ minutes, stirring once, until melted and smooth. (Or melt in a small saucepan over low heat, stirring until smooth.) Let stand for 1 minute.

4. Holding the stick, dip the apple into the hot caramel, turning until coated all over and the caramel is used up. (If needed, use a small metal spatula to help spread the caramel.) Place on the greased paper. Refrigerate for 5 minutes.

5. Meanwhile, melt the remaining 10 caramels and 1½ teaspoons of water as above. Dip the apple a second time. Refrigerate for 10 minutes.

6. While the apple chills, microwave the chocolate and cream in a medium-size microwave-safe bowl on High for 1 to 1½ minutes, stir until melted and smooth. (Or melt in a small saucepan over very low heat. Stir until smooth.)

7. Put the chopped nuts on a plate. Dip the apple into the chocolate mixture to coat, using a small spatula to help spread chocolate. Dip the bottom into the nuts, then roll the sides gently in the nuts to coat. Spoon the remaining nuts over the top of the apple.

8. Refrigerate on waxed paper for 2 hours or until hard. Wrap in plastic wrap and refrigerate for up to 1 week. When ready to eat, unwrap, leave at room temperature for 20 minutes for caramel to soften, then cut into wedges.

APPENDIX

EQUIPMENT, INGREDIENTS & TECHNIQUES

PANS

CAKE PANS: Round cake pans range in depth from 1½ to 4 inches and in diameter from 6 to 22 inches. We recommend two-pan sets of 9 x 1½ or 2 inches and 8 x 1½ or 2 inches. Also include at least one 8 x 8 x 2-inch or a 9 x 9 x 2-inch square pan (good brownie pans), and one 13 x 9 x 2-inch and a 11 x 7 x 1½-inch baking pan or dish. Buy the best, heaviest pans you can afford. Inexpensive pans may warp when exposed to heat but high-quality ones will last for a lifetime of baking.

COOKIE (BAKING) SHEETS: Essential for baking cookies and pastries, among other things, these are flat metal sheets with the barest of rims or a rim on only one end. They are designed to allow the oven heat to reach the batter or dough from every direction. Their level surface allows cookie dough to spread. Buy heavy-duty baking sheets; thin ones will warp in the oven and cause uneven baking. Dark-colored pans absorb heat and therefore cookies will brown more quickly when baked on them. Many home bakers prefer nonstick baking sheets, and if you bake a lot of cookies, buy a few of the nonstick

kind to complement the other sheets. Double-layer insulated baking sheets are wonderful investments, as their construction practically guarantees that no cookie will ever have an overbrowned bottom. Select as large a cookie sheet as will fit in your oven with a 2-inch margin on all sides for proper convection. You'll want at least two cookie sheets, one to cool while the other is in the oven baking.

JELLY ROLL PAN: A flat rectangular pan with 1-inch sides. Most jelly roll pans are 15½ x 10½ x 1 inch, although some are slightly smaller and others slightly larger. These are used to bake sponge cakes to be used for cake rolls, plus sheet cakes and some bar cookies. Jelly roll pans are also referred to as half-sheet pans.

LOAF PANS: Standard loaf pans are 9 x 5 x 3 inches and may be made of metal or glass. Mini loaf pans measure 6 x 3¼ x 2 inches. Metal loaf pans produce loaf cakes and quick breads with more evenly browned crusts; cakes and breads baked in glass loaf pans may brown before they are thoroughly baked.

MUFFIN PANS: Standard muffin pans have 12 or 24 cups, each holding 6 to 7 tablespoons of batter. The pans are also made in mini and large cup sizes.

PIE PLATES: Pie plates may be metal, ceramic, or glass. (Be aware that glass pie plates absorb heat

EQUIVALENT PAN SIZES

Always try to use the size and shape of the pan recommended in a recipe. If, however, you do not have the right size or wish to vary it, you may use the chart below to find a substitute that will hold the same volume. The volume of the pan is measured by the amount of liquid it holds when filled to the rim, not the amount of batter. Remember that if a substitute pan is deeper, it will require a longer baking time.

PAN SIZE	VOLUME	PAN SIZE	VOLUME
8 x 1½-inch round cake pan	4 cups	9 x 5 x 3-inch loaf pan	8 cups
8 x 2-inch round cake pan	6 cups	10 x 2½-inch springform pan	9 cups
9 x 1½-inch round cake pan	6 cups	9 x 9 x 2-inch square pan	10 cups
11 x 7 x 1½-inch baking pan	6 cups	9 x 2½-inch springform pan	10 cups
8½ x 4½ x 2½-inch loaf pan	6 cups	9 x 3-inch Bundt pan	12 cups
9 x 2-inch round cake pan	8 cups	10 x 3½-inch tube pan	12 cups
8 x 8 x 2-inch square pan	8 cups	13 x 9 x 2-inch baking pan	12 cups

more quickly than metal pie plates; therefore, a pie will bake slightly faster in a glass plate.) They are available in 8- to 11-inch diameters with sloping sides. Having both a 9- and a 10-inch pie plate will accommodate most recipes. For deep-dish pies, use a pie plate with at least a 2-inch depth.

SOUFFLÉ DISHES: Soufflé dishes are round and deep and have straight sides so that a soufflé can rise straight and tall. Made of glass, stoneware, or porcelain, they range from 1- to 4-quart capacities.

SPRINGFORM PAN: A round baking pan with a high straight side that can be released with a clamp. We recommend having a 9 x 2½- or 3-inch and a 10 x 2½- or 3-inch springform pan (good for cheesecakes).

TART PANS: Fluted, round tart pans are manufactured with either removable or permanent bottoms in diameters ranging from 4½ to 12 inches, and range from ¾ to 1½ inches deep. We recommend having a 9- or 10-inch tart pan with a removable bottom. Individual tartlet pans or molds are made from lightweight tinned steel and come in a variety of styles. They are sold singly or in sets.

TUBE PANS: These include angel-food cake pans (with removable bottoms), fluted tube pans, Bundt pans, and kugelhopf pans. They can be used interchangeably as long as they share a capacity. Tube pans range from 1½ quarts to 4 quarts. Be sure to have at least one 2-quart and one 3-quart tube pan (for more, see Glossary, page 331).

OTHER EQUIPMENT

CAKE TESTERS: These are thin metal skewers to insert into a cake to test its doneness. The rule of thumb is that if the cake tester comes out dry, with no crumbs clinging to it, the cake is done. A thin bamboo skewer, a wooden toothpick, or a small knife may be used to test cakes, too.

CANDY THERMOMETER: These thermometers range from 100° to 400°F and may also be called deep-frying thermometers. Buy those with the mercury bulb and column mounted on a protective metal casing with a clip so that it can be attached to the side of a pan. Never let the bulb touch the bottom of the pan or the reading will be inaccurate.

COOKIE AND BISCUIT CUTTERS: Usually made of metal so that the cutting side holds its edge, some inexpensive cutters are also molded in plastic. Cookie cutters come in a wide variety of shapes; biscuit cutters are always round.

CUSTARD CUPS: Usually made of tempered glass (most in the U.S. are manufactured by Pyrex), custard cups also may be ceramic. The two most common sizes hold 6 or 8 ounces when filled to the brim (for more, see *Ramekins* in the Glossary, page 331).

DOUBLE BOILER: A double-decker pot in which the top portion fits snugly over the bottom, leaving enough room for several inches of water in the bottom. You can make your own double boiler by setting a large metal bowl over a pot of simmering water (but not touching the water). The purpose is to provide indirect, gentle heat for cooking or melting.

ELECTRIC MIXERS: Both hand-held electric mixers and heavy-duty standing mixers work well to blend most cake batters and cookie doughs, although standing mixers work better on large quantities and heavy batters. Hand-held electric mixers can be used with nearly any bowl or pan. Standing mixers are equipped with their own bowls.

FOOD PROCESSOR: An essential piece of equipment in today's kitchen, a food processor is wonderful for blending, chopping, and grinding, and can be a great time saver. Some can make batters, bread, and pastry doughs (check the manual). Buy the best food processor with the largest capacity you can afford.

MEASURING SPOONS AND CUPS: Measuring spoons and dry-measure cups are sold in nests with exact measurements. Dry measuring cups, ranging from ¼ cup to 1 cup, are designed so they can be filled to the brim, then leveled off with a straight-edge. Measuring spoons are made of metal or plastic and range from ¼ teaspoon to 1 tablespoon. Liquid-measure cups range in size from 1 cup to 4 cups (or more) and are made of clear glass or plastic with the measuring increments listed on the sides so they can be read at eye level. (For more, see Measuring, page 325.)

MIXING BOWLS, SPOONS, AND SPATULAS: Mixing bowls may be plastic, glass, ceramic, or metal. They generally are large-mouthed and hold from 1 to 4 quarts or more. Mixing spoons are wooden, plastic, or metal. Wooden spoons are good for many mixing tasks, particularly those over heat, since the wood does not conduct heat. Try to keep the wooden spoons used for sweet preparations separate from those used for savory—these may retain the taste of garlic and onions. Rubber scrapers, also called rubber spatulas, are great for scraping batter from bowls and for gently stirring (folding) ingredients together. Have several. Thin, flexible metal cake spatulas (more narrow than pancake turner-style spatulas) are excellent for frosting cakes and lifting dough from flat surfaces. Have a few with flat handles and a few with crooked handles, also called offset spatulas.

OVENS AND OVEN THERMOMETERS: You should never rely on the built-in oven setting alone as a gauge of an oven's temperature because sometimes it can be off as much as 50° to 100°F. This can seriously affect baked goods. To check accuracy, invest in a small metal mercury-type oven ther-mometer. Place the thermometer on the center rack and heat the oven for 15 minutes. If the thermo-meter reading doesn't agree with the oven setting, you will know that your oven is not accurately calibrated and you'll need to compensate. For example: If the oven is set for 350°F and the thermometer reads 325°F, you will know that your oven is off by 25°F. Therefore when a recipe calls for 350°F, set your oven for 375°F to compensate.

Always heat the oven for 15 minutes before starting to bake. Check your auxiliary thermometer to verify the temperature before baking anything.

Most ovens have a hot spot, which is easily detected by how baked goods brown. To ensure even baking, rotate baked goods from one shelf to another or from front to back after half the baking time has passed. Do this only if you must, because moving batters can sometimes affect their rising.

PASTRY BAG AND TIPS: Plastic or fabric triangular-shaped bags designed to hold frosting or another substance for decorative piping onto cakes and confections. Pastry bags are fitted with removable tips with variable shapes and sizes of openings depending on the design desired.

PASTRY BLENDER: A tool fitted with rigid, curved wires used to cut fat into flour.

PASTRY BRUSH: Small, bristled brush used to spread syrups over warm cake layers or to brush the edges of pastry with egg washes or cold water. Also a small, soft-bristled dry brush used to brush flour and other powdery ingredients from the surface of doughs and baked cakes.

PASTRY SCRAPER: A tool fitted with a flat, rigid metal plate and used to scrape dough from coun-tertops and boards. Also made of more flexible plastic.

ROLLING PINS: Heavy, high-quality smooth wooden rolling pins are best for working with pie crusts and other doughs. Many bakers prefer French-style rolling pins, which taper at the ends and have no handles. Others like American-style rolling pins with handles that turn on ball bearings. For fine pastry work, marble rolling pins are recommended because they stay cool.

STRAINERS AND SIFTERS: These are perforated containers for sifting flour and other dry ingredients or straining solids from liquids. They may be fashioned from very fine wire mesh (sifters) or, at the other end of the spectrum, from metal or plastic with relatively large holes (strainers).

WHISKS: Wire whisks vary in size, with the largest

being called balloon whisks, a nomenclature that refers to the whisk's shape. Whisks are useful for smoothing out and mixing batters and for incorporating dry ingredients.

INGREDIENTS

FLOUR

When we call for flour we mean wheat flour—although a number of other grains are milled into flour, too. Wheat is milled to make all-purpose flour, cake flour, whole-wheat flour, bread flour, and pastry flour. In the recipes included here we use *only all-purpose flour, whole-wheat flour, and cake flour.*

All-purpose flour may be bleached or unbleached, but regardless of the processing it always appears bright white and either will behave as well as the other. Which to buy is a personal preference; bleached flour is slightly more processed than unbleached. (This processing accelerates the flour's necessary aging so that bleached flour can reach the supermarket shelves more quickly.) White flour is milled from the endosperm of the wheat berry, which surrounds the center of the grain and contains no oil. Manufacturers produce all-purpose flour so that it is uniform in consistency and capabilities, regardless of where it is bought. This ensures that the home baker will get excellent results whether a recipe is prepared in Florida, Massachusetts, Colorado, or California. Most published recipes calling for flour depend on all-purpose flour, unless otherwise specified.

Whole-wheat flour is less processed than all-purpose flour because during milling the germ and bran are left intact. This produces flour that looks beige instead of white. Baked goods made with whole-wheat flour are slightly heavier, taste vaguely nutty, and may be denser. Consequently, whole-wheat should never be substituted for all-purpose flour. The oil in the germ causes the flour to turn rancid after a few months of storage.

Cake flour is milled from soft wheat with very few gluten-forming abilities and a high level of starch. This results in a very tender, soft crumb. It should not be substituted for all-purpose flour or whole-wheat flour. Some cake flour is self-rising, which means baking powder and salt are incorporated into the flour. Do not use self-rising cake flour unless the recipe calls for it. And if a recipe does call for self-rising cake flour, be sure to use it.

Buy flour as you need it. Store the unopened sacks in a cool, dry cupboard, and once opened transfer the flour to a glass or ceramic canister with a tight-fitting lid. Whole-wheat flour keeps for 6 months and all-purpose and cake flours for up to one year. Both keep slightly longer in the refrigerator or freezer but will attract moisture. Let them reach room temperature before using.

SUGARS

Most of WOMAN'S DAY's recipes call for granulated sugar—the white sugar sold in every market and small grocery in the nation and clearly an effective sweetener. Confectioners' sugar, also called powdered sugar, has added cornstarch and is used for making classic frostings and for decorating.

Brown sugar contains added molasses and is slightly acidic. Both light and dark brown sugar will clump when exposed to the air. Store them in a tightly closed sealable plastic bag in a cool, dry place. While in most recipes light and dark brown sugar can be used interchangeably with little effect on texture or baking time and nominal effect on flavor, neither should be substituted for granulated sugar unless specified.

Because sugar has no fats or oils, it keeps extremely well without spoiling. Store it in the paper sack or cardboard box it comes in or transfer it to a glass or ceramic canister. Keep it in a cool, dry cupboard rather than the refrigerator, where the high moisture level will encourage clumping.

FATS AND OILS

In most recipes we rely on salted or unsalted butter or margarine, although throughout the book you will find recipes calling for solid vegetable shortening or oil as well. Unless we call for "either butter or margarine" in a recipe, they cannot necessarily be used interchangeably. Butter is made from milk's natural sweet cream and contains 80 percent butterfat. Regular margarine is made to resemble butter and has a minimum of 80 percent vegetable oil.

Each contains 100 calories per tablespoon (14 grams). Both produce baked goods that brown nicely, have a pleasing texture, and taste good. Because advanced food technology has allowed manufacturers to produce low- and reduced-fat stick margarines, it is not accurate to assume that stick margarine is higher in fat than tub or liquid margarine. Therefore, always read the nutritional information on the package before buying margarine. Do not substitute light margarine, which has less than 40 percent oil, or fat-free margarine, which has less than a half gram of fat per serving, for regular margarine in baked goods. They contain far too much moisture to ensure success. However, reduced-fat margarines, with at least 60 percent oil, work well in most traditional recipes and can be used in place of regular margarine or butter unless a recipe is very dependent on precise amounts of fat, such as recipes for pastry crust or rich butter cookies.

Solid vegetable shortenings made from vegetable oil are preferred by many for pie crusts, biscuits, and other recipes that in the past might have called for lard. These fats produce light, tender crusts and crumbs and because of their semisolid state are easy to work with. However, they are most successfully cut into dry ingredients when they have been chilled first.

Solid vegetable shortenings and some margarines are also referred to as "partially hydrogenated." This refers to the process that converts the oil into a solid and stable state by injecting hydrogen gas into it under pressure. Unfortunately, this procedure makes the oils more saturated and therefore undesirable for anyone concerned with his or her cholesterol levels. Saturated fats raise blood cholesterol. As a rule, saturated fat is found in animal products such as butter, lard, cream, and, to a lesser extent, egg yolks, although it is also present in tropical oils such as coconut and palm oil.

Not too many recipes in this book call for oil, but when they do we at WOMAN'S DAY generally prefer monounsaturated flavorless oils such as canola, safflower, sunflower, and peanut. Unsaturated fats help lower total cholesterol in the blood, but monounsaturated fats have an advantage over polyunsaturated: they lower only LDL ("bad") cho-

lesterol levels while leaving HDL ("good") cholesterol levels alone. Conversely, polyunsaturated fats lower both LDL and HDL levels, making no distinction between the two.

Store butter and margarine in the refrigerator or freezer. Oils and solid vegetable shortening will keep in a cool, dark cupboard for several months or longer.

EGGS

In our recipes we use grade A large eggs. Whether the eggs have brown or white shells makes no difference but it is advisable to buy eggs as fresh as possible and to store them correctly. And because of the slight danger of salmonella contamination, it's important to handle and prepare eggs carefully.

A packing date is stamped on every carton of eggs, reflecting the day of the year the eggs are packed. In other words, eggs packed on January 2 would carry the number 2, while those packed on June 15 would carry the number 166, since June 15 is the 166th day of the year. Eggs keep for 4 to 5 weeks beyond the packing date. Always store them in their cartons (the Styrofoam or cardboard provides extra insulation) and always refrigerate them.

Salmonella enteritidis occurs in less than 1 percent of the eggs sold in the United States. While it is rarely dangerous, it is certainly unpleasant: Those infected with the bacterial organism suffer from gastrointestinal distress and fever.

Salmonella will not grow at temperatures below 40°F (the temperature of most home refrigerators) or above 160°F; the danger zone is considered to be between 40° and 140°F. When cooking and baking with eggs, be sure they are heated to at least 160°F or, if necessary, heat them to 140°F and hold them at this temperature for three and a half minutes. However, home cooks need not fuss with thermometers or worry unduly as long as the eggs in a recipe are baked or cooked under normal circumstances (cakes, cookies, custards, quick breads, and so on). Other commonsense practices include never leaving eggs at room temperature for longer than 2 hours, using only clean and unbroken eggs, and removing any bits of shell that fall into a mixture with a clean utensil and *not* with another piece of shell. (The bacteria is carried on the outside of eggshells.) Finally, buy eggs from a market with high turnover.

EGG SUBSTITUTES

Most egg substitutes are approximately 80 percent egg whites combined with other ingredients to replace the yolks. They provide a cholesterol-free product to use in baking and cooking in place of cholesterol-heavy whole eggs. (An egg yolk contains about 200 mg of cholesterol and 7 grams of fat; egg whites are cholesterol-free and extremely low in fat.) For most culinary needs, egg substitutes are very reliable.

Most egg substitutes come in liquid form. Beside egg whites, they may include nonfat milk, soy, vegetable oil, emulsifiers, and gums. A few egg substitutes contain no egg products at all and are called "egg replacers." These are made mainly from soy. Read the label to determine exactly what is in the product. For example, some contain MSG and so are not recommended for anyone sensitive to it. Egg substitutes and replacers are sold in cartons in the refrigerated or frozen sections of the supermarket. If frozen, let them thaw in the refrigerator. Use ¼ cup of liquid egg substitute to replace 1 whole egg.

Powdered egg substitutes are usually made of the dried egg whites, although egg-free products are also available. Look for powdered egg products in the health food store, some supermarkets, and specialty food stores. Some catalogues also sell them. These dry products keep very well in the cupboard.

DAIRY PRODUCTS

Dairy products provide tenderness, texture, and flavor to many baked goods and desserts. No longer are we limited to whole milk, heavy cream, and full-fat cheeses when we consider dairy products—we can choose from an impressive array of reduced- and low-fat dairy products, including low-fat and nonfat yogurt, sour cream, cream cheese, cottage cheese, and ricotta cheeses. If a reduced-fat or nonfat dairy product will work in any one of our recipes, it will be listed as an option in the ingredient list.

Milk is sold with varying amounts of fat, including whole (or full fat), 2 percent, 1 percent, ½ percent, skim, and nonfat. Unless otherwise instructed, whole and low-fat milk can be used interchangeably in baking. Store milk in the carton in the refrigerator. Buttermilk is often used in recipes because its mild acidity reacts with baking soda and provides a pleasant flavor and texture. True buttermilk is the liquid that is extracted from cream when it is churned into butter and is very low in fat. Today, buttermilk usually is made by adding a culture to skim milk. Since few people today drink buttermilk and therefore do not have it on hand, it is useful to know that powdered, dry buttermilk, sold in most supermarkets, is a long-lasting and good substitute.

Cream, too, is sold with varying amounts of fat. Half-and-half is an equal mixture of whole milk and cream and has from 10 to 18 percent milkfat. Light cream has from 18 to 30 percent milkfat and is sometimes referred to as coffee cream or table cream. Whipping cream has a milkfat content of between 30 and 36 percent and may be called light whipping cream. Heavy cream has a milkfat content of between 36 and 40 percent and may be called heavy whipping cream. Neither half-and-half nor light cream can be whipped; both whipping cream and heavy cream whip to billowy clouds, with heavy cream creating slightly richer, firmer mounds. Cream should be stored in the coldest section of the refrigerator, which usually is near the back of the lowest shelf. It keeps for about a week past its "sell-by" date.

Evaporated milk is milk that has had about 60 percent of its water removed. It is sold in cans and can be stored at room temperature until it is opened. After it is opened, it should be refrigerated and used within several days. Do not use evaporated milk as a substitute for other milk products unless it is diluted as directed on the label. Evaporated skim milk is also available.

Sweetened condensed milk is milk that has had about 50 percent of its water removed; it is about 40 percent sugar. It is not suitable as a substitute for other milk products. It is sold in cans and can be stored at room temperature until it is opened. After it is opened, it should be refrigerated and used within several days. Nonfat sweetened condensed milk is also available.

LEAVENERS

This book includes no recipes that call for yeast, which is used in bread-making and for several kinds of coffee cakes and breakfast pastries. We rely on the so-called chemical leaveners: baking soda and its close cousin, double-acting baking powder. These leaven when they are mixed with liquid by releasing gases that lighten the batter. We also include numerous recipes that are leavened solely by the air beaten into eggs and egg whites.

Baking soda is an alkali that in order to perform its leavening magic must react with an acid, such as sour milk, buttermilk, yogurt, citrus juice, or molasses. Baking powder is a mixture of alkali and acid and therefore will leaven a batter without the addition of an acidic ingredient. Double-acting baking powder, the kind used in our recipes and also most available to the consumer, reacts with liquid to initiate the leavening process and then again in the oven when the batter is exposed to heat.

Both baking soda and baking powder keep well for several months if stored in a cool, dark cupboard. Do not store them in the refrigerator, where they will attract moisture. (The open box of baking soda placed in the refrigerator to minimize odors should definitely not be used in recipes!) To test if an aging box of baking soda or baking powder is active, mix a generous pinch with tepid water to see if it fizzes. If so, it's fine. If the white powder settles to the bottom of the container with no bubbling, it is too old to use and should be discarded.

NUTS

Nuts add flavor and texture to many baked goods. They may be shelled and whole with the skin on (natural or unblanched) or without the skin (blanched). Though most nuts are sold both salted and unsalted, most recipes require unsalted nuts. It is possible to substitute one type of nut for another, but do consider the flavor, texture, and oiliness of the kind of nut called for when considering a substitution. Nuts keep best in the refrigerator or freezer.

Almonds are available in a wide array of styles: whole natural or blanched, slivered almonds, which are cut into matchsticks, or sliced, cut into thin flakes. Sliced almonds are available unblanched or blanched. In general, using unblanched almonds will add texture and color to a finished product.

Hazelnuts are most often sold with the skins on, but most recipes call for skinned hazelnuts. Buy them without the skins if you can. To remove the skins from hazelnuts, see page 325.

Pecans and walnuts are available shelled as halves or chopped or a mixture of the two called "pieces."

Macadamia nuts are especially high in fat and therefore perishable. Look for them in vacuum-packed cans or jars. If you can only find the salted variety, rinse them well, place in a single layer on a cookie sheet, and bake at 325°F for about 5 minutes to dry them out.

SPICES AND EXTRACTS

Common spices used in baking and dessert making and therefore found in the pages of this book are easy to find in supermarkets and keep well for several months in cool, dark cupboards. Allspice tastes like a mixture of cinnamon, cloves, and nutmeg and is often found in fruit desserts. Cinnamon, by far the most popular dessert spice, is sold ground; the rolled bark of the plant is sold as cinnamon sticks of varying lengths. Ginger is sold fresh, dried and ground, or crystallized. Crystallized ginger has been cooked and sugared and is used mainly to garnish desserts. Nutmeg is sold grated or fresh, which means as a whole seed. For the best flavor, we advise buying whole nutmegs and grating them as you need the spice. (You can use the smallest holes on a box grater or purchase a small nutmeg grater.)

Vanilla is a familiar and popular flavor used in numerous desserts—including chocolate desserts, whose flavor is mysteriously accentuated by vanilla's delicate yet rich essence. Vanilla beans, sold in the pod, are richer tasting than extract, although for most baking needs, pure vanilla extract is easier to use. Do not buy imitation vanilla—it does not taste nearly as good and the cost savings are minimal.

Other extracts include almond, lemon, and orange, as well as more esoteric flavorings sold in specialty stores but not used in our recipes. Extracts lose potency when exposed to light, so store them in dark bottles in a dark, cool cupboard. If stored properly, they will keep indefinitely.

HELPFUL TECHNIQUES

MEASURING

Measuring cups are designed for either dry or liquid ingredients. As a rule, measuring cups for dry ingredients are nested metal or plastic cups that hold a precise amount, usually beginning with a ¼ cup and ending with 1 cup. Liquid measures are clear glass or plastic cups with the amounts indicated on the sides.

To measure flour and confectioners' sugar accurately, spoon it lightly into the cup until it overflows, then level it with the back of a knife or edge of a spatula. Scooping the flour or tapping it into the cup will alter the amount.

Measure liquids in clear glass measuring cups. Put the cup on a flat surface, fill it, then bend down to eye-level with the markings to read it.

To measure baking powder, baking soda, and ground spices, dip the spoon right into the container. Fill it to overflowing, then sweep off the excess as you would for flour.

Brown sugar is one thing that you pack into a measuring cup, just until it's level with the top.

Sour cream and yogurt should be measured in nested cups. Shortening also needs to be pressed into the measuring cup, to eliminate air. If you're not up to the mess, use sticks of solid vegetable shortening.

An entire stick of butter or margarine equals ½ cup or ¼ pound; and ⅛ of a stick equals 1 tablespoon. Use a sharp knife to cut off the amount needed, following the markings on the wrapper.

Measure dry ingredients over a sheet of waxed paper rather than the mixing bowl. This way it is easy to return spills to the containers, and you won't have to start from scratch if something spills into the bowl.

TOASTING NUTS

Toasting nuts releases their natural oils and makes them more flavorful. Toasting also helps to keep nuts crisp. It's an easy procedure that makes a big difference. In our recipes, we call for toasted walnuts, pecans, almonds, macadamia nuts, and hazelnuts.

To toast nuts: Heat the oven to 350°F. Spread the nuts in a single layer on a jelly roll pan or cookie sheet with a rim. Bake them for 5 to 10 minutes, until they begin to brown and turn fragrant. Stir or shake the nuts once or twice during toasting. Remove the nuts to a cool baking sheet or flat plate to cool completely. If allowed to cool on the hot baking sheet, they will continue to cook.

A small amount of nuts can be toasted in a frying pan. Spread them in a dry pan set over medium-high heat and toast for 5 to 8 minutes, shaking the pan frequently until the nuts are lightly browned and fragrant. Cool on a baking sheet or flat plate.

Whole almonds and hazelnuts may require an additional 4 to 5 minutes to toast. Hazelnuts will turn golden beneath their skin, which must be removed after toasting. To do so, wrap the nuts in a clean, dry kitchen towel and let them cool. Put them in a sieve and rub the nuts with the towel and

BAKING WITH ROOM-TEMPERATURE INGREDIENTS

When butter, margarine, cream cheese, and eggs are at room temperature, they will swell to a greater volume and are more easily blended than when they are cold. Batters for cakes and cookies benefit from room-temperature ingredients. When a recipe calls for butter, margarine, or cream cheese to be softened (meaning it should yield to gentle pressure without feeling squishy-soft), remove it from the refrigerator about 1 hour before you will need to use it. Or if you haven't planned

far enough in advance, you can use the microwave. Cut the butter, margarine, or cream cheese into small pieces and put it into a microwave-safe bowl. Microwave on Low at 30-second intervals, stirring, until just softened but not melted. Eggs need about 1 hour to come to room temperature. Don't use the microwave to warm them up quickly—they will explode. Instead, place the egg(s) in a bowl of lukewarm water and they will be ready to use in about 5 minutes.

your fingers to remove as much as possible of the loosened skins.

Nuts in their shells keep for several months in a cool, dry place. Refrigerate shelled almonds, pecans, and walnuts in an airtight container for up to 6 months or freeze for up to 1 year. Shelled hazelnuts and macadamia nuts will keep airtight in the refrigerator for up to 1 month or in the freezer for up to 6 months.

TOASTING COCONUT

To toast coconut: Heat the oven to 350°. Spread shredded coconut on an ungreased jelly roll pan or cookie sheet with a rim. Toast for 8 to 10 minutes, or until golden, stirring occasionally. Place the pan on a wire rack to cool.

GREASING PANS

Vegetable shortening, unsalted butter, margarine, or nonstick vegetable oil cooking spray can all be used to grease a pan so that baked goods will not stick. Spread a thin layer of fat over the bottom and up the sides of the pan, remembering that too much results in overbrowning. At high oven temperatures, salted butter will brown excessively, too.

Many recipes suggest greasing and flouring a pan. In that case, add a few tablespoons of flour to the greased pan, and shake the pan to distribute the flour lightly and completely. Then, holding the pan over the sink, tap out the excess so that all that is left is a thin, even film. (For some dark-colored desserts, a dusting of cocoa powder is preferable to flour.)

Lining the bottom of a cake pan with waxed paper or parchment paper ensures that the cake does not stick to the pan. Many bakers recommend doing this even if a recipe does not say to. Begin with a thin layer of fat on the bottom and sides of the pan and then press a paper round or rectangle cut to fit the bottom of the pan over the fat. Rub more fat on the paper and then sprinkle it with flour, tapping out the excess. When the cake is baked and turned out onto a rack to cool, the paper peels off easily.

SEPARATING EGGS

When separating eggs, do not use the old-fashioned method of sliding the yolk back and forth between the broken shell halves. This is a good way to pick up microscopic bacteria still on the shell. (Of course, any bacteria will be killed by the heat if the eggs, for example, are being used in a cake batter.) For the same reason, it is not a good idea to separate eggs in your hands either. Instead, invest in an inexpensive egg separator, a small perforated gadget that allows the egg whites to drain while holding the yolk.

BEATING EGG WHITES

When beating egg whites, begin with room-temperature whites without a speck of yolk. (To guarantee that the whites will be yolk-free, separate each egg white into a small bowl, then transfer it to the beating bowl. This way, if the yolk breaks as you're separating, you won't contaminate all the whites.) Put them into a clean, dry glass or metal bowl and use clean, dry beaters or whisks. Whites can increase six to eight times in volume, but even a tiny bit of fat from a yolk or from the equipment will inhibit them. If the recipe calls for soft peaks, beat the whites only until they pile softly or, when the beater is lifted, the peaks curl over slightly. If the recipe calls for stiff peaks, beat the whites until they no longer slip if the bowl is tilted and, when the beaters are lifted, the peaks stand straight up. An acidic stabilizing agent such as cream of tartar or lemon juice added at the beginning of beating will make the whites more stable—helpful if they are being folded into a batter. If adding sugar, begin adding 1 or 2 tablespoons at a time once the whites begin to foam. Add it slowly so that it does not weigh down the whites.

HIGH-ALTITUDE BAKING

Baking at altitudes higher than 3,000 feet can be tricky. Recipes developed at sea level don't work as well at high altitudes. Baked goods may have a porous, dry crumb and rise too high, overflowing the pan. You can avoid these problems by adjusting your recipes following the guidelines below. (It's important to note that these guidelines are not absolutely precise and you may have to experiment a little before you are completely comfortable converting sea-level recipes to high-altitude ones.)

At 3,000 feet:

- Reduce baking soda and/or baking powder by ⅛ teaspoon for every teaspoon.
- Reduce sugar by 1½ teaspoons to 1 tablespoon for every cup.
- Increase liquid by 1 to 2 tablespoons for every cup.
- Beat egg whites to soft peaks instead of stiff peaks.
- Increase the oven temperature by 25°F and shorten the baking time slightly.

At 5,000 feet:

- Reduce baking soda and/or baking powder by ⅛ to ¼ teaspoon for every teaspoon.
- Reduce sugar by 1½ teaspoons to 2 tablespoons for every cup.
- Increase liquid by 2 to 4 tablespoons for every cup.
- Beat egg whites to soft peaks instead of stiff peaks.
- Increase the oven temperature by 25°F and shorten the baking time slightly.

At 7,000 feet:

- Reduce baking soda and/or baking powder by ¼ teaspoon for every teaspoon.
- Reduce sugar by 1 to 3 tablespoons for every cup.
- Increase liquid by 3 to 4 tablespoons for every cup.
- Beat egg whites to soft peaks instead of stiff peaks.
- Increase the oven temperature by 25°F and shorten the baking time slightly.

LOW–FAT BAKING

There are no hard and fast rules for low-fat baking. Fat plays such an important role in baking that it's not easy to reduce the amount and maintain flavor and texture. But here are some general tips for replacing some of the fat in baked-good recipes:

- Use egg whites for *some* of the whole eggs. As a general rule, two egg whites will equal one whole egg.
- Replace *some* of the butter or oil with applesauce or mashed or puréed fruit such as bananas, prunes, or dates.
- Use buttermilk instead of cream or whole milk. It can also be used in place of *some* of the oil and butter.
- Coat baking pans with nonstick cooking spray instead of using butter or shortening.
- Opt for reduced-fat or fat-free dairy products such as sour cream, yogurt, and cream cheese when a recipe calls for it.

GUIDE TO CHOCOLATE

Chocolate seduces the palate as few other foods do. It is a favorite component of desserts, as a simple candy bar, a rich creamy mousse, or a dark tender cake. It's true that a few people seem immune to the glory of chocolate, but far more are enchanted by it, rarely passing up an opportunity to indulge. Chocolate is the ultimate luxury food—seductive, dark, and tempting.

Not all chocolate is alike. Depending on how it is manufactured, it will taste and behave differently in cooking and baking. There is also a range in quality. While more expensive chocolate is smoother and richer, it is not always necessary in the kitchen. If you have access to a top-quality imported chocolate and want to use it in a recipe where its superior flavor and texture won't be masked, go ahead and splurge. But familiar and less expensive supermarket brands of unsweetened and semisweet chocolate are delicious in most preparations. Find a brand you like; the more you cook with it, the more familiar you will become with its properties. While it is essential to use the type of chocolate called for in a particular recipe (unsweetened cannot be used in place of semisweet, for example) and helpful to understand the differences among chocolates, the goal is to enjoy the chocolatey end result.

FROM BEAN TO BAR

Cocoa beans grow on trees in tropical countries that belt the globe near or on the equator. Although native to Central America, the trees now thrive in Africa, Indonesia, parts of South America, and even in Hawaii. Their cultivation has become a major agricultural endeavor, one that feeds an ever growing demand for chocolate worldwide.

Once the cocoa beans are harvested, they are left in the field to ferment. Next they are roasted, shelled, and crushed into a meaty mass called nibs. At this point the nibs are ground into the substance known as chocolate liquor, which is approximately 50 percent cocoa butter and which, when hardened, becomes bitter or unsweetened chocolate. To make cocoa powder, most of the cocoa butter is extracted and then the liquor is ground and sifted.

The extracted cocoa butter is used later to manufacture different varieties of chocolate. For example, semisweet and bittersweet chocolate are made by blending chocolate liquor with varying amounts of sugar, cocoa butter, flavorings such as vanilla, and emulsifiers such as lecithin. Milk chocolate is made much the same way, the major difference being that milk solids are added to the chocolate. Premium chocolate products contain high amounts of cocoa butter rather than another fat. They also are made from beans that have been fermented and roasted to a manufacturer's specifications—much like coffee.

During processing, chocolate is "conched" and permitted to mellow. Conching is a process in which the warm chocolate is kneaded between massive rollers while other ingredients are incorporated. The longer the chocolate is conched, the finer its final grain and texture and, in most circumstances, the better the chocolate is. Chocolate generally is conched for 12 to 72 hours. Following conching, the chocolate is ready to be packaged or mixed with other ingredients to make any number of chocolate and confectionery products.

CARING FOR AND WORKING WITH CHOCOLATE

BUYING CHOCOLATE: When chocolate leaves the factory it is in temper, which means the cocoa butter crystals are stabilized so that the chocolate shines with its characteristic gloss and breaks with a satisfying snap. Unless the chocolate is improperly stored, it will hold its temper until it is melted for cooking and baking.

When buying chocolate, buy it from a busy store with good turnover. Avoid dusty chocolate bars pulled from the back of the shelf; instead, buy fresh-looking bars that are well wrapped. In some gourmet shops, expensive chocolate is sold in unevenly sized chunks broken from a larger block. This chocolate is usually *couverture* (covering) chocolate, which is very high in cocoa butter and is best for candy making and enrobing, although it can be used for some baking.

Do not substitute one kind of chocolate for another in a recipe. If the recipe calls for unsweetened chocolate, bittersweet or semisweet will not work. Milk chocolate, because of the unstable milk solids, is very rarely used for baking and should not be substituted. This is also true for cocoa. If the recipe requires alkalized, or Dutch-process, cocoa powder, you are best advised to use it rather than natural or nonalkalized cocoa powder.

STORING CHOCOLATE: Store solid chocolate (bars and blocks) at cool room temperature with moderate humidity (65°F and 50 percent relative humidity are ideal). Wrap it first in foil and then in plastic. Do not freeze or refrigerate the chocolate; the humidity can cause sugar bloom and may alter the taste and texture of the chocolate. When correctly stored, dark chocolate can keep for about 10 years, milk and white chocolate for up to 1 year.

CHOPPING CHOCOLATE: Use a large sharp knife to chop squares or bars of chocolate. Begin with cool-room-temperature chocolate and chop it on a dry, clean cutting board.

MELTING CHOCOLATE: Melt chopped chocolate or chocolate chips in the top of double boiler or in a microwave. Because chocolate burns easily, melt it gently and slowly; the actual temperature of the chocolate during melting should not exceed 100° to 110°F. If using a double boiler, set the top portion over water that is barely simmering because even a droplet of water or a wisp of steam can cause seizing, in which the chocolate becomes dry and grainy and unworkable. The temperature of the water should be between 120° and 140°F. To prevent seizing, take care that the water does not touch the bottom of the top portion of the double boiler and that it never boils. When chocolate is melted with cream, butter, or another ingredient, seizing is not a problem, although the water should still be kept at a very low simmer during melting and stirring.

To melt chocolate in the microwave, put chopped chocolate or chocolate chips in a microwave-safe container and melt on Medium (50 percent) power, checking after the first minute and then returning to the microwave for 20 seconds at a time, if necessary. Do not expect the chocolate to melt to a liquid pool; instead, it will soften and turn shiny and only upon stirring become smooth. Keep close watch because the chocolate can scorch.

MAKING CHOCOLATE CURLS: To make decorative chocolate curls, warm a bar or square of chocolate in the microwave set on Medium (50 percent) power, 20 seconds at a time, just until it softens but is not melting. Alternatively, hold the chocolate 5 to 6 inches from a light bulb for 6 or 7 minutes. Using a paper towel, grip the chocolate at one end and use a vegetable peeler to scrape tight curls onto a baking sheet lined with waxed paper. Refrigerate the curls until ready to use. If the chocolate bar or square is too cool, the peeler will produce shavings rather than curls. (Of course, shavings, too, can be used to decorate.)

PIPING CHOCOLATE: Slightly cooled melted chocolate can be piped using a pastry bag and a plain tip. You can also spoon melted chocolate into a plastic bag, snip off a corner to expose a small opening, and then squeeze the chocolate through the hole. With a small enough hole, you can produce a narrow line.

CHOCOLATE GLOSSARY

ALKALIZED COCOA POWDER: Cocoa powder processed with an alkali to neutralize the natural acidity of chocolate is labeled "alkalized," "treated with an alkali," and "Dutch-process." It looks darker and has a milder flavor than nonalkalized cocoa.

BAKING CHOCOLATE: Unsweetened or bitter chocolate.

BITTERSWEET CHOCOLATE: Chocolate liquor sweetened with sugar and blended with cocoa butter, lecithin (an emulsifier), and flavorings such as vanilla or vanillin. Bittersweet chocolate must be at least 35 percent chocolate liquor. Can be used interchangeably with semisweet chocolate. Also called dark chocolate.

CACAO: The cacao tree grows in South and Central America, Africa, Southeast Asia, and the West Indies and is cultivated for its seed pods, which are used to produce chocolate.

CHOCOLATE BLOOM: Both powdery-looking white blotches and grainy, rough surfaces are considered chocolate bloom. The former, fat bloom, is caused by warmth; the latter, sugar bloom, is caused by dampness. Bloom is not harmful and when the chocolate is melted, it disappears.

CHOCOLATE LIQUOR: Pure unsweetened mash of ground cocoa beans. When hardened, it is unsweetened or bitter chocolate.

COCOA: Powder made from chocolate liquor with most of the fat removed. It is available either alkalized ("Dutch-process") or nonalkalized ("natural").

COCOA BUTTER: Fat naturally occurring in the cocoa bean that is first extracted and then returned to chocolate in varying amounts depending on the manufacturer and type of chocolate.

CONCHING: Rolling chocolate between heavy rollers to refine it while ingredients such as sugar and milk solids are added. The length of conching affects the chocolate's texture.

COUVERTURE: Dark chocolate with a high percentage of cocoa butter (from 32 to 39 percent) used for coating, hand-dipping, and molding because it melts so smoothly and forms a thin, shiny shell.

DARK CHOCOLATE: Sweetened chocolate liquor with milk solids. Also called bittersweet and semisweet chocolate.

DUTCH-PROCESS COCOA: Cocoa powder that has been treated with an alkali. It has a darker color and a milder flavor than cocoa powder that has not been treated.

LECITHIN: A natural substance (a member of the phospholipid family) that emulsifies fats. Chocolate manufacturers use it to emulsify, or smooth out, the chocolate.

MILK CHOCOLATE: Chocolate containing milk solids, sugar, cocoa butter, and flavorings such as vanilla or vanillin (artificial vanilla).

NONALKALIZED COCOA POWDER: Cocoa powder that has not been treated with an alkali. It has a lighter color and a stronger chocolate flavor than alkalized cocoa powder. Also called natural cocoa powder.

SEIZING: When melted chocolate lumps and hardens; occurs when water or moisture accidentally comes in contact with the hot chocolate.

SEMISWEET CHOCOLATE: Chocolate liquor sweetened with sugar and blended with cocoa butter, lecithin (an emulsifier), and flavorings such as vanilla or vanillin. Semisweet chocolate must be at least 35 percent chocolate liquor and therefore is often exactly the same in composition as bittersweet chocolate. Can be used interchangeably. Also called dark chocolate.

SWEET CHOCOLATE: Chocolate that is 15 percent chocolate liquor and blended with sugar, cocoa butter, milk solids, and flavorings. Also called German sweet chocolate, after a man named German who first produced the chocolate in a factory near Boston at the end of the last century. Cannot be substituted for dark chocolate.

TEMPERED CHOCOLATE: Chocolate with stable cocoa butter crystals. Tempered chocolate is necessary for candy making, enrobing (coating), and molding. Chocolate is in temper when it leaves the manufacturer. When melted, chocolate is out of temper.

UNSWEETENED CHOCOLATE: Baking or bitter chocolate.

WHITE CHOCOLATE: Made from cocoa butter, sugar, milk solids, lecithin, and flavorings, it is not really chocolate because it contains no chocolate liquor.

GLOSSARY

ALMOND PASTE: A soft, uncooked blend of ground almonds, sugar, and egg whites. See *Marzipan*.

ANGEL-FOOD CAKE: A cake made with beaten egg whites, sugar, flour, and flavorings, angel-food cakes are always fat-free. It is baked in a tube pan with feet, also called an angel-food cake pan.

BAIN-MARIE: A water bath for baking. A bain-marie is made by placing a pan or dish of food in a larger, shallow pan and then adding enough hot water to the larger pan to come about halfway up the sides of the smaller dish. The cooking is done in the oven.

BAKING POWDER: A chemical leavener. It is called "double-acting" because it works twice: once when it comes in contact with liquid and again when it comes in contact with heat.

BAKING SODA: A chemical leavener. Recipes that call for baking soda as the only leavening agent will always include an acidic ingredient such as yogurt, lemon or orange juice, or molasses, since baking soda will only react in the presence of an acid.

BATTER: An uncooked mixture of dry and liquid ingredients that is thin enough to pour from a pan or drop from a spoon. Batter is thinner than dough.

BEAT: The quick, steady motion used to in-corporate air into batters and doughs, while mixing ingredients together. May be done by hand with a whisk or spoon or, more commonly in baking recipes, with an electric beater.

BLIND-BAKED: Term used to describe a pie or tart shell baked empty, before filling. The blind-baked pie shell may be baked further after filling or not, depending on the recipe.

BRÛLÉ: French for "burned." Describes a dessert, such as a custard, which has been sprinkled with sugar that is then caramelized by passing it under the broiler.

BUNDT PAN: A style of tube pan with fluted sides.

BUTTER CAKE: Also called a "plain" or "American layer" cake, a butter cake has a high amount of fat (usually butter) in relation to eggs.

BUTTERCREAM: A smooth and creamy frosting made with confectioners' sugar, butter, milk, and sometimes egg yolks. It can also be flavored. Swiss meringue buttercream is a rich, velvety smooth frosting made by heating egg whites and sugar and then beating them to a stiff meringue while adding butter a piece at a time.

CAKE ROLL: A sponge-type cake that is baked in a jelly roll pan, then spread with a filling and rolled into a cylinder or log shape. Also known as a *roulade* (roo-LAHD).

CARAMEL: Sugar heated slowly until it liquefies and turns color. The same word is also used for the rich, chewy candy made by the long, slow cooking of cream, sugar, and butter. Caramelized sugar is used to coat molds for custards and ice creams, as a glaze for pastries and cakes, and as a flavoring for sauces. Caramel candy is commonly sold as small, wrapped squares.

CHEESECAKE: A rich, dense cake made with a batter of primarily cream cheese or another cheese such as ricotta or cottage cheese, which may have a crumb or pastry base. Cheesecakes are usually baked, but not all require baking.

CHIFFON CAKE: A light, airy cake leavened with beaten egg whites (meringue) and made with cooking oil (rather than butter or another flavorful fat) and egg yolks.

COAT THE BACK OF A SPOON: The point at which a mixture is thick enough to form a visible film on a spoon. Usually a custardlike consistency is necessary to "coat the back of a spoon."

COFFEE POWDER AND ESPRESSO POWDER: The freeze-dried granules used to make instant coffee are useful in baking. In general, espresso powder is stronger than coffee powder. Powder dissolves more easily than granules in batters, although both dissolve quickly in hot or boiling water.

CREAM: To beat fats such as butter or vegetable shortening (usually with another ingredient such as sugar) until smooth, fluffy, light in color, and increased in volume. This technique is usually done with an electric mixer.

CRIMP: To create a decorative pattern on the edge of pie pastry using a fork, your fingers, or a pastry crimper. If a pie has a double crust, it also refers to sealing the edges of the top and bottom crust together to form a decorative edge.

CRUMB COAT: A thin first layer of frosting that seals the cake's surface so that the next and final layer of frosting may be applied easily without the worry of picking up stray crumbs during the process.

CURDLE: To separate into lumpy curds and liquid. Eggs will curdle when exposed to too-high heat, as will dairy products. Milk and cream will also curdle when combined with acid foods such as lemon juice or wine; this is the process by which cheese-making begins.

CUSTARD: A smooth dessert, similar in texture to pudding, made with milk, sugar, eggs, and flavorings and cooked very gently so that the eggs do not separate (curdle). A custard can be baked or stirred on the stovetop.

CUT IN: To incorporate cold, solid fat into a dry ingredient, such as flour, until the mixture resembles coarse crumbs. Most cooks use either two kitchen knives, a pastry blender, or their fingertips to cut fat into flour.

DOT: To sprinkle or scatter small pieces of one food over the surface of another. In baking, this generally refers to the best way to distribute butter.

DOUGH: The substance created when dry and liquid ingredients are mixed together to form a cohesive mass that holds together by itself. Dough is thicker than batter.

DUST: To lightly coat food with a sprinkling of a dry ingredient, such as confectioners' sugar or cocoa, for visual appeal and flavor.

FILM: The membranelike covering that forms on top of custards or puddings when they cool. Also called a "skin."

FLUTE: To make a decorative pattern on the edge of a pie shell or other pastry.

FOLD: To gently combine, usually with a rubber spatula, two mixtures with different densities, such as beaten egg whites and creamed batter, so that they lose neither air nor volume.

FONDANT: A sugar preparation cooked to the soft ball stage. Poured fondant can be bought from a specialty bakers' supply house. It is heated and poured over a frosted cake to form a thin, smooth sheath perfect for intricate piping and decorating. Rolled fondant is a stiff mixture of confectioners' sugar, corn syrup, glycerin, water, and gelatin and is used as a sweet, smooth covering for cake or to make decorative shapes.

FROTH: Foamy light bubbles accumulated on the surface of a thin batter or other mixture.

GARNISH: To decorate or embellish a dish with complementary and attractive food, such as mint sprigs, whipped cream, or chocolate shavings.

GENOISE (jen-WAHZ): A French-style sponge cake made by gently heating eggs so that they expand to maximum volume when they are beaten. Melted butter is added to genoise batter, resulting in a light, delicate, and versatile cake.

GLAZE: To apply a thin, glossy coating to a sweet or savory food that, after setting or cooking, will provide a smooth, shiny surface. A common glaze for desserts is a mixture of confectioners' sugar and milk. Melted jam is also used as a glaze.

GRANITA: A frozen mixture of water, sugar, and fruit juice, wine, or coffee that is stirred during freezing to aerate the mixture. Granitas differ from sorbets in that they are generally more granular and are not made in ice cream machines. Also called ice.

GRATE: To turn solid food into particles by rubbing it against a serrated utensil, such as a common kitchen grater. Foods may also be grated in rotating graters, food mills, and food processors.

HULL: To remove the inedible stems and leaves from strawberries and other fruits.

ICE CREAM: A sweet mixture of cream, sugar, flavorings, and sometimes eggs or gelatin that is agitated to incorporate air as it freezes.

KNEAD: To mix dough with the hands, a mixer fitted with a dough hook, or in a bread machine so that the dough forms a cohesive mass and, at the same time, the gluten in the flour begins to develop.

LADYFINGER: A small oval-shaped sponge cake. These cakes are often sandwiched together with a filling and are used in trifles.

LIGHTEN: To add a lighter ingredient, such as beaten egg whites or whipped cream, to a heavier mixture, such as a cake batter or custard-base, to reduce the density of that mixture.

LUKEWARM: A temperature between hot and cool, usually between body temperature (98°F) and 105°F.

MACERATE: To soften fruit and/or release its liquid by soaking it in liqueur or sprinkling it with sugar.

MARBLE: To combine two mixtures (usually batters) of equal weight just enough to create a marbleized, or swirly, effect.

MARZIPAN: Like almond paste, marzipan is a confection made from finely ground blanched almonds, sugar, and egg whites. Almond paste is used in baking, whereas marzipan, which is already cooked, is used as is to mold fanciful shapes for eating as candy or for decorating cakes. Both marzipan and almond paste can be purchased in the baking section of large supermarkets or specialty gourmet shops.

MERINGUE: A foam of beaten egg whites and sugar whisked until the mixture holds its shape. There are two types of meringue: Soft meringue has less sugar and is used as a topping for pies. Hard meringue has more sugar and is used to make pie and tart shells, dessert cases, and other confections.

MOUSSE: Sweet mousses are made with chocolate, fruit, or another flavoring combined with whipped cream or beaten egg whites to form a smooth, rich, creamy dessert. Often fortified with gelatin. A mousse may be chilled or frozen.

NEUFCHÂTEL: Light cream cheese sold in brick form. It has a similar taste and appearance to cream cheese, but has less milkfat and more moisture.

PARE: To peel or skin with a small knife or vegetable peeler.

PASTRY: An unleavened dough made from flour, water, and a solid fat such as butter or vegetable shortening. It is commonly used to make pie and tart crusts.

PEAKS: The shape held by beaten egg white or whipped cream when the beaters are lifted up from its surface.

PEEL: The colored outer portion of the skin of a citrus fruit, but not the bitter white pith beneath, which contains the flavorful oils. Also called zest.

PETIT FOUR (petty for): A bite-size cake (usually sponge cake) glazed with several layers of icing and delicately decorated.

PHYLLO DOUGH: Of Greek origin, these paper-thin sheets of pastry made from flour and water are always fat-free and are used in layers to make desserts, appetizers, and main dishes. Commercially frozen phyllo dough is readily available. Also spelled filo.

PIPE: To squeeze a soft mixture (such as frosting) through a pastry bag or tube to make decorative shapes or borders.

PLUMP: To soften and rehydrate dried fruits by soaking them in hot water.

POUNDCAKE: A rich loaf cake with a fine crumb traditionally made with equal weights of eggs, flour, sugar, and butter.

PRALINE: Caramelized sugar, often mixed with chopped nuts, that once hardened is broken into pieces or ground into powder for decoration, flavoring, and crunch.

PUDDING: A soft, smooth dessert, made with milk, sugar, and eggs, and sometimes thickened with flour, cornstarch, or tapioca, that is cooked on top of the stove, steamed, or baked.

PUFF PASTRY: A dough made from flour, water, and a high proportion of butter. The butter is worked into the dough by a series of rollings and foldings, resulting in a pastry that has numerous paper-thin layers of dough and butter. While it bakes, the butter melts, creating steam and causing the dough to rise to spectacular heights. Commercially frozen puff pastry is readily available.

PURÉE: To blend in a blender, process in a food processor, or force through a food mill until food is smooth and lump-free.

RAMEKIN: A small ovenproof dish used for individual portions of baked or chilled foods. Ramekins resemble soufflé dishes and are usually made of ceramic or porcelain.

RIBBON: The stage at which batter forms a ribbon-like shape when a small amount is allowed to fall from a spoon or from lifted beaters.

ROULADE: See *Cake Roll.*

SCALD: To heat liquid, such as milk, until it almost boils and just begins to form tiny bubbles around the edge of the pan. Solid foods are scalded by being dropped in boiling water for a few moments.

SCRAPE DOWN: To use a rubber spatula or spoon to remove batter, whipped cream, or another mixture from the sides of the bowl during mixing.

SHERBET: A frozen confection made from sugar, fruit, and milk that is agitated during freezing to incorporate air.

SHRED: To cut into flat strips using a knife or a shredder.

SHORTBREAD: A rich, buttery cookie made from butter, sugar, and flour and sometimes flavorings. It has a tender, crumbly texture.

SHORTCAKE: A layered dessert of biscuits (sponge cakes or slices of poundcake are also used), fruit, and whipped cream. The biscuit for the dessert is also called a shortcake.

SIFT: To remove lumps and aerate dry ingredients by passing them through a mesh sifter or strainer.

SIMMER: To boil very gently so that the liquid produces small, occasional bubbles around the edges of the pan and across the surface of the liquid.

SNIP: To cut food with kitchen shears or scissors into small pieces.

SORBET (sor-BAY): A frozen confection made from water, sugar, and fruit juice that is agitated during freezing to incorporate air. Sorbets may be made in ice cream machines or in shallow trays and stirred with a fork several times during freezing. They generally are smoother than granitas.

SPONGE CAKE: A cake with very little fat in proportion to the eggs, which are separated and beaten to a foam before being incorporated into the batter. This method provides the cake with its characteristic light texture.

STEEP: To soak an ingredient in hot water so that its flavors are released into the water, or in order to soften it.

STRAIN: To filter food by pouring or pressing it through a fine wire sieve or strainer.

TEMPER: To heat or warm food carefully and gently so that it may be incorporated into preparations requiring longer cooking. Eggs are often tempered to prevent their curdling by being mixed with a little hot liquid before they are stirred into a sauce or a soup.

TORTE: A dessert or savory constructed of round layers. Also a rich cake made with very little or no flour but with ground nuts or bread crumbs.

TRIFLE: An English dessert that consists of layers of ladyfingers or cake slices sprinkled with sherry or brandy, fruit or jam, and pudding or custard, then topped with whipped cream.

TRUFFLE: A French candy made from melted chocolate, butter, cream, sometimes eggs, and flavorings. The mixture is formed into small balls and rolled in cocoa, confectioners' sugar, or nuts, or dipped in chocolate. Truffle is also the name of an edible fungus that grows underground and is prized for its aroma and delicate flavor (and is not used in dessert-making!).

TUBE PAN: A deep, straight-sided cake pan with a hollow central tube, sometimes with feet. Also called an angel-food cake pan.

TURNTABLE: A device for cake decorating on which cake layers can be rotated during frosting and piping.

ULTRAPASTEURIZED: The commercial process by which heavy cream is heated to a high temperature (up to 300°F) to kill microorganisms that cause souring. This stabilizes the product and increases its shelf life. Ultrapasteurized cream does not whip as well as other cream, although it will whip.

UPSIDE-DOWN CAKE: A cake that is baked in a pan in which fruit, sugar, and butter are arranged in the bottom before the cake batter is poured on top. The fruit caramelizes during baking so that when the cake is inverted after baking, the fruit creates a glaze and decorative topping. The most common is pineapple upside-down cake.

WEEPING: When beaten uncooked egg whites break down and release a watery liquid. This usually happens upon standing. Meringue toppings, such as is used to top a lemon meringue pie, can weep also during baking.

WELL: A hollow depression made in dry ingredients into which liquid ingredients are poured before being incorporated with the dry ingredients.

WHIP: To beat with a whisk or beater until the mixture increases in volume.

ZEST: The colored outer portion of citrus fruit peel containing the flavor oils, but not the white portion beneath it, called the pith, which is bitter.

EQUIVALENTS & CONVERSIONS

EQUIVALENTS (All amounts are approximate)

Bread crumbs: 1 slice fresh bread = ½ cup fresh crumbs
1 slice toasted bread = ¼ cup dried crumbs

Butter: ⅛ pound = 2 ounces = 4 tablespoons = ¼ cup =
½ stick
¼ pound = 4 ounces = 8 tablespoons = ½ cup =
1 stick
½ pound = 8 ounces = 16 tablespoons = 1 cup =
2 sticks

Chocolate: 1 ounce = 1 square = 2 tablespoons grated

Cocoa powder: ¼ pound = 4 ounces = 1 cup

Cream cheese: One 3-ounce package = 6 tablespoons
One 8-ounce package = ½ cup

Eggs: 1 large egg yolk = 1 tablespoon
1 large egg white = 2 tablespoons
4 to 5 large eggs = 1 cup
7 to 8 large egg whites = 1 cup
14 to 15 large egg yolks = 1 cup

Flour: ¼ ounce unsifted flour = 1 tablespoon
2½ ounces unsifted flour = ½ cup
5 ounces unsifted flour = 1 cup
3¾ ounces sifted cake flour = 1 cup

Gelatin: 1 (¼-ounce) envelope = 1 scant tablespoon

Lemons: 1 medium lemon = 3 tablespoons juice
1 medium lemon = 2 teaspoons grated peel

Limes: 1 medium lime = 2 tablespoons juice
1 medium lime = 1 teaspoon grated peel

Milk: 1 (14-ounce) can condensed milk = 1¼ cups
1 (5⅓-ounce) can evaporated milk = ⅔ cup

Oranges: 1 medium orange = ⅓ cup juice
1 medium orange = 3 tablespoons grated peel

Sugar: ½ ounce granulated sugar = 1 tablespoon
1¾ ounces granulated sugar = 4 tablespoons (¼ cup)
3½ ounces granulated sugar = ½ cup
5 ounces granulated sugar = ¾ cup
7 ounces granulated sugar = 1 cup
7 ounces brown sugar = 1 cup packed
4 ounces unsifted confectioners' sugar = 1 cup
3½ ounces sifted confectioners' sugar = 1 cup

CONVERSIONS FOR WEIGHTS AND MEASURES
(Metric amounts are the nearest equivalents)

Liquid measures:
1 teaspoon = 5 milliliters
1 tablespoon = 3 teaspoons = 15 milliliters
⅛ cup = 2 tablespoons = 1 fluid ounce = 30 milliliters
¼ cup = 4 tablespoons = 2 fluid ounces = 60 milliliters
½ cup = 8 tablespoons = 4 fluid ounces = 120 milliliters
1 cup = 16 tablespoons = 8 fluid ounces = 240 milliliters
1 pint = 2 cups = 16 fluid ounces = 480 milliliters
1 quart = 4 cups = 32 fluid ounces = 960 milliliters (.96 liter)
1 gallon = 4 quarts = 16 cups = 128 fluid ounces = 3.84 liters

Weights:
1 ounce = 28 grams
¼ pound = 4 ounces = 114 grams
1 pound = 16 ounces = 454 grams
2.2 pounds = 1,000 grams = 1 kilogram

Page numbers in **boldface** refer to photographs; page numbers in *italics* refer to illustrations.

A

Alkalized cocoa powder, 329. *See also* Chocolate
Almond(s), 324
 Apricot Linzer Tart, 135
 cake
  Chocolate-, with Dark Chocolate Glaze, 171-72
  Chocolate-Orange Sponge, 285-86
  Sliced, 179
 Chocolate-Covered Toffee, 311-12
 Chocolate-Orange Cups, 308
 cookies
  Amaretti, 286
  Austrian Linzer Cookies, **303**, 307
  Biscotti, Cinnamon-, 44-45
  Congo Bars, 31, **34**
  Fudgy Low-Fat Brownies, 24
  Glaze, Honey-, Butter Strips with, 298
  Lemon Softies, 22-23
  Raspberries with Amaretti Cream, 220
  Shortbread, 43-44
 French Bread Pudding, 142-43
  Low-Fat, 142
 Ice Cream, Coffee-, 54
 paste, 331
 -Peach Parfait, 246
 Raspberry Linzer Tart, 135-36
 Rice Pudding, Baked, 140-41
 storing, 179
 Tart, 134-35
 Toasted, -Apple Ice Cream Topping, 84
 toasting, 325
Almost-Margarita Pineapple, 246
Amaretti, 286
 Cream, Raspberries with, 220
Ambrosia, 218-19
Angel food cake, 331
 Big Bang Cupcake Cake, 286-87
Anise seeds, storing, 38
Apple(s), 129. *See also* Applesauce
 Baked, Orange-Glazed, 237
 Brown Betty, 238
 Caramel, 291
 with Custard Sauce, 236-37
 Dessert à la Waldorf, 246
 Double-Dipped Chocolate Caramel, 316

Apple(s), (*cont.*)
 Dunking, 246
 Fritters, 297-98
 Ice Cream Topping, Toasted Almond-, 84
 Kuchen Bars, 28
 pie
  apples for, 100
  Cider, 99-100, **110**
  Crunch, 99
  Date, and Pecan, 295
  Phyllo, 100-1
  Quick-Fix Caramel, 246
  Sorbet, 63
  storing, 199
  Streusel Coffeecake, 199-200
  Tart, Free-Form, **110**, 129
  Upside-Down Cake, 198-99
  Walnut Crisp, **226-27**, 244
Applesauce
 Bars, Whole-Wheat, 32
 Cake with Caramel Glaze, 174-75
 Saucy Raisin-Toast Triangles, 246
Apricot
 Bars, Crispy, 49-50
 Linzer Tart, 135
Austrian Linzer Cookies, **303**, 307

B

Bain-marie, 331
Baked Almond Rice Pudding, 140-41
Baking. *See also* Techniques
Baking chocolate, 329. *See also* Chocolate
Baking powder, 204, 324, 331
Baking soda, 204, 324, 331
Baking techniques. *See also* Techniques
 high-altitude, 326-27
 low-fat, 327
Banana(s)
 buying and storing, 231
 Cinnamon-Scented, in Honey Yogurt, 246
 Cream Cake, **192**, 210
 Custard Tart, 133-34
 Frozen, Chocolate-Covered, 64
 Fudge, Peanut Butter and, 312
 Ice Cream, Strawberry-, 57-58
 Lickety Split, Blueberry-, 246
 Nippy Nibbles, 64
 Poundcake, 196
 Shake, 87
  Low-Fat, 87
 Sorbet, Pineapple-, 60
 Split with Fudge Sauce, **72**, 86

Bananas (*cont.*)
 Sugared Split, 64
 -Toffee Ice Cream Cake, **73**, 78-79
 Treat, Frozen Yogurt, 246
 Tropical Smoothie, 246
Batter, 331
Beat, defined, 331
Berry(ies). *See also specific kinds*
 Cassis, Watermelon-, 219
 Cornmeal-Honey Shortcakes with, 204
 Melon and, with Strawberry Sauce, 221
 Pavlova, **187**, 213-14
 Tart, Two-, **116**, 127
 washing, 58
Beverages
 Banana Shake, 87
  Low-Fat, 87
 ice cream sodas, 86
  Mocha, 88
  Low-Fat Orange-and-Cream, 87
  Orange-and-Cream, 87
 Tropical Smoothie, 246
Big Bang Cupcake Cake, 286-87
Big Maccake, 252-53, **262**
Biscotti, Cinnamon-Almond, 44-45
Biscuit(s). *See also* Shortcakes
 Cherry-Pear Cobbler, 240
 cutters, 319
 Peach Cobbler, 239
 storing, 202
Bittersweet chocolate, 329. *See also* Chocolate
 Truffle Tart, 136
Blackberries. *See also* Berry(ies)
 Fragrant Fruit with Raspberry Sherbet, 222, **228**
Black and White Brownies, 27
Blind baked, 331
Blondies, 26, **34-35**
Blueberry(ies), 98. *See also* Berry(ies)
 -Banana Lickety Split, 246
 Big Bang Cupcake Cake, 286-87
 Cantaloupe "Mousse," 157-58
 Cobbler, Peach-, 239
 Fourth of July Sundae, 88
 Fruit Melba, 234
 Ice Cream Sauce, Lemon-, 85
 Individual Cheesecake Flags, 288
 -Lemon Ice Cream, 58-59
 Melon and Berries with Strawberry Sauce, 221
 Melon Toss, 246

Blueberry(ies) (*cont.*)
New York–Style Cheesecake, 189, 206
Nippy Nibbles, 64
Pie with Cornmeal Crumb Topping, 98–99
-Plum Crisp, 245
-Spice Coffeecake, 201–2
Starry Shortcake, 288–89
Trifle, Strawberry-, **149**, 159
Two-Berry Tart, **116**, 127
Boston Cream Pie, 182–83, **190**
Box of Crayons Cake, 254–55, *255*, **266**
Bread crumbs, 238
Bread Pudding, 142
Almond French, 142–43
Low-Fat, 142
Chocolate, 143
Lemon Custard, 141–42
Low-Fat, 141
Broiled Brown-Sugared Oranges, 246
Broiled Pineapple Rounds, 246
Brownie(s)
baking techniques, 23
Black and White, 27
Blondies, 26, **34–35**
Chocolate Nut, 23
Fudgy Low-Fat, 24
Ice Cream Cake, Seven-Layer, 77–78
Ice Cream Loaf, No-Bake, 77
Nut Slices, 48
Shortbread, 29–30
storing, 24
Brûlé, 321
Rice Pudding, 140
Strawberry, 225, 236
Bundt cake, 181
pan, 331
Vanilla Buttermilk, 181–82
Bunny Cake, **268**, 269–70, *270*
Butter
cake, 331
Citrus, 315
Honey-Maple Spice, 315
Raspberry, 315
Buttercream, 331
Bow Cake, 274
Fluffy Vanilla, Yellow Cake with, 167–68
Buttermilk, 169
Bundt Cake, Vanilla, 181–82
Butterscotch
Ice Cream Sauce, 85
Pudding, 146–47
Buying and storing food. *See also*
Freezing food; Storing food

Butterscotch (*cont.*)
bananas, 231
chocolate, 328–29
dairy products, 323
eggs, 157, 322–33
egg substitutes, 323
extracts, 324
fats and oils, 321–22
flour, 32, 321
grapefruit, 218
honeydew, 234
kiwifruit, 224
leaveners, 324
mangoes, 235
nuts, 123, 125, 324
oranges, 218
papayas, 223
peaches, 220
pears, 240
pineapple, 218, 241
plums, 245
raspberries, 221
spices, 324
strawberries, 67, 232
sugars, 321
Cacao, 330
Cake, 161–214. *See also* Cheesecake;
Coffeecake; Ice cream cake; Quick
breads; Shortcakes; Silly cakes
Applesauce, with Caramel
Glaze, 174–75
apple
Streusel Coffeecake, 199–200
Upside-Down, 198–99
baking tips, 203
banana
Cream, **192**, 210
Poundcake, 196
Big Bang Cupcake, 286–87
Carrot, 175
with Cream Cheese Frosting, 175
chocolate
-Almond, with Dark Chocolate
Glaze, 171–72
Bars, Frosted Fudge, 183–84
Espresso, 180
Graham Icebox, 214
Meringue Torte, Frozen, 67–68
-Mocha Cherry, 169–70, **186**
Mocha-Hazelnut Roll, 212–13
Mousse Roll, 210–11
One-Bowl, 164–65, **190–91**
-Orange Cups, 308
-Orange Sponge, 285–86
Pine Cone, 299–300, **304**

Cake: chocolate (*cont.*)
Pudding, 144–45
Pumpkin-, 289–90, **304**
-Raspberry Heart, 278–79, *278*, **301**
Cranberry Pecan Loaves, 314
cupcakes
Chocolate-Peanut Butter, 193–94
Lemon, 184–93
decorating, 164, 181, 256
with flowers, 259
with pastry bag, 272
Gingerbread with Citrus
Sauce, 178
Holiday Pecan, 292–93
Layer, Triple-Lemon, 165–66, 185
Lemon Poppy Seed, with Lemon
Glaze, 197–98
Maple-Coconut Pecan, 177
microwave
Chocolate Pudding, 145
Cocoa Snack, 172
Maple-Coconut Pecan, 177
Peanut Butter Crumble, 176
No-Bake Petits Fours, 305
Nut, with Fruit Sauce, 284–85
Orange Chiffon, with Nectarines, 208–9
Orange Chiffon Easter Basket, 280–82
pans, 318
Peanut Butter Crumble, 176
Petite Gingerbreads, 313–14
Poundcake, 194–95
roll, 331
scraps, using, 274
Sliced Almond, 179
Spice Layer, with Pecan Frosting, 168–69
storing, 165
testers, 319
tortes, 68
Tropical Fruitcakes, 314
Vanilla Buttermilk Bundt, 181–82
yellow
Boston Cream Pie, 182–83, **190**
with Chocolate Cream
Frosting, 167
with Fluffy Vanilla Buttercream, 167–68
Candy, 313. *See also* Confections
Sea Glass, 312–13
thermometer, 319
Cantaloupe, 230
"Mousse," 157–58

Cappuccino-Chocolate Chunk Ice
  Cream, 56-57
Caramel, 331
  Apple(s), 291
    Double-Dipped Chocolate, 316
    Quick-Fix, 246
  Banana-Toffee Ice Cream
    Cake, **73**, 78-79
  Clusters, 50
  Coconut Flan, 148-53, **150-51**
  Crème, Coffee, 147-48
    Make-It-Easy, 147
  Glaze, Applesauce Cake with, 174-75
Mexican Mocha Flan, 153-54
  pans for making, 153
  Pie, Chocolate Truffle, 120-21
  stages of, 148
  Waffle Sundae, 88
Carlyle the Crocodile, 253-54, *254*, **264**
Carnival Cones, 88
Carrot Cake, 175
  with Cream Cheese Frosting, 175
Cereal
  Caramel Clusters, 50
  Crispy Apricot Bars, 49-50
  crushing, 49
  Frozen Strawberry Daiquiri Pie,
    66-67
  Nutty Granola Cookies, 20-21
  Peanut Butter and Jelly Cookies, 49
  Pear Granola Crisp, **226-27**, 244
Cheesecake, 331
  baking tips, 208
  Chocolate, **189**, 205
  cutting, 207
  Flags, Individual, 288
  freezing, 206
  Lemon, Flag Bars, 287-88
  Lemony, 208
  New York-Style, **189**, 206
  No-Bake Vanilla Yogurt, **188**, 207
Cherry(ies)
  Bombe, 88
  Cake, Chocolate-Mocha, 169-70, **186**
  -Cheese Tart, 128
  Chocolate-Covered, 279-80
  Cobbler Bars, 28
  Dip, 246
  Ice Cream Bombe, **69**, 82
  -Pear Cobbler, 240
  Pie, Rhubarb-, 96
  pitting, 195
  "Ravioli," Chocolate, 41
  Ruby-Red Ice Cream Sauce, 85
  Sauce, Lemon-, for Poundcake, 195

Chiffon cake, 331
  Orange, Easter Basket, 280-82
  Orange, with Nectarines, 208-9
Chilled Pineapple-Mango Soup, 235
Chocolate, 171
  bloom, 330
  Boston Cream Pie, 182-83, **190**
  Bread Pudding, 143
  cake(s)
    -Almond, with Dark Chocolate
      Glaze, 171-72
    Bars, Frosted Fudge, 183-84
    Cheesecake, **189**, 205
    Chip Shortcakes, Strawberry-
      Peach, 203
    Espresso, 180
    Graham Icebox, 214
    Holiday Pecan, 292-93
    Microwave Cocoa, 172
    Microwave Pudding Cake, 144-45
    -Mocha Cherry, 169-70, **186**
    Mocha-Hazelnut Roll, 212-13
    Mousse Roll, 210-11
    One-Bowl, 164-65, **190-91**
    -Orange Cups, 308
    -Orange Sponge, 285-86
    -Peanut Butter Cupcakes, 193-94
    Pine Cone, 299-300, **304**
    Pudding Cake, 144-45
    Pumpkin-, 289-90, **304**
    -Raspberry Heart, 278-79,
      278, **301**
    Seven-Layer Brownie Ice Cream,
      77-78
    Soufflé Cake, Warm, 173
  Caramel Apple, Double-Dipped, 316
  cookies
    Black and White Brownies, 27
    Blondies, 26, **34-35**
    Brownie Nut Slices, 48
    Brownie Shortbread, 29-30
    Cherry "Ravioli," 41
    Chip, Oatmeal-, 18
    Cinnamon-Almond Biscotti, 44-45
    Cocoa-Mint Wafers, **303**, 310
    Congo Bars, 31, **34**
    Crackle Tops, 39-40
    Jumbles, Double, 14-15
    Lemon Bars, 29
    Nut Brownies, 23
    Peanut Rounds, 46-47
    Pretzels, 41
    Sandwiches, 41
    Shortbread, 43
    Walnut Chunk Cookies, 14

Chocolate: cookies (*cont.*)
    Zebras, 25
  -Covered Cherries, 279-80
  -Covered Frozen Banana, 64
  -Covered Toffee, Almond, 311-12
  Cream Frosting, Yellow Cake
    with, 167
  decorating with, 329
  -Dipped Fruit and Cookie
    Wreath, 300-5
  Fondue, 160
  Fudge, Easy Triple-, 312
  glossary of, 329-30
  guide to, 328-30
  ice cream, 55
    Banana Split with Fudge
      Sauce, **72**, 86
    Bombe, **69**, 82
    Carnival Cones, 88
    Cherry Bombe, 88
    Chunk, Cappuccino-, 56-57
    Loaf, Ladyfinger, **76**, 79
    Loaf, No-Bake Brownie, 77
    Low-Fat, 58
    -Peanut Butter-Cup Sundae,
      Double, 83
    Soda, Mocha, 88
    Sundae, Low-Fat, 83
    Sundae, Mocha, 83
    Super-Rich, 55
  Leaves (cookies), 41
  leaves for decorating, 212
  liquor, 330
  Marbled Truffles, 280
  melting, 329
  Meringue Torte, Frozen, 67-68
  Mexican Mocha Flan, 153-54
  Milk, 330
    Mousse, 156
  Mousse, Rich, **152**, 155
  pies
    Cream, Double, 105-6
    Mississippi Mud, 104-5
    Pastry for a Single-Crust, 93-94
    -Peanut Mousse, **112**, 118-19
    -Raspberry Chiffon, 108
    Ribbon Coconut Cream, 282-83
    Truffle Caramel, 120-21
    -Vanilla Mousse, **112**, 119-20
  Pudding, 145-46
  sauce
    Hot Fudge, 84
    Orange Sherbet Loaf with, 80
    -Peanut Butter Ice Cream, 84
  tarts

Chocolate: tarts (*cont.*)
Bittersweet, Truffle, 136
-Strawberry, 125-26
tempered, 330
Christmas desserts
Austrian Linzer Cookies, **303**, 307
Chocolate-Dipped Fruit and Cookie
Wreath, 300-5
Chocolate-Orange Cups, 308
Cinnamon Triangles, **303**, 310
Cocoa-Mint Wafers, **303**, 310
Coconut Crispies, **303**, 306
Cranberry Icebox Cookies, 309
Fruitcake Squares, **303**, 311
No-Bake Petits Fours, 305
Pine Cone Cake, 299-300, **304**
Spice Cookie Cutouts, 303, 308-9
Spiral Cookies, 303, 306-7
Cinnamon, 237, 324
-Almond Biscotti, 44-45
-Peanut Butter Cookies, 15-16
-Scented Bananas in Honey
Yogurt, 246
Triangles, **303**, 310
Twists, Flaky, 45-46
Citrus fruit. *See also specific kinds*
Butter, 315
Sorbet Cups, 88
zest (peel), 335
grating, 102, 118
Coat the back of a spoon, defined, 331
Cobbler, 238
Cherry-Pear, 240
Peach, 239
-Blueberry, 239
Pineapple-Macadamia, 241
Cocoa, 183, 328-330. *See also* Chocolate
-Mint Wafers, **303**, 310
Coconut
Ambrosia, 218-19
Banana Custard Tart, 133-34
Carrot Cake, 175
with Cream Cheese Frosting, 175
Congo Bars, 31, **34**
Cream Pie, Chocolate Ribbon,
282-83
Crispies, **303**, 306
Flan, 148-53, **150-51**
Ice Cream, Pineapple-, 54
Nest-Egg Cookies, 284
Pecan Cake, Maple-, 177
Microwave, 177
Piña Colada Sorbet, 59-60
Pineapple-Macadamia Cobbler, 241
shelling, 219

Coconut (*cont.*)
toasting, 132, 166, 325
Triple-Lemon Layer Cake, 165-66
Tropical Fruitcakes, 314
Coffee
-Almond Ice Cream, 54
Cappuccino-Chocolate Chunk Ice
Cream, 56-57
Chocolate Espresso Cake, 180
Chocolate-Mocha Cherry Cake,
169-70, **186**
Crème Caramel, 147-48
Make-It-Easy, 147
crushing beans, 147
forms of, 331
Granita, 64-65
Mexican Mocha Flan, 153-54
Mocha Chocolate Sundae, 83
Mocha-Hazelnut Roll, 212-13
Mocha Ice Cream Soda, 88
No-Bake Brownie Ice Cream
Loaf, 77
Seven-Layer Brownie Ice Cream
Cake, 77-78
Coffeecake. *See also* Cake
Apple Streusel, 199-200
Blueberry-Spice, 201-2
German Crumb, 200-201
Cold Pumpkin Soufflé, 295-96, **302**
Compote
Dried Fruit, 231-32
Melon, 230
Plum and Walnut, 229
Conching, 330
Condensed milk, 31, 323
Confections
Almond Chocolate-Covered
Toffee, 311-12
Chocolate-Covered Cherries, 279-80
Chocolate-Orange Cups, 308
Easy Triple-Chocolate Fudge, 312
Marbled Truffles, 280
Peanut Butter and Banana
Fudge, 312
Peppermint Stick Fudge, 312
Popcorn Balls, 291
Sea Glass Candy, 312-13
Congo Bars, 31, **34**
Cookie(s), 11-50
baking sheets, 318
baking techniques, 14, 16, 17, 19, 20,
21, 22, 48
bar, 25, 30
Apple Kuchen, 28
Black and White Brownies, 27

Cookies: bar (*cont.*)
Blondies, 26, **34-35**
Butter Strips with Honey-Almond
Glaze, 298
Cherry Cobbler, 28
Chocolate Lemon, 29
Chocolate Nut Brownies, 23
Cinnamon Triangles, **303**, 310
Congo, 31, **34**
Fig, **33**, 37-38
Fruitcake Squares, **303**, 311
Fudgy Low-Fat Brownies, 24
Individual Cheesecake, 288
Lemon, 28-29
Lemon Cheesecake Flag
Bars, 287-88
Raspberry-Hazelnut, 30-31
Whole-Wheat Applesauce, 32
Zebras, 25
Biscotti, Cinnamon-Almond, 44-45
Caramel Clusters, 50
Cherry "Ravioli," 41
Chocolate Crackle Tops, 39-40
Chocolate Pretzels, 41
Coconut Nest-Egg, 284
cutters, 319
drop
Amaretti, 286
Chocolate Walnut Chunk, 14
Cinnamon-Peanut Butter, 15-16
Coconut Crispies, **303**, 306
Double Chocolate Jumbles, 14-15
freezing dough, 50
Lacy Oatmeal, 16
Lemon Softies, 22-23
Lemon Softies with Lemon
Icing, 22
Peanut Butter and Jelly, 49
Praline Chip, 18-19
White Chocolate Walnut
Chunk, 14
Whole-Wheat Raisin, 19-20
icebox
Brownie Nut Slices, 48
Chocolate Peanut Rounds, 46-47
Cocoa-Mint Wafers, **303**, 310
Cranberry, 309
Lemon-Ginger Crisps, 47-48
Oatmeal Spice, 17
Orange-Poppy Seed, 297, 303
Spiral, 303, 306-7
Ice Cream Zoo, 88
mailing, 26
Mexican Wedding Cakes, 38
Molasses Crinkle, **36**, 42

Cookie(s): icebox (*cont.*)
  Nutty Granola, 20-21
  Oatmeal-Chocolate Chip, 18
  packaging tips, 307
  Pecan Thumbprint, 43
  Raspberries with Amaretti Cream, 220
  rolled
    Austrian Linzer, **303**, 307
    Chocolate Leaves, 41
    Chocolate Sandwiches, 41
    Cut-Out, 283-84
    Cutouts, Spice, **303**, 308-9
    Flaky Cinnamon Twists, 45-46
  shortbread
    Almond, 43-44
    Brownie, 29-30
    Chocolate, 43
    Cornmeal, 40
    Orange-Hazelnut, 44
  Soft Sugar, 21
  storing, 39
  Walnut Thumbprint, 42-43
  Wreath, Chocolate-Dipped Fruit
    and, 300-5
  Yo-yos, 88
Cooking techniques. *See* Techniques
Cornmeal
  Crumb Topping, Blueberry Pie
    with, 98-99
  -Honey Shortcakes with Berries, 204
  Shortbread Cookies, 40
  storing, 40
Couverture, 328, 330
Cranberry(ies), 309
  Crimson Pie, 293-94
  Icebox Cookies, 309
  Pecan Loaves, 314
  -Raspberry-Orange Gelatin, 233
  Ruby-Red Ice Cream Sauce, 85
Cream (dairy), 323
  whipping, 106, 159, 160
Cream, defined, 332
Cream cheese, 333
  Cherry-Cheese Tart, 128
  Lemony Cheesecake, 208
  New York-Style Cheesecake, **189**, 206
  softening, 27
Creamy Hawaiian Fruit Cups, 246
Crimp, defined, 332
Crisp, 238
  Apple Walnut, **226-27**, 244
  Nectarine, 242
  Pear Granola, **226-27**, 244
Crispy Apricot Bars, 49-50
Crumb coat, 332

Crumble, 238
  Plum Oatmeal, **226-27**, 242-43
Crunch, 238
Cupcakes
  Chocolate-Peanut Butter, 193-94
  Lemon, 184-93
Curdle, 332
Custard(s), 137-60, 332. *See also* Pie
  baked vs. stirred, 154
  Boston Cream Pie, 182-83, **190**
  Bread Pudding, Lemon, 141-42
    Low-Fat, 141
  Coconut Flan, 148-53, **150-51**
  Coffee Crème Caramel, 147-48
    Make-It-Easy, 147
  cooling, 155
  cups, 319
  doneness of, 145
  Mexican Mocha Flan, 153-54
  Pumpkin Crunch, 154-55
  Sauce, Apples with, 236-37
  tips for making, 154
Cut in, defined, 332
Cut-Out Cookies, 283-84

D

Dairy products, 323. *See also specific kinds*
Dark chocolate, 330. *See also* Chocolate
Date(s)
  Apple, and Pecan Pie, 295
  Dessert à la Waldorf, 246
  Petite Gingerbreads, 313-14
  Sauce, Rum-, for Poundcake, 195
Decorating, 294
  cakes, 164, 181, 256
  with chocolate, 329
  chocolate leaves, 212
  with flowers, 259
  with pastry bags, 272, 320
Desert Delight, 246
Dessert à la Waldorf, 246
Dot, defined, 332
Double boiler, 319
Double Chocolate Cream Pie, 105-6
Double Chocolate Jumbles, 14-15
Double Chocolate-Peanut Butter Cup
  Sundae, 83
Double-Dipped Chocolate Caramel
  Apple, 316
Dough, 332
Dried fruit. *See also specific kinds*
  Compote, 231-32
  Fruitcake Squares, **303**, 311
  Tropical Fruitcakes, 314

Dunking Apples, 246
Dust, defined, 332
Dutch-processed cocoa, 330

E

Easter desserts
  Chocolate Ribbon Coconut
    Cream Pie, 282-83
  Coconut Nest-Egg Cookies, 284
  Cut-Out Cookies, 283-84
  Orange Chiffon Easter Basket
    Cake, 280-82
Easy Triple-Chocolate Fudge, 312
Edible cake flowers, 259
Eggs, 322-23. *See also* Meringue
  baking, 104
  beating, 182, 184, 285, 326
  safe handling, 168, 322-23
  separating, 285, 326
  storing, 157
Egg substitutes, 201, 323
Electric mixers, 319
Equipment, 318-21
  acid ingredients and cookware, 118
  bain marie, 146, 331
  cake pans, 170, 254, 318, 319, 331
  candy thermometer, 180, 319
  food processor, 171, 319
  ice cream machine, 65
  measuring volume of baking
    dish, 143
  nutmeg graters, 200
  ovens and oven thermometers, 310
  pans for making caramel, 153
  pastry bags, 272, 320
  pie plates, 93, 318-19
  ramekin, 334
  skillets as baking pans, 198
  springform pans, 81, 319
  tart pans, 128, 319, 325
  turntable, 325
  water baths, 146, 331
Equivalents, 336
Espresso. *See* Coffee
Evaporated milk, 323
Extracts, 324

F

Fabulous Vanilla Ice Cream, 54, **72**
Fast and Fresh Pineapple Sherbet, 246
Fats and oils, 321-22
Fig(s), 37
  Bar Cookies, **33**, 37-38
  Desert Delight, 246
  storing dried, 27

Film, defined, 331
Flaky Cinnamon Twists, 45-46
Flaky Pastry for Tarts, 92-93
Flan
    Coconut, 148-53, **150-51**
    Mexican Mocha, 153-54
Flavored butters, 315
Flavoring oils, 313
Flour, 32, 321
Flowers, for cake decorating, 259
Flute, defined, 331
Fold, defined, 332
Fondant, 332
Fondue, Chocolate, 160
Food processor, 171, 319
Food safety and eggs, 168, 322-23
Fool, 159
    Tropical Mango, 158-59
Fourth of July desserts
    Big Bang Cupcake Cake, 286-87
    Fourth of July Sundae, 88
    Individual Cheesecake Flags, 288
    Lemon Cheesecake Flag Bars, 287-88
    Starry Shortcake, 288-89
Fragrant Fruit with Raspberry Sherbet, 222, **228**
Free-Form Apple Tart, **110**, 129
Freezing foods
    cheesecake, 206
    coconut, 219
    cookie dough, 50
    phyllo, 101
Fresh Fruit Terrine, 224
Fritters, Apple, 297-98
Frosted Fudge Cake Bars, 183-84
Frosting cakes, 164
Frosty, **265**, 271-72
Froth, defined, 332
Frozen Chocolate Meringue Torte, 67-68
Frozen desserts, 51-88. *See also* Granita; Ice cream; Sherbet; Sorbet; Yogurt, frozen
    Cherry Bombe, 88
    Chocolate-Covered Frozen Banana, 64
    Chocolate Meringue Torte, 67-68
    Frozen Strawberry Daiquiri Pie, 66-67
    Frozen Yogurt Banana Treat, 246
    low-fat, 63
    Nippy Nibbles, 64
    Spaceship, 88
    Sugared Split Bananas, 64
    Yo-yos, 88

Frozen Strawberry Daiquiri Pie, 66-67
Frozen Yogurt Banana Treat, 246
Fruit, dried. *See* Dried fruit
Fruit, fresh. *See also specific kinds*
    Chocolate Fondue, 160
    Layered, with Raspberry Sauce, 230-31
    Lemony Cheesecake, 208
    Melba, 234
    Salad, Tropical, 223-24
    Terrine, 224
Fruitcake(s)
    Squares, **303**, 311
    Tropical, 314
Fruit desserts, 215-46. *See also specific fruits*
Frying tips, 298
Fudge
    Easy Triple-Chocolate, 312
    Peanut Butter and Banana, 312
    Peppermint Stick, 312
Fudgy Low-Fat Brownies, 24

G

Garnish, defined, 332
Gelatin, 233
    Cranberry-Raspberry-Orange, 233
    Spaceship, 88
    Strawberry-and-Cream, 232-33
Genoise, 332
Georgia Peach Sundae, 83
Geranium leaves, scented, 222
German Crumb Cake, 200-201
Gifts from the kitchen
    Almond Chocolate-Covered Toffee, 311-12
    Citrus Butter, 315
    Cranberry Pecan Loaves, 314
    Double-Dipped Chocolate Caramel Apple, 316
    Easy Triple-Chocolate Fudge, 312
    Honey-Maple Spice Butter, 315
    Peanut Butter and Banana Fudge, 312
    Pear Quick Breads, 315
    Peppermint Stick Fudge, 312
    Petite Gingerbreads, 313-14
    Raspberry Butter, 315
    Sea Glass Candy, 312-13
    Tropical Fruitcakes, 314
Ginger, 324
    Crisps, Lemon-, 47-48
    Gingerbread with Citrus Sauce, 178
    Gingered Plums and Mango, 222-23
    Peanut Butter Crumble Cake, 176
    Microwave, 176

Ginger (*cont.*)
    Petite Gingerbreads, 313-14
Gingerbread(s)
    with Citrus Sauce, 178
    Petite, 313-14
    -Pumpkin Ice Cream Roll, 296
Gingered Plums and Mango, 222-23
Glaze, defined, 332-33
Gloria Glowworm, 250-51, *251*, **262**
Glossary, 321-25
    chocolate, 329
Graham crackers, 214
    Chocolate Graham Icebox Cake, 214
Granita, 332
    Coffee, 64-65
    Raspberry-Lemon, 63-64, **71**
Granola
    Caramel Clusters, 50
    Cookies, Nutty, 20-21
    Crisp, Pear, **226-27**, 244
    Frozen Strawberry Daiquiri Pie, 66-67
Grapefruit
    choosing, 218
    In-the-Pink, 246
    Sorbet, Strawberry-, 61, **70**
Grapes
    Creamy Hawaiian Fruit Cups, 246
    Nippy Nibbles, 64
    Sour, 246
Grate, defined, 333
Greasing pans, 326

H

Halloween desserts
    Caramel Apples, 291
    Popcorn Balls, 291
    Pumpkin-Chocolate Cake, 289-90, **304**
Hanukkah desserts
    Apple Fritters, 297-98
    Butter Strips with Honey-Almond Glaze, 298
    Orange-Poppy Seed Cookies, 297, **303**
Hazelnut(s), 324
    Bars, Raspberry-, 30-31
    Bittersweet Chocolate Truffle Tart, 136
    buying, 125
    Providence Nut Pie, 107-8
    Roll, Mocha- 212-13
    Shortbread, Orange-, 44
    toasting, 325-26
High-altitude baking, 326-27
Holiday desserts, 275-316

Holiday Pecan Cake, 292-93
Honey
 -Almond Glaze, Butter Strips
  with, 298
 -Maple Spice Butter, 315
 Pumpkin Pie with Orange Whipped
  Cream, 292
 Shortcakes, Cornmeal-, with
  Berries, 204
 -Topped Papaya Fans, 246
 Yogurt, Cinnamon-Scented Bananas
  in, 246
Honeydew melon
 buying and storing, 234
 Fruit Melba, 234
 Mint Julep Sorbet, 62, **74**
 Summer Fruit with Brown Sugar
  Cream, 221
Hot Dog, What a Cake!, 257-58,
 257-58, **263**
Hot Fudge Sauce, 84
Hull, defined, 333

I

Ice cream, 51-88, 333. *See also* Frozen
 desserts; Granita; Sherbet; Sorbet;
 Yogurt, frozen
 Blueberry-Lemon, 58-59
 Bombe, **69**, 82
  Cherry, 88
 cake
  Banana-Toffee, **73**, 78-79
  Loaf, Ladyfinger, **76**, 79
  Loaf, No-Bake Brownie, 77
  Roll, Gingerbread-Pumpkin, 296
  Seven-Layer Brownie, 77-78
 Cappuccino-Chocolate Chunk, 56-57
 Carnival Cones, 88
 chocolate
  Low-Fat, 58
  Super-Rich, 55
 Coffee-Almond, 54
 Fabulous Vanilla, 54, **72**
 machines, 65
 Party Clown, 88
 Peach, 55-56, **70**
 pie
  Peach-Raspberry, 65
  Strawberry Mousse, 121-22
 Pineapple-Coconut, 54
 ripening, 56
 Shake, Banana, 87
  Low-Fat, 87
 soda, 86
  Mocha, 88

Ice Cream: soda (*cont.*)
  Orange-and-Cream, 87
   Low-Fat, 87
 softening, 82
 still-freeze method, 62
 storing, 79, 86
 Strawberry, 54
  -Banana, 57-58
  -and-Cream Gelatin, 232-33
 sundae
  Banana Split with Fudge Sauce,
   72, 86
  Double Chocolate Peanut
   Butter-Cup, 83
  Fourth of July, 88
  Georgia Peach, 83
  Low-Fat Chocolate, 83
  Mocha Chocolate, 83
  Peach Melba, 83
  Red, White, and Blue, 83
  Tropical, 83
  Waffle, 88
 techniques for making, 58
 Yo-yos, 88
 Zoo, 88
Individual Cheesecake Flags, 288
Ingredients, about, 321-24. *See also*
 Buying and storing food; Glossary;
 Storing Food
 anise seeds, 38
 apples, 100
 cantaloupe, 230
 caramel, 148
 chocolate, 171
 cinnamon, 237
 cocoa, 183
 cranberries, 309
 dairy products, 31, 169, 323
 eggs, 322-33
 egg substitutes, 201, 323
 extracts, 324
 fats and oils, 321-22
 figs, 37
 flavoring oils, 313
 flour, 321
 graham crackers, 214
 kiwifruit, 224
 leaveners, 204, 324
 lemon, 193
 macadamia nuts, 123
 mangoes, 235
 maple syrup, 107
 mascarpone, 131
 meringue, 133
 molasses, 42, 178

Ingredients (*cont.*)
 nectarines, 209
 nutmeg, 200
 nuts, 324
 oats, 243
 papayas, 223
 peanut butter, 15
 pears, 240
 phyllo pastry, 101
 pineapple, 241
 pistachio nuts, 47
 plums, 229
 puff pastry, 130
 raspberries, 220
 scented geranium leaves, 222
 sour milk, 178
 spices, 324
 sugar, 214, 242, 321
In-the-Pink Grapefruit, 246

J

Jack-O'-Lantern Cake, **268**, 270-71
Jam/jelly
 Apricot Linzer Tart, 135
 Austrian Linzer Cookies, **303**, 307
 Cookies, Peanut Butter and, 49
 Orange-Strawberry Swirl Pie, 66, **75**
 Pecan Thumbprint Cookies, 43
 Raspberry-Hazelnut Bars, 30-31
 Raspberry Linzer Tart, 135-36
 Walnut Thumbprint Cookies, 42-43
Jelly roll pan, 318
Jolly Wally Walrus, 250, **268**

K

Keep on Truckin' Cake, 255-56, *255*,
 264
Key Lime Pie, 117-18
Kiwifruit, 224
 Fragrant Fruit with Raspberry
  Sherbet, 222, **228**
 -Lime Sorbet, 60-61, **70**
 peeling, 61
Knead, defined, 333
Knife techniques. *See also* Techniques
 apple coring, 129
 bar cookie cutting, 25
 chocolate chopping, 329
 kiwifruit peeling, 61
 pineapple, 60

L

Lacy Oatmeal Cookies, 16
Ladyfinger(s), 333
 Ice Cream Loaf, **76**, 79

Ladyfinger(s) (*cont.*)
    Strawberry Shortcake Parfaits, 232
Lattice Peach Pie, 97, **115**
Layered Fresh Fruit with Raspberry
    Sauce, 230-31
Layered Melon Sherbet Cake, 81-82
Leaveners, 324
Lecithin, 330
Leftover cake scraps, 274
Lemon
    Bars, 28-29
        Chocolate, 29
    -Blueberry Ice Cream Sauce, 85
    Cheesecake Flag Bars, 287-88
    -Cherry Sauce for Poundcake, 195
    Cream, Mascarpone, Tartlets, 131-32
    Cupcakes, 184-93
    Custard Bread Pudding, 141-42
        Low-Fat, 141
    Gingerbread with Citrus
        Sauce, 178
    -Ginger Crisps, 47-48
    Granita, Raspberry-, 63-64, **71**
    grating peel, 102
    Ice Cream, Blueberry-, 58-59
    Individual Cheesecake Flags, 288
    Layer Cake, Triple-, 165-66, **185**
    Lemony Cheesecake, 208
    Meringue Pie, 103-4, **113**
    Mousse with Raspberry Sauce, 157
    Pie, Sour Cream, 102-3
    Poppy Seed Cake with Lemon
        Glaze, 197-98
    Softies, 22-23
        with Lemon Icing, 22
    Sponge Pudding, 144
    yield of juice and peel, 193
Lemony Cheesecake, 208
Lighten, defined, 333
Lime
    grating peel, 118
    Mousse Schaumtorte, 133-34
    Pie, Key, 117-18
    Sorbet, Kiwi-, 60-61, **70**
    Tropical Mango Fool, 158-59
Loaf pans, 318
Low-fat baking, 327
Low-Fat Banana Shake, 87
Low-Fat Chocolate Ice Cream, 58
Low-Fat Chocolate Sundae, 83
Low-Fat Lemon Custard Bread
    Pudding, 141
Low-Fat Orange-and-Cream
    Soda, 87
Lukewarm, 333

M

Macadamia nut(s), 123, 324
    Cobbler, Pineapple-, 241
    Mango Custard Tart, 123
    Tropical Fruit Salad, 223-24
Macerate, defined, 333
Mailing cookies, 26
Make-It-Easy Bunny Cake, 270, *270*
Make-It-Easy Coffee Crème
    Caramel, 147
Make-It-Easy Jack-O'-Lantern
    Cake, 271
Make-It-Easy Watermelon Cake, 260
Mango(es), 235
    Custard Tart, 123
    Fool, Tropical, 158-59
    Frozen Strawberry Daiquiri Pie,
        66-67
    Gingered Plums and, 222-23
    Soup, Chilled Pineapple-, 235
Maple
    Butter, Honey-, 315
    -Coconut Pecan Cake, 177
        Microwave, 177
    -Pecan Pie, 107
    syrup, 107
Marble, defined, 333
Marzipan, 333
Mascarpone, 131
    Lemon Cream Tartlets, 131-32
Measuring spoons and cups, 319-20
Melon. *See also specific kinds*
    and Berries with Strawberry
        Sauce, 221
    Compote, 230
    Sherbet Cake, Layered, 81-82
    Toss, 246
    Well-Dressed, 246
Meringue, 333
    Berry Pavlova, **187**, 213-14
    hard vs. soft, 133
    Lime Mousse Schaumtorte, 133-34
    pattern making, 213
    Pie, Lemon, 103-4, **113**
    Torte, Frozen Chocolate, 67-68
Metric conversions, 336
Mexican Mocha Flan, 153-54
Mexican Wedding Cakes, 38
Microwave cake
    Chocolate Pudding, 144-45
    Cocoa Snack, 172
    Maple-Coconut Pecan, 177
    Peanut Butter Crumble, 176
Milk, 323. *See also* Dairy products
    souring, 178

Milk (*cont.*)
    sweetened condensed, 31, 323
Milk chocolate, 330. *See also* Chocolate
    Mousse, 156
Mint
    Julep Sorbet, 62, **74**
    Peppermint Stick Fudge, 312
    Wafers, Cocoa-, **303**, 310
Mississippi Mud Pie, 104-5
Mixing bowls, spoons, and spatulas, 320
Mocha
    Cherry Cake, Chocolate-, 169-70, **186**
    Chocolate Sundae, 83
    Flan, Mexican, 53-54
    -Hazelnut Roll, 212-13
    Ice Cream Soda, 88
Molasses, 42, 178
    Crinkle Cookies, **36**, 42
Mousse(s), 137-60, 333
    Cantaloupe, 157-58
    Lemon, with Raspberry Sauce, 157
    Milk Chocolate, 156
    pie
        Chocolate-Peanut, **112**, 118-19
        Chocolate-Vanilla, **112**, 119-20
        Strawberry, 121-22
    Rich Chocolate, **152**, 155
    Roll, Chocolate, 210-11
    Schaumtorte, Lime, 133-34
    White Chocolate, 155
Muffin pans, 318

N

Nectarine(s), 209
    Crisp, 242
    Orange Chiffon Cake with, 208-9
    -Raspberry Tart, **109**, 126-27
    with Rum Cream, 218
    Sundae, 246
    in Wine, **226**, 229
Neufchâtel, 333
New York-Style Cheesecake, **189**, 206
Nippy Nibbles, 64
No-Bake Brownie Ice Cream Loaf, 77
No-Bake Petits Fours, 305
No-Bake Vanilla Yogurt Cheesecake,
    188, 207
Nonalkalized cocoa powder, 330.
    See also Chocolate
Nut(s), 324. *See also specific kinds*
    Cake with Fruit Sauce, 284-85
    Double-Dipped Chocolate Caramel
        Apple, 316
    grinding, 171
    Pie, Providence, 107-8

Nuts *(cont.)*
 Popcorn Balls, 291
 toasting, 325-26
Nutmeg, 200, 324
Nutty Granola Cookies, 20-21

O

Oatmeal cookies
 -Chocolate Chip, 18
 Coconut Crispies, **303**, 306
 Lacy, 16
 Spice, 17
Oats
 Blueberry-Plum Crisp, 245
 Coconut Crispies, **303**, 306
 Lacy Oatmeal Cookies, 16
 Nectarine Crisp, 242
 Oatmeal-Chocolate Chip Cookies, 18
 Oatmeal Spice Cookies, 17
 Plum Oatmeal Crumble, **226-27**,
  242-43
One-Bowl Chocolate Cake, 164-65,
 190-91
Orange(s), 218
 Ambrosia, 218-19
 -and-Cream Soda, 87
  Low-Fat, 87
 Broiled Brown-Sugared, 246
 Chiffon Cake with Nectarines, 208-9
 Chiffon Easter Basket Cake, 280-82
 Citrus Butter, 315
 Cups, Chocolate-, 308
 Gelatin, Cranberry-Raspberry-, 233
 Gingerbread with Citrus Sauce, 178
 -Glazed Baked Apples, 237
 -Hazelnut Shortbread, 44
 Ice Cream Bombe, **69**, 82
 Nut Cake with Fruit Sauce, 284-85
 -Poppy Seed Cookies, 297, **303**
 Sherbet Loaf with Chocolate Sauce, 80
 Sponge Cake, Chocolate-, 285-86
 -Strawberry Swirl Pie, 66, **75**
 Whipped Cream, Honey Pumpkin
  Pie with, 292
Ovens, 320
Oven thermometers, 320

P

Pandowdy, 238
Pans, 318-19
Papaya(s), 223
 Creamy Hawaiian Fruit Cups, 246
 Fans, Honey-Topped, 246
Pare, defined, 333
Party Clown, 88

Passion fruit
 Peach Passion, 219-220
Passover desserts
 Amaretti, 286
 Chocolate-Orange Sponge
  Cake, 285-86
 Nut Cake with Fruit Sauce, 284-85
Pastry, 333. *See also* Pies(s); Tart(s)
 Chocolate, for a Single-Crust
  Pie, 93-94
 for a Double-Crust Pie, 92
 phyllo, 101, 333
 pie, 93, 94, *95*
 puff, 130, 334
 for a Single-Crust Pie, 92
 tart, 127
  Flaky, 92-93
  Sweet, 94-95
Pastry bag, 272, 320
Pastry blender, 320
Pastry brush, 320
Pastry scraper, 320
Peach(es), 220
 -Blueberry Cobbler, 239
 Cobbler, 239
 Ice Cream, 55-56, **70**
 melba, 83
  Sundaes, 83
 New York-Style Cheesecake, **189**, 206
 No-Bake Vanilla Yogurt Cheesecake,
  188, 207
 Parfait, Almond, 246
 Passion, 219-220
 peeling, 97
 Pie, Lattice, 97, **115**
 -Raspberry Ice Cream Pie, 65-66
 Sundae, Georgia, 83
Peaks, 333
Peanut(s). *See also* Peanut butter
 Banana Split with Fudge Sauce,
  72, 86
 Mousse Pie, Chocolate-, **112**, 118-19
 Rounds, Chocolate, 46-47
Peanut butter, 15
 and Banana Fudge, 312
 Chocolate-Peanut Mousse Pie, **112**,
  118-19
 Chocolate Peanut Rounds, 46-47
 Cookies, Cinnamon-, 15-16
 Crumble Cake, 176
  Microwave, 176
 Cupcakes, Chocolate-, 193-94
 Cup Sundae, Double Chocolate-, 83
 Ice Cream Sauce, Chocolate-, 84
 and Jelly Cookies, 49

Pear(s), 240
 Cobbler, Cherry-, 240
 Granola Crisp, **226-27**, 244
 Jubilee, 246
 Melba, 246
 Pie, Phyllo, 100, **111**
 Pineapple-Poached, 234-35
 Quick Breads, 315
 Upside-Down Tarts, Walnut, 130
Pecan(s), 324
 cake
  Blueberry-Spice Coffeecake, 201-2
  Holiday, 292-93
  Maple-Coconut, 177
  Microwave Maple-Coconut, 177
 cookies
  Blondies, 26, **34-35**
  Lacy Oatmeal, 16
  Mexican Wedding Cakes, 38
  Praline Chip, 18-19
  Thumbprint, 43
 Frosting, Spice Layer Cake with,
  168-69
 Loaves, Cranberry, 314
 pie
  Apple, Date, and, 295
  Chocolate Truffle Caramel, 120-21
  Maple-, 107
 Pumpkin Crunch Custard, 154-55
 Tropical Fruitcakes, 314
 Waffle Sundae, 88
Peel, citrus, 102, 118, 333
Peppermint Stick Fudge, 312
Petite Gingerbreads, 313-14
Petit fours, 333
 No-Bake, 305
Phyllo, 101, 333
 Apple Pie, 100-1
 Pear Pie, 100, **111**
Pie(s), 89-136
 apple, 100
  Date, and Pecan, 295
  Cider, 99-100, **110**
  Crunch, 99
  Phyllo, 100-1
 Blueberry, with Cornmeal Crumb
  Topping, 98-99
 chocolate
  Cream, Double, 105-6
  Pastry for a Single-Crust, 93-94
  -Peanut Mousse, **112**, 118-19
  -Raspberry Chiffon, 108
  Ribbon Coconut Cream, 282-83
  Truffle Caramel, 120-21
  -Vanilla Mousse, **112**, 119-20

Pie(s) (*cont.*)
Crimson, 293-94
crumb crusts, 122
frozen
Orange-Strawberry Swirl, 66, **75**
Peach-Raspberry Ice Cream, 65
Strawberry Daiquiri, 66-67
fruit, 96
Honey Pumpkin, with Orange
Whipped Cream, 292
Key Lime, 117-18
Lattice Peach, 97, **115**
Lemon Meringue, 103-4, **113**
Maple-Pecan, 107
Mississippi Mud, 104-5
pans, 93
pastry, 93, 94, *95*
Chocolate, for a Single-Crust
Pie, 93-94
for a Double-Crust, 92
for a Single-Crust, 92
Phyllo Pear, 100, **111**
plates, 318-19
Providence Nut, 107-8
Raspberry Chiffon, 108-17
Rhubarb-Cherry, 96
Sour Cream Lemon, 102-3
Strawberry Mousse, 121-22
vs. tarts, 126
Zucchini "Apple," 101-2
Piña Colada Sorbet, 59-60
Pineapple, 60, 218, 241
Almost-Margarita, 246
Ambrosia, 218-19
-Banana Sorbet, 60
Carrot Cake, 175
with Cream Cheese Frosting, 175
-Coconut Ice Cream, 54
-Macadamia Cobbler, 241
-Mango Soup, Chilled, 235
Piña Colada Sorbet, 59-60
-Poached Pears, 234-35
Rounds, Broiled, 246
Sherbet, Fast and Fresh, 246
Tropical Fruit Salad, 223-24
Tropical Smoothie, 246
Pine Cone Cake, 299-300, **304**
Pipe, defined, 333
Pistachio nuts, 47. *See also* Nuts
Lemon-Ginger Crisps, 47-48
Peach Melba Sundaes, 83
Plum(s), 229
buying and storing, 245
Crisp, Blueberry, 245
and Mango, Gingered, 222-23

Plum(s) (*cont.*)
Oatmeal Crumble, **226-27**, 242-43
and Walnut Compote, 229
Plump, defined, 333
Popcorn Balls, 291
Poppy seed(s)
Cake, Lemon, with Lemon Glaze,
197-98
Cookies, Orange-, 297, **303**
storing, 197
Poundcake, 194-95, 333
Banana, 196
Nectarines with Rum Cream, 218
sauces for, 195
tips for making, 196
Praline, 333-34
Chip Cookies, 18-19
Providence Nut Pie, 107-8
Pudding, 137-60, 334. *See also* Custard;
Flan; Mousse
Banana Cream Cake, **192**, 210
bread, 142
Almond French, 142-43
Chocolate, 143
Lemon Custard, 141-42
Low-Fat Almond French
Bread, 142
Low-Fat Lemon Custard
Bread, 141
Butterscotch, 146-47
cake
Chocolate, 144-45
Microwave Chocolate, 144-45
Chocolate, 145-46
cooling, 155
doneness of, 145
Lemon Sponge, 144
Rice, 140
Baked Almond, 140-41
Brûlé, 140
Puff pastry, 130, 334
Starry Shortcake, 288-89
Walnut Pear Upside-Down Tarts, 130
Pumpkin
-Chocolate Cake, 289-90, **304**
Crunch Custard, 154-55
Gingerbread-, Ice Cream Roll, 296
Pie, Honey, with Orange Whipped
Cream, 292
Soufflé, Cold, 295-96, **302**
Purée, 324, 334

Q

Quick Breads, Pear, 315
Quick-Fix Caramel Apples, 246

R

Raisin(s)
Chocolate Walnut Chunk
Cookies, 14
Cookies, Whole-Wheat, 19-20
German Crumb Cake, 200-201
Lemon Softies, 22-23
with Lemon Icing, 22
-Toast Triangles, Saucy, 246
White Chocolate Walnut
Chunk Cookies, 14
Whole-Wheat Applesauce
Bars, 32
Ramekin, 334, 324
Raspberry(ies)
with Amaretti Cream, 220
Butter, 315
Chiffon Pie, 108-17
Chocolate-, 108
Fruit Melba, 234
-Hazelnut Bars, 30-31
Heart Cake, Chocolate-,
278-79, *278*, **301**
Ice Cream Pie, Peach-, 65
-Lemon Granita, 63-64, **71**
No-Bake Vanilla Yogurt
Cheesecake, **188**, 207
Peach Melba Sundaes, 83
Pear Melba, 246
sauce
Layered Fresh Fruit with,
230-31
Lemon Mousse with, 157
Ruby-Red Ice Cream, 85
Summer Fruit with Brown Sugar
Cream, 221
tart
Linzer, 135-36
Nectarine-, **109**, 126-27
Two-Berry, **116**, 127
Red, White, and Blue Sundae, 83
Rhubarb-Cherry Pie, 96
Ribbon, defined, 324, 334
Rice Pudding, 140
Baked Almond, 140-41
Brûlé, 140
Rich Chocolate Mousse, **152**, 155
Ricotta cheese
Chocolate Cheesecake, **189**, 205
Nectarines with Rum Cream, 218
Rolling pins, 320
Ruby-Red Ice Cream Sauce, 85
Rum
Cream, Nectarines with, 218
-Date Sauce for Poundcake, 195

S

Salad, Tropical Fruit, 223-24
Sauce
  ice cream
    Butterscotch, 85
    Chocolate-Peanut Butter, 84
    Hot Fudge, 84
    Lemon-Blueberry, 85
    Ruby-Red, 85
  poundcake
    Lemon-Cherry, 195
    Rum-Date, 195
Saucy Raisin-Toast Triangles, 246
Scald, defined, 334
Scented geranium leaves, 222
Scrape down, defined, 334
Sea Glass Candy, 312-13
Seizing, defined, 330
Semisweet chocolate, 330. *See also*
  Chocolate
Serving suggestions, 294
  brownies, 24
  chocolate mousse, 121
Seven-Layer Brownie Ice Cream
  Cake, 77-78
Sherbet, 334
  Cake, Layered Melon, 81-82
  Fast and Fresh Pineapple, 246
  Frozen Strawberry Daiquiri
    Pie, 66-67
  Gingered Plums and Mango, 222-23
  Ladyfinger Ice Cream Loaf, **76**, 79
  Orange, Loaf with Chocolate
    Sauce, 80
  Orange-Strawberry Swirl Pie, 66, **75**
  Peach Passion, 219-220
  Raspberry, Fragrant Fruit
    with, 222, **228**
  vs. sorbet, 61
  Spaceship, 88
  Summer Rainbows, 88
Shortbread, 334
  Almond, 43-44
  Chocolate, 43
  Cookies, Cornmeal, 43
  Orange-Hazelnut, 44
Shortcake(s), 334
  Cornmeal-Honey, with Berries, 204
  Starry, 288-89
  Strawberry, 202-3
    Parfaits, 232
    -Peach Chocolate-Chip, 203
Shred, defined, 334
Sift, defined, 334
Sifters, 320

Silly cakes, 247-74
  Big Maccake, 252-53, **262**
  Box of Crayons, 254-55, *255*, **266**
  Bunny, **268**, 269-70, *270*
  Buttercream Bow, 274
  Carlyle the Crocodile, 253-54,
    254, **264**
  decorating tips, 256
  Frosty, **265**, 271-72
  Gloria Glowworm, 250-51, **262**
  Hot Dog, What a Cake!, 257-58,
    257-58, **263**
  Jack-O'-Lantern, **268**, 270-71
  Jolly Wally Walrus, 250, **268**
  Keep on Truckin', 255-56, *255*, **264**
  Make-It-Easy Bunny, 270, *270*
  Make-It-Easy Jack-O'-Lantern, 271
  Make-It-Easy Watermelon, 260
  Stack-of-Gifts, **267**, 273-74, *273*
  Sunflower, 256-57, **261**
  Tomato-in-the-Sun, 258-59, **268**
  Watermelon, 260, **262**
  A Whale of a Cake, 251-52, *252*, **264**
Simmer, 324, 334
Sliced Almond Cake, 179
Snip, defined, 334
Soft Sugar Cookies, 21
Sorbet, 334
  Apple, 63
  Banana Split with Fudge
    Sauce, **72**, 86
  Cups, Citrus, 88
  Fourth of July Sundae, 88
  Frozen Strawberry Daiquiri
    Pie, 66-67
  Kiwi-Lime, 60-61, **70**
  Mint Julep, 62, **74**
  Piña Colada, 59-60
  Pineapple-Banana, 60
  vs. sherbet, 61
  Spaceship, 88
  still-freeze method, 62
  Strawberry-Grapefruit, 61, **70**
Soufflé
  Cake, Warm Chocolate, 173
  Cold Pumpkin, 295-96, **302**
  dishes, 319
Soup, Chilled Pineapple-Mango, 235
Sour Cream Lemon Pie, 102-3
Sour Grapes, 246
Sour milk, 178
Spaceship, 88
Spice Cookie Cutouts, **303**, 308-9
Spice Layer Cake with Pecan
  Frosting, 168-69

Spices, 324
  anise seeds, 38
Spiral Cookies, **303**, 306-7
Sponge cake, 334
  Chocolate-Orange, 285-86
Sponge Pudding, Lemon, 144
Springform pans, 319
Stack-of-Gifts Cake, **267**, 273-74, *273*
Starry Shortcake, 288-89
Steep, defined, 334
Still-freeze method for ice creams and
  sorbets, 62
Storing food. *See also* Buying and
  storing food; Freezing food
  anise seeds, 38
  apples, 199
  brownies, 24
  cake, 165
  cookies, 30, 39
  cornmeal, 40
  figs, dried, 27
  ice cream, 79, 86
  nuts, 179, 326
  poppy seeds, 197
  sugar syrup, 81
Strain, defined, 334
Strainers, 320
Strawberry(ies). *See also* Berry(ies)
  -Banana Ice Cream, 57-58
  Big Bang Cupcake Cake, 286-87
  -Blueberry Trifle, **149**, 159
  Brûlé, **225**, 236
  buying and storing, 67, 232
  Chocolate-Dipped Fruit and Cookie
    Wreath, 300-5
  -and-Cream Gelatin, 232-33
  Custard Tart, **114-15**, 124-25
  Daiquiri Pie, Frozen, 66-67
  -Grapefruit Sorbet, 61, **70**
  Ice Cream, 54
  Mint Julep Sorbet, 62, **74**
  Mousse Pie, 121-22
  Nut Cake with Fruit Sauce, 284-85
  Sauce, Melon and Berries with, 221
  Shortcakes, 202-3
    Parfaits, 232
    -Peach Chocolate Chip, 203
    Starry, 288-89
  Swirl Pie, Orange-, 66, **75**
  Tart, Chocolate-, 125-26
  Tropical Smoothie, 246
Substitutions
  brown sugar, 242
  pans, 318
Sugar, 321

Sugar (*cont.*)
 brown, 242
 superfine, 214
 syrup, storing, 81
Sugar Cookies, Soft, 21
Sugared flowers for cake decorating, 259
Sugared Split Bananas, 64
Summer Fruit with Brown Sugar
  Cream, 221
Summer Rainbows, 88
Sunflower Cake, 256-57, **261**
Super-Rich Chocolate Ice Cream, 55
Sweet chocolate, 330. *See also* Chocolate
Sweetened condensed milk, 31, 323
Sweeteners. *See also* Honey; Maple
 molasses, 42
 sugar, 214, 242, 321
Sweet Pastry for Tarts, 94

T
Tart(s), 89-136
 Almond, 134-35
 Apricot Linzer, 135
 Banana Custard, 133-34
 Bittersweet Chocolate Truffle, 136
 Cherry-Cheese, 128
 Chocolate-Strawberry, 125-26
 Free-Form Apple, **110**, 129
 fruit, 124
 Lime Mousse Schaumtorte, 133-34
 Mango Custard, 123
 Mascarpone Lemon Cream
  Tartlets, 131-32
 Nectarine-Raspberry, **109**, 126-27
 pans, 128, 319
 pastry, 127
  Flaky Pastry for, 92-93
  Sweet Pastry for, 94-95
 Raspberry Linzer, 135-36
 removing from pan, 136
 Strawberry Custard, **114-15**, 124-25
 Two-Berry, **116**, 127
 vs. pies, 126
 Walnut Pear Upside-Down, 130
Tartlets, Mascarpone Lemon
 Cream, 131-32
Techniques, 325-27. *See also* Glossary
 bread pudding, 142
 brownies, 23
 cake, 203
 candy-making, 313
 caramel, 148
 cereal crushing, 49
 cheesecake, 208
 chocolate, 329

Techniques (*cont.*)
 citrus peel grating, 108, 118
 coconut toasting, 132, 166, 326
 coffee bean crushing, 147
 cookies, 14, 16, 17, 19, 20, 21,
  22, 48
 cream cheese softening, 27
 crumb crusts, 122
 crumb making, 49, 205, 238
 crumbles, 243
 custards, 146, 155, 154
 decorating, 164, 181, 272
 doneness of puddings and
  custards, 145
 eggs, 104, 182, 184, 285, 326
 fruit pie, 96
 fruit tarts, 124
 frying, 298
 gelatin, 233
 greasing pans, 326
 high-altitude baking, 326-27
 ice cream, 56, 58, 62
 low-fat baking, 327
 measuring, 326
 meringue, 133
 nuts, toasting, 325-26
 peach peeling, 97
 pie pastry, 93, 94, *95*
 poundcake, 196
 souring milk, 178
 vanilla chip melting, 120
 whipping cream, 106, 159, 160
Temper, defined, 334
Tempered chocolate, 330
Terrine, Fresh Fruit, 224
Thanksgiving desserts
 Apple, Date, and Pecan Pie, 295
 Cold Pumpkin Soufflé, 295-96, **302**
 Crimson Pie, 293-94
 Gingerbread-Pumpkin Ice Cream
  Roll, 296
 Holiday Pecan Cake, 292-93
 Honey Pumpkin Pie with Orange
  Whipped Cream, 292
Toasted Almond-Apple Ice Cream
 Topping, 84
Toffee, Almond Chocolate-Covered,
 311-12
Tomato-in-the-Sun Cake, 258-59, **268**
Torte, 68, 335
 Frozen Chocolate Meringue, 67-68
Trifle, 159, 335
 Strawberry-Blueberry, **149**, 159
Triple-Lemon Layer Cake, 165-66, **185**
Tropical Fruitcakes, 314

Tropical Fruit Salad, 223-24
Tropical Mango Fool, 158-59
Tropical Smoothie, 246
Tropical Sundae, 83
Truffle(s), 335
 Caramel Pie, Chocolate, 120-21
 Marbled, 280
 Tart, Bittersweet Chocolate, 136
Tube pans, 319, 325
Turntable, 325
Two-Berry Tart, **116**, 127

U
Ultrapasteurized, 335
Unsweetened chocolate, 330. *See also*
 Chocolate
Upside-down cake, 335
 Apple, 198-99
Upside-Down Tarts, Walnut Pear, 130

V
Valentine's Day desserts
 Chocolate-Covered Cherries, 279-80
 Chocolate-Raspberry Heart Cake,
  278-79, *278*, **301**
 Marbled Truffles, 280
Vanilla, 324
 Buttercream, Fluffy, Yellow Cake
  with, 167-68
 Buttermilk Bundt Cake, 181-82
 chips, melting, 120
 Ice Cream, Fabulous, 54, **72**
 Mousse Pie, Chocolate-, **112**, 119-20
 Yogurt Cheesecake, No-Bake,
  188, 207

W
Waffle Sundae, 88
Walnut(s), 324. *See also* Nut(s)
 Apple Streusel Coffeecake, 199-200
 Brownie Nut Slices, 48
 Carrot Cake, 175
  with Cream Cheese Frosting, 175
 Chocolate Nut Brownies, 23
 Chunk Cookies, Chocolate, 14
 Chunk Cookies, White Chocolate, 14
 Cinnamon Triangles, **303**, 310
 Compote, Plum and, 229
 Crisp, Apple, **216-17**, 244
 Easy Triple-Chocolate Fudge, 312
 German Crumb Cake, 200-201
 Nut Cake with Fruit Sauce, 284-85
 Oatmeal Spice Cookies, 17
 Pear Upside-Down Tarts, 130
 Providence Nut Pie, 107-8

Walnut(s) (*cont.*)
  Thumbprint Cookies, 42-43
  Whole-Wheat Applesauce Bars, 32
  Zebras, 25
Warm Chocolate Soufflé Cake, 173
Watermelon
  -Berry Cassis, 219
  Cake, 260, **262**
  Melon and Berries with Strawberry
    Sauce, 221
Weeping, defined, 335
Well, defined, 335
Well-Dressed Melon, 246
A Whale of a Cake, 251-52, *252*, **264**
Whip, defined, 335
Whipping cream, 106, 159, 160
Whisks, 320-21
White chocolate, 330. *See also*
  Chocolate
  Crispy Apricot Bars, 49-50
  -Dipped Fruit and Cookie
    Wreath, 300-5
  Easy Triple-Chocolate Fudge, 312
  Marbled Truffles, 280
  Mousse, 155
  Walnut Chunk Cookies, 14
Whole-wheat
  Applesauce Bars, 32
  flour, storing, 32
  Raisin Cookies, 19-20
Wine, Nectarines in, **226**, 229

Y

Yellow cake. *See also* Cake
  Boston Cream Pie, 182-83, **190**
  with Chocolate Cream Frosting, 167
  with Fluffy Vanilla Buttercream,
    167-68

Yogurt
  Cantaloupe "Mousse," 157-58
  Cheesecake, No-Bake Vanilla,
    188, 207
  Cherry Dip, 246
  Creamy Hawaiian Fruit
    Cups, 246
  Dessert à la Waldorf, 246
  frozen
    Banana Treat, 246
    Blueberry-Banana Lickety
      Split, 246
    Chocolate Meringue Torte, 67-68
    Ice Cream Bombe, **69**, 82
    Ladyfinger Ice Cream
      Loaf, **76**, 79
    Low-Fat Banana Shake, 87
    Low-Fat Orange-and-Cream
      Soda, 87
    Mocha Ice Cream Soda, 88
    No-Bake Brownie Ice Cream
      Loaf, 77
    Peach Melba Sundaes, 83
    Seven-Layer Brownie Ice Cream
      Cake, 77-78
    Strawberry-and-Cream Gelatin,
      232-33
    Strawberry Daiquiri Pie, 66-67
  Honey, Cinnamon-Scented Bananas
    in, 246
  Nectarine Sundae, 246
  Plum and Walnut Compote, 229
  Strawberry Mousse Pie, 121-22
Yo-yos, 88

Z

Zest, 102, 118, 335
Zucchini "Apple" Pie, 101-2

PHOTO CREDITS

Abbreviations: T–Top; M–Middle;
B–Bottom; L–Left; R–Right

Calvo, Ben: 110T, 188
Koenig, Lisa: 71, 149, 187, 225
Goldspink, Edmund: 112, 150-1, 192,
  262M
Maas, Rita: 301
Needham, Steven Mark: 33, 70, 226L,
  228, 304T
Pilossof, Judd: 110B, 186, 303
Turner, Tim: 114-5, 152
Uher, John: 34L, 34-5, 36, 69, 72T, 72B,
  73, 74, 75, 76, 109, 111, 113, 115R,
  116, 185, 189T, 189B, 190L, 190-1,
  226-7, 261, 262T, 262B, 263, 264T,
  264M, 264B, 265, 266, 267, 268TL,
  268TR, 268BL, 268BR, 302, 304B